Comic Relief

Edited by SARAH BLACHER COHEN

Comic Relief

Humor in Contemporary American Literature

UNIVERSITY OF ILLINOIS PRESS
Urbana   Chicago   London

"Toward a Definition of Black Humor," by Max F. Schulz, from his *Black Humor of the Sixties* (Athens: Ohio University Press, 1974). Reprinted by permission of the author and Ohio University Press. ©1974 by the Ohio University Press.

Portions of "Saul Bellow's Humane Comedy," by Allen Guttmann, are revised from a version published in his book, *The Jewish Writer in America* (New York: Oxford University Press, 1971), pp. 189–198, 201–210. Permission to revise has been given by Oxford University Press. ©1971 by Oxford University Press.

Second printing, 1979

LIBRARY OF CONGRESS CATALOGING IN PUBLICATION DATA

Main entry under title:

Comic relief.

Bibliography: p.
1. American literature—20th century—History and criticism—Addresses, essays, lectures. 2. American wit and humor—History and criticism—Addresses, essays, lectures. I. Cohen, Sarah Blacher.
PS438.C6   1978   817'.5'409   78–16510
ISBN 0-252-00576-7

For Gary

Acknowledgments

The idea for this book grew out of a Modern Language Association seminar on contemporary American humor. Those papers which were read generated such enthusiasm that I wanted to make them, and other treatments of the subject, available to a larger audience. The essays written for this collection I chose from authorities on the various kinds, concerns, and practitioners of recent American humor. The contributors were most generous in sharing their insights, cooperative about clarifying obscurities, and extremely good humored throughout the project.

Members of the English department of the State University of New York at Albany were especially helpful. Chairman John Gerber, his predecessor, Walter Knotts, and administrative assistant, Ann Weinberg, assigned me convenient teaching schedules and in many other ways supported my endeavors. Undergraduate student Judy Lillienthal located useful articles and found recondite information; graduate student Roger Sheffer expertly assisted me in compiling the bibliography. Kathy Overocker and Linda Sajan were excellent typists.

A fellowship and grant from the State University of New York Research Foundation facilitated the completion of this book. My thanks to the Foundation for its financial aid and encouragement.

Once again members of the University of Illinois Press were indispensable co-workers. I am indebted to editor Richard L. Wentworth for his exacting standards and good taste, to assistant editor

Ann Lowry Weir for her meticulous sense of language, and to Christie Schuetz for her inventive promotional skills.

My husband, Gary, was there when I needed him. He deliberated with me; he consoled me; he laughed with me.

Albany, New York —SARAH BLACHER COHEN

Contents

Leid macht auch Lachen.
—JEWISH PROVERB

The worst returns to laughter.
—SHAKESPEARE

The most acutely suffering animal on earth invented laughter.
—NIETZSCHE

Will a day come when the race will detect the funniness of these juvenilities and laugh at them—and by laughing at them destroy them? For your race, in its poverty has unquestionably one really effective weapon—laughter.
—MARK TWAIN

The comic alone is able to give us the strength to bear the tragedy of existence.
—IONESCO

Obliged to choose between complaint and comedy, I choose comedy as more energetic, wiser and manlier.
—SAUL BELLOW

Jokes grow best on the graves of old anxieties.
—MARTIN GROTJAHN

SARAH BLACHER COHEN

Introduction:
The Variety of Humors

Historians of American humor have shown that the greatest burgeoning of American comedy occurred during the Jacksonian democracy, from the Civil War years to 1900, and in the 1930's.[1]
That two of these periods were times of great duress for the country
strongly suggests that travail gives rise to humor, which expresses
people's rage at the senseless turn of events and dissipates their
gloom. Since the multitudes are generally too demoralized to originate a humor bracing enough to sustain them, they rely on their
comic artists to transform disaster into drollery. During and after the
bitter Civil War years, people looked to the "literary comedians"
and their sardonic scion, Mark Twain, to expose the skulduggery
and hoot it out of existence. Yet with all their arsenal of folly—their
deadpan method of delivery, their grammatical violations, their
"inspired idiot" poses, their caustic vernacular wit—they did not
succeed. Their laughter, in the words of Twain's *Mysterious
Stranger*, did not blow the "colossal humbug . . . to rags and atoms
at a blast," but it did make the public see "the comic side of a
thousand low-grade and trivial things"[2] and thereby made their lot
more bearable. Similarly, during the grim Depression years the

[1]See Walter Blair, *Native American Humor* (San Francisco: Chandler, 1960), and Jesse
Bier, *The Rise and Fall of American Humor* (New York: Holt, Rinehart and Winston, 1968).
[2]Mark Twain, *The Mysterious Stranger and Other Stories* (New York: Harper & Brothers,
1922), pp. 131–132.

1

slapstick film antics of W. C. Fields, the Marx Brothers, and Charlie Chaplin evoked belly laughs in people who temporarily forgot their bellyaches. They witnessed the plights of rascals and tramps and fleetingly indulged in the Hobbesian laughter of feeling superior toward those more wretched than themselves. On the printed page they relished the *dementia praecox* humor of Benchley, Thurber, and Perelman and identified with the "perfect neurotics" they created. By reading exaggerated versions of their own psychic mishaps in the domestic and occupational spheres, they discovered a degree of mirth in their own adversity.

During World War II, when the nation was defeating the Fascist aggressors and our economy thrived by keeping the "world safe for democracy," no distinctive American humor emerged. There was instead a continuation, with slight difference, of types that already existed. Walter Blair in "Laughter in Wartime America" describes these types as the "humor of the irresponsibles," the "humor of the rugged individualists," and the "humor of the poor little men."[3] Since people's anger was directed at a distant, bizarre enemy— mechanical, goose-stepping "Krauts" and yellow-skinned, slant-eyed "Japs"— the antic muse on the home front did not have to be particularly bellicose. Nor did she have to be anxious or skeptical, since Americans wholeheartedly believed in the country's integrity and had confidence in the military leadership. People could afford to enjoy light, diversionary humor.

The post–World War II period changed all that. It fell far short of the hopes of most Americans. The fighting against the Axis powers had ended, but the full impact of the Holocaust, its barbarity initially too terrible to comprehend, now weighed heavily on survivors. The nuclear destruction of Hiroshima and Nagasaki shamed and terrified us. The Cold War grew colder, global skirmishes grew hotter, and apocalypse seemed around the corner. Political figures offered no remedy. McCarthy fanaticism, Eisenhower timidity, slain Kennedy idealism only heightened our anxiety. Race riots, assassinated civil rights leaders, rampant crime and indifference, mounting automation and unemployment made American life scarcely endurable. This was not the "new frontier," the "great society" that had been promised us.

A common response of the mid-twentieth-century American

[3] Walter Blair, "Laughter in Wartime America," *College English*, 6 (April, 1945), 362.

writer to what Elizabeth Bishop described as "our worst century so
far" was a feeling of shocked disbelief and inability to make sense of
the nightmarish happenings. The truth was stranger than any fiction.
The writer, to quote Philip Roth, had "his hands full in trying to
understand, describe, and then make *credible* much of American
reality. It stupefies, it sickens, it infuriates, and finally it is even a
kind of embarrassment to one's own meager imagination."[4] And for
a time many American writers did not choose to deal with this insane
reality in their work. Instead, the "sick comedians" stepped forward
to serve as the lunatic commentators of our collective lunacy, a role
they assumed with a vengeance. Defying McCarthy censorship and
the surface decency it enforced, the Lenny Bruces and Mort Sahls
gleefully mentioned the unmentionable—the drug abuse, sexual
perversion, bigotry and gratuitous violence of respectable folks.
With newspapers and recent history as their sources, they joked
about H-bomb fallout, neo-Nazism, failed Russian-American
détente, Vatican corruption, political self-interest. Their aim was
deflationary: to show that presumably normal Americans were as
grotesque as the monsters of Charles Addams's art, and just as cruel
to each other. Their creed, if they had one, was Lenny Bruce's:
"Everything is rotten—mother is rotten, God is rotten, the flag is
rotten."[5] Their language was also rotten, the foulest four-letter
words that would make a Henry Miller blush. Their favorite kind of
comedy was scatological to convey their excremental vision of
things. Their preferred comic technique was rapid, improvisational,
and escalating in intensity. Its characteristic form was the *shpritz*,
the spontaneous outburst of venom and wit which sprayed performer
and onlooker alike. Their attitude toward audiences was hostile.
They slaughtered every sacred cow they could corral and flaunted
their carcasses before the pained owners. As one British critic
observed, the "American sickniks gouge the customers where they
are most sensitively vulnerable, insult them to their wincing faces,
and nightly implant the nagging unease that the barbecue pit is the
abyss."[6] Upholding no ethical norm, they censured for the perverse

[4]Philip Roth, "Writing American Fiction," *Commentary*, 3 (March, 1961), reprinted in
Roth, *Reading Myself and Others* (New York: Farrar, Straus and Giroux, 1975), p. 120.
[5]Quoted in Albert Goldman, "The Comedy of Lenny Bruce," *Commentary*, 36 (October,
1963), 316.
[6]Kenneth Allsop, "Those American Sickniks," *The Twentieth Century*, 170 (July,
1961), 98.

delight of censuring. For this reason they lost their appeal. They became so outrageous in their mockery, so excessive in their nihilism that audiences became surfeited with their invective. No longer appreciated, the sick comedians either self-destructed or vanished.

But they did not disappear permanently. Just as the oral comic tradition precedes and is a major source of written comedy, so the material and techniques of the sick comedians of the 1950's were absorbed by the black humor novelists who followed them. The "sickniks," however, were not the black humorists' only progenitors. The contributions of more distant American relatives —Melville's wry ambiguities, Twain's satanic laughter, West's grotesque apocalypses—enriched the blackness of their comic vision. French influences were also contagious, especially André Breton's 1939 version of *humour noir,* which was more a frame of mind than a genre for ridiculing the foibles of society and the absurdities of the universe. By and large, however, black humor was, as Max Schulz convincingly proves, a "phenomenon of the 1960's, comprising a group of writers who share a viewpoint and an aesthetics for pacing off the boundaries of a nuclear-technological world intrinsically without confinement." Who these writers were was determined by the critic who was categorizing them. If he was Bruce Jay Friedman, a wise-cracking black humorist himself, who wanted to earn some quick dollars from an anthology, he would lump together his own short story, works by Thomas Pynchon, Joseph Heller, J. P. Donleavy, Charles Simmons, John Rechy, Edward Albee, John Barth, Terry Southern, James Purdy, Conrad Knickerbocker, Louis-Ferdinand Céline, and, for want of a better label, call them black humorists. Though these writers possessed some similarities, Friedman admitted that their "visions are so private and unique" that they "would not know or perhaps even understand one another's work if they tripped over it."[7] Offering fuller, more scholarly definitions of the black humorist were critics Alfred Kazin, R. W. B. Lewis, Ihab Hassan, Robert Scholes, Brom Weber, Hamlin Hall, and Max Schulz, each with his own list of representative authors and special favorites. But whomever they designated as black humorists, these writers, confronting a prepos-

[7]Bruce Jay Friedman, Foreword to *Black Humor* (New York: Bantam Books, 1965), pp. vii–viii.

terous world, all created more preposterous fiction to assert the supremacy of their imagination. They devised more nefarious conspiracies, nonsensical wars, lurid sexual assaults, outlandish sacrileges than those which occurred daily. To convey these distortions, they used broad parodies, political caricature, comic-book mayhem, gothic horror, hoaxes, obfuscations—any means to reflect and outrival the absurdity engulfing them. They did so presumably to alert the public to the madness in their midst. Also, by exaggerating this madness, they hoped to gain control over it, or at least to protect themselves from it through the distance of their art. But critics faulted them for being too distant; they accused them of fabricating cartoon worlds with slapstick catastrophes in order to avoid dealing with the complexities and anguish of the real world. They charged them with being ineffectual satirists who were so caught up with the ingenuity and flagrancy of their mockery that they neglected to subtly delineate the objects of their scorn. Once touting black humor as the most original American literary contribution since World War II, critics now found it an exhausted art, an overworked and underdeveloped form of iconoclasm. Perhaps a more serious criticism of black humor was that it had ceased to be funny. Weary of this crazy kind of comedy which identifies "itself with the very tension and terror it once did so much to alleviate," James Thurber asked the question on the minds of many: "How long can the needle of the human gramaphone stay in the rut of *Angst* without wearing out and ending in the repetition of goulish gibbering?"[8] Obviously there are some black humorists whose needles have not become stuck and are not creating gibberish. Vladimir Nabokov, known for his lexical drollery and cosmopolitan grotesques, is a master of diabolical comedy. As wily author, he leads his readers to anticipate one outcome and then, through narrative ruses, totally reverses their expectations. In *Lolita* and *Pale Fire,* Nabokov cannily dismantles or gleefully decimates the "everyday world, everyday fantasies and everyday literary conventions"; what remains, claims Richard Pearce, is a "tantalizing verbal surface suspended over a black hole." Thomas Berger and John Barth employ what Stanley Trachtenberg terms "the comedy of decomposition." In *Vital Parts* Berger shows the risible consequences of having a splintered self,

---

[8]James Thurber, "The Future, If Any, of Comedy," *Harper's* (December, 1961), pp. 40, 45.

and in *Little Big Man* he presents mythic parodies of American history. In *Lost in the Funhouse* Barth reveals the comic breakdown of the fictional process itself, whereby the stories cease to perform a mimetic function but are concerned with their own narrative viability and progression. There are other black humorists such as John Hawkes, Thomas Pynchon, James Purdy, and Robert Coover, whose achievements are significant enough to warrant extended analysis, were this a book devoted only to black humor. And undoubtedly there are more black humorists waiting in the wings, soon to display their dark mirth. Therefore, it is premature to say that black humor has expired. The corpus is still too lively for the critics to send out death notices.

What does seem certain is that smudges of black humor have rubbed off onto other kinds of humor in contemporary American literature, notably that of science fiction. The kind of cosmos frequently depicted in science fiction is one without God, or one in which humans or advanced mechanical creatures aspire to be God. Such a cosmos resembles the absurd universe satirized by the black humorists. Also science fiction, especially the work of Kurt Vonnegut, mockingly points up the similarities between the bizarre happenings of outer space and the equally bizarre occurrences of our own world. In *Slaughterhouse-Five,* for example, Vonnegut makes us accept as believable and comic both the incredible antics of the Trafalmadorians and the Allies' firebombing of Dresden. Thus David Ketterer concludes that "a more twisted form of humor . . . akin to the horrific, tragic or absurd" is increasingly found in serious science fiction.

But for all its novelty and sensational effects, the fantasy humor of alternate worlds is not nearly as amusing as the realistic humor of certain regions of this country. From 1830 to 1867 Down East or Yankee humor prevailed, with its laconic analyses of politics and its dialect stories of peddlers outwitting foreigners and country rubes alike. During the same period, the Old Southwest humorists made even a greater stir, with their exuberant tall tales of shifty lowlife baiting "uppity" Northerners, tangling with fierce beasts, and reveling in their bodily functions and bawdy acts. This humor influenced recent southern literature and made the region, known for its tragic sense, prominent for its earthy and tough-minded comic sense as well. The most polished writers—William Faulkner, Flannery O'Connor, Erskine Caldwell—employed Old Southwestern humor not only for its quaint local charm or as facile comic relief from the austerities in their fiction. They also used that mode, Hugh Holman contends, "as a means of permitting the realistic portrayal of characters and actions that might otherwise have overwhelmed us with their crudeness or with their horror." Faulkner, through the magnifying lens of vernacular comedy, showed the Snopses to be a rascally but risible pack of varmints. Caldwell, focusing on the hyperactive sexuality of his characters, made them seem more like ludicrous animals than desperate human beings. And O'Connor, drawing her "large and startling figures" of spiritual misfits, emphasized how limited and yet how laughable they were. But whoever was the object of their scrutiny, these writers used Old Southwestern humor to achieve a necessary distance and thus saw things more clearly.

From the South emerged another kind of comic spirit—the disguised plantation humor of the black slaves. In folktales they created Brer Rabbit as their hero, that weak and helpless creature who appeared to cower before more formidable adversaries. But they also endowed him with the capacity to survive and triumph. A practical joker, trickster, and wit, he often got the better of bigger and stronger animals. By identifying with the victorious Brer Rabbit, the slaves secretly felt superior to their white masters. Most of the time, however, they acted the fool to please those who held the whip and allowed black-face minstrels to portray their seemingly droll lot. After emancipation and even during the Harlem Renaissance of the 1920's, blacks still employed a highly camouflaged form of humor. Langston Hughes's Simple, a Harlem factory worker, became the representative comedian. An outwardly genial bar-stool philosopher, for twenty years he cleverly mocked national policy and private lives. But because he sounded slightly inebriated and his Harlem argot was so entertaining in its own right, whites responded to his criticism with amusement, not anger. Only after World War II, when blacks had more power and pride in themselves, did they cease to hide behind the mask of an inoffensive comedy. Wit became the unimpeded outlet for their hostility. As performers like Dick Gregory, Flip Wilson, and Godfrey Cambridge became more virulent in their clowning, so black writers became more savage in their ironies, more iconoclastic in their satire. Ralph Ellison, Leroi Jones, and Ishmael Reed, as Charles Nichols convincingly shows, now laughed openly and defiantly at what *they* found funny.

Jewish humor was also the salvation of the powerless against the powerful. The Jews of Eastern Europe from whom the majority of twentieth-century Jewish-American comic performers and writers descended were victims of a ludicrous irony: they were divinely designated to be Chosen People, yet they were treated like rejects. To fill the gap between glorious expectation and miserable reality, they wryly deprecated their persecutors and bittersweetly mocked themselves. In jests, their adversaries were dimwitted and besotted; in turn, they themselves were *schlemiels, schnorrers* and *luftmenschen*: bunglers, beggars, and failed speculators. When they immigrated to America, their marginal status again prompted them to make comedy out of constraint. But this time their Jewish jokes were not limited to *shtetls*; they told them before the delighted audiences of burlesque and vaudeville halls and later devised elaborate comic routines for radio, TV, and movies. Yet they still employed the staples of ghetto humor. Their English, like Yiddish, was earthy and verbose. They mimicked the same losers and magnified their plights. They needled the audience and jabbed at their own vulnerabilities. These comics made America receptive to Jewish wit and acted in part as the models for Jewish-American writers, even for the most cerebral of them, Saul Bellow. Though Allen Guttmann is correct in arguing that Bellow's real subject since *Augie March* has been "the mind's comical struggle with ideas," the characters he creates and the language he employs owe much to Old and New World Jewish humor. The importuners in his novels, Allbee and Tamkin, who insist they are entitled to others' good fortune, are latter-day versions of *shtetl schnorrers*. Leventhal and Wilhelm, whose cumbersome bodies continually trip them up, resemble *klotzes,* the clumsy oafs of Jewish slapstick. The mad antics of Henderson and Humboldt are like the zany bits of the *meshuggah,* the crazy buffoon of the Borscht Belt. But the most frequent comic character appearing in Bellow's fiction is the *schlemiel* as masochist, his intelligent yet chronic mistake-making creature who revels in his misery. Similarly, Bellow's style is Yiddish-inspired. His prose, like the speech of his ghetto ancestors, is crowded with the most farfetched mock-heroic allusions to point up the humorous discrepancies between his fallible characters and the grand figures of Bible, myth, and history. His prose contains the comic juxtaposition of many levels of discourse. Like Yiddish, with its "fusion of the secular and the sacred,"[9] Bellow's language teems with gutter clarity and philosophic obscurity. His characters also utilize the Yiddish "humor of verbal retrieval, the word triumphant over the situation."[10] The sprightly metaphors and agile wit at their command temporarily enable them to spring free of their troubles.

Bellow displays a fondness for the Yiddish past, his immigrant Jewish parents, and his melting-pot slum childhood. As Herzog says, "his heart was attached with great power" to the Napoleon Street Jewish ghetto of his youth. Not so with Philip Roth. He writes of third-generation Jews with few endearing memories of family solidarity and meaningful religious experience. Quasi-assimilated, they revile more than revere the Jewish heritage. Alexander Portnoy is, of course, Roth's most vociferous and hilarious reviler, and *Portnoy's Complaint* is his brutally candid and ingeniously comic treatment of what it means to be Jewish in America. As Sheldon Grebstein vividly shows, Roth draws upon many sources for inspiration and technique: the "live" performances of "aggressive-self-destructive Jewish stand-up comedians," the harrowing "sit-down" comedy of Franz Kafka, the "colloquial seriocomic monologue" as practiced by Sinclair Lewis, radio and film scenarios, advertising jargon, and racy Yiddish dialect. The end result is the most painfully funny account to date of the Jewish family romance as told by the guilt-ridden Jewish son.

The Jewish daughter was slower at writing down her complaints and embellishing them with comedy. She was not alone in her delay. "Women had played no essential part in the long sequence of the comic spirit in America,"[11] wrote Constance Rourke. Perhaps it would be more precise to say that women were not originators of American comedy, but they certainly have been the butt of it. In WASP and Jewish-American literature alike, they have appeared as ludicrous whipping-girls, hilarious harridans, and ridiculous sex objects. With no humorous tradition of their own which retaliates against a common enemy, women have been hard pressed to turn

---

[9]Maurice Samuel quoted in Sarah Blacher Cohen, *Saul Bellow's Enigmatic Laughter* (Urbana: University of Illinois Press, 1974), p. 19.

[10]Maurice Samuel quoted *ibid.*, p. 20.

[11]Constance Rourke, *American Humor* (New York: Harcourt, Brace, 1931), p. 118.

their wit outward. Some of the recent Jewish women writers facilely jest at their own and other women's expense, thus reinforcing the notion that females are silly incompetents. Others, like Erica Jong, treat men as comic foils and seek to outrival them in their Rabelaisian accounts of female sexuality. Only a few of them, like Cynthia Ozick, feel sure enough of their powers to leave the women's section of the literary synagogue to wryly portray what's happening in the rest of the Jewish world. Likewise, Mary McCarthy is called "raging Mary" or "lady with a switchblade" for slicing away at the political and social pretensions of Gentile society. In her comedies of manners and ideas she ridicules oppressive males and weak-willed women as well. Because of this double-edged attack, Wendy Martin finds McCarthy's satire "complex and varied" and ultimately more revealing of the subtleties of women's experience in the twentieth century.

There is no denying, however, that Mary McCarthy's minority status has provided her and other contemporary women writers with a vantage point from which to mock the majority culture. Similarly, Afro-American and Jewish-American writers have made comic capital out of their position as marginal and invisible men. Since humor often depends on outsiders making fun of insiders, it is very difficult for insiders to discover what is laughable about themselves. So it has been with the WASP establishment. During the eighteenth, nineteenth, and early twentieth centuries, they were the principal literary jesters. They determined what was to be laughed at, and the severity of the laughter. But since World War II there have been so many plebeian mirthmakers exposing their patrician follies that the WASPs have had to abdicate their position as the clown princes of American humor. The greatest joke has been played on them. Once the majority humorists, they are now the minority—but not the silent minority. Creative writer George Garrett, with his quirky definition of WASPs and his whimsical analysis of their humor, contributes his own sample of it. As critic, he finds WASP humor sparsely represented in the country's more serious writers. From discussing those authors whose relationship with the comic muse is strained and uneasy, Garrett singles out midwestern Wright Morris and southern R. H. W. Dillard, who risk being seen in the muse's company and have a rousing good time as well. Garrett also discovers large concentrations of WASP humor "just outside the official precincts of literary respectability" in the new journalism. Tom Wolfe is for him the Twain of the times, who with his updated Protestant satire keeps WASP humor burning brightly.

In addition to ethnic comic writers stealing the show from their WASP counterparts, there has been an upsurge of a nonpartisan kind of comedy—college humor—appealing to all races, creeds, classes, regions, and genders. Not a new phenomenon, it has existed from the 1920's on and has grown in popularity as Americans have become more regressive in their needs and more juvenile in their tastes. Its most representative work, and the one which most influenced future sophomoric wits, was Max Shulman's *Barefoot Boy with Cheek* (1944). This first-person parodic narrative with its risible nomenclature and zany anecdotes begat increasingly wilder imitations of itself. Earl Rovit describes the emerging college humor as elephantinely subtle, rhetorically clumsy, "deliberately grotesque," "defiantly irresponsible," "amorphously sentimental," and "buoyantly paranoid." Rovit also acknowledges the charms of this adolescent comedy, but he worries that it and the audience it caters to will remain at an arrested state of development.

This is not a concern of Sanford Pinsker in his discussion of the urban tall tale. Though it is seemingly a variant of college humor practiced by some of the same comic writers whom Rovit dubs adolescent, Pinsker finds this urban brand of mirth an "artful stretching of the truth," where rueful "*under*compensations" of city dupes replace the riotous "*over*compensations" of frontier heroes. Current high-brow American literature has its share of *angst*-ridden protagonists who exaggerate their woe with Kafkaesque glee. But no one can outwhine or tally up more bodily and psychic damages than the leading fall-guy of popular literature and film—Woody Allen. By boasting of the countless defeats which befall him, he amuses audiences with his ineptitude. His hyperbolic imagination of disaster also takes the scare out of city life and, for a short time, makes it more funny than fearsome. This is the added social value of urban tall tale humor. It may be immature, but it ensures our balance in dangerous places.

The humor of recent American experimental writing is also grounded in popular culture. Indeed, its primary concern, according to Philip Stevick, is with representing "certain attitudes toward, and treatments of, the shared mass cultural objects of our world," or

what he refers to as the *dreck* of our lives. In the works of Donald
Barthelme and Stanley Elkin, two of the more prominent trash
collectors of postmodern fiction, their characters are immersed in a
world of hackneyed advertising slogans, the camp art of tasteless
movies and sentimental songs, tantalizing brand names, defective
merchandise, political cant. The authors do not judge this junk as
meaningless, but playfully exhibit a naive fascination with its garish
surface. By making *dreck* so prominent in their fiction, they re-
vitalize their art and, in the process, introduce new comic effects for
the refuse-besieged audience to appreciate.

Camp is also one of the principal ingredients in the humor of
contemporary American drama—only there it joins forces with
cruelty and colloquialism to make the most virulent comic impact.
Prior to the merging of these three C's, genteel social comedy, the
mechanical humor of vocational types, and predictable situation
comedy prevailed in nineteenth- and twentieth-century American
drama. In the last few years, however, plays have appeared which
defy the conventional definitions of stage comedy. In the works of
Edward Albee, Arthur Kopit, John Guare, Rochelle Owens, Sam
Shepard, Megan Terry, and Ed Bullins, a preverse kind of humor
erupts unexpectedly in the most serious contexts. As Ruby Cohn
describes it, this humor alternates between "verbal flagellation,"
colloquial triviality, and the many excesses of camp, "especially its
obstreperous self-consciousness of itself as play."

The element of play for its own sake is equally conspicuous in
certain kinds of contemporary American poetry. The New York
school of poets such as Kenneth Koch and John Ashbery refuse to be
shackled to a serious art whose most important function is to convey
meaning. Since they believe there is a "gap between words and
things," John Vernon finds, they "release words to play on their
own, joke around, display themselves, invent, shuffle, entertain."
Like the experimental prose writers, they lace their poems with
images from popular culture, with abundant clichés, with references
to camp sentimentality and nostalgia. A second group of poets, with
A. R. Ammons and John Berryman in their ranks, enlists humor as a
detective to aid in the capture of elusive meanings in their poems. It
upsets their equilibrium, takes them on detours, compounds their
confusions, but ultimately leads them to important thematic discoveries. Humor, however, need not always be so purposive in

contemporary American poetry; often its waggish twists and turns, which delight but defy analysis, are reason enough for its existence.

E. B. White would agree with this position. Leery of humor critics and their deadly commentary, he once complained: "Humor can be dissected as a frog can, but the thing dies in the process and the innards are discouraging to any but the pure scientific mind." The humor critics in this book are not guilty of this offense. With their fresh and probing essays, they have kept contemporary American humor alive. The frog may not be the celebrated one from Calaveras County, but it is still bright-eyed and jumping.

MAX F. SCHULZ

Toward a Definition of Black Humor

Conrad Knickerbocker is its theoretician, Bruce Jay Friedman its field commander. Yet neither they nor their fellow partisans can agree on a common article of faith or theater of operations. Black humor is a movement without unity, a group of guerrillas who huddle around the same campfire only because they know that they are in Indian territory. Even though they grudgingly concur about the enemy, they anarchistically refuse to coordinate their attack. Desperate men, not only have they abandoned the safety of received opinions, but they have also left to the news media the advance positions of satirical shock treatment, charging instead the exposed flanks of undiscovered lands "somewhere out beyond satire," which require "a new set of filters" to be seen.[1]

The irony is that Friedman inadvertently gave literary respectability and philosophical cohesion to the group, when he patched together thirteen pieces (short stories and excerpts from novels, including one of his own, "Black Angels") for Bantam Books in 1965 and nonchalantly entitled them *Black Humor*. The other twelve writers on whom he had perpetrated this travesty were Terry Southern, John Rechy, J. P. Donleavy, Edward Albee, Charles Simmons, Louis-Ferdinand Céline, James Purdy, Joseph Heller,

---

[1]Bruce Jay Friedman, Foreword to *Black Humor* (New York: Bantam Books, 1965), p. x. The same essay with slight changes is reprinted as "Those Clowns of Conscience" in *Book Week*, July 15, 1965.

Thomas Pynchon, Vladimir Nabokov, Conrad Knickerbocker, and John Barth. The venture was an exercise in book-making. Friedman's novels had had good critical reception but modest sales; he had a living to earn, a family to support. Much to his surprise, he found himself tarred with his own black label. Dumbfounded (like one of his fictional characters) to learn that someone was indeed listening, he soon regretted his part in this bit of carpentry for the trade. The tag was applied to his own fiction until he winced when he heard the words. What he had ended up with were "thirteen separate writers with thirteen separate, completely private and unique visions," he admitted with ingratiating candor as early as his foreword to the collection, "who in so many ways have nothing at all to do with one another and would not know or perhaps even understand one another's work if they tripped over it."[2]

Despite Friedman's protestations and a subsequent effort to describe his play *Scuba Duba* with the more critically usable phrase "tense comedy," the black humor tag seems to have stuck. If, however, the term is to have any critical usefulness, aside from an opaque impressionistic meaning, it must be more clearly defined than hitherto. For as a term black humor *is* vague. It fails to distinguish among the genres. It fails to differentiate the contemporary movement from the many past instances of similar literary reactions to human experience. It fails to focus the means (plot, character, thought, and diction) and the end (effect on reader: laughter, tears, etc.) of literary expression, as Friedman's alternative "tense comedy" attempts more successfully to do. Indeed, black humor needs a definition that will be not only inclusive but also exclusive.

Although several attempts have been made to define black humor, the results have been elusive and chimerical. (1) Despairing of any substantive formula, Friedman opted for a mystery that has been around as long as the human mind has had an iconoclastic itch to peel back disguises and to probe "thoughts no one else cares to think."[3] (2) Robert Scholes[4] tried to channel Friedman's all-out purchase on history by shifting to formalist concerns and identifying black humor with the recurrent intellectual reaction of artists to the limitations of realism. As with the painterly aims of some modern artists, black humorists, he believes, are absorbed by the possibilities of playful

[2]*Ibid.*, pp. vii–viii.
[3]*Ibid.*, p. xi.
[4]Robert Scholes, *The Fabulators* (New York: Oxford University Press, 1967), pp. 35–46.

and artful construction. They are master fabulators in the tradition of the Romance and its baroque configurations. Like Plato's "all-in-one," unfortunately, Scholes's "fabulation" becomes in practice a nondiscriminating standard, subsuming in its alembic all "artful contrivance," for is not the artist by nature a maker of patterns? Are not the stark fables of Isaac Bashevis Singer as contrived as the mannered convolutions of Vladimir Nabokov? Surely Scholes's already disparate group of fabulators, ranging from Lawrence Durrell to John Hawkes, could not deny membership to the master fabulator—and ironist—Henry James. *Hic reductio ad absurdum!* If, on the other hand, Scholes sees this fabulation as a game to be enjoyed in part for its own sake, a decadence appreciated by a developed taste for the sophisticated, the artful—as his emphasis on Nabokov and Barth as arch-fabulators would suggest —then the moral position of a Henry James or the social gesture of a Bruce Jay Friedman, a Louis-Ferdinand Céline, a Terry Southern, or a Kurt Vonnegut becomes an important distinction. This is not to deny that Nabokov and Barth have their serious themes, or that Friedman has his aestheticism, but to suggest that the ways Nabokov and Barth handle their subjects loom larger in their calculations than the stylisms of Friedman loom in his. In any final analysis, the verbal conundrums of Nabokov and Barth would appear more the stance of the aesthete than the verbal uniqueness of Friedman. And Scholes's definition would seem inevitably to polarize the practitioners of black humor into at least two groups distinguishable by the formalist means they employ. (3) Conrad Knickerbocker in his groundbreaking essay[5] diminishes the black humorist to *poéte maudit,* a scorpion to the status quo, so full of the poison of self-loathing for the "specially tailored, ready-to-wear identities" given to us by TV, movies, the press, universities, the government, the military, medicine, and business, that he mortally stings himself, pricking the surrogate skin of society.[6]

[5]Conrad Knickerbocker, "Humor with a Mortal Sting," *New York Times Book Review,* 69, pt. 2 (September 27, 1964), 3, 60–61. Cf. Richard Schickel, "The Old Critics and the New Novel," *Wisconsin Studies in Contemporary Literature,* 5 (1964), 26–36.

[6]Other attempts to deal with black humor include Richard Kostelanetz, "The Point Is That Life Doesn't Have Any Point," *New York Times Book Review,* 70 (June 6, 1965), 3, 28–30; reprinted as "The American Absurd Novel" in *The World of Black Humor,* ed. Douglas M. Davis (New York: E. P. Dutton, 1967), pp. 306–313; Davis's introduction to the volume; Robert Buckeye, "The Anatomy of the Psychic Novel," *Critique,* 9 (1967), 33–45; Charles D. Peavy, "Larry McMurtry and Black Humor: A Note on the Last Picture Show," *Western American Literature,* 2 (1967), 223–227; Koji Numasawa, "Black Humor: An American

We unnecessarily compound the problem of determining what black humor is when we try, like Scholes, to see it as a universal attitude of mind, periodically emerging in the history of literature. Such a *via media* leads to an impasse not unlike that reached by those critics who make romanticism and classicism out to be constant modes of apprehending human experience. More limiting, certainly, but more useful in the long run is to recognize that black humor is a phenomenon of the 1960's, comprising a group of writers who share a viewpoint and an aesthetics for pacing off the boundaries of a nuclear-technological world intrinsically without confinement. Equally useful is to discriminate black humor from the oral techniques of sick humor and from the dramatic conventions of the theater of the absurd, even though it shares with these modes of expression some of the same assumptions about our century. In this respect, Hamlin Hill's essay,[7] which deals with the confrontation of humorist and audience, analyzes the technique of such stand-up comedians as Mort Sahl, Mike Nichols, and Lenny Bruce and the sick humor of Jules Feiffer and Paul Krassner, rather than the literary form of black humor; hence it somewhat unwittingly helps in discriminating sick humor from black humor, but not in defining black humor, which was purportedly its intention. And *Catch-22,* widely heralded as a black humor novel, actually derives as much from absurdist theater as from black humor fictional strategies. Written in the late forties and early fifties for the most part (although not published until 1961), its disregard of time and space, repetitiveness of speeches, stichomythia of commonplaces, and exercises in disproportion (that is, the substitution of the trivial as vehicle for and purveyor of the serious) link it more to the plays of Ionesco and Beckett, which cry out against a complex world, than to the elegant

---

Aspect," *Studies in English Literature* (University of Tokyo), 44 (1968), 177–193; Eugene McNamara, "The Absurd Style in Contemporary American Literature," *Humanities Association Bulletin* (Canada), 19 (1968), 44–49; Burton Feldman, "Anatomy of Black Humor," *Dissent* (March-April, 1968); reprinted in *The American Novel Since World War II,* ed. Marcus Klein (New York: Fawcett, 1969), pp. 224–228; Joseph J. Waldemeir, "Only an Occasional Rutabaga: American Fiction since 1945," *Modern Fiction Studies,* 15 (1969–70), 467–481; Brom Weber, "The Mode of Black Humor," in *The Comic Imagination in American Literature,* ed. Louis D. Rubin (New Brunswick, N.J.: Rutgers University Press, 1973), and my article on "Black Humor" in *Encyclopedia of World Literature in the Twentieth Century,* ed. Frederick Ungar and Lina Mainiero (New York: Ungar, 1975), IV, 45–49.

[7]Hamlin Hill, "Black Humor: Its Causes and Cure," *Colorado Quarterly,* 17 (1968), 57–64.

fictional structures of Barth, Borges, Grass, Nabokov, and Pynchon which wittily parody that same world. A similar transitional work is Donleavy's *Ginger Man* (1955), which displays its Angry Young Man genesis as much as it anticipates the black humor stance.

The possibility that black humor differs from existentialism in its view of man is less easy to determine, yet I think an effort to discriminate between the two should be made. Basically, both posit an absurd world devoid of intrinsic values, with a resultant tension between individual and universe. The existentialist, however, retains implicitly a respect for the self. Although existence precedes being, to exist is to act (even for Beckett's almost immobile characters), and to act is to assert the self. The negation of many possibilities in favor of one choice of action thus becomes a heroic primal assent to life, as in Camus' portrait of Sisyphus. More often than not with the French existentialists, action leads to cosmic despair rather than to joyous wholeness of being. Nevertheless, the realization of self, as with Meursault in Camus' *Stranger,* Moses in Bellow's *Herzog,* and Rojack in Mailer's *American Dream,* is potentially present in the act of overcoming the negation of life by way of the assertion of self. Thus, while one finds in existentialism a rejection of suprapersonal law, dogma, and social order, one finds retained a grudging hard-won faith in the dignity and ordering capacity of the individual; whereas black humor smiles at the human penchant for conceptualizing chimeras into existence and then mistaking them for incontrovertible absolutes.

With black humor, choice poses the primary difficulty. This is the consequence of a shift in perspective from the self and its ability to create a moral ambience through an act to emphasis on all the moving forces of life which converge collectively upon the individual. But to affirm all possible forces in the likelihood that an act can be self-creating is to deliver oneself up to skepticism that the self is anything but chimerical. Such is the plight of Barth's heroes. Yet this refusal to confirm either a suprapersonal or a personal order does not leave the black humorist despairing. He remains dissociated, hanging loose (or, as has been suggested about Friedman, "hanging by his thumbs"[8]), coolly presenting individual efforts to realize oneself in relation to the outer world, with the focus less on the

[8]Josh Greenfield, "Bruce Jay Friedman Is Hanging by His Thumbs," *New York Times Magazine,* January 14, 1968.

individual than on the world of experiences, less on the agony of struggle to realize self than on the bewildering trackless choices that face the individual.

Nor are its grotesqueries heirs to those of surrealism. The latter assumes the validity of the human consciousness in its reliance on the processes of dreaming for its substance. If the subconscious mind includes a certain amount of internal disorder, this is realized aesthetically in the techniques of surrealism, as well as in those of expressionism and stream of consciousness. Contrariwise, external disorder, meaningless social disorder, is codified as "absurdity" in existentialist fiction.[9] Here black humor finds its logical home.

Divergence from traditional comedy and satire further characterizes black humor. New comedy, according to Northrop Frye's "Argument of Comedy,"[10] always worked toward a reconciliation of the individual with society. Either the normal individual was freed from the bonds of an arbitrary humor society, or a normal society was rescued from the whims imposed by humor individuals. As might be suspected, Frye finds lurking beneath this realignment of social forces the yearly triumph of spring over winter. He sees the victory of normality over abnormality as a formalized celebration of the archetypal pattern of death and resurrection. In the marriage of the young hero, in his triumph over the old lecher (*senex*), in the freeing of the slave, new comedy rehearsed the victory of life over death.

Black humor stops short of any such victory. It enacts no individual release or social reconciliation; it often moves toward, but ordinarily fails to reach, that goal. Like Shakespeare's dark comedies, black humor condemns man to a dying world; it never envisions, as do Shakespeare's early and late comedies, the possibilities of human escape from an aberrant environment into a forest milieu, as a ritual of the triumph of the green world over the waste land. Thus, at the conclusion of Bruce Jay Friedman's *Stern,* the protagonist is as alienated from "the kike man" and the suburban neighborhood he lives in as he was at the outset. Despite his efforts at *rapprochement,* he and society persist in the bonds of abnormality

---

[9]Mark Spilka discusses these distinctions in *Dickens and Kafka: A Mutual Interpretation* (Bloomington: Indiana University Press, 1963), p. 262.

[10]Northrop Frye, "The Argument of Comedy," in *English Institute Essays 1948* (New York, 1949), pp. 58–73; reprinted in *Theories of Comedy,* ed. Paul Lauter (New York: Doubleday, 1964), pp. 450–460, from which I quote.

separating each other. The same comic divisiveness holds true for Benny Profane in Thomas Pynchon's *V.*, for Lester in Charles Wright's *Wig*, for Oskar in Günter Grass's *Tin Drum*, and for the narrator in Leonard Cohen's *Beautiful Losers*, to name a few of the many instances to be found in this fiction.

Black humor's denial of social reconciliation or individual release is epitomized in the vision of Louis-Ferdinand Céline, who "worked the same beat," Friedman admiringly acknowledges, "thought all your thoughts . . . was dumbfounded as many times a day as you are, long before you were born."[11] In *Journey to the End of the Night* the best that Bardamu can offer as a summation of his "aimless pilgrimage" through this "truly appalling, awful world" is that "life leaves you high and dry long before you're really through."[12] With numbness of heart, Bardamu acknowledges that neither person nor house can speak to him, that no one can find another in the darkness through which each is condemned to travel a long way alone. Céline heralds the dead end of the eighteenth-century social and political ideal of the *philosophes*, memorably epitomized in William Godwin's boast that society is a collection of individuals.[13] The many black humorists today who look on him as ur-progenitor continue to push farther into the Célinesque darkness—incredible as that seems—in their determined exploration of the permutability of urban existence and the paralysis of human indifference.

The divisiveness of society is certainly one consequence of the individualizing bent of Protestant humanism of the past five hundred years, but other causes peculiar to our century are equally discernible. One need only to contrast the Rome of Plautus and the London of Shakespeare to the New York of Friedman and the Los Angeles of Pynchon to see the change in social cohesion that has taken place. Whereas the Plautean Romans and the Shakespearean Londoners were members of cities whose districts added up to coherent and whole communities with identifiable classes and cultures, Friedman's New Yorkers and Pynchon's Angelenos live in cities no longer with centers, connected to each other by subways and free-

[11]Friedman, *Black Humor*, p. viii.

[12]Louis-Ferdinand Céline, *Journey to the End of the Night* (New York: New Directions, 1960), pp. 504, 459.

[13]William Godwin, *An Enquiry Concerning Political Justice* (1793), ed. Isaac Kramnick (New York: Penguin, 1976), bk. II, ch. 2.

ways. Although they live elbow to elbow, they are separated by vast distances from the places of personal relationships: work, church, parental homes, recreation. Friedman's Everyman, Stern, daily faces a harrowing multi-houred trip to the office, among indifferent (or outright hostile) fellow commuters. Angelenos spend equal numbers of hours speeding down ribbons of concrete, each encased in his metal cocoon of an automobile, cut off from the intimate sounds of human voices and smells of human bodies, permitted only the occasional blurred glimpse of a face through two panes of window glass as they whisk past one another. Benny Profane —Pynchon's man profaned—yo-yoing on the Times Square– Grand Central Station subway shuttle, embodies the ultimate directionlessness of life in the modern city. In constant motion, he lacks destination. Extended into the cosmos, and even more pointless ultimately, are Billy Pilgrim's peregrinations (in Vonnegut's *Slaughterhouse-Five*) between Earth and Tralfamadore. Like Bardamu's restless movements from France to Africa to America back to France, life describes a pointless journey with death as the only true destination. It is this disjunctive world that moves the black humorist, in part, to arrest the traditional comic reconciliation of individual and society.

Black humor differs also from current existentialist views of man in refusing to treat his isolation as an ethical situation. Friedman slyly ribs Stern's effort to offset his fearful solitariness. In the last scene of the novel, for example, Stern's self-conscious embrace of wife and child in the nursery becomes a parodic tableau of the holy family, mistimed and miscued:

> Now Stern walked around the room, touching the rugs to make sure they wouldn't fall on his son's face. Then he said, "I feel like doing some hugging," and knelt beside the sleeping boy, inhaling his pajamas and putting his arm over him. His wife was at the door and Stern said, "I want you in here, too." She came over, and it occurred to him that he would like to try something a little theatrical, just kneel there quietly with his arms protectively draped around his wife and child. He tried it and wound up holding them a fraction longer than he'd intended.[14]

Céline's dry tone and Parisian argot are similarly scornful of any

[14]Friedman, *Stern* (New York: Simon and Schuster, 1962), p. 191.

mask other than the comic. With a matter-of-factness that suggests the laconic air of boredom (incongruously belied by the precipitous torrent of words), Bardamu recounts his indifference to life:

> Whatever people may care to make out, life leaves you high and dry long before you're really through.
>
> The things you used to set most store by, you one fine day decide to take less and less notice of, and it's an effort when you absolutely have to. You're sick of always hearing yourself talk. . . . You abbreviate. You renounce. Thirty years you've been at it, talking, talking. . . . You don't mind now about being right. You lose even the desire to hang on to the little place you've reserved for yourself among the pleasures of life. . . . You're fed up. From now on, it's enough just to eat a little, to get a bit of warmth, and to sleep as much as you can on the road to nothing at all. . . . The only things that still mean anything very much to you are the little regrets, like never having found time to get round and see your old uncle at Bois-Colombes, whose little song died away forever one February evening. That's all one's retained of life, this little very horrible regret; the rest one has more or less successfully vomited up along the road, with a good many retchings and a great deal of unhappiness. One's come to be nothing but an aged lamppost of fitful memories at the corner of a street along which almost no one passes now.[15]

"If you're to be bored," Bardamu concludes, "the least wearisome way is to keep absolutely regular habits." Not suicide! That would be a nonsensical gesture of metaphysical despair or of archaic heroics. Todd Andrews reaches the same decision at the end of Barth's *Floating Opera* when he recognizes that if there is no good reason why he should go on living, there is also no reason why he should die. This conception of its protagonist as the common man *manqué* is what makes black humor a somewhat limited vision capable of the specific aberrations of comedy, rather than the universal condition of tragedy.

We can gauge the degree of detachment practiced by black humor if we compare these examples with the contrary moral renunciation of mankind that fires Schrella's decision at the conclusion of Heinrich Böll's *Billiards at Half-Past Nine*. A fugitive from Nazi Germany, Schrella has returned to his native city after an exile of more than twenty years. But he does not plan to stay. Unlike the rest of his countrymen and such black humor figures as Stern, he resolutely

[15]Céline, *Journey*, pp. 459–460.

resists accommodation with the destructive powers of the past which persevere in the continuing forces of the present. As a continuing moral protest, he persists in his rooming-house and hotel existence.

> "I'm afraid of houses you move into, then let yourself be convinced of the banal fact that life goes on and that you get used to anything in time. Ferdi would be only a memory, and my father only a dream. And yet they killed Ferdi, and his father vanished from here without a trace. They're not even remembered in the lists of any political organization, since they never belonged to any. They aren't even remembered in the Jewish memorial services, since they weren't Jewish. . . . I can't live in this city because it isn't alien enough for me . . . my hotel room's exactly right. Once I shut the door behind me, this city becomes as foreign as all the others."[16]

Billiards at Half-Past Nine is black enough in its vision of man; but its fervid crusade to alter human nature, and its desperate rejection of society until such moral regeneration takes place, give it a tragic rather than comic mask. When he wishes, of course, Böll can write what passes for black humor. In *The Clown* he depicts the deterioration of Hans Schnier, a social misfit who cannot adjust to the hypocrisy of postwar Germany. Whereas Dostoevsky's Idiot spirals tragically heavenward, Böll's Clown winds down through Biedermeier instances of insult to a beggar's cushion in the Bonn train station. Like the irreverently treated heroes of *God Bless You, Mr. Rosewater* and *The Sot-Weed Factor,* Schnier the "wise fool" proves to be more foolish than wise. But even at this ebb tide of his life, Schnier (unlike Schrella) continues to seek out human company.

Like Böll's Clown, the protagonist of black humor does not despair with the savage bitterness of Nathanael West's Miss Lonelyhearts. Nor does he remain aloof, dismissing society with cold imperviousness, like Evelyn Waugh's Dennis Barlow. Rather, he worries about his place in it. Only after repeated rebuffs in his search for a relationship with others does he accept his empty existence with an angry shrug like Ferdinand Bardamu. He may be a booby like Friedman's Stern, a *naïf* like his Joseph, an anti-hero like Céline's Bardamu, a silly like Vonnegut's Eliot Rosewater, a pervert like Nabokov's Humbert Humbert, a clown like Heller's Yossarian, a fool like Barth's Ebenezer Cooke, a rogue like Berger's Jack

---

[16]Heinrich Böll, *Billiards at Half-Past Nine* (New York: McGraw-Hill, 1963), ch. 13.

Crabb, a dropout like Grass's Oskar, a dupe like Pynchon's Herbert Stencil—but he is never an untouched innocent like Waugh's Paul Pennyfeather, a dismembered scapegoat like West's Lemuel Pitkin, or an unwitting gull like Swift's Gulliver. At the end of *Decline and Fall* Paul Pennyfeather returns to college unchanged by his scarifying mishaps. At the end of *A Cool Million* Lemuel Pitkin is without thumb, leg, eye, teeth, scalp—indeed, his very existence; yet he is, ironically, a heroic witness to the American dream of success. The black humor protagonist is not, like these satiric foils, an authorial lens for analyzing the real, corrupt object of the satire. Nor does detachment mean for him withdrawal from the world, as it does for Gulliver, Candide, or Dennis Barlow. He is at once observer of, and participant in, the drama of dissidence, detached from and yet affected by what happens around him. Extremely conscious of his situation, he is radically different from the satiric puppets of Waugh and West, who bounce back like Krazy Kat from every cruel flattening as smooth and round as before, their minds unviolated by experience. His—and the author's—gaze is, more often than not, concentrated on what Conrad Knickerbocker has called the terrors and possibilities of the world we have brought into being in this century, and of the self-knowledge that this leads us toward.[17] His prison-house loneliness, forced upon him by existence, becomes a Célinesque journey to the end of the night.

The moral quality of society—the aim of satire—is not, according to Northrop Frye, the point of the comic resolution of an individual and a group.[18] Nor is it the objective of black humor, which resists any final accommodation. As Scholes notes, the black humorist is concerned not with what to do about life, but with how to take it.[19] This is not to say that he has no moral position, but only to suggest that this position is *implicit*. He may challenge the trances and hysterias of society, as Conrad Knickerbocker suggests,[20] but he does not ordinarily urge choice on us. He seeks, rather, a comic perspective on both tragic fact and moralistic certitude. In extreme instances (for example, some of Kurt Vonnegut's writings), this attitude of mind will lead to the novel's refusal to take seriously its implied moral position. *The Sot-Weed Factor* has been faulted for its

[17]Knickerbocker, "Humor with a Mortal Sting," p. 61.
[18]Frye, "The Argument of Comedy," in *Theories of Comedy*, p. 453.
[19]Scholes, *Fabulators*, p. 43.
[20]Knickerbocker, "Humor with a Mortal Sting," p. 61.

abdication of responsibility to answer the questions it raises about intrinsic values, and *Catch-22* for its central evasiveness as regards war, for its not having a point of view, an awareness of what things should or should not be.[21] Such is the ultimate ethical and aesthetic chaos that these novels risk in their rage for an inclusive purchase on reality.

The skepticism of the black humorist suggests an explanation for the distinctly metaphysical bent and American identity of this fiction. Can a writer convinced of the truth of a closed ethical, philosophical, or religious system conceptualize human experience in the terms of black humor? I think not. Undeviating acceptance of Christianity would surely make it impossible to produce an anti-God novel like Robert Coover's *Universal Baseball Association Inc.— J. Henry Waugh, Prop.,* other than as an unconvincing pastiche. His ardent Catholicism prompts Heinrich Böll to castigate his bourgeois characters for giving their allegiance to the German economic miracle rather than to the Catholic religious values they nominally profess, and accounts for *The Clown*'s suffering from artistic and philosophical confusion and ultimately for not corresponding to the black humor novels considered here. Günter Grass also professes to be a Catholic. His social skepticism, however, qualifies his religious dogmatism. In *The Tin Drum* he contains the two perspectives of Catholicism and black humor, content with a simple balance of contraries, especially the dichotomies of guilt and innocence, tempter and tempted, the Christlike and the satanical, the Dionysian (Oskar's fascination for Rasputin) and the Apollonian (Oskar's attraction to Goethe), without compulsion to reconcile them.[22] His concentration on the outward-oriented world of objects—the tin drum, fizz powder, the smells of the women in Oskar's life, the cartridge case, the skat playing of Oskar's parents, his grandmother's petticoats —contributes to this intellectual neutrality, since objects are basically inimical to ideas, or to the resolution of ideas.[23] Consequently

[21]Cf. Robert Garis, "What Happened to John Barth?" *Commentary,* 85 (October, 1966), 80–82; Earl Rovit, "The Novel as Parody: John Barth," *Critique,* 6 (1963), 77–85; John M. Muste, "Better to Die Laughing: The War Novels of Joseph Heller and John Ashmead," *Critique,* 5 (1962), 16–27; and John Wain, "A New Novel about Old Troubles," *Critical Quarterly,* 5 (1963), 168–173.

[22]See Leslie A. Willson, "The Grotesque Everyman in Günter Grass's *Die Blechtrommel,"Monatshefte,* 18 (1966), 131–138.

[23]See W. G. Cunliffe, "Aspects of the Absurd in Günter Grass," *Wisconsin Studies in Contemporary Literature,* 7 (1966), 311–327.

Grass's novels observe the frame of reference of black humor despite his commitment to traditional beliefs.

The literary tradition of the German and English novels also militates against the inconclusive version of life presented in the black humor novel. The German *Bildungsroman,* or *Entwicklungsroman,* presupposes a set of social, as well as moral and ethical, values, a substantive goal toward which the protagonist progresses in preparation for his adult role in the community. *The Tin Drum* conforms to this genre but parodies its fixed principles in its conception of Oskar's being born with awareness, of his being as cognizant of his world at three as at thirty, and in its uncertainty (and plurality) of point of view.[24] The English novel of manners similarly assumes a collective relevance, established social classes, and codes of conduct—a context within which narrative conflict is developed. The American novel, short on *Entwicklung* and manners, is more receptive to the inconclusive exploration of ontological and epistemological questions of being, growth, and knowledge. In this respect, the black humor novel continues the quest of the *Pequod,* its route updated and its procedure modernized.

It is probably not accidental that the two European writers, other than Grass and Céline, who are identified with black humor —Vladimir Nabokov and Jorge Luis Borges—exhibit a disillusioned cosmopolitanism acquired by the accidents of choice and of history that transcends the literary and cultural suppositions of their Russian and Argentinian heritages. To them have been "given bad times in which to live"[25] in greater measure than is man's normal lot; and their excruciating sense of the instability of life pervades the texture and substance of their fiction. "We are creatures of chance in an absolute void," "the *true* Present . . . . an instant of zero duration," Nabokov has Van Veen exclaim in *Ada* "—unless we be artists ourselves." Only in "the act of artistic correction" is "the pang of the Present"[26] given durability. Heirs of this century's national tensions and philosophical uncertainties, their stories are parodies of man's mistaken faith, historically and philosophically,

[24]Cf. *ibid.,* and Robert Maurer, "The End of Innocence: Günter Grass's *The Tin Drum,* " *Bucknell Review,* 16 (1968), 45–65.

[25]From Borges's tribute to his Argentine forbear Juan Crisóstomo Lafinur, in the Prologue to "A New Refutation of Time," in *Labyrinths: Selected Stories and Other Writings,* ed. Donald A. Yates and James E. Irby (New York: New Directions, 1964), p. 218.

[26]Vladimir Nabokov, *Ada* (New York: McGraw-Hill, 1969), pp. 324, 417, 418.

in cultural continuity and ideational permanence. It is not accidental that Kurt Vonnegut has waited longest of the black humorists for recognition. His novels are not organized according to one fictional model but follow multiple modes, at once novel of manners, confessional journal, science fiction, social satire, detective story, soap opera, and slick magazine tale. The resultant farrago of literary syntaxes has bewildered and offended both British and American readers, whose expectations are never consistently satisfied. At any rate, black humor has remained, with the exception of the few European writers mentioned, a predominantly American phenomenon of the sixties, whose anxieties proceeding from pluralism, conformity, and an irresolute value system give it both its method and its subject.

RICHARD PEARCE

Nabokov's
Black (Hole) Humor:
Lolita and *Pale Fire*

The Enchanted Hunters is not only the name of the hotel where Humbert Humbert first consummated his love with Dolores Haze, or where Lolita first seduced the hungry Humbug; it is also the name of a school play built upon a multiplicity of seductions and deceptions, not the least of which was the seduction of the leading lady by the playwright Clare Quilty, who, Lolita insisted to her hummocky stepfather, was just some old woman. In the play a farmer's daughter, acted by Lolita, has gotten hold of a book on hypnotism and persuades six red-capped, identically dressed hunters (a banker, a plumber, a policeman, an undertaker, an underwriter, and an escaped convict) that their past lives were only dreams or nightmares from which she has aroused them. But the seventh hunter, a poet, insists that she and the entertainment are his invention. In the end, "barefooted Dolores was to lead check-trousered Mona [Humbert had insisted that male parts be "taken by female parts"] to the paternal farm behind the Perilous Forest to prove to the braggart she was not a poet's fancy, but a rustic down-to-brown-earth lass."[1]

In a filmed interview Nabokov describes the joy he takes in such creative deception: "the first thrill of diabolical pleasure that you have in . . . discovering that you have somehow cheated creation by

---

[1] Vladimir Nabokov, *Lolita* (New York: Berkley, 1966), p. 184. Subsequent page references will be made directly in the text.

creating something yourself."[2] The thrill is diabolical, first, because what he creates is independent of prior creation and defiant of ultimate "reality." It is also diabolical because the cheating entails a deconstruction of prior creation—a canny dismantling or gleeful decimation of the everyday world, everyday fantasies, and everyday literary conventions. Nabokov's "thrill of diabolical pleasure" is like the thrill that animated the Roman Saturnalia and that found its medieval expression in the Feast of Fools, the miracle plays, and the *sotie* drama. By reflecting on three points in the medieval development of diabolical comedy, we may gain a perspective on Nabokov's achievement.[3]

The Feast of Fools was an English New Year's revel that loosened traditional restraints, allowing the release of a joyful demonic energy. To use a medieval trope, "the world was turned upside down": priests and clerks wore monstrous masks, ate blood puddings during mass, played dice on the altar, leaped through the church, drove through town in shabby carts regaling everyone with "infamous performances . . . indecent gestures and verses scurrilous and unchaste."[4]

In the English miracle plays the diabolical comic impulse became more formalized, and as the energy became more controlled and more comic, it became more threatening. Pilate amused the spectators by toying with his wife before calling Jesus before him; devilish tormentors would blindfold Christ and make Him guess who scourged Him last, or make a farce out of fitting His body onto a cross that had been carelessly made the wrong size. The devils and tormentors were energetic, inventive, comic, skillful, and successful. By "turning their work into sport" they presented "Hell to their victims as an unending, varied game." In their malicious play they achieved an experience of evil—the destruction of divine order. And yet they also succeeded in bringing the biblical drama to life.[5]

In France, which did not tolerate fools in its church or clowning with its liturgy, the diabolical comic impulse was secularized in

[2]Robert Hughes, *Vladimir Nabokov*, National Education Television Film, 1966.

[3]The concept of diabolical comedy has developed from my thinking since the publication of my *Stages of the Clown: Perspectives on Modern Fiction from Dostoyevsky to Beckett* (Carbondale: Southern Illinois University Press, 1970). The germ of this essay will be found in ch. 6.

[4]E. K. Chambers, *The Mediaeval Stage* (Oxford: Oxford University Press, 1903), p. 294.

[5]T. McAlindon, "Comedy and Terror in Middle English Literature: The Diabolical Game," *Modern Language Review*, 40 (July, 1965), 321–332.

year-round fool societies and formalized in their *sotie* drama. The fools in these plays were as skillful in their acrobatics as they were with their verbal wit. Turning handsprings in the midst of the satiric banter, they would gleefully defy the laws of gravity and grammar as well as social convention. And in the end a comic free-for-all would bring a "jerry-built new world tumbling about their ears."[6] The *sotie* fools, that is, realized their vitality and exercised their mental and physical skills in the total destruction of the ordinary world.

In the Feast of Fools, the miracle plays, and the *sotie* drama, creative vitality is achieved through the playful release of destructive energy, the diabolical thrill of turning life into a game, the comic urge toward disorder and nihilistic destruction. In the end the world is turned upside down, order is destroyed, reality is undermined by a comic force that is at once threatening and enlivening. And, as the force becomes more threatening and enlivening, its manipulators become more daring and skillful. The diabolical thrill, then, derives from the exercise of skills that destroy social and psychological orders, leaving only the game or the act—or an arbitrary and precarious order that evinces skillful control and creative daring, and that undermines our security while awakening our senses, feelings, and intellects.

One of the most vivid modern realizations of the diabolical impulse I have been trying to define is in Nabokov's *Ada*—in the extraordinary act that Van Veen performed in the guise of Mascodagama. It began with an empty stage, when, "after five heartbeats of theatrical suspense, something swept out of the wings, enormous and black . . . a shapeless nastiness," which precipitated in the audience "something similar to the 'primordial qualm' ":

> Into the harsh light of its gaudily carpeted space a masked giant, fully eight feet tall, erupted, running strongly in the kind of soft boots worn by Cossack dancers. A voluminous, black shaggy cloak of the *burka* type enveloped his *silhouette inquiétante* . . . from neck to knee or what appeared to be those sections of his body. A Karakul cap surmounted his top. A black mask covered the upper part of his heavily bearded face. The unpleasant colossus kept strutting up and down the stage for a while, then the strut changed to the restless walk of a caged madman, then he whirled, and to a clash of cymbals in the orchestra

[6]Enid Welsford, *The Fool: His Social and Literary History* (London: Faber and Faber, 1935), p. 231. Also see Barbara Swain, *Fools and Folly during the Middle Ages and the Renaissance* (New York: Columbia University Press, 1952), ch. 6.

and a cry of terror (perhaps faked) in the gallery, Mascodagama turned over in the air and stood on his head.

In this weird position, with his cap acting as a pseudopodal pad, he jumped up and down, pogo-stick fashion—and suddenly came apart. Van's face, shining with sweat, grinned between the legs of the boots that still shod his rigidly raised arms. Simultaneously his real feet kicked off and away the false head with its crumpled cap and bearded mask. The magic reversal "made the house gasp."[7]

The "magic reversal" is more than the discovery of Van right side up when we thought him upside down; it is a reversal that destroys our sense of which way is up, our normal frame of reference, our sense of "reality." Mascodagama upright—ugly, massive, erratic, masking upside down Van—is threatening. Van upside down— bouncing on his hands like a pogo stick, playing the upright giant —is comic. Mascodagama coming apart is frightening. Van kicking away Mascodagama's fake head is comic—but he is also frightening, because at this point we recognize the union of the strange colossus and the familiar Van, of the erratic and the controlled, of the menacing and the impish. When the mask and costume and performance have been recognized for what they are, all our links with "reality" have been destroyed: all that remains is flat stage and Van's shining face and diabolical grin. And even this reality is undermined by the narrator's ironic style. The narrator, who has no place within the world of the novel, has told us that only "the work of a poet" could describe Van's extraordinary act (especially a poet of the "Black Belfry group"). The ultimate diabolical act, then, is the work of the narrator-poet: the work itself, the verbal surface—which is like a stage whose wings do not open to an outside world. Or a mask that only masks another mask worn by an actor cavorting over a black hole, fully aware of the danger but taking joy in the fact that he has made the hole and his precarious act.

Nabokov's diabolical strategy is to create a recognizable world and then undermine or deconstruct every possible vantage from which we might form judgments. In the end he leaves us with a rich and tantalizing verbal surface suspended, as it were, over a black hole. His singular achievement, then, might be called black-hole humor. This critical metaphor leads from the diabolical tradition to the tradition of modernism, which develops the potential of discon-

---

[7]Vladimir Nabokov, *Ada* (New York: McGraw-Hill, 1969), pp. 183–184.

tinuity, as well as to the imaginative defiance and daring of modern astronomers who first postulated and then discovered a "black hole" in space. I will apply it to two of Nabokov's important and interestingly related novels: *Lolita,* where we are cunningly led along the shifting surface and trapped in its discontinuities by a narrator who is always beyond our grasp; and *Pale Fire,* where we encounter a black hole that is not metaphorical but literal and physical—and that may have led Robbe-Grillet to admire Nabokov and say that this book "comes very close to expressing my feelings."[8]

Lolita (1955) was Nabokov's twelfth novel, the third written in English after his departure from Europe in 1940. "It had taken me some forty years to invent Russia and Western Europe," he tells us in his epilogue, "now I was faced by the task of inventing America" (p. 283). What Nabokov invented was the drive—and aimless driving—toward some evanescent ideal which had obsessed American novelists from Fitzgerald to Kerouac; the speech and manners of an adolescent girl, which few American writers had even looked at; the American motelscape, just before it gave way to the superhighways; the drugstore, before its soda fountain was replaced by the dirty-book rack (which the paperback industry created for the likes of *Lolita*); the department store, with its "touch of the mythological and the enchanted" (p. 100); the bohemian surburban housewife; the progressive girls' school. Much of *Lolita* is like *Sister Carrie* or *An American Tragedy,* where Dreiser deliberately recorded details of those American institutions he knew would become historical. Thus, the Haze house is a "white-frame horror . . . looking dingy and old, more gray than white—the kind of place you know will have a rubber tube affixable to the tub faucet in lieu of shower" (p. 36). And Humbert jots down his early recollections "on the leaves of what is commercially known as a 'typewriter tablet' " (p. 40). But the realistic details in *Lolita* are magnified, and at times singularly distorted, by the lens of Humbert Humbert's language, which is the product of a foreign consciousness. A row of parked cars are "like pigs at a trough" (p. 108). A fire hydrant is seen as "a hideous thing, really, painted a thick silver and red, extending the red stumps of its arms to be varnished by the rain which like stylized blood dripped

[8]"An Interview with Alain Robbe-Grillet, Conducted by David Hayman," *Contemporary Literature,* 16 (Summer, 1975), 276.

upon its argent chains. No wonder that stopping beside those nightmare cripples is taboo" (pp. 98–99).

Humbert Humbert's foreign consciousness is due to more than his European upbringing and his perverse sensibilities. He is made foreign, and removed from our reach, by the "bizarre cognomen . . . his own invention . . . this mask—through which two hypnotic eyes seem to glow" (p. 6). He is removed, that is, by the persona, created by a narrator whose real identity and ultimate purpose are slyly kept beyond our reach. Moreover, he is doubly removed, from the outset of the novel, by being such a persona in a memoir edited by the improbable John Ray, Jr., Ph.D., who has been awarded the Poling Prize for a "modest" work, "Do the Senses Make Sense?" (p. 5). Indeed, the foreword, being a parody of that device used to establish verisimilitude ever since *The Scarlet Letter*, destroys any bridge between the world of the novel and the world where the daily papers are supposed to have carried references to Humbert's crime.

The novel proper is cast as a memoir, a form usually written in a style of sincerity if not modesty, and usually designed to reveal the personality of its author and the tenor of his time through a coherent sequence of selected events and ponderings. It is also cast in the form of a quest, and Humbert's quest has two models, which are also kinds of memoirs. The first is Dante's: from the inspiration of his nymphet Beatrice to the beatific vision, which Humbert encounters as "the melody of children at play, nothing but that, and so limpid was the air that within this vapor of blended voices, majestic and minute, remote and magically near, frank and divinely enigmatic —one could hear now and then, as if released, an almost articulate spurt of vivid laughter, or the crack of a bat, or the clatter of a toy wagon" (p. 280). The second quest model is Melville's *Moby-Dick*. If, on first thought, Humbert's nymphet (especially as she is likened to a butterfly) makes an improbable white whale, and the Humbert-Quilty double is a far cry from Ishmael-Ahab, ponder a layer lower, reader—at least upon Humbert's historical, anthropological, and scientific digressions, which realistically ground and epically magnify the proportions of his nymphet and his quest.

That these forms are not copied but parodied destroys the possibility of a coherent protagonist and comprehendible goal—or effects a deconstruction of our normal expectations, perceptions, and conclusions. The novel's underlying metaphor also contributes to this deconstruction. Diana Butler has pointed out the relationship between Humbert's passion for nymphets and Nabokov's own passion for butterflies;[9] indeed, Lolita's peculiar attraction, Humbert's thrills of discovery, and his pangs of horror and guilt are all evoked through the implicit and pervasive metaphor of Lolita as prize butterfly. Moreover, Alfred Appel, Jr., has described how metamorphosis, which characterizes both the butterfly and the nymphet, also characterizes the form of the novel, the development of Lolita from a girl into a woman, Humbert's lust into love, and a crime into a redeeming work of art. In the end, "the reader has watched the chrysalis come to life."[10]

But to see the beautiful butterfly at the end of the multiple transformations should not obscure the stages of destruction, or deconstruction, in the process. Humbert Humbert acknowledges: "I knew I had fallen in love with Lolita forever; but I also knew she would not be forever Lolita. She would be thirteen on January 1. In two years or so she would cease being a nymphet and would turn into a 'young girl,' and then, into a 'college girl'—that horror of horrors" (p. 62). Lolita is as changeable and transient as a butterfly; the narrator's accomplishment is not in capturing, but evoking her in an equally changeable and transitory form—a form composed of perspectives that are successively and gleefully destroyed. The pattern of deconstruction may be analyzed into two contradictory planes, which we might call endless multiplication and continual forward movement.

In *Lolita*'s opening paragraphs, we are given a fine example of Nabokov's style:

> Lolita, light of my life, fire of my loins. My sin, my soul. Lo-lee-ta: the tip of the tongue taking a trip of three steps down the palate to tap, at three, on the teeth. Lo. Lee. Ta.
>
> She was Lo, plain Lo, in the morning, standing four feet ten in one sock. She was Lola in slacks. She was Dolly at school. She was Dolores on the dotted line. But in my arms she was always Lolita. [p. 11]

The style is perhaps best characterized by its repetitive variation, its

---

[9]Diana Butler, "Lolita Lepidoptera," *New World Writing*, 16 (1960), 58–84.

[10]Alfred Appel, Jr., "*Lolita:* The Springboard of Parody," *Wisconsin Studies in Contemporary Literature*, 8 (Spring, 1967), 204–241; also in *Nabokov: The Man and His Work*, ed. L. S. Dembo (Madison: University of Wisconsin Press, 1967), pp. 106–143.

ability—through rhythm, sound patterns, puns, precision—to cause us to see an image in multiple flashes. The multiplicity is increased by relating Lolita to Humbert's first love, Annabel, and to the innumerable nymphets in literary history. It is increased even more by the innumerable variations of the same scene of lovestruck Humbert courting the tough-minded and tough-hearted Lolita. The four-page catalog of "Sunset Motels, U-Beam Cottages, Hillcrest Courts, Pine View Courts, Mountain View Courts, Skyline Courts, Park Plaza Courts, Green Acres, Mac's Courts" (p. 134) is one of the most incisive evocations of the American landscape in the 1950's. But it is also a dramatic means to convey the multiple and identical scenes that took place during a year and over the expanse of three thousand miles.

Still another way that Nabokov effects an experience of multiplicity is through the device of the double. Nabokov may be indebted to Stevenson, Poe, Gogol, and Dostoevsky, but he does not follow them in using the double to explore psychic dimensions of a main character's personality. Clare Quilty, the writer, man of the stage, debauchee, driver of an Aztec-red convertible, is not a projection of the hero: there is no need for a projection in Humbert's full confession. Clare Quilty is a parody and a comic repetition of Humbert Humbert. He mocks the hero, he arouses fresh sympathy for the hero—and he also conveys the impression that Humbert is not unique but one of many. The world is full of nymphets, and nympholepts as well.

The result of Nabokov's tricks of style, structure, and characterization is that we are led through a series of freshly evoked and quickly shattered experiences, which are nearly identical and which take place in a world of nearly identical backdrops. Nabokov destroys our preconceptions of time and space. As we think back, we almost feel as if time were composed of the same moment being repeated over and over, and as if space were pieced together from identical motelscapes.

This is not a complete description of our response, though, for the novel also depends on its continuing forward movement through both time and space. We are fascinated by Nabokov's "verbal diddle,"[11] we are affected by the multiplicity, we become lost in the

[11]John Hollander, "The Perilous Magic of Nymphets," *On Contemporary American Literature*, ed. Richard Kostelanetz (New York: Avon, 1964), pp. 477–480.

intricate labyrinths, we are led on by the style, which, as Nabokov says of Gogol, follows "the dream road of his superhuman imagination"[12]—but our most immediate concern is what happens next to Humbert Humbert. Will Humbert make contact with Lolita? How will he take care of Charlotte? What will happen when he arrives at Lolita's camp? When will he seduce his nymphet? Will he get caught by the police? Will the red convertible catch up? Will he find his runaway love? Will he get Quilty? If the first main dimension of the novel's structure is endless multiplication, the second is continual forward movement. The multiplication works at cross purposes to the forward movement but does not impede it. Rather, it creates an eccentric rhythm very much like that which Nabokov attributes to Gogol's "Overcoat": "a combination of two movements: a jerk and a glide. Imagine a trapdoor that opens under your feet with absurd suddenness, and a lyrical gust that sweeps you up and then lets you fall with a bump into the next traphole."[13]

Nabokov's eccentric rhythm achieves its climax in the meeting of the doubles. This obligatory scene is demanded by the novel's continuing forward movement, and yet, after the scene with Dolly Schiller which eliminates Humbert's motivation, it is wholly gratuitous. Humbert fires into the thick pink rug. Quilty continues his banter until, in the midst of a banal question, he throws himself on the avenging gunman. "We rolled all over the floor, in each other's arms, like two huge helpless children. He was naked and goatish under his robe, and I felt suffocated as he rolled over me. I rolled over him. We rolled over me. They rolled over him. We rolled over us." Humbert's second shot sends Quilty into the music room, his fingers wiggling in the air, his rump heaving rapidly, where, after a struggle over the door, he sits down at the piano and plays "several atrociously vigorous fundamentally hysterical, plangent chords, his jowls quivering, his spread hands tensely plunging, and his nostrils emitting the soundtrack snorts which had been absent from our fight." Struck in the side by Humbert's third bullet, Quilty rises from his chair "higher and higher, like old, gray, mad Nijinski, like Old Faithful . . . head thrown back in a howl, hand pressed to his brow, and with his other hand clutching his armpit as if stung by a hornet." Humbert chases him down the hall "with a kind of double,

[12]Vladimir Nabokov, *Nikolai Gogol* (Norfolk, Conn.: New Directions, 1944), p. 144.
[13]*Ibid.*, p. 142.

triple, kangaroo jump . . . bouncing up twice in his wake, and then bouncing between him and the front door in a ballet-like stiff bounce." "Suddenly dignified, and somewhat morose," Clare begins to ascend the broad stairs: "I fired three or four times in quick succession, wounding him at every blaze; and every time I did it to him, that horrible thing to him, his face would twitch in an absurd clownish manner, as if he were exaggerating the pain . . . [and] he would say under his breath, with a phoney British accent—all the while dreadfully twitching, shivering, smirking, but withal talking in a curiously detached and even amiable manner: 'Ah, that hurts, sir, enough! Ah, that hurts atrociously, my dear fellow. I pray you, desist.' " But the chase continues from room to room until Humbert corners the "blood-spattered but still buoyant" Quilty in his bed and shoots him through the blanket at close range: "a big pink bubble with juvenile connotations formed on his lips, grew to the size of a toy balloon, and vanished" (pp. 271–278).

We have been swept up and let fall with a bump into the final traphole. This scene—which is the climax of the novel, coming just a few pages before the end—momentarily destroys our recollection of Humbert's evocations of the nymphet, the delights of his tentative conquests, the perceptions of her special grace, the poignancy of his meeting with Dolly Schiller. After Humbert's total acceptance of Lolita's metamorphosis, there is no explaining his need for vengeance or the slapstick treatment of the gruesome scene. The violent shift in perspective completely destroys the already shifting foundations of the novel; it causes us to doubt the confusing impressions of the narrator that we have built up, as it were, from scratch. What are we to make of a world where perversity is the only form that love can take, where the grotesque is the only form of beauty, where madness is the only form of sanity, where obsession is the only form of freedom, where destruction is the only form of living? And what are we to make of Humbert Humbert, the hero, the victim, the creator of this world? Is he the comic-pathetic Romantic, forever in search of the unattainable? Is he the true and tender lover of Lolita and Dolly Schiller? Is he the mad sadist, the avenger-killer of Clare Quilty?

The final diabolical shift in perspective forces us to question not Humbert Humbert's grasp of reality, but our own. Quilty dies, Dolly dies, Humbert dies. But the narrator who has gleefully destroyed everything in sight—like the medieval devils and fools,

Dostoevsky's double, and Melville's confidence man—continues to haunt us.

Shifting perspectives are common in modern literature. What distinguishes *Lolita* is the narrator's diabolically comic strategy and stance—or his black-hole humor. The narrator's strategy is black in its ontological defiance and gratuitous but creative deconstruction that evoke the "thrill of diabolical pleasure." It is comic in its satiric range and sheer playfulness. And it is marked by the trapholes in its narrative continuum that trip us and cause us to shift perspectives, that take us by surprise and destroy our equilibrium, that undermine our bases for psychological and moral judgment.

The narrator's stance—how and where the narrator stands in relation to his story—also effects a kind of diabolical comedy marked by what we might call a black hole. This is not the trap into which the reader is swept, but the encounter of absence. Indeed, that encounter of absence—or the dramatic presence of absence—is like the encounter of a "black hole" in space, which is caused by a star so massive that its field of gravity has collapsed it to virtually nothing. The narrator of *Lolita* is continually present in the novel. He engages us with his verbal wit, comic destructiveness, and diabolical control. He leads us through an evanescent, undermined, but nonetheless positive experience of longing and love. He is all the while before us—but has cunningly kept himself beyond our reach by his "bizarre cognomen," his subjugation to the improbable John Ray, Jr., and his creation of a persona who changes continually and discontinuously.

In *Pale Fire* (1962)[14] we encounter a hole that is not metaphoric but literal and physical. This is the empty space—the blank pages—between the poem "Pale Fire," presumably written by John Shade, and the commentary, presumably written by Charles Kinbote. On one side of the hole are 999 lines of heroic couplets which focus on the poet's love for his wife, the catastrophe of his daughter's possible suicide, and his experience of death and rebirth. On the other side of the hole is a set of notes six times as long as the poem, illuminating those allusions which Shade's wife ("the domestic censor") convinced the poet to suppress or disguise: the "glorious friendship" between Shade and Kinbote, and the story of

---

[14]Vladimir Nabokov, *Pale Fire* (New York: Berkley, 1968). Page references will be made directly in the text.

Charles the Beloved, King of Zembla, who was forced to escape his homeland and take up a post incognito at Wordsmith College, where he lived in constant fear of the assassin who started from Zembla on the day when Shade's poem was begun.

The hole in the text opens the question of relationships while, at the same time, obviating any answer. It precludes any certainty about the relationship between the poem and the story that was supposed to inspire it, between Shade and Kinbote, between Charles Kinbote and Charles the Beloved, between Wordsmith College in America and the Kingdom of Zembla, between Kinbote (whose name in Zemblan means regicide) and Gradus (the would-be regicide), between Jakob Gradus and Jack Gray (whom Kinbote confuses with Gradus and who accidentally kills Shade while aiming at Kinbote, whom he has mistaken for the judge who sentenced him to the Institute for the Criminal Insane).

Let us begin with the empty space as a simple physical presence—intrusion. The hole between the poem and commentary opens a rudimentary physical problem: which way does the book go? Should we, with customary respect for the poetic text and our linear habit of mind, read the poem first, and then the commentary? Should we follow the editor's advice to read the commentary first, and then the poem—along with the notes? Or should we start with the poem and turn to the notes as the spirit moves us? Whichever choice we make, we will continually return to an experience of the book as a physical object divided in two parts, and we will inevitably find ourselves reading in two directions. The empty space divides the poem absolutely from the commentary and compels us to turn back and forth between them. Moreover, as each note grows longer, let's be frank about it, we forget the word or line being annotated, not to mention the stanza or context. And we may find ourselves reading the poem backward, or up the page until we discover where the unit of meaning begins. Certainly, though, we begin to wonder about the actual subject or center: is it Shade the poet, or Kinbote the commentator? We discover that the book is designed to frustrate our sense of center—or that the only center we can know is the empty space that secures our forefinger as we flip between the poem and commentary.

Actually, there are three holes in *Pale Fire*: the first between the foreword (which, in the scholarly tradition, describes the manuscript) and the book's editorial apparatus; the second between the

poem and the commentary; and the third between the commentary
and the index, which refers us back far less to the poem than it does to
the notes. On first reading, of course, we hardly see the blank pages;
we expect these clear demarcations in such a text. But by the time we
finish *Pale Fire,* we discover that they mark not rational divisions,
but complete separations, the central separation governing the other
two. If we now think about the text as a whole, we may describe
these separations, empty spaces, holes, as presences in our reading
experiences—to be encountered just as we usually encounter characters, action, description, dialogue, discourse, rhythm, or diction.

I am focusing on *Pale Fire* as a physical object not only to
illuminate an important dimension of our reading experience, but
also to suggest a relationship between the choices of physical directions and the sets of psychological, epistemological, and ontological
judgments we will implicitly make—or between the direction in
which we read the book and what the book means. For example,
suppose, as a kind of thought experiment, we try to design an ideal
reading of *Pale Fire.* How should we proceed? The first choice
confronts us at the end of the foreword, when we turn to the empty
pages that precede the poem. The editor has advised us to suspend
our customary priorities and begin with the commentary. But what
gives the editor the authority to advise us? He starts his foreword
with the cool objectivity of an authoritative scholar (pedant), but
soon his enthusiasm begins to intrude. We begin to wonder about the
judgments of a man who has been compelled to leave an improbable
New Wye and assume an incognito, who recalls a "glorious
friendship" not mentioned in the poet's obituary (p. 73), who
treasures his first glimpse (from his second-story window) of "the
poet's slippered foot" (p. 15), who records the first words spoken to
him by the poet—the laconic suggestion that he "try the pork" (p.
13)—and the poet's spontaneous utterance when a snowflake fell
upon his watch—"crystal to crystal" (p. 14).

When, in our thought experiment, we pause in the empty space
between the foreword and the poem, we discover that nothing we
have read so far guarantees the right way to go on. The foreword has
destroyed our sense of direction, or normal procedure; it has compelled us to make a decision and, at the same time, denied us any
way of telling right from wrong. The decision we make at this
conscious moment in our thought experiment, about which way to

go through the novel, will imply at least a tentative judgment about Kinbote as a critical authority and, hence, about the judgments he makes within his commentary.

One of the judgments we may pause to consider, even before we get to the poem, is aesthetic. Is the poet's spontaneous utterance "crystal to crystal," when the snowflake lands upon his watch, poetry or posturing? And, we should ask as we read Shade's poem, is "Pale Fire" an elegant display of wit that fuses mundane reality with poetic fancy—as many readers contend? Or is it a preposterous display of egoism that puffs up stupid perceptions with poetic rhetoric—as may be suggested by such a mundane metaphor as "TV's huge paper clip" (p. 24); by the fingernail clippings in which he discovers "flinching likenesses" of his grocer's son, the college astronomer, a tall priest, and an old flirt (p. 28); by the details that would be overlooked by his "staid biographer"—the apparatus he designed for shaving in the bath, a "hinge-and-screw affair, a steel support / Running across the tub to hold in place / The shaving mirror right before his face / And with his toe renewing tap-warmth, he'd / Sit like a king there, and like Marat bleed" (pp. 46–47); and by the discovery that his affinity with the woman who, like him, had died and been reborn, was based on a misprint in the newspaper account of her vision—"*Mountain,* not fountain. The majestic touch. / Life Everlasting—based on a misprint! / I mused as I drove homeward: take the hint" (p. 44).

The aesthetic judgment—whether "Pale Fire" is a good or bad poem—determines how we read the book. It determines whether the poet or the commentator is being parodied. Therefore, it determines the ultimate narrator, controlling intelligence, arranger, who—while felt as a dramatic presence—is kept beyond our grasp, or within the empty spaces. The question of the ultimate narrator is opened in the lacuna of the poem's putative last line; indeed, we might see the hole between the poem and commentary opening not in the pages between them, but in the space after line 999, which the heroic couplet form obliges to be filled in. Kinbote insists that line 999, "Trundling an empty barrow up the lane," was to be followed by a repetition of line 1, "I was the shadow of a waxwing slain," thus completing a perfect circle—and, we might add, completing the juncture between the mundane and the poetic. But there is another choice opened by the lacuna. The commentary ends with Shade, who has become a shadow of Kinbote, being slain, if not "by the false azure in the windowpane" (line 2), then by the false reflection in the mind of the (imagined?) assassin. We may, therefore, see a bridge between the commentary and the poem, or a joining of the poem and the commentary into a perfect circle and, as a result, a unity of the poet and commentator.

But who is the primary narrator, guiding intelligence, arranger? The answer depends upon an aesthetic judgment. Readers who judge the poem to be an elegant work of art see Shade as the primary narrator, a poet capable of imagining the fantastic Kinbote and adding what his character Kinbote tells us is the human counter-part to the poem. Readers who assume the poem to be ridiculous see the primary narrator as Kinbote, a poet *manqué* or a paranoid, who has appropriated Shade's text and/or fantasized an ideal or two ideal selves.

But the aesthetic judgment is not so simple, nor, therefore, is the locus of the primary narrator. The poem is neither elegant nor stupid. It is wildly comic but capable of constraining the most ornate diction and the most mundane perceptions, the most sophisticated allusions and the most slapstick descriptions within its tightly controlled meter. And the effect is most striking when the poem is read aloud.

Once we have developed a taste, like Aunt Maude's, "For realis-tic objects interlaced / With grotesque growths and images of doom" (p. 25), once we laugh at the images and admire the interlacing, a signal question arises. Where in the world of *Pale Fire* do we find a character capable of such wit, such wild flights and mixtures, such control? Not in the dull gray poet characterized by Kinbote. Not in the persona of Kinbote as he exists in the commentary or in the foreword, who is so limited by his zeal and paranoia. And not in the persona of the poem, who takes his dull life so seriously and who enjoys his posturing as much as Kinbote admires it. We do not find the controlling intelligence in the foreword, the poem, the commen-tary, or the index.

Indeed, in the last paragraph of the commentary the narrator distinguishes himself from his fictional personae. He has just told us that his "work is finished": his "poet is dead" and he wonders (or postulates the inquiry of a "gentle young voice"), "What will *you* be doing with yourself, poor King, Poor Kinbote?" Now he invokes God's help "to rid myself of any desire to follow the example of two other characters in this work . . . . I may assume other disguises, other forms, but I shall try to exist.'' Perhaps more important, he will remain inseparable from the counterpart, who ''has already set out . . . and presently . . . will ring at my door—a bigger, more respectable, more competent Gradus'' (pp. 212–213).

We may discover a clue to the controlling intelligence when the poet describes the major catastrophe of his life, his daughter's death or suicide. He refers to the improbable geography of his region:

> People have thought she tried to cross the lake
> At Lochan Neck where zesty skaters crossed
> From Exe to Wye on days of special frost. [p. 36]

Further, when called to lecture at the Institute of Preparation for the Hereafter, he notes his temporary move from ''New Wye / To Yewshade'' (p. 36).

Here not the poet but the poem calls attention to itself as a product of language, indeed of letters. Here the poem moves from the highest flights of poesy to the lowest ground of reality: the physical units that compose it. Here the book calls attention to itself as a physical object composed of discrete parts and empty spaces, composed primarily of a poem and a commentary and a hole between them. The hole in the center not only keeps the poem and commentary apart and the various doubles from ever merging. It also obscures the guiding intelligence who has engaged us by his comic powers, changing reflections, and diabolical control.

A ''black hole'' is not only what astronomers call the absence they encounter in empty space. It is also an imaginative concept arrived at through the daring and skill of human intelligence able to deconstruct normal forms and expectations and play with the possibility (indeed, necessity) of a star so massive as to collapse in on itself—before this phenomenon could be searched for, let alone confirmed.

The black holes in *Lolita* and *Pale Fire* function in a similar manner—except that they implode not in outer space, but in the realm of human experience. As a result, they threaten the bases not only of rational explanation, but also of humane judgment. In *Lolita* the narrator, laughing diabolically in the narrative black holes, leads us through an experience of longing and love while undermining our ability to measure it against traditional norms. In *Pale Fire* the narrator, laughing diabolically within the hole separating the poem from the commentary, denies us—indeed, forces us to continually question—all physical, psychological, epistemological, and aesthetic guidelines. The hidden narrators of *Lolita* and *Pale Fire* have cheated creation by creating a new life in each fiction—and by generating a new life in the readers who, denied the security of habit, must see and decide for ourselves.

STANLEY TRACHTENBERG

Berger and Barth:
The Comedy
of Decomposition

Traditionally the comic spirit had been defined by its power of reconciliation, an ordering tendency that attempts to make the chaotic nature of the world more livable. Its action may be governed by an individuating or a collective norm. But whether, as in the first instance, the comic hero opposes his fate or, as in the second, submits to it, he succeeds in establishing his humanity against that agency which seeks to overthrow it—which is to say, life itself. As such, his triumph cannot be permanent, any more than comedy can allow permanent injury to befall its antagonists. But if the futurity which comedy guarantees is temporary, it is no less substantial. For the hero of the comic novel, the extension of possibilities traditionally presents itself in social terms. He struggles to understand what society is, to learn the difference between its real values and the disguises in which those values are expressed. Only then can he form an idea of his relationship to it and so discover the valid claims it makes on him, as well as where he can successfully urge his own desires against them. His antithesis is not a tragic counterpart but a comic foil, a figure of vulnerability. This figure may appear innocent of the disaster that strikes him, a dupe such as Pickwick or a helpless improvident like Micawber; or he may be the victim of his own thwarted design, a comic villain, Blifil, for example, or more recently Mink Snopes or Henry Armstid of Faulkner's *The Hamlet*.

Whatever his function, the attitude toward the comic figure continues to assert the triumph of the human over his nonhuman adversary, whether that adversary appears in mechanical form or as a force of nature. For if nature is living, as Susanne Langer argues, it is also purposeless and so mechanical. To it comedy brings a teleology that supports human vitality in its struggle to maintain itself.[1]

Currently, however, a difference can be seen in comic fiction, one in which the individual is so radically thrown back on himself as to threaten the existence not only of his social reality but also of the idea of self which allows him to define it. He discovers that his suffering is immedicable, and that his attempt to locate an alternative to his condition only confronts him more starkly with the formlessness responsible for it. The comic notion of the hero merges with that of the dupe. Even so affirmative a novelist as Saul Bellow, whose Herzog insists that he has "had it with the victim bit," makes fun of the comic attempt to order the disparate elements of experience into a coherent synthesis. "One of the sources of comedy in my books," Bellow notes, "is the endless struggle of people to make sense of life and to sort out all the issues and get the proper historical perspective on oneself."[2]

This comic view of the historical impulse marks a distinct shift from the modernist recognition that the sequential nature of language resists the simultaneity with which reality is experienced. Opposed to middle-class society, which structured itself upon that sequence, modernism turned instead to the processes of individual consciousness as a source of narrative truth; to make such private consciousness accessible, it relied on the structuring faculty of myth. The contemporary sensibility, however, finds itself more isolated from or within the world of objects. The perceiving consciousness is unable to discover in the material world any clues to its concealed meaning. Neither myth nor metaphor is adequate to establish some correspondence between public and private visions.[3] Reality becomes composed or decomposed into splintered versions, all equally fictive, all equally real.

[1] See "The Great Dramatic Forms: The Comic Rhythm," in Susanne Langer, *Feeling and Form* (New York: Scribner's, 1953), pp. 326–350.

[2] Robert Cromie, "Saul Bellow Tells (among Other Things) the Thinking behind Herzog," *Chicago Tribune Books Today,* January 24, 1956, p. 9.

[3] For a persuasive account of how the contemporary imagination rejects the modernist use of myth as a structuring principle, see Richard Wasson, "Notes on a New Sensibility," *Partisan Review,* 36 (1969), 460–477.

This decomposition has led the critic and theologian Nathan Scott, Jr., to the striking observation that current literature refuses to compete with reality. Scott takes the phrase from Musil's *Man without Qualities,* and by it I understand him to mean the absence of narrative forms by which experience can be ordered. Drawing on Kafka's mordant parable of a man who elevates self-denial literally into an art, Scott terms this literature a "hunger art," an art which makes no inferences, draws no conclusions, accepts no current frame of reference, repudiates any inherited one. It is an art of displacement which hesitates to reconstruct reality, or even to frame it. At its most positive, such an art asks us to receive mystery, rather than to dispel it.[4]

Hunger art, then, is distinct from modernism in that it not only begins without making sense of things but ends that way as well. Random situations replace connected plot and, with it, the fixed meanings that society affords. We lose the sense of narrative continuity, of telling a story, and focus instead on the manner in which the story is told—the voice, the lexical tensions, the ambiguity of text. Memory, association, nostalgia, legend, and myth, the painter Barnett Newman explains, are impediments from which the post –World War II generation struggled to free itself.[5]

The flattening of values emerges in the modern artist's concern with the surface of his canvas, with bringing his subject closer to the picture plane, until it almost collides with the reality it formerly reflected. In fiction, this reflexive tendency similarly promotes the autonomy of structure. Language is extended to accommodate multiple meanings, chronology is rearranged, points of narrative reference are liberated. This strategy does not mean there is no longer a sense that fiction is distinct from reality. Far from it. The difference between them, in fact, becomes so exaggerated, so pressing that no one version of reality can impose itself as authentic and so compel the belief which allows imaginative constructions to correspond to life. Modernism attempts to conceal the fact that reality is unapproachable through language. In contrast, contemporary fiction is characterized by an insistence on the reality of its own artifice.

For comedy, the consequences of that insistence is that it no

[4]Nathan Scott, Jr., "The Conscience of the New Literature," *Negative Capability* (New Haven: Yale University Press, 1969) pp. 53–54.

[5]Barnett Newman, "The Sublime Is Now," *The Tiger's Eye,* December, 1948, p. 53.

longer becomes possible to extend life beyond the limits to which it is normally subject, to extend it beyond even the borders of the page. There remains no vital center of consciousness, no unified self around which a sequential order of events may be gathered, much less transcended. Instead, the personality is broken into disconnected and so mechanical states of being, no more integral than the relations between the various objects of experience against which they are thrust. There are worse things than death after all—things against which comedy attempts to secure us. The dizzying search for some principle that will order the numerous possibilities of identity turns out to be one of them.

As a consequence, the reassurance which comedy provides now issues not from a vision of wholeness as a sanative norm, but from the possibilities for getting along with fragments that don't fit together, for seeing oneself in a funhouse mirror that distorts the figure in front of it or (worse) reflects no figure at all. At the same time, this distortion itself proves vulnerable to some continuing if not clearly articulated dissatisfaction with its own image, thus keeping the center of comic affirmation off balance, shifted both toward and away from the fictive reflections of actuality.

This comic decomposition becomes manifest in the paradigmatic fiction of Thomas Berger, whose most ambitious single work to date, *Little Big Man,* like Barth's *Sot-Weed Factor* or *Giles Goat-Boy,* to name two prominent examples of the genre, relies on a strategy of mythic parody to account for the main thrust of its comic development. Berger's subject is not the American West but the myth that has grown up around it; thus his work plays against, rather than extends what otherwise has served as perhaps our most representative source of comedy. Here we are given the memoirs of Jack Crabb, supposedly the 111-year-old sole white survivor of the Battle of Little Big Horn. Crabb's account covers a twenty-four-year period. When he is ten years old he is captured and raised by the Cheyenne Indians, and he continuously returns to the tribe between various careers in white society as a gambler, army scout, gold seeker, and buffalo hunter. Nothing in Crabb's narrative, however, is the way it is pictured in the classic Western formulations of Owen Wister or Zane Grey. Crabb wears elevator shoes, cheats at cards, and deserts when the odds are against him. Other heroic figures are similarly reduced by the parodic strategy of contrasting their legendary exploits with the prosaic personal details of their lives. Wild Bill Hickok, for example, is obsessively concerned with the technical considerations of gunfighting and kills from ambush; George Armstrong Custer is growing bald. Crabb himself underscores the unreality of Western myth. "When you run into a story of more than three against one and one winning," he remarks, "then you have a lie."[6]

The romantic notions of the Indian that have been fixed in American literary tradition since James Fenimore Cooper are similarly parodied. Though occasionally capable of great dignity, the Indians in *Little Big Man* are more often childlike and comically superstitious. Chief among them is Old Lodge Skins, who appears initially in an old plug hat, trying to keep his blanket from falling off. Almost immediately thereafter he becomes drunk in the classic tradition of the silent film comedian. One drink and he topples over backward, kicking his heels together so that one of his moccasins flies off. Lodge Skins is not, however, a baggy-pants comedian; he continues to grow as a moral guide until, by the end of the novel, it is his wisdom that establishes a comic basis for it. This basis emerges from the idea that meaning can exist without rational understanding and is grounded in the Indian's belief in circularity. "The buffalo eats grass [Lodge Skins says], I eat him, and when I die, the earth eats me and sprouts more grass. Therefore nothing is ever lost, and each thing is everything forever, though all things move" (p. 433). In contrast, the white world is formed on a linear pattern. White men, Lodge Skins goes on to say, "live in straight lines and squares." By this he means that the white world values only the end, rather than celebrates the process of life. "Winning is all they care about," he explains, "and if they can do that by scratching a pen across paper or saying something into the wind, they are much happier" (p. 433). When this interpretative approach to experience is imposed on the Indian's more natural responses, an even greater discontinuity results. After the restlessness that followed a treaty of peace imposed by the whites on warring Indian tribes, Lodge Skins advises the Crow that "We used to like you when we hated you . . . . Now that we are friends of yours, we dislike you a great deal" (p. 434). It is against this context that he utters his dying prayer for the Every-

---

[6]Thomas Berger, *Little Big Man* (New York: Dial Press, 1964). Subsequent page references are indicated in the text.

where Spirit to "Take care of my son [Crabb] here, and see that he does not go crazy" (p. 437).

Crabb, too, despite—perhaps because of—the diminished perspective from which he witnesses events, is invested with a good deal of the novel's moral authority. He is the sardonic figure of the vernacular tradition against which the excesses of romantic myth are comically exposed. Yet even this authority is undercut by the device which frames his narrative. Traditionally the frame device, as Kenneth Lynn has noted, established a social point of view against which the idiosyncratic observer was made to appear funny.[7] In *Little Big Man,* the reportorial voice outside the action is that of Ralph Fielding Snell, who transcribes Crabb's story from taped interviews. Snell, however, is particularly sensitive about his own image, and his overly literal attempts to authenticate Crabb's account confirm the general impression of comic fussiness which he gives. Significantly, he is forced to delay publication of the story for ten years while recovering from a mental breakdown triggered by a challenge to his inheritance. The suggestion that Snell's literal approach to experience may be no more legitimate than the seemingly exaggerated events he relates prevents the reader from adopting a definitive attitude toward either. Despite its vernacular diction, Crabb's account is no more real than the myths it parodies. Along with Snell's pedantic frame, the totality of the novel makes a comic statement of the impossibility of taking seriously any one version of history, even its own.

This parodic assumption is echoed in Crabb's inability to reconcile the split in his own personality between his Indian upbringing and his white heritage. Crabb thus echoes the confrontation between the red man and the white in Cooper's fiction, while trading upon its assurances for comic effect. For Cooper, the separation between races is based on each's unique "gifts" and is subject to a divine order. Appropriate action, then, is relative to a man's condition: yet the ritual function that Natty Bumppo serves in reassuring society of its belief in possibility contrasts with his pragmatic recognition of what is expected of him as a social being. His initiation from youth to hunter further establishes a parallel conflict with his romantic innocence—his refusal to marry, really to mature—so that an

[7]Kenneth Lynn, *Mark Twain and Southwestern Humor* (Boston: Little, Brown, 1959), pp. 64–65.

inadvertent comedy of contrasting styles is set up between myth and reality.

In *Little Big Man,* these contradictions are incorporated into the comic structure of the narrative. During the battle of Little Big Horn, Custer observes, "It is to be regretted that the character of the Indian as described in Cooper's interesting novels is not the true one" (p. 410). Custer is, of course, partly right, but his absent-minded preoccupation with such abstract subjects during battle preempts his ability to direct or even to be aware of what is going on around him, and so comically turns his observation back on his own heroic posture. The values that, in Western myth, are conventionally associated with the red and white cultures similarly undergo comic reversal. Crabb is humiliated on becoming a Cheyenne warrior, confessing with unconscious irony that "You could seldom find a man back in town who didn't think an Indian even lower than a black slave" (p. 74). At the same time, he accepts at face value the Cheyenne custom of referring to themselves as the Human Beings. What this means, he subsequently learns, is that they believe in the living quality of all things—in contrast to whites, who feel that "everything is dead: stones, earth, animals, and people, even their own people" (p. 214). By the final battle, Crabb recognizes that the circumstances of the two races have become exchanged: "A peculiar reversal of roles took place that day upon the Little Big Horn. Reno had been sent to charge the village and instead was himself charged. Custer, going to envelop the enemy, had got it done to his own self. In their last great battle the Indians fought like white men was supposed to, and we, well, we was soon to arrive at the condition in which we had planned to get them, for this wasn't the terrain for cavalry and our order commenced to dissolve somewhere along that flight" (p. 402).

The dissolution of order is a particularly apt metaphor for what has happened both to the sequence of history and to the individual psyche that a collective history sustains. Exaggerated so that they seem larger than life, the characters of Crabb, Lodge Skins, Hickok, and Custer do not achieve mythic stature because they are unable to order experience. Instead, they are reduced to shadow projections of myth, doubles, whose independence of myth comically prohibits Crabb from arriving at a convincing acceptance of his identity either as an Indian or as a white.

Though found in folklore as well as in the earliest forms of literary expression, the theme of the double received its most striking formulation in the nineteenth-century psychological romances of E. T. A. Hoffmann and Adalbert von Chamisso, and in its development by Poe, Stevenson, Melville, Conrad, and Dostoevsky, among others, for whom the double serves as a device both for exploring subjective reality or states of mind and for projecting alternative moral possibilities or states of being. Sometimes real, sometimes imaginary, the double engages the self with the dilemma of ambivalence or of suppressed desires. He may, as Otto Rank contends, appear initially in response to a narcissistic desire for immortality, an identical self who projects the future. Alternatively, he may attempt to disown responsibility for certain of his actions, an opposing self who links man to his perishable past.[8] The double thus brings to consciousness the unacceptable desires of the ego or pursues the self with the unwanted knowledge of death, which can never, finally, be evaded. The wicked queen in *Snow White*, for example, attempts to summon an eternal image of youth in a magic mirror. Conversely, Dorian Gray displaces onto a portrait the corrupt, mortal element of his being, just as Superman, in a comic inversion, projects that human quality on his inept alter ego, Clark Kent.

A representative either of instinct or of repression, then, the double characteristically takes the form of opposition between a social self and a repressed instinctual impulse, projecting either immortality or the limits to which it is subject. Sometimes longed for, as in a pact with the devil, the double can equally be retributive, a reaction to the consciousness of guilt. In either case, pursued or pursuer, the double is subject to the mechanical compulsiveness which Freud noted in the uncanny quality that attaches to duplication.[9] Challenging the conscious or social self with an anarchic impulse, and further embodying that impulse in the form of an automaton who attempts to impose himself on the living, the double invites comic treatment. Conversely, when the double is credited

---

[8]Otto Rank, *The Double: A Psychoanalytic Study,* trans. Harry Tucker, Jr. (Chapel Hill: University of North Carolina Press, 1971). In addition to this seminal study, see also Rank, "The Double as Immortal Self," *Beyond Psychology* (New York: Dover, 1958), pp. 62–101; Ralph Tymms, *Doubles in Literary Psychology* (Cambridge: Bowes & Bowes, 1949); and Robert Rogers, *A Psychoanalytic Study of the Double in Literature* (Detroit: Wayne State University Press, 1970).

[9]Sigmund Freud, "The Uncanny," *The Complete Psychological Works,* standard ed., trans. James Strachey (London: Hogarth Press, 1955).

with a vital quality, as in romance, any comic intention must be directed at the repressive agency. Turkey and Nippers, for example, reflect the comic counterparts of Melville's Bartleby and the lawyer, one pair at odds but complementary, the other sympathetic but irrevocably disjunctive. For the overall tone of a fictional construct to be comedic, the personal or social norms of the individual must be reconciled with the metaphysical imperatives of the double—the shadow united with the self—or else the double must be confirmed as a foreign element, an imposter or (better yet) the unwitting victim of mistaken identity. In the confusion, the normal restrictions of social behavior are temporarily suspended, as in *The Amphytrion* in the first instance, *The Menaechmi* in the second.

Where the result of such an attempt is ambiguous, as in Saul Bellow's *Victim,* or where the psychological fact of doubling is itself suspect, as in the fiction of Vladimir Nabokov (who has insisted that there are no real doubles in his novels), the problem of comedy shifts from the assertion of humanity to its discovery. Here it assumes a darker, often solipsistic tone. In Ellison's *Invisible Man,* for example, the narrator suggests that he is the double of the reader. Turning society upside down, he claims to speak for the deepest level of its consciousness, the level of dream and nightmare. This black reflection shapes itself to, as much as it is shaped by, the white image, alternately vulnerable and heroic, perhaps heroic finally because vulnerable. The intimacy of Ellison's relation between shadow and substance establishes a comic perspective in contrast to the treatment of the shadow in American cultural iconography, where its association with mortality is reinforced by a Puritan view of the corrupt nature concealed within material form. At least as far back as Poe and Hawthorne, then, the shadow or mirror image has been treated as sinister or life denying, even when, as in a popular radio program of the 1930's, such a figure was co-opted to enforce social values.

In contemporary fiction, however, it is those values which appear inimical to life, the shadow which presses its own claim to authenticity. Stretching toward the social world with a mixture of anxiety and condescension, it hopes to obtain at least the appearance of a buried vitality. Yet as a projection of the same dark source, the social figure can neither draw strength from reconciliation with the shadow nor obtain relief from the confusion it licenses. Its stubborn if bewildered insistence on restoring the validity of its own vision, or at least maintaining the illusion of that validity, counterpoints opposing claims. Those claims and the proliferation of sources from which they issue establish a comic tension that transforms the shadow from a threatening presence to a funny one.

Such a comic transformation animates Berger's *Vital Parts,* the final novel of a trilogy in which Carlo Reinhart struggles to accept moral responsibility for his life against the social backgrounds of post–World War II Germany and then the American Midwest of the fifties and sixties.[10] At the outset of the novel, Reinhart is confronted by an alter ego in Bob Sweet, a former high school classmate, who serves as a figure of potency, a complement to Reinhart's time-bound progress. In contrast, Reinhart is out of work, henpecked, behind in his TV payments. Having long since lost faith in his own judgment, he is apprehensive even about opening his mail or answering the telephone, either of which is likely to confront him with unpaid bills. This sense of failure is focused particularly in the grossness of his large body and by the sense of mortality with which it confronts him. "I am just a guy," Reinhart sadly admits, "who regardless of what he thought at twenty knows at forty-four only that he will die" (p. 41). Reinhart's slim hopes for survival are nourished by the ironic conception of it as possible only by accomplishing something both useless and too small to be noticed. Correlatively, he personalizes the indifference of nature to the human demand that it have meaning. Reinhart thus justifies his failure by persuading himself that, in order to be loved, he must be non-threatening.

For Sweet, such humility is self-destructive. "You might one day," he warns Reinhart, "be killed by someone else's statement to the effect that you do not exist" (p. 209). Sweet, whose school years were marked by acne, a tendency toward masturbation, and a reputation for physical cowardice, now displays an aggressive self-confidence that parallels Reinhart's earlier interest in physical development. Indifferent to guilt, he is able to satisfy his instinctual

[10]Page references to Berger's *Vital Parts* are cited in the text and are taken from the New American Library edition (New York, 1970). The other two novels in the trilogy are *Crazy in Berlin* (1958) and *Reinhart in Love* (1962). Berger has indicated that the novels were not initially envisioned as a unified construct, but that the central character was more or less a convenient device around which he was able to group independent thematic concerns. Still, there is a sense of continuity, however accidental, in their development. In *Crazy in Berlin,* Reinhart, through betrayal, accepts moral ambiguity in place of the innocence he had previously insisted on bringing to experience. In *Reinhart in Love,* he is similarly led to the conviction that, despite its doubleness, social life offers a satisfying pattern for working out human destiny. "After all," he concludes, "that's all there is."

longings without the burden of social restraint. Sweet's mastery of kung fu, his black-faced Omega wristwatch, his chauffeur-driven Bentley combine to make him an embodiment of Reinhart's dream of power, "a man of his own age and background and apparently omnipotent and all knowing" (p. 21). Sweet thus confronts Reinhart with the dualism of consciousness that characterizes the psychological double, ultimately with the confusion of identity itself.

Sweet recognizes dislocation as the norm. "Nobody believes in God anymore," he explains, "but neither is there an ultimate faith in science" (p. 103). As a result, Sweet devotes himself to survival isolated from meaningful experience, financing experiments in which people are frozen into states of suspended animation until more permanent life-sustaining means become available. Despite his disclaimer, then, Sweet does rely on science, an indication that though his commitment to a neutral mode of existence is sincere, his methods are those of a confidence game. Reinhart confirms this deception by his discovery that the grain elevators which supposedly house Sweet's commodity holdings actually contain gravel. Earlier he had learned that Sweet artificially maintained his virility by taking monkey-gland injections from an unlicensed medical assistant, and that his youthful appearance, seemingly resistant to time, is in reality synthetic. Sweet wears a toupee, a corset, dentures, and glasses that lack corrective lenses. Without these props, his features blur into the indistinct regularity of an amateur cartoon drawing. Sweet's insubstantiality is further suggested by his childhood unwillingness to look in a mirror and is confirmed in the design of his freezing room, which is lighted so that no shadows can be cast. Reinhart is nonetheless convinced of Sweet's legitimacy by his authoritative manner and shows his eagerness to accept a Faustian bargain by blotting out his own reflection in a bathroom mirror.

The revelation of Sweet as mechanically imitating living matter suggests a theme which Bergson saw at the heart of comedy, and one which appears in American fiction at least as far back as Poe and continues through Nathanael West and, more recently, Thomas Pynchon.[11] Typically it is a feature of social satire, as in Poe's story "The Man That Was Used Up," where it comments on the unjus-

[11]R. W. B. Lewis has also called attention to this motif in "Days of Wrath and Laughter," *Trials of the Word* (New Haven: Yale University Press, 1965), pp. 232–233. This transformation of persons into things is symptomatic of the apocalyptic mood that Lewis sees in the fiction of Nathanael West.

tified nineteenth-century optimism and its faith in science and technology, or as in West's later burlesque of the American Dream in *A Cool Million*. Projected onto a double image, such artificiality allows Berger to take a comic view not only of the cultural celebrations of apocalypse, but also of a sustaining individuality, including the literary convention of the double through which it is announced. These intentions are combined in the image of the double presented by Reinhart's son, Blaine, whose values are so antagonistic to his father's that Reinhart suspects the two of them "may be figments of each other's imagination" (p. 380). In this struggle, Blaine takes the role Northrop Frye sees structuring the comic myth. A younger figure defeats an older one who unnaturally competes with him for sexual or life-sustaining goals, a myth which, for Frye, symbolizes the seasonal renewal of life.

Blaine successfully frustrates his father's voyeuristic interest in the girl next door, replaces him in his mother's affection, and even wins the sympathy of Reinhart's own mother. Yet Reinhart's fear of aging and death lead him to pursue this image of his own youth as much as to resist its triumph. Reinhart denies the Oedipal nature of this conflict. "Only squares," he writes to his son, "still believe that the father-figure embodies the threat of emasculation" (p. 350). Blaine, for his own part, comically reverses the Freudian conditions of family romance by rejecting the conventional signals of vitality. Perversely, he associates himself instead with a passive principle. Boasting of his bisexuality, he affects a snug-hipped style of dress and long flowing hair that, added to his slim physique, lead Reinhart to mistake him for a girl. Rather than struggling for individuating features, Blaine submerges himself in his generation, characteristically speaking in the first-person plural. "Maybe it would be accurate to say your crowd is yourself," Reinhart decides, associating this impulse with the central tradition of the culture. In the resulting social confusion, the young thus prove old. When Reinhart, in a gesture of both love and anger, cuts his son's hair, he discovers he has lost his own strength and is driven from his home. This inversion reveals Reinhart's struggle with Blaine to be not so much irrelevant, as he claims, as definitive of the new comic norms. With Blaine established as a mirror image of age, Reinhart's failure to reconcile himself with this double can remain funny.

In a subsequent attempt to recover his youth, Reinhart revisits his childhood home, now occupied by yet another double. This time it is a black, Splendor Gallant, who, like Sweet, is a former classmate of Reinhart's. Now dying of cancer, Splendor has volunteered for Sweet's freezing process. Splendor protests against the impersonality of death, refusing to accept it as natural. "Death," he argues, "is an absence, and not a presence, not a hooded figure hacking you down with a scythe—actually an attractive image; were Death an antagonistic personage, intent on imposing his will, we would have known how to defeat him long since" (p. 325). Formerly himself a confidence man who had unsuccessfully collaborated with Reinhart in a number of attempted swindles (chronicled in *Reinhart in Love*), Splendor identifies the changed nature of reality. "We live in a remarkable time," he observes, "the phony is constantly turning into the real and vice versa" (p. 185). Though Splendor acknowledges that the equation of rhetoric with reality had always formed part of the American tradition, he insists that, unlike the current generation, an older one was able to make the distinction.

Splendor's judgment is confirmed by his son Raymond, who serves as a counterpart to Blaine. Like his father, whose name originally had been Sylvester Mainwaring, Raymond changes his identity. He becomes Captain Bruno Storm, the leader of a group of black activists. A manifestation of the double, Storm's anarchic protest is enthusiastically welcomed into social consciousness. He is invited to address a meeting of the bar association, at which he calls his audience scum and boasts of his intention to gun them down while raping their wives and sisters. He receives a standing ovation. Though society thus exploits rather than assimilates Storm's anger, their celebration of it succeeds in neutralizing him. "I comply, man," he informs Reinhart grimly, "I pay cash for everything and the draft board has a cardiogram made by a member of the AMA in good standing on which my heart murmur is registered" (p. 330). In contrast to this belligerent conformity, Reinhart notes, it is the midwestern Protestant who orbits the moon.

The reversal of roles is echoed by Reinhart's wife, Genevieve, who supports the family while maintaining a childlike affection for her father, whom she thinks of as "the greatest daddy that ever lived." Like Reinhart's Maw, who converts the vital instinct of life into a nonhuman reflex, Genevieve responds to life mechanically, projecting herself into a movie version of it that surfaces in her confused idiomatic speech and in the disjunctiveness of her thought. Genevieve's displacement of human values with impersonally mechanical ones is underscored by her own alter ego, Gloria, a prostitute who forgets her customers within minutes after they leave and who figuratively turns into a dial tone when Reinhart suggests over the phone that he pay her by check. "She wanted," Reinhart concludes, "no document that confirmed his existence as a person. She dealt solely in human parts, never whole entities" (pp. 76–77). Like Storm's, however, this response is no longer an underground element of society but its norm. Gloria is, in fact, a middle-class housewife whose linen suit reminds Reinhart of his wife's, and who complains of high rent, her dentist's bills, and the cost of sending her daughter to Girl Scout camp. Even her morality is genteel, marked by indignation at dirty language and an objection to legalized prostitution, which she considers not only an economic threat but also a Communist attempt to undermine conventional values.

With Sweet's secretary, Eunice, Reinhart does find temporary insulation against his sense of growing older. Claiming to be her employer's daughter, Eunice initially treats Reinhart as though he were her father. Later she becomes his mistress. Though like Blaine, Eunice adopts an anti-social manner; she is concerned above all with how things look. When Reinhart tells her he has a son her age, the first thing she wants to know is how he dresses. Changing her own appearance constantly, Eunice betrays a desperate urgency to remain contemporary. "I hate this place," she admits of a discotheque to which she brings Reinhart, "but it happens to be where it's at" (p. 164). Movies, she insists, "present the characteristic atmosphere of our kinetic time, along with rock. Words are out" (p. 100), and she later confides that "Jews are out. Blacks may not last much longer" (p. 267). While making love to Reinhart, she announces that she doesn't believe in "the validity of individuals." Adopting this series of roles in place of identity, Eunice, as Reinhart claims of her generation, allows the theatrical to substitute for a sense of order. Her real father proves to be a transvestite psychiatrist, whose ability to twist compromising situations into absurdly normal ones leads Reinhart to label him "a quick change artist in more ways than one." Even Eunice's nymphomania proves to be a pose. What she really wants, she admits, is to get married and live a conventional suburban life.

Eunice's confession, however, does little to reassure Reinhart. He remains subject to the same uncertainties he formerly voiced to his imaginary childhood alter ego, Jim Jackson. A "ruthless critic of his creator," Jackson reappears when Genevieve's announcement that she wants a divorce leads Reinhart to think of suicide. Exposing Reinhart's strategy of compensating for failure by a pose of moral superiority, Jackson attempts to taunt Reinhart out of his resolve. This continued reversal of roles between the double and the social figure affords a comic contrast to the relationship which Otto Rank assigns to them. For Rank, the double "measures on the one hand the distance between the ego-ideal and the attained reality; on the other, it is nourished by a powerful fear of death and creates strong tendencies toward self-punishment, which also imply suicide."[12] Reinhart's suicidal impulse is encouraged not by his double, however, but by the conviction of his competitive failure in society. Intimidated further by Sweet's bullying, he agrees to let himself be frozen when even his attempt to kill himself is frustrated. Despite its ultimate promise of immortality, the choice, he realizes, means a more immediate death. Predictably, the decision frees him from the fear of social sanctions and, unembarrassed by his fantasies, he adopts a youthful lifestyle in which he had earlier personified them. Wearing tight, mod clothes and a toupee and driving a Jaguar, Reinhart echoes the frantic changes of appearance through which Eunice has disguised her own middle-class anxiety. Each now mirrors the other's soul, rather than his demon. After initially evidencing her discomfort with this change, Eunice takes off with Reinhart in dreamlike pursuit, unable to catch her though she runs from him in high heels.

Eunice's disappearance sends Reinhart back to Splendor, with whom he shares the past and who consequently provides reassuring evidence of continuity. Though Reinhart admires the mixture of manipulation and philosophic acceptance with which Splendor confronts his death, he is convinced that even this posture is helpless to prevent it. Uncomfortable with the illusion he must maintain that Splendor will recover, Reinhart abruptly cuts short his visit. The gratification he feels in the cheerfulness of Negro smiles may, he suspects, finally rest in their ability to "relieve you of the dark apprehensions with a show of white" (p. 329). Even in the promise

[12]Rank, *The Double*, p. 77.

of immortality held out by the double, then, Reinhart senses the waiting terror of death. Rather than overwhelming him, however, this knowledge permits Reinhart to revise his estimate of what it means to be human, even at the expense of his ability to identify a consistent or essential quality to his life, a quality without which the expectation of continuity vanishes into a series of disconnected roles or states of being.

Reinhart's acceptance of this decomposition paradoxically allows him to make a new life with his daughter, Winona. Despite deep mutual affection, their encounters with one another had been characterized by accidental collisions "from which each recoiled in equal degree" (p. 41). Like her father, Winona has been so consistently victimized that he sees her as someone who "could be considered as himself as a pudgy female of sixteen" (p. 42). Ignored by her mother, abandoned by her friends, Winona lives in a world of her own devising, so vaguely related to this one that she is hit by a truck as she crosses a street. Significantly, Winona is frightened by the shadow world of TV, which she objects to having left on while she is asleep. Her refusal to acknowledge the doubleness of life serves as a model for Reinhart; he draws strength from her uncritical acceptance of him, which "uniquely refused to confirm his self-hatred" (p. 45).

In rejecting all offers extended by Sweet, Reinhart, too, repudiates this shadow world, limiting the dimension of his existence instead to the present moment, which, he decides, is all he knows. Reinhart's experience has confirmed the absence of any meaningful connection between himself and his environment, suggesting the reality of any personal relationship to be problematic as well. The movement his adventures describe comes to rest not in the notion that personality is integral and made up of seamed parts, but in the recognition that the shadow is separable from the self and equally vulnerable to mortality. The loss of coherence between the various aspects of self comically fragments the notion of identity and thus fictionalizes the existential concept of authenticity as a shaping condition of it. Reinhart overcomes the self-limiting burden of guilt by accepting a qualified judgment about how complex a creature man is or needs to be, and what his chances are for extending himself into the future.

Traditionally, whatever pattern the splitting of the self took, its

importance, as Claire Rosenfield has shown, was that it revealed an
inner life not responsive to reason and a corresponding reluctance
by the conscious mind to acknowledge that life. The split revealed,
in other words, a psychic struggle whose outcome determined
the nature of reality.[13] That struggle becomes the basis for a comic
variation by John Barth, who, in *Lost in the Funhouse,* establishes
the narrative itself as an authorial alter ego and uses it to play on the
multiple possibilities of self-definition. Though conventionally the
interior reality of comic fiction reverses the conditions of limit and
possibility that obtain in the real world, it continues to rely on that
world for the ground of its meaning. In turn, life becomes the
beneficiary of thematic discovery. For Barth, fiction continues to
accommodate this historical correspondence, continues in other
words to tell a story; however, it must at the same time reflect the
contemporary sense that individual characters no longer inform or
are informed by society, and consequently they must abandon the
conventional structuring of plot.[14] In *Lost in the Funhouse* Barth
resolves this contradiction by making the subject of his fiction into
the difficulty he experiences writing it. Rejecting mimetic correspondence, the stories in *Lost in the Funhouse* parody those conventional literary forms which, by reflecting life, attempt to establish
some link between its random occurrences and the human perception
of them. The parody takes the form of attributing an intention to the
narrative. The stories become separate doubles of each other as well
as of the author/narrator, attempting to extend not his life but their
own narrative continuity. Such an extension rejects the function of
myth, as Richard Wasson identifies it, for the modern sensibility in
resisting the disordering, ultimately destructive progression of
history.[15] Rather than structuring experience or subordinating it to
the discipline of human consciousness, Barth's funhouse entraps
that consciousness and, despite its struggles, ultimately displaces it
in the world of nature. It is that self-conscious struggle that accounts
for much of the comic tension. Fiction anticipates and so preempts
authorial intention. A sperm cell, a tape deck, a disembodied voice,

[13]Claire Rosenfield, "The Shadow Within: The Conscious and Unconscious Use of the
Double," *Daedalus* (Spring, 1967), reprinted in *Stories of the Double,* ed. Albert J. Guerard
(Philadelphia: J. B. Lippincott, 1967), pp. 311–331.

[14]Barth theorizes about the difficulty of responding both to history and to the sensibility of
his own time in an interview conducted by Joe David Bellamy in *The New Fiction* (Urbana:
University of Illinois Press, 1974), p. 14.

[15]Richard Wasson, "Notes on a New Sensibility," pp. 460–462.

a poet all give promise of writing stories in which they themselves
are to become characters. In this manner *Lost in the Funhouse* both
qualifies and complements the assertion that the double is no more
resistant to time than the social being.

In establishing fiction as both antagonist to and constituent of the
self, Barth parallels a conflict that evolves in his earlier novels
between an innocent figure who searches for a single interpretation
of experience and a knowledgeable if amorphous one who is able to
assume a multitude of roles. In *End of the Road,* this opposition exists
between the doubled pair Joe Morgan/Jake Horner and an unnamed
Negro doctor; in *The Sot-Weed Factor,* between Ebenezer Cooke
and Henry Burlingame; in *Giles Goat-Boy,* between Giles and
Harold Bray. While each of these figures, along with minor paired
opposites, functions as an independent consciousness, severally
they constitute aspects of a single identity. In *Lost in the Funhouse,*
that identity emerges in the struggle between narrator and narrative,
with each story replicating itself through a series of interior frames
that attempt to detach themselves from the narrator's control.

Though Barth has maintained that the stories are arranged serially,
Max Schulz is surely right in noting that such an arrangement does
not provide the fictive scaffolding for a protagonist's psychological
growth.[16] Schulz sees the tales as constituting a parodic development
of the nineteenth-century *Bildungsroman*. Yet the discoveries made
are confined exclusively within the narrative framework, really *to*
that framework; they do not extend to the characters at any stage of
their successive appearance, much less to an analogic world beyond
them. This reflexive pattern is anticipated in the ''Frame Tale,''
which begins the collection. The story proper consists solely of
instructions which direct the reader to match up the ends of a
Moebius strip that repeats the legend, ''Once upon a time there was a
story that began.''[17] The story includes directions for assembling the
strip—Barth's initial parody of fictional method—and the parenthetical promise that the story is to be continued. Such continuation is
not linear but cyclical. It does not lead to further stories in the
collection, nor does it allow an extensional analogy. Instead it

[16]Max Schulz, ''Characters (Contra Characterization) in the Contemporary Novel,'' in
Theories of the Novel, ed. John Halperin (New York: Oxford University Press, 1974),
pp. 141–154.

[17]Page references noted in the text in parentheses are taken from John Barth, *Lost in the
Funhouse* (New York: Bantam, 1969).

redirects the anticipation of successive events back to its own fictive beginnings.

This reflexive movement is continued in "Night Sea Journey." Anticipating his authorial conception, a single sperm cell wonders, "Is the journey my invention? Do the night, the sea exist at all, I ask myself, apart from my experience of them?" (p. 3) The uncertainty with which the narrator regards experience is linked to his fear of destruction by his own Maker, or father, who, in turn, he suspects may be subject to the will of some even more encompassing figure, a source simultaneously of creation and annihilation. One form of resistance is biological, a regeneration of self. For the swimmer/hero of the narrative, however, such natural reproduction offers at best only a qualified immortality. Against its "weak vitality," and despite the temptation of love which is ultimately self-destructive, he decides to become "tale bearer of a generation." The multi-leveled phallic pun is crucial to the authorial and ultimately to the narrative intention. Faced with the senselessness of his journey, of all journeying, the speaker appeals to the reader as double, or to "whoever echoes these reflections." Even sexual potency, he insists, depends upon maintaining the integrity of the narrative process.

The separation between real and fictive modes of experience is further explored in "Autobiography," in which the narrative voice emerges through a tape recorder that both reverses and distorts it. The suggestion of Oedipal ferocity in "Night Sea Journey" is here allowed to surface in terms of fictional method. Echoing the author, whose dissatisfaction with the lack of a subject leads him to think of turning off the machine, the tape similarly pleads to be terminated. "I'm his bloody mirror," it exclaims bitterly (p. 34). The tale-bearing function has absorbed the tale itself and comes to rest in the process by which the story gets told. Despite its desire to imitate a more conventional historical reality, the tape finds itself involved solely with the problems of exposition. In fact, the machine reveals that it may be exclusively a narrative device. Even if it proves to be merely a shadow of authorial hesitancy, the tape resolves finally to "mutter to the end, one word after another, string the rascals out" (p. 37). The act of composition becomes its own justification, the referent of meaning pointed further from reality. "My last words," the tape concludes tautologically, "will be my last words" (p. 37). This philosophic acceptance, even anticipation, of its own end is deceptive and stems as much from fiction's inability to dissociate itself from fact as it does from dissatisfaction with the nature of its own formal development.

In "Petition," fiction again struggles for a disjunctive autonomy against a dominant physical reality. One Siamese twin pleads to be separated from its more public counterpart. "He's incoherent but vocal," the petitioner complains of his twin, "I'm articulate but mute" (p. 59). The struggle of the fictional twin to free himself from the limiting body of reality is focused in the fraternal rivalry for Thalia, a lady contortionist. This sexual triangle is one of Barth's standard motifs, typically initiated by a compliant husband or conducted with his knowledge, if not encouragement. The seemingly reluctant or indifferent lover thus acts as a sexually proficient alter ego for a paternal figure and, at the same time, realizes without guilt the son's desire to possess a maternal one. As reality approaches a social norm, Thalia's ability to mediate between the competing claims of the brothers diminishes, if, in fact, it ever existed. Though the petitioner becomes apprehensive about being absorbed by his alter ego, he, too, finds death preferable to the increasingly strained acts of the imagination that lead him to discover (or to imagine he has discovered) within Thalia a fictional counterpart to his own existence.

"Lost in the Funhouse" climaxes the attempt to construct a self-sustaining fiction as a consolation for the necessary exclusion from love. The story relates the circumstances of a family outing held, appropriately, on Independence Day. Thirteen-year-old Ambrose resolves to turn the incidents he lives through into the material of fiction. In doing so, he interposes pedantic explanations of literary style along with narrative descriptions of character and incident. The naiveté of these copybook rules is underscored by the tentative method of composition, which relies on repetitive expression, uncompleted predicates, and alternative, even contradictory characterization and plot development. While reflecting the hesitancy of the immature author, however, the story ironically employs these techniques to suggest the disordered reality from which they are drawn. This intention is most strikingly focused in the gathering metaphor of the funhouse, which sustains the physical action while objectifying the process by which the action is fictionalized. Ambrose indirectly comments on this reversal in his observation that the customary use of initials or blanks in nineteenth-century fiction enhanced the reality of illusion only by exaggerating its artificiality. This concentration on the processes of fiction allows him to distance his subject from a threatening reality whose least detail he is unable to forget, and which pursues him through the funhouse with the knowledge that "Husbands and wives often hated each other; parents didn't necessarily love their children" (p. 87).

In the funhouse Ambrose is separated from his alter egos, cigar-smoking, insensitive Uncle Karl and Ambrose's coarse, exuberant brother Peter, whom Karl resembles. Both echo the life-grasping force of the ribald twin in "Petition." In contrast, Ambrose, like his father, is a "minstrel in reverse," becoming paler, more insubstantial as the day advances.

What begins as fun threatens to turn to tragedy. Ambrose's isolation from the conditions of actuality leads him to become concerned about losing himself entirely in his own reflection. He experienced that concern obliquely even on the trip to the funhouse, suggesting his ambivalence by alternate preference for sunlight or shadow. Once inside, he sees "more clearly than ever, how readily he deceived himself into supposing he was a person" (p. 90). His attention to the construction of the story paradoxically threatens his chances of completing it. He wonders if he will ever get out of the funhouse, which, he realizes, may not rescue him from the apprehensions of reality after all. No matter how he twists in the distorting mirrors, he finds his head will always get in the way so that he is unable to see himself go on forever. "The necessity for an observer," he concludes, "makes perfect observation impossible" (p. 90).

Nonetheless, Ambrose finally contents himself with the funhouse as preferable to the reality beyond in which no one chooses to be what he is. Any experienced sailor, he sees, is aware that the idea is not to get through the funhouse, but to take advantage of its protective darkness. There the rising and falling plot line, however serpentine, can be sustained more firmly than its biologically phallic equivalent under a boardwalk or behind a toolshed, where Ambrose has his first experience with sex. Ambrose accepts this knowledge reluctantly and against the mocking echo of the fat lady's mechanical laughter advertising the funhouse. This interior laughter is equally at the expense of reality which, transformed into an image whose own substance becomes problematic, recedes before the self-reflecting mirrors of the funhouse.

The various possibilities of narrative independence are similarly the subject of the remaining stories, "Echo," "Title," "Life Story," and "Menelaiad." In "Echo," several strategies are offered to separate the omniscient author from the story. Narcissus escapes his admirers by losing himself in the cave of Tiresias, who, as a composite of history and prophecy, is unsure of his own identity. Tiresias' own response is repetition, through which words lose their usual meanings and become detached from external reality. In an echo of shadow-like motion, Tiresias describes the result as "a tale of shortcomings, lengthened to advantage" (p. 97). Within the tale, Narcissus and Echo represent two ways of framing reality—one subjective and self-absorbing, the other objective and self-effacing. The narrative thus withdraws from all identity so that the narrator decides it is finished before it starts. This judgment, however, is accurate only if the self-knowledge to which it refers is limited to the characters' point of view. For the reader and the narrator, those points of view themselves determine the meaning by detaching the narrative from any external and so deadening future.

In "Title," the narrator depends on the idea of frustrated expectation to sustain the comedy. Insisting that convincing fiction can no longer utilize standard notions of plot or theme, he invites an unnamed female companion to fill in the resulting blanks of his story, for which he provides convenient syntactic forms. These forms, ironically, constitute the dramatic action, building a comic tension against the auditor's desire for more conventional development. The narrator thus inverts the standard comedy routine in which, typically, a singer or musician is prevented from beginning his performance, a starving man from eating a meal spread before him. Having begun his story, the narrator searches for a series of technical devices which will permit him to keep it going. He finds these chiefly by calling attention to his difficulty in writing, substituting random verbal association for recognizable progression of incident. Though this technique parodies linear structure, it does support a spiral one, a comic spinning of form against thematic statement that defers an ending even as it reaches a conclusion.

In both "Life Story" and "Menelaiad," the narrative posture becomes increasingly fictionalized. In the former, an author recognizes that, as a mirror for social realism, fiction is no longer viable. At the same time, he is anxious to continue "without discarding what he's already written" (p. 113). What farcically complicates his dilemma is the suspicion that he may himself be a character in someone else's fiction. Unable to arrive at meaning in the processes of living and dying, he finds it difficult to write about them other than as aspects of his creative impotence or its sexual counterpart. He, too, then is increasingly distanced from reality in an unending series of novels about characters writing novels. Additional references to other fictional worlds, including some of Barth's own, locate the evolving narrative exclusively within its own fictional frame. This frame is dryly reinforced by ascribing to the narrator a preference for the circumstantial realism of Updike or Simenon, a joke which gets its point from Barth's acknowledged sympathy for the "irrealism" of Borges and Beckett.[18] That fiction be able to maintain itself in some way as a counterpart to experience is, however, necessary for continuity, despite the recognition that "the old analogy between Author and God, novel and World, can no longer be employed" (125). Once again the comedy emerges from the struggle to reconcile these contradictory impulses. To do so, the narrative must allow for an alternative relation between itself and its reader, whom the narrator apostrophizes as "You dogged, uninsultable, print-oriented bastard" (p. 123). It does this by coiling back inside itself. Separating the mediate from the ultimate author, it allows both to put a final period to their stories.

"Menelaiad" reverses this basic situation by constructing the narrative in a series of receding internal frames that struggle to reach the borders of that reality which encloses them. These protean forms of fiction displace the narrator. "This isn't the voice of Menelaus," he admits, "this voice *is* Menelaus, all there is of him" (p. 127). Menelaus' attempt to reconcile himself with Helen once more translates literary accomplishment into a sexual frame of reference. This time the triangle is seen from the husband's point of view, rather than the lover's; the attempt to make certain of his wife's affection becomes the matter of his story, and the need to delay that assurance the means by which he can extend it and so maintain his existence. To do so, he adopts the disguise of Proteus, who is in turn absorbed into the recitation of his own capture. The narrative thus comes

[18]Bellamy, *New Fiction*, p. 4.

finally to grip the storyteller, even as he wrestles with it to pin down his own meaning. Though it carries a suggestion of autoeroticism from which the narrator himself abruptly calls for respite, the triumph of the fiction allows Helen to insist that she had never betrayed her husband or left her home, except as a shadow projection of that fiction. The narrative voice ultimately finds itself submerged in its own fiction, but though it becomes obscure, finally grows blank, it continues in whatever form it assumes to permit the author's survival and, along with it, that of the now fictionalized reality of love.

In "Anonymiad," fiction has the same temporal restrictions as the world outside. A nameless Mycenaen minstrel finds himself marooned on an Aegean island by one of those paired doubles whose "gluttony for life's delights" contrasts with the minstrel's own unworldliness. During his isolation he invents alternative circumstances for it, whose drama, he comes to see, lies in getting where he is in life. The actuality of his situation comically blends with the fictions he creates, fictions which are themselves based on anterior fictions he thinks of as real. By means of such fictions, the minstrel discovers, he is able to "achieve a lovely truth which actuality obscures—especially when I learned to abandon myth and pattern my fabrications on actual people and events: Menelaus, Helen, the Trojan War" (p. 186). Describing these self-sustaining works as his "enciphered spirit," the minstrel casts them adrift in wine jars, where each floats "realer than the gods, its significance objective and undecoded as the stars" (p. 188). Cut off from social reality, however, his imagination runs dry. "Was there any new thing to say," he wonders, "new way to say the old" (p. 188). When he tries to load one jar with more than one of his fictions, the burden proves too great; both sink. The failure of fiction to support multiple interpretations of life and the minstrel's correlative isolation from what he thinks of as the real world cause him to lose interest in his continuing existence. When a manuscript is washed ashore, he is uncertain whether it is his own swept back to him, the work of someone similarly marooned, or even a critique of his earlier efforts. In any case, what he finds is illegible, empty of meaning. Only by accepting this emptiness, however, is the minstrel encouraged to renew his own literary efforts. His own lack of identity gives his work its direction and so provides it with a name. Independent of the life it mirrors, fiction becomes distanced both internally and on the literal space of the page. There, as it gains a reality no longer afforded to its author, its claim to immortality proves equally tentative. Though it thus offers a self-mocking reminder of the limits it both announces and hopes to transcend, such a condition, comically enough, is the best man can hope for in the otherwise wasting day that anticipates his long night to come.

These compromised and uncertain resolutions reflect the contemporary inability to hold in a unified construct the things hurtling at us from outside ourselves and those which rush to meet them from within. The shadow is sprung loose from its sensible counterpart. Free of restraint, it parodies the totality of vision which attempts to locate man within an environment responsive, if not to what he does, at least to how he perceives it. In place of the self, it is this dark figure who now struggles to redefine what being human means—how tightly man is bound to the objects that surround him, or how loose he swings. Its claim to an independent reality, however, makes the shadow vulnerable to disorder, rather than solely a representative of it. Correspondingly, man in the natural world finds he is denied access to that refuge the shadow once afforded. In its consequent reduction, the human figure, too, becomes comic.

Nonetheless, there remains a resilience, farcical in nature, in which the outraged victim, flattened by a door sprung shut or by a safe dropped from the top of a building, recovers without visible scars, eager to start a fresh scheme to eliminate his mocking tormentor. Reinhart's discovery that, like himself, his shadow is vulnerable to history allows its loss to remain funny—though the joke ultimately is at his own expense. His completeness, like that of Chamisso's Peter Schlemihl, proves partial rather than whole. But at least he is still around and, if with little more than good will, still curious to see what he can do against the circumstances that threaten to make his desires irrelevant to his fate. Similarly, Menelaus; through his fictional odysseys, the minstrels in his perishable manuscript cling to the possibility that they may endure despite their apparent isolation from the physical world in which such endurance matters. It is this stubborn insistence on life, however transformed, that affirms the vital principle, a principle on which comedy, in whatever state of decomposition, must finally depend.

DAVID KETTERER

Take-Off to Cosmic Irony:
Science-Fiction Humor
and the Absurd

Science fiction is not characteristically, or at least not intention-
ally, a humorous literature. Some might even argue that humor,
along with sexual and romantic experience, is inappropriate to
science fiction. The notion of humor includes the notion of what it is
to be human, and the sense has long reigned that any concern with
human beings in science fiction is severely secondary.[1] Critics have
experienced a similar feeling of inconsistency with regard to these
lines from Chaucer's *Troilus and Criseyde,* following Troilus' death
and his ascent to "the eighthe spere:"

> And down from thennes faste he gan avyse
> This litel spot of erthe . . .
>
>   . . . .
> And in hymself he lough right at the wo
> Of hem that wepten for his death so faste. [V, 1814–22]

There is a comparable well-known passage in *Paradise Lost,* when
Christ applauds God's amused reaction to Satan's situation:

>   Mighty Father, thou thy foes
> Justly has in derision, and secure
> Laugh'st at their vain designs and tumults vain. [V, 735–37]

---

[1]The semantic equation between humor and disposition or mood in the "theory of humors"
provides the clearest basis for the association of the humorous with the human. What is
potentially funny about the phlegmatic, choleric, sanguine, or melancholic man is, of course,
the matter of imbalance and exaggerated posture. Ben Jonson considerably expanded the range
of such temperaments in his humor comedies.

It has been argued that, since dead Troilus and God both transcend the human state, laughter is an unbefitting or somehow tasteless response. But the fact is that writers who wish to create "other worlds" cannot do so without recourse to the human world in which they live. However disguised, such writers, whether Milton or the authors of science fiction, cannot escape the element of anthropomorphic projection. That the laughter of Troilus and God is fundamentally ironic is, therefore, a most appropriate reflection of the ironic situation in which the creator of other worlds finds himself.

As I shall argue, if there is a form of humor which is generic to science fiction, that form is irony. My overall purpose, however, is to discuss the possibilities of humor in science fiction and to demonstrate, in conclusion, the importance of irony. Along the way, I distinguish between the kinds of humor which figure in superior and serious science fiction (the humor of realization, absurdist humor, and conscious irony) and the kinds of humor which result either from not taking the genre seriously or from a basic lack of humor on the part of the author (slapstick, parody, and unconscious cliché). But first there are significant connections to be made between various comedic aspects of science fiction and related forms of literature.

I begin this survey in comparative terms because science fiction is best understood as an aspect of a larger literary structure. In *New Worlds for Old: The Apocalyptic Imagination, Science Fiction, and American Literature,* I distinguish between a sequence of three imaginative structures which depend upon a reader's conventionalized understanding of the intended relationship between the "worlds" writers create and the world of general experience.[2] A writer within the mimetic tradition is concerned with creating "worlds" directly imitative of, and therefore credible in relation to, the "real" world. A writer within the fantastic tradition, including the writer of overt allegories, of what are normally called fantasies, and of certain kinds of comedy, is concerned with creating "worlds" which are significantly different from the "real" world and which, *on a literal level,* are intended to exist in an incredible relationship with that "real" world. A writer within the apocalyptic tradition draws on both mimetic and fantastic strategies to create other "worlds" which are significantly different from the "real" world,

[2]David Ketterer, *New Worlds for Old: The Apocalyptic Imagination, Science Fiction, and American Literature* (Bloomington: Indiana University Press, 1974).

yet which are intended as existing in a credible relationship with it. The assumption of credibility as a reading convention is signaled either by an appeal to rationality, largely the technique of extrapolation and analogy in the case of science fiction; or by an appeal to faith, in the case of, say, *The Divine Comedy* and *Paradise Lost*. Within the apocalyptic imagination, theoretical distinctions can be drawn between visionary or mystical worlds outside of space and time; other worlds, often satirical, in space and time; and, third, formulations which have the effect of describing the present "reality" in other "philosophical" terms: new definitions of man, reality, and the nature of an outside manipulator or god.

The genre of science fiction is remarkable for its assimilative capacity; hence the notorious plethora of definitions in answer to that misguided question, What is science fiction? The definitions make much more sense as answers to the question, What are the different kinds of science fiction? The initials "sf" may sometimes be translated as "speculative fiction" or even, to instance the latest invention, as "structural fabulation."[3] To see science fiction as an aspect of a larger imaginative structure which includes visionary, metaphysical, and surrealist literature, writings which attempt to capture "the sublime" and some forms of satire, is to immediately gain an idea of the different forms which science fiction can take. Apocalyptic literature now appears to be capable of a fluidity and adaptability which is not characteristic of the fatigued mimetic tradition, underpinned as it is by a dated epistemology. We are in a situation where mainstream fiction is drawing on some of the techniques and furniture of science fiction, while science fiction itself is metamorphosing to a point where the applicability of the label often seems questionable.

Given this state of affairs and allowing that the best science fiction

[3]See Robert Scholes, *Structural Fabulation: An Essay on Fiction of the Future* (Notre Dame, Ind.: Notre Dame University Press, 1975). Whatever reservations I have about Scholes's term, I am pleased to see that he does distinguish between science fiction and fantasy. For Scholes it is a matter of the relationship between sublimation and cognition. In the case of fantasy or pure romance, the emphasis is on sublimation with minimal cognition. With science fiction there is either a balance or an emphasis on cognition. I take as further corroboration for my position the fact that Scholes appears to envision a large formal totality—didactic romance—which includes or develops into speculative fabulation, dogmatic fabulation, and structural fabulation (essentially a name for serious science fiction). The special relationship he ponders between structural fabulation and dogmatic fabulation comes close to paralleling my concept of the apocalyptic imagination.

tends to be serious, it may be useful to outline the theoretical possibilities for humor in science fiction in terms of the various comedic forms which can be appreciated as feeding into the genre. First, if one can speak of such a thing as the "plot" of science fiction, it seems that such a plot is comic in the technical sense that *The Divine Comedy* is comic. It ends happily. I would argue that the bulk of science fiction adheres to a consensus plot which parallels that of the Book of Revelation. After a dystopian situation comes world catastrophe, followed by a post-catastrophe interlude. Space travel offers an escape from such disaster, a potential immortality. That promise culminates in a kind of visionary utopia, science fiction's equivalent of the celestial city. The works of Olaf Stapledon, A. C. Clarke, and more recently Ursula K. Le Guin point to such a comedic outcome. Balancing the visionary emphasis in science fiction is the satiric. The alien viewpoint in science fiction is frequently used for satiric purposes, and obviously satire is a form which can involve humor. The best examples of satiric humor in recent American science fiction are to be found in the works of Frederick Pohl and C. M. Kornbluth (particularly the novel on which they collaborated, *The Space Merchants*), William Tenn (*Venus and the Seven Sexes, The Masculine Revolt*), Robert Sheckley (*Journey Beyond Tomorrow, Do You Feel Anything When I Do This?*), John T. Sladek (*The Muller-Fökker Effect*), and, inevitably, Kurt Vonnegut, Jr. (*Welcome to the Monkey House, Cat's Cradle*, etc.).

For example, a domestic kind of satire exists in Robert Sheckley's "Street of Dreams, Feet of Clay." The protagonist, Carmody, is tempted to leave the horrors of New York and sample the pleasures of Bellwether, which claims to be the perfect city—too perfect, as it turns out. To avoid impersonality, Bellwether "was created with a voice and an artificial consciousness."[4] But in conversation with Carmody, the over-solicitous city reveals itself as having the personality of the stereotyped nagging Jewish mother. There is a limit to how much goodness a person can take; like all the other potential residents, Carmody soon flees the city, but not without taking with him one irritating anxiety: " 'Have a nice trip!' Bellwether called after him. 'Don't worry about me, I'll be waiting for you.' "[5]

Humorous science fiction is on the increase, but were it not for the

[4] "Street of Dreams, Feet of Clay," reprinted in *World's Best Science Fiction 1969*, ed. Donald A. Wollheim and Terry Carr (New York: Ace, 1969), p. 15.
[5] *Ibid.*, p. 25.

works of Vonnegut, it would not have become so popular. Because I may assume a kind of familiarity with Vonnegut, which is not true of most of the science fiction writers I might wish to discuss, I shall frequently refer to his works for the various facets of science fiction humor. For the moment he may serve to introduce the issue of the role of humor in the science fiction/fantasy debate. Vonnegut's reluctance to align himself with the world of science fiction is well-known and not surprising. He spent a good many years getting out of that literary ghetto. It might indeed be argued (although I disagree, for reasons that will become apparent) that, like much humorous "science fiction," Vonnegut's work is actually a species of fantasy. One way to be funny in "science fiction" is not to take the genre seriously, to write on a subjunctive level which implies this is all too ridiculous to bear any literal relationship to the known world. The technique of extrapolation easily lends itself to the *reductio ad absurdum* or the empty game. Many humorous time-travel stories are of this kind and properly belong in the category of fantasy—not because time travel is itself implausible, but because the possibilities are not treated seriously.[6]

Time-travel tales frequently exist in that grey area between science fiction and fantasy. Alfred Bester's story "The Men Who Murdered Mohammed" is an example. The protagonist attempts to dispose of his unfaithful wife by jumping into a time machine and killing her ancestors, only to discover that there is no universal time continuum. He can only travel and act in his individual continuum; in so doing, he commits chronicide and becomes a ghost. Another example is David Gerrold's *Man Who Folded Himself,* hailed as the ultimate time-paradox story. The folded man is able to enjoy a homosexual relationship with another temporal self. Central in both these stories is the element of play, which creates humor and gives the impression of fantasy rather than science fiction.

A reader would have somewhat the same reaction to Frederic Brown's very clever, very funny story entitled "Placet Is a Crazy Place." Brown creates an eccentric planet "that does a figure-eight orbit around two dissimilar suns," a situation that gives rise to periodic hallucinations on the part of the terrestrial inhabitants:

[6]The semantic argument that science fiction is actually a form of fantasy is a red herring. Strictly speaking, both fantasy and reality are passé terms. Neither can exist outside an intending consciousness. If critical discourse is to continue, the intending consciousness of an author in this regard must be taken into account.

"Placet is the only known planet that can eclipse itself twice at the same time, run headlong into itself every forty hours, and then chase itself out of sight. "[7] The buildings which the colonists have erected are regularly shaken by "birds" flying "underground." The "birds' " molecular structure is "so dense that ordinary matter is as tenuous to them as air is to us. "[8] From the "birds' " point of view, the human colony exists on top of Placet's atmosphere! The problem of the shaking buildings is solved by making the foundations hollow and therefore equivalent to a vacuum for the "birds."

I have said that humor is associated with the human, but there is a slapstick humor related to the inhuman or mechanical. Clearly, there is plenty of room in science fiction for a Jacques Tati kind of mechanical mayhem. Such zaniness occurs in Philip José Farmer's "Riders of the Purple Sage." The protagonist approaches a door: "The door, detecting, amplifying, and transmitting the shifting but recognizable eidolon of epidermal electrical fields to the activating mechanism, balks. Chib is too upset. Magnetic maelstroms rage over his skin and distort the spectral configuration. The door half-rolls out, rolls in, changes its mind again, rolls out, rolls in. "[9] Likewise, the human mimicry of robots may be treated comically. But, as with game playing, this type of humor, if extended, will tend to transform science fiction into fantasy.

Spoof science fiction has its roots in the literary hoax and the tall tale, both traditions highly relevant to the development of American science fiction. Oddly enough, the importance of these humorous forms in the history of science fiction has barely been recognized although, given a moment's thought, the connection is obvious, particularly in the case of the literary hoax. Literary hoaxes may be of essentially two kinds. Either a writer may attempt a literary forgery—to pass off his own writing as Shakespeare's, for example—or he may attempt to put over as factual an account of some extraordinary phenomenon or incident. The extraordinary quality ensures that the second type of hoax easily transforms itself into science fiction. The *New York Sun* frequently published such pieces in order to boost its circulation. Locke's "Moon Hoax" and

[7] "Placet Is a Crazy Place," originally published in *Angels and Spaceships* (1954), reprinted in *Best SF Two: Science Fiction Stories*, ed. Edmund Crispin (London: Faber and Faber, 1956), p. 87.

[8] *Ibid.*, p. 94.

[9] "Riders of the Purple Sage," in *Dangerous Visions*, ed. Harlan Ellison (New York: New American Library, 1975), p. 43.

Poe's "Balloon Hoax" and "The Unparalleled Adventure of One Hans Phaall" are the best known examples. What the hoax form is to Poe, the tall tale tradition is to Twain and such science-fictional works as *A Connecticut Yankee in King Arthur's Court* and "Three Thousand Years among the Microbes." Both Poe and Twain use the hoax and the tall tale with a philosophical seriousness that puts the works I have mentioned in the "apocalyptic" tradition and in affinity with science fiction, rather than with fantasy. Vonnegut is the heir of Twain and it is, I believe, his essential philosophical seriousness which makes him an apocalyptic writer and at times a writer of science fiction. However, my present point is only that the hoax and the tall tale are two of the elements that feed into the humorous potential of science fiction. Of the three figures that Hugo Gernsback pointed to as the founders of science fiction—Poe, Verne, and Wells—only Poe aspired regularly toward humor. Perhaps the line from Poe to Twain to Vonnegut explains the continuing comic element in American science fiction.

Much that is funniest in "science fiction" is unintentional, stems indeed from a lack of humor. The clichés and stereotypes of the genre have become established to the point that an author may find himself writing parody unconsciously. Undoubtedly the clearest, hoariest example is that line, "There are things man was not meant to know," or variations thereof. It is the very lack of humor accompanying such utterances which provokes mirth. Since *The War of the Worlds,* formula science fiction has treated us to innumerable invasions of Earth by superior aliens equipped with fearsome powers. In *The Sirens of Titan* Vonnegut works a parodic inversion on this tradition. The invasion from Mars organized by Niles Rumfoord is hopelessly inadequate—the puniest threat from space in science fiction. On a realistic level, the outcome, with "Martians" (actually, conscripted humans) strung up from lampposts, is tragic, but on the level of parody the event makes for fine humor.

The absurdity of plotting and the flatness of characterization in bad science fiction provide obvious targets for parody. One familiar result is the figure of the "mad scientist." However disturbing and dangerous such a person might be in reality, on paper he is invariably comic. Presumably, it is impossible to write about rockets thrusting into the void without some consciousness of sexual innuendo, were it not for the lack of simple human awareness and insensitivity to language on the part of some science fictioneers. Vonnegut's science-fiction hack writer, Kilgore Trout, as the putative author of Philip José Farmer's *Venus on the Half-Shell,* proffers the following description of his hero's reaction to his spaceship: "It lay broadside to him and, as usual, the sight of it disturbed him. He could never put his mental finger on the reason. It was about six hundred feet long, its main length cylindrical shaped. The nose however was bulbous, and its stern rested on two hemispheres. These housed the engines which drove the *Hwang Ho.* "[10] Vonnegut himself brings the whole issue out into the open in a story called "The Big Space Fuck," included in an anthology entitled *Again, Dangerous Visions.* In the realm of much science fiction, sex would seem to be the most dangerous vision of all.

In a field as inbred as science fiction, the work of the better-known writers is frequently "taken off." The colorful galaxy-spanning extravaganzas of Alfred Bester appear to parody the kind of "space opera" associated with E. E. "Doc" Smith. Harry Harrison's *Bill,, the Galactic Hero* parodies the militaristic set-up in Heinlein's *Starship Troopers.*

It is necessary, however, to distinguish between "science-fiction" works whose overall intention is parodic, and science-fiction works containing parodic elements.[11] The former works belong to the class of parody, not science fiction. Strictly speaking, then, a book like *Venus on the Half-Shell* is not an example of humorous science fiction, it is an example of parody. In Vonnegut's own books the element of undiluted parody is largely confined to wry synopses of Kilgore Trout stories with such titles as "Pan-Galactic Three-Day Pass" and "Maniacs in the Fourth Dimension." The tyrannizing growth of parody in *Breakfast of Champions* appears to signal the exhaustion of Vonnegut's talent, but the Trout synopses work well as exaggerated versions of a context which is something more than parody, in that it expresses a realistic species of truth. In *Venus on the Half-Shell* (the title alludes to Botticelli's

[10] Kilgore Trout, *Venus on the Half-Shell* (New York: Dell, 1974), p. 36.
[11] See William L. Godshalk, "Alfred Bester: Science Fiction or Fantasy?" *Extrapolation,* 5 (1975), 149–155. Godshalk speaks of the element of parody in Bester and appears to assume that parodies are also fantasies. Because the important factor in a parody is the relationship between two literary worlds and not between a literary world and "reality," such a form, in my terms, is outside the parameters which distinguish mimetic, fantastic, and apocalyptic literature.

"Birth of Venus") this vitalizing context is missing—it is all Trout. One indication that the author recognizes his book's lack of substance is provided by the many references to farting, belching, and bad smells: "Terrestrials had a reputation as the most odiferous race in the universe."[12] That the author should associate this book with foul winds may have been encouraged by Vonnegut's tendency of late to refer to himself as an "old fart."

There is, of course, something Swiftian about this motif (to revert to critical delicacy), and that no doubt is the reason why "Trout" regularly rehearses the tales of another science-fiction writer named Jonathan Swift Somers III. This formal regression exemplifies the coded "literary" nature of parody. Paralyzed from the waist down, Sommers's heroes are similarly handicapped except for Ralph von Wau Wau, who is a dog. Some of the funniest passages in the book describe the adventures of "Sommers' basketcase hero, John Clayter," who gets around in a prosthetic spacesuit.[13] But in spite of the excellent imitation of Vonnegut's inconsequential style, the parodic nature of the book as a whole stretches the joke much too thin. Occasional moments of real hilarity—the Clayter stories, the absurdly detailed descriptions of bizarre aliens, and accounts of comic biological symbiosis systems—are insufficient to boost the "take-off" of the whole.

However limited an artistic form, the evidence of parody in science fiction may be a positive phenomenon. And here science fiction may include the notion of a kind of literature which could not exist without the prior existence of science fiction. According to the Russian formalists, parody plays a key role in the development of literature, the metamorphosis of forms. Boris Eichenbaum writes:

> In the evolution of each genre, there are times when its use for entirely serious or elevated objectives degenerates and produces a comic or parodic form . . . the serious interpretation of a construction motivated with care and in detail gives way to irony, pleasantry, pastiche; the connections which serve to motivate a scene become weaker and more obvious; the author himself comes on stage and often destroys the illusion of authenticity and seriousness; the construction of a plot

[12]Trout, *Venus on the Half-Shell*, p. 24.
[13]*Ibid.*, p. 138.

becomes a playing with the story which transforms itself into a puzzle or an anecdote. And thus is produced the regeneration of the genre: it finds new possibilities and new forms.[14]

This is a strikingly exact description of the current situation in the science fiction I have described. Further defining the nature of literary evolution, Roman Jakobson observes that "Genres which were originally secondary paths, subsidiary variants, now come to the fore, whereas the canonical genres are pushed towards the rear."[15] It may be at least suspected, then, that parodic "science fiction" represents the death knell of bad, superficial and cliché-ridden science fiction and promises the emergence of vitalized, related but perhaps unrecognizable mutations. Certainly we appear to be in a situation where the writer of serious science fiction must protect himself against fossilized forms by a judicious edge of parody and irony.

The difference between good and bad science fiction has much to do with the degree of realization. Ideas are only meaningful in relation to human beings who are themselves meaningful. The best science fiction to date and, it is to be hoped, the good work to come is and will be inhabited by real people as well as real aliens and robots. The human element will no longer be a secondary consideration; it will exist in equal if sometimes antithetical relationship to the more abstract cerebral tapestry characteristic of the genre. It is, of course, axiomatic that writers who care about people will care about humor and make it an indispensable element of the fully realized scene. Having drawn attention to some examples of science fiction where the humor depends ultimately on the artistic limitations, it is now appropriate to note examples of the kind of humor to be associated with artistic ability—in particular, humor as an aspect of characterization. While not typical of current science fiction as a whole, there already exist examples of the kind of realization that I am projecting. Theodore Sturgeon's work tends in this direction, as does that of R. A. Lafferty. However, success here is to be measured outside the narrow world of science fiction readers. The best known example is probably *A Canticle for Leibowitz* by Walter M. Miller, Jr.

[14]Quoted by Robert Scholes in *Structuralism in Literature: An Introduction* (New Haven: Yale University Press, 1974), pp. 87–88.

[15]*Readings in Russian Poetics,* ed. Ladislay Matejka and Krystana Pomorska (Cambridge: Harvard University Press, 1971), p. 85.

This book is about man's apparent inability to free himself, millennium after millennium, from a cyclic process of nuclear self-destruction and stumbling renewal—not exactly a laughing matter. But there is irony here, the one species of muted humor that is essentially generic to science fiction. There is also a more full-blooded humor deriving from the nature and reactions of realized characters trapped in a realized scene. Most of the action centers on the monks of Leibowitz (something's changed!) Abbey who venerate, study, and attempt to preserve the artifacts of pre-catastrophe civilization. The novel begins with an almost farcical dance of misunderstanding between a naive, ridiculously pious novice, Brother Francis, and a mysterious, spindly pilgrim. Thinking the crochety old pilgrim is a manifestation of Satan, Brother Francis spatters him with holy water:

> This surprise attack on the Powers of Darkness and Temptation produced no immediate supernatural results but the natural results seemed to appear *ex opere operato*. The pilgrim-Beelzebub failed to explode into sulfurous smoke, but he made gargling sounds, turned a bright shade of red, and lunged at Francis with a bloodcurdling yell. The novice kept tripping on his tunic as he fled from flailing of the pilgrim's spiked staff, and he escaped without nail holes only because the pilgrim had forgotten his sandals. The old man's limping charge became a skippity hop.[16]

This is not the kind of mechanical slapstick which renders the scene unbelievable, but the kind of human slapstick which makes it true.

The character of the abbot, Dom Jethrah Zerchi, is best illustrated by his comically combative, St. George–like attitude toward machinery: "The dragon was an Abominable Autoscribe, and its malignant enormity, electronic by disposition, filled several cubical units of hollow wall space and a third of the volume of the abbot's desk. As usual, the contraption was on the blink."[17] This incongruous combination of religious fervor and prosaic ignorance, of doubtful value in the business of electrical repair, gives the reader real insight into Zerchi's mind: "His only claim to competence at the repair of polylinguistic transcription devices lay in his proud record of once having extracted a dead mouse from the information storage circuitry, thereby correcting a mysterious tendency on the part of

---

[16]Walter M. Miller, Jr., *A Canticle for Leibowitz* (New York: Bantam, 1961), pp. 5–6.
[17]*Ibid.*, p. 203.

the machine to write double syllables.''[18] Not being able to find a mouse this time, Zerchi retreats from the engagement after an electric shock throws him to the floor.

This form of incidental humor by virtue of realization is most easily illustrated in terms of characterization but it is not limited to that alone. The degree to which a writer has succeeded in getting inside his future or alternate world may be measured, in large part, by his ability to see and communicate its funny aspects. Any daily newspaper, past, present, or future, will find room for humorous items. Of course, to be appreciated by the reader, the comedy inherent in a particular situation must be filtered through a human viewpoint. We come back, then, to the importance of character realization. To the extent that a narrator or reflecting consciousness is susceptible to the humorous element in his environment, he will help to establish the reality both of that environment and of himself. Such intermittent humor, while an essential ingredient of good science fiction, is very much a matter of means rather than ends. It is time to consider the science-fictional possibilities of sustained comic vision. Does there exist a consistently humorous science fiction which is not actually fantasy or parody?

A shared potential for subversion suggests that the marriage between humor and science fiction is not as unnatural as it might at first seem. Science fiction, whether basically satiric, visionary, or philosophic in picturing alternatives to a present reality, has the effect of subverting the status quo. Humor has been exploited as an instrument of subversion by many writers. There is indeed a clear tradition of such humor in American literature, making for a virtual equation between comedy and apocalypse.[19] Little Satan in Twain's *Mysterious Stranger* speaks of the apocalyptic power of laughter: "Power, money, persuasion, supplication—these can lift at a colossal humbug—push it a little—weaken it a little, century by century; but only laughter can blow it to rags and atoms at a blast. Against the assault of laughter nothing can stand."[20] Here are

[18]*Ibid.*, p. 204.

[19]See R. W. B. Lewis, "Days of Wrath and Laughter," in *Trials of the Word: Essays in American Literature and the Humanistic Tradition* (New Haven: Yale University Press, 1965), pp. 184–235. To some extent Robert Scholes covers the same ground in *The Fabulators* (New York: Oxford University Press, 1967).

[20]*Mark Twain's "The Mysterious Stranger" and the Critics*, ed. John S. Tuckey (Belmont, Calif.: Wadsworth, 1968), p. 69.

the roots of black humor in response to an absurd universe. Here also is a fertile area of overlap between science fiction and mainstream fiction.

Characteristically, science fiction presents a universe without God, a universe in which men aspire to be gods. Such a universe can easily slip into the sort of absurdist universe we often appear to live in. In spite of the religious setting in *A Canticle for Leibowitz,* there is little evidence of God and much evidence of a fundamental absurdity. In fact, the old pilgrim observes Brother Francis as a Sisyphus figure in the act of rolling a stone—albeit to help construct a shelter. The Sisyphus comparison is strongly reinforced by the overall context of pointless repetition. However, my essential point is that man's philosophical position in an absurd cosmos is one that translates freely into science fiction, as does the concomitant human reaction of black humor.

A sense of the absurd makes possible the humorous science fiction of Kurt Vonnegut and prevents it from being classified as fantasy. The difference is between the *reductio ad absurdum* used purely for its comic effect, and the same device used as an expression of the philosophical absurd. The bizarre situations and events in *The Sirens of Titan, Cat's Cradle,* and the short stories collected in *Welcome to the Monkey House* reflect a universe which is equally bizarre. However incredible it may appear, the world of Vonnegut's science fiction is intended to exist in a credible relationship with the "real" world because that "real" world is likewise incredible. Thus, in *Slaughterhouse-Five* the science-fictional world of Tralfamadore becomes as absurdly believable as the fire-bombing of Dresden. In his preface to *Welcome to the Monkey House,* Vonnegut refers to a conversation with a college professor: "I asked him what the very lowest grade of fiction was, and he told me, 'Science fiction.' I asked him where he was bound in such a rush, and learned that he had to catch a Fan-Jet. He was to speak at a meeting of the Modern Language Association in Honolulu the next morning. Honolulu was three thousand miles away."[21] The reality of Vonnegut's absurdist world is not compromised by a framework of allegory such as exists in, say, John Barth's *Giles Goat-Boy.* The overt allegorical schema makes Barth's book comic fantasy and not comic science fiction. Within my subdivisions of the apocalyptic imagination, absurdist

[21]Kurt Vonnegut, Jr., *Welcome to the Monkey House* (New York: Dell, 1970), p. x.

science fiction belongs among those works which present the present world in other terms by virtue of an extreme philosophical reinterpretation of the nature of reality.

The prominence of black humor in the American fiction of the 1960's is a large part of the explanation for the increased output of humorous science fiction and, in lesser part, an explanation for the current academic interest in science fiction. Only the absurd creations of science fiction seem to equal the absurd reality of a book like Bruce Jay Friedman's *Stern*. This affinity comes to a focus with Vonnegut and leads critics to wonder whether *Cat's Cradle* is best described as science fiction or black humor. Equally blurred are the distinctions between satire, parody, and black humor. Black humor is a form of satire and, since what is being satirized is a hackneyed reality, parody may ironically become a form of "realism."

A couple of stories from Vonnegut's *Welcome to the Monkey House* will illustrate the mixed quality of black humor–science fiction. "Harrison Bergeron" describes a future world where human equality is legislated. People of more than average intelligence, beauty, or whatever are correspondingly handicapped. For example, ballerinas "were burdened with sashweights and bags of birdshot, and their faces were marked, so that no one seeing a free and graceful gesture or a pretty face would feel like something the cat dragged in."[22] In clichéd dystopian fashion, one man, Harrison Bergeron, rebels against the system, only to be shot dead by the Handicapper General.

In "Tomorrow and Tomorrow and Tomorrow" the satiric target is overpopulation and medically prolonged life. The problem is how to wean Gramps, aged one hundred and seventy-two, from his anti-gerasone so that Lou and Em can come into their inheritance. The two reminisce about the old days before "processed seaweed" and "processed sawdust," when "You didn't have to wait for somebody to die to get a bed or chairs or a stove or anything like that."[23] This is the kind of situation which has been told straight in innumerable science-fiction stories, perhaps most notably in Harry Harrison's *Make Room, Make Room,* translated to the screen as *Soylent Green.*

In an absurdist universe, conventional reality is shown to be a sham. The ironic disparity between man's sense that existence is

[22]*Ibid.*, p. 8.
[23]*Ibid.*, p. 296.

meaningful, primarily in a religious sense, and the realization that he exists in a universe devoid of human meaning constitutes the absurd. The almost conventionalized science-fiction discovery that human reality is somehow counterfeit provides for a similar experience. A master of this species of absurdist science fiction is Philip K. Dick. His work is characterized by grim comedy and metaphysical wit, the type of wit exemplified in a title like *Do Androids Dream of Electric Sheep?* In Dick's surreal metaphysical world, the mechanical and the organic, the material and the spiritual are interchangeable; human beings turn out to be robots, worlds turn out to be hallucinations or fakes. Life is a cruel comedy of errors. Like the poetry of Donne, Dick's fiction deals in bizarre and witty juxtapositions.

Juxtapositions frequently result in irony, the one "humorous" element that I consider to be virtually a generic aspect of science fiction. Certainly, dystopian fiction, a major subspecies of science fiction, is ironic by definition. Equally, the cosmic laughter of the chrono-synclastic infundibulated (therefore transcendent) Rumfoord in *The Sirens of Titan,* no less than the cosmic laughter of God and Troilus with which I began, is ironic. Of course, all fictions rely on plot reversals which could be called ironic (peripeteia and irony exist hand in glove). What is distinctive about science-fiction irony is that it resides not so much in incident or character as in the confrontation of alternate worlds or realities. The relationship between the known and the unknown, basic to science fiction, is inevitably ironic. The humor evoked by such irony is rarely raucous, it is more often wry, tragic, or, like black humor, simply expressive of the absurd.

A well-known example of the operation of irony in science fiction is H. G. Wells's *Time Machine.* Here the irony has two foci. On the one hand, there is a teasing irony associated with the Time Traveler's repeatedly inaccurate attempts to formulate his understanding of the future in which he finds himself. On the other, there is the overriding and sober irony that what the Time Traveler's contemporaries take to be progress is actually the cause of human regression. Humanity has undergone a split "evolution" into the ineffective Eloi and the bestial Morlocks, because of the advance of civilization and comfort—upper-class comfort, that is.

In American literature, Vonnegut's *The Sirens of Titan* provides the best examples of science-fiction irony. Indeed, this book is perhaps the supreme example of science-fiction humor. In it are all the various elements I have described: satiric humor (aimed at such targets as fundamentalist religion and dehumanization), the *reductio ad absurdum* (the "dirty" definition of a chrono-synclastic infundibulum in *A Child's Cyclopaedia of Wonders and Things to Do*), parody (of whizz-bang "space opera" as practiced by the likes of A. E. van Vogt), the humor of realization (the character of Boaz, for example), and the absurd (Rumfoord's new religion based on the concept of God the Utterly Indifferent). The plot spirals around two absurd ironies. First, the reader gradually discovers that all of human history has been manipulated for their own ends by robots on the planet Tralfamadore, in a distant galaxy. Human history is thus stripped of all human meaning. The Tralfamadorians have been intent on rescuing one of their kind named Salo; eons ago he was forced to land on Titan, one of the moons of Saturn, when his spaceship developed a fault. Salo was engaged in carrying a message of greeting from one end of the universe to the other. The second irony reverses the scale of the first. It turns out that the piece of junk metal which a boy named Chrono has worn around his neck as a charm will function as the spare part required to get Salo's ship on its way again. All of human history has been geared to getting Chrono to Titan with his "good luck piece."

Reality-switching ironies of this kind are well suited to the short story form. That the science-fiction short story has long been in a healthy condition may have something to do with the fact that ironic conclusions, as opposed to merely trick endings, generally work effectively in a restricted format. In van Vogt's "Enchanted Village" an Earthman stumbles across a "dead" Martian village. His presence activates the mechanical servitors and, during the course of the tale, the village appears to adapt itself to his human needs. Only with the final sentence—the reference to the intruder's swishing tail—does the reader realize that the outsider has adapted himself to the village and has become a Martian. In Ray Bradbury's little masterpiece, "Kaleidoscope," a rocket ship breaks up just outside Earth's atmosphere. As one of the spacesuited crew plunges toward Earth, he wonders if anyone will see his meteoric demise. He is in fact observed as a shooting star by a mother and her son: " 'Make a wish,' said his mother. 'Make a wish.' "[24]

The work of Frederick Brown offers several examples of this sort of irony. In "Answer" a computer, asked about the existence of God, replies, *"Now* there is a God!"[25] The following story, attributed to Brown, is complete: "After the last atomic war, Earth was dead; nothing grew. The last man sat alone in a room. There was a knock on the door . . . "[26] Could a story, any story, as short as this one exist without the presence of irony?

As is the nature of irony, none of these punch lines is simply funny unmixed with complicating tones. Indeed, the whole issue of humor, and of humor in science fiction, is more complicated than it may at first appear. The simplistic response that good science fiction is serious literature and therefore not a vehicle for humor does not fit the facts. A serious worldview does not preclude the possibility of humor. It is, however, necessary to reaffirm that the bulk of science fiction is not given to sustained humor. Sustained "straight" humor can only exist in science fiction that degenerates into fantasy or parody. But a more twisted form of humor, where what is funny is akin to the horrific, tragic, or absurd, is compatible with and increasingly evident in serious science fiction. Science fiction may contain laughs, but it must contain other things as well. Like apocalyptic literature generally, it concerns itself both with the human which is potentially funny and with the enveloping non-human which, taken on its own terms, is not. If what I have called the "plot" of science fiction, culminating in the vision of man at home in the entire cosmos, is expansive, the humor of science fiction defines and often mocks the limitations of man, the worlds he creates, and the world he inhabits.

[24]Ray Bradbury, *The Illustrated Man* (New York: Bantam, 1957), p. 41.
[25]Quoted by Brian W. Aldiss in *Billion Year Spree: The True History of Science Fiction* (New York: Schocken, 1973), p. 234.
[26]Quoted by Sam J. Lundwall in *SF: What It's All About* (New York: Ace, 1969), p. 13.

C. HUGH HOLMAN

Detached Laughter in the South

"I have found that any fiction that comes out of the South is going to be called grotesque by the Northern reader—unless it is grotesque, in which case it's going to be called realism,"[1] declared Flannery O'Connor, who also asserted that "The woods are full of regional writers and it is the great horror of every serious southern writer that he will become one."[2] Thus, in her wry way, she marked off a body of writing uniquely associated with the southeastern United States, asserted that it had differences deeper than the local-color qualities of a section of the nation, and expressed her stubborn pride in those differences.

The average reasonably well-informed northern reader may want to debate O'Connor's definition of realism, but he will certainly agree that southern writing in this century has been different. Even if he shares the arch provincialism of New York City that has led Richard Gilman to say, "The time is long past when southern writers were either at the center of American literature or powerful influences on the flank,"[3] when you say "southern writing" to this

[1]Flannery O'Connor, "Some Aspects of the Grotesque in Southern Literature," in *The Added Dimension: The Art and Mind of Flannery O'Connor*, ed. Melvin J. Friedman and Lewis A. Lawson (New York: Fordham University Press, 1966), p. 273.

[2]Flannery O'Connor, "The Fiction Writer and His Country," in *The Living Novel: A Symposium*, ed. Granville Hicks (New York: Macmillan, 1957), p. 160.

[3]Review of *The Surface of Earth*, by Reynolds Price, in *New York Times Book Review*, June 29, 1975, p. 1.

average northern reader, he thinks he knows what to expect. It is the Gothic, revelling deliciously and lasciviously in its horrors. It is the historical, restoring past glories now gone with the wind. It is the idealized and the sentimental, so sickly sweet that he feels as though he had swallowed *Love Story* at one gulp. It is the grotesque, depraved, and deformed. Occasionally, too, it is the indignant and the socially aware. But this northern reader seldom gets from the words "southern writing" a picture that has a substantial comic dimension. This is surprising, because for the last hundred and fifty years the comic has been a major, though often ignored, segment of the southern literary imagination.

O'Connor has other surprises for this northern reader. While acknowledging the label of "grotesque" for her characters, she disavows its applicability and asserts a realistic intention. And if her northern reader means "grotesque"—a southern characteristic which he does recognize and expect—in the currently fashionable sense of the term, he is likely to see it as "an outgrowth of contemporary interest in the irrational, distrust of any cosmic order, frustration at man's lot in the universe,"[4] an element of "black humor," when it is comic, a form of distortion whose purpose is expressionistic, not representative. If O'Connor is correct, what he sees as grotesque and expressionistic in southern writing is something quite different.

To understand that difference, it is necessary here, as it is with many things southern, to go back for a moment into the past. To a degree unthinkable for any other section of a nation with a history as short as that of the United States, the South has preserved and cherished its temporal continuities. In a time of discontinuities, the South has revered tradition and community. In a world that, by and large, pants passionately after the new and the untried, the South has adapted the received and the known to the needs of the present and the future. Nowhere is this essentially conservative attitude more clearly expressed than in its literature, where it reveres history, gothicism, sentimentality, and formalist criticism—the primary modes of its writers in the nineteenth century. That this traditionalism is also true of its comic writing should be no surprise, for the irreverent but conservative muse of comedy is the muse of

[4]C. Hugh Holman, *A Handbook to Literature,* 3rd ed. (Indianapolis: Bobbs-Merrill, 1972), p. 246.

limitations, of restraints, of tradition, the portrayer of human limitations and frailties rather than superhuman aspirations and ideals—at
least so it has often been, and so it is in the American South. To look
at humor in the recent South, it is necessary to see it as a continuation
of traditional comic writing in the region, even though the South has
frequently been viewed as an arena exclusively dedicated to tragedy
or cruel exploitation or sickeningly pious sentiment. What has comedy, committed as she is to mocking the discrepencies between
appearance and reality, to do with so self-deluding a region as the
South? Such a view is peculiarly unhistorical, for few would deny
the ribald life and triumphant vigor of that group of nineteenth-
century writers whom we call the humorists of the Old Southwest,
and only those whose sense of history is too weak to instruct them in
the chronological course of the westward-moving frontier in the
early nineteenth century will fail to see that that flood of writing was
produced in Georgia, Mississippi, and Alabama—in what was the
southwestern frontier before the Civil War. Augustus Baldwin
Longstreet's *Georgia Scenes* (1835) is the comic portrayal of a
backwoods culture in Georgia. Joseph Glover Baldwin's *Flush
Times of Alabama and Mississippi* (1853) is an amusing record of the
rascality, ignorance, and depravity of life on that wild and roaring
frontier. Johnson Jones Hooper's *Some Adventures of Captain
Simon Suggs* (1845) follows a rascal's wild, picaresque adventures
on that frontier. George Washington Harris's sketches about Sut
Lovingood, an exuberant and uninhibited denizen of Tennessee,
were collected as *Sut Lovingood Yarns* (1867). And there are many
others, most notably Thomas Bangs Thorpe, whose *Big Bear of
Arkansas* is almost the archetype of a brand of humor resting
upon dialect and tall tale and comic character. It was a rich strain of
earthy humor which these writers—mostly lawyers, politicians,
and journalists—produced as an avocation on the Old Southwestern frontier.[5]

These early southern humorists have a number of common characteristics. The writer, either in his own person or through a narrative
persona, usually belongs to a social class quite different from and
superior to that of the frontier wild life which he describes. He

---

[5]A fine representative collection of these humorists, with a perceptive introduction, is
Humor of the Old Southwest, ed. Hennig Cohen and William B. Dillingham (Boston:
Houghton Mifflin, 1964; reprinted, Athens: University of Georgia Press, 1976).

remains consistently the outsider and the observer who brings to bear upon the subjects of his portrayal a set of standards, a level of culture, and a facility with language quite out of keeping with the subjects being described. Each narrator depends upon this social and cultural distance to make possible the representation of crudities, cruelties, and depravities that would otherwise have been almost unbearably shocking to the reader to whom the work is addressed. The mode in which these writers worked was neither Gothic nor sentimental; it was detached, cool, amused, generally tolerant, and often sardonic. They reported to a society back home on what was happening on the wild frontier, but these reports became historical only after the westward movement had passed and had left them as its records. The primary method which these writers employed was the realistic portrayal of an extravagant and wild life, done with great exuberance and a peculiar delight in the vitality and the strangeness of idiomatic speech on the Old Southwestern frontier. Tall tales were one of the hallmarks of this kind of humor, and folk heroes like Davy Crockett and Mike Fink paraded their might across the pages of these books. The primary method, however, was literal reporting of the strange and wonderful doings of the natives, colored by a certain amount of amused extravagance, in reports sent back to an urbane and civilized society.

This was not the only form of humor in the South during the nineteenth century. George Bagby wrote wittily and comically in the *Southern Literary Messenger,* and others imitated the quiet wit of the English periodical essays. Nevertheless, the uniquely southern form of humor dealt with this frontier. Humor was relied on to make the portrayal of this coarse, rough life palatable and enjoyable, rather than horrifying and sickening, for it could easily have been a subject for Gothic treatment. For example, William Gilmore Simms worked essentially in the Gothic tradition in many of his novels. In 1835 and 1836, in his attempts to portray the Loyalist forces during the American Revolution, he piled up the terrors to which they were submitted by their Whig adversaries and the horrors which they later perpetrated in revenge, making themselves into creatures of terror, drinkers of blood, frightening outlaws. However, by the middle 1850's Simms had virtually abandoned the Gothic approach. In his last two Revolutionary novels, *The Forayers* (1855) and *Eutaw* (1856), he shifted to the comic portrayal of these depraved people, creating a great host of far from lovable but certainly laughable and impressive rascals and ruffians who represented the Tory forces. For him, comedy became an effective medium for downgrading the seriousness of hated causes and for attacking the character of those he disliked.[6]

In this century, the South has produced two kinds of humor not greatly different from those of Bagby and the Old Southwest humorists. The humor practiced by James Branch Cabell and Ellen Glasgow in Virginia and by Robert Molloy and Josephine Pinckney around Charleston is essentially that of the novel of manners or of urbane fantasy. Charming and witty, it exists only because the Virginia Tidewater and the Carolina Low Country still had a code of manners sufficiently firm to enable the comedy of manners to be constructed around it. Perhaps the finest writing in this tradition done by any Southerner was by Ellen Glasgow in her Queenborough trilogy, *The Romantic Comedians* (1926), *They Stooped to Folly* (1929), and *The Sheltered Life* (1932).[7]

Opposed to this kind of polished and witty humor, there has also existed a raucous, ribald, and extravagant humor which is the realist's way of dealing with the unbearable or intolerable aspects of life without shifting into the tradition of the Gothic or the tragic. It is a kind of humor that depends, as had that of the Old Southwest, upon the difference in social class and learning between the putative narrator and the subject. It has its roots in aspects of the social condition which constitute affronts to human dignity and arouse the deepest and most penetrating anger, or in cosmic conditions that dwarf and stunt human beings. It controls and shapes these affronts, this anger, or this vision by establishing a redeeming comic distance.

To attempt to deal with the humor of William Faulkner is a task for a book, not for a section of an essay, so I shall use him not as a subject for analysis, but as an object to point to before going on to my two representative writers. William Faulkner can be considered the "compleat" southern writer, for he has demonstrated with a high degree of artistry and accomplishment almost every mode of south-

---

[6]See C. Hugh Holman, "Simms's Changing View of Loyalists during the Revolution," *Mississippi Quarterly,* 29 (Fall, 1976), 501–513.

[7]These novels are dealt with as comedies of manners in C. Hugh Holman, "April in Queenborough: Ellen Glasgow's Comedies of Manners," *Sewanee Review,* 82 (Spring, 1974), 263–283, reprinted with annotations in *Ellen Glasgow: Centennial Essays,* ed. M. Thomas Inge (Charlottesville: University Press of Virginia, 1976), pp. 108–130.

ern fiction which exists in this century. He dealt with Gothic horrors and extravagances in *Sanctuary* (1931). He carried the historical novel to its highest limits of artistic success in *Absalom, Absalom!* (1936). He made art out of the idealized and sentimentalized view of the Civil War in *The Unvanquished* (1938). He dealt with the peculiar mixture of symbolism and naturalism that we associate with the South in *Light in August* (1932) and *The Sound and the Fury* (1929). In the Snopes trilogy—*The Hamlet* (1940), *The Town* (1957), and *The Mansion* (1960)—he carried realistic comedy to its highest accomplishment in this century, working in the tradition of the frontier humorist. Those who call *The Hamlet* the finest comic novel produced by a southern American certainly can feel some confidence in their judgment. It is worth noting that *The Hamlet* is in four parts; Parts I and IV deal with the comic theme of barter, and Parts II and III deal with the novel's other major theme, love.[8] Thus the serious elements of the novel are enclosed by the comic. This use of the comic tone to restore an equitable world is not unusual for Faulkner; the opening and concluding chapters of *Light in August,* dealing with Lena Grove, serve a similar although more restricted function, setting the tragic horrors of the main portion of that novel in a perspective against a comic pastoral.[9] But the Snopes trilogy is loaded with scenes of extravagant humor. The Snopeses themselves are thoroughly in keeping with the natives of the Old Southwestern frontier of Longstreet and Baldwin, and there may be a close relationship between Flem Snopes, the leader of the Snopes clan, and Johnson Jones Hooper's Simon Suggs. The Snopeses represent the lowest class. They swarm over the land, almost seeming to crawl from under stones and rotten logs, and gradually take possession of it. Under the coldly acquisitive leadership of Flem Snopes, they move from the small country community of Frenchman's Bend into the town, and finally to the triumphant possession of the once-

[8]See Melvin Beckman, *Faulkner: The Major Years* (Bloomington: Indiana University Press, 1966), pp. 139–159, for an excellent, succinct treatment of the structure and themes of *The Hamlet.* See Olga W. Vickery, *The Novels of William Faulkner,* rev. ed. (Baton Rouge: Louisiana State University Press, 1964), pp. 167–208, for an examination of the themes of love (or sex) and money in the Snopes trilogy. See Warren Beck, *Man in Motion: Faulkner's Trilogy* (Madison: University of Wisconsin Press, 1961), for a most detailed (but perhaps overly solemn) treatment of the trilogy.

[9]For an explication of the functional role of the Lena Grove story, see C. Hugh Holman, "The Unity of Faulkner's *Light In August,* " in his *The Roots of Southern Writing: Essays on the Literature of the American South* (Athens: University of Georgia Press, 1972), pp. 149–167. The essay was first published in *PMLA,* 72 (March, 1958), 155–166.

glorious South. *The Hamlet* is a loosely linked series of episodes about the Snopeses and their way of life, breaking into separate episodes. Some of those, first published as short stories and episodes in other of the Yoknapatawpha novels, represent an almost pure survival of the characters, actions, and mode of Old Southwestern humor, even being recounted by a narrator, V. K. Ratliff, from a position of superior knowledge. One such is the story of how Ab Snopes was bested by Pat Stamper, a horse-swap story of a sort that goes back to Longstreet's *Georgia Scenes*.[10] Perhaps the funniest story that Faulkner ever wrote, "Spotted Horses," appears as an episode in *The Hamlet*. It recounts the events that befell Frenchman's Bend when Flem Snopes brought in a band of wild, untamable Texas horses and sold them to the men of the community.[11] That novel closes with a tale of "salting" treasure in the old Frenchman's place in Flem's efforts to sell it to Ratliff. In *The Mansion,* a novel generally quite inferior to *The Hamlet,* there are redeeming pieces of comic delight, such as the episode when Byron Snopes sends his four wild and uncivilized children to visit kinsmen in Jefferson. They almost burn Clarence Snopes at the stake. In another incident Clarence, running for Congress, is making a speech; Ratliff has two boys brush Snopes's trousers with branches saturated with dog urine, so the dogs line up to lift their legs on his trousers while he is speaking. Clarence is eliminated from the race on the grounds that the district shouldn't be represented by a man whom every "dog that happens by can't tell from a fence post." In *The Hamlet* there is the tall tale of Flem Snopes outwitting the Devil in Hell and gaining ownership of the infernal regions.

Faulkner uses these episodes and many others like them to fashion a picture of his mythical county, firmly embedded in specific people and actions and described with great intensity. Throughout this picture of what the South had fallen to and of those who controlled it in the years between 1865 and 1915, Faulkner used humor because it allowed him to describe these people and their way of life without treating them either with the Gothic horrors which they might have

[10]William Faulkner, *The Hamlet* (New York: Random House, 1940), pp. 28–53. This episode was originally published as "Fool about a Horse," *Scribner's,* 100 (August, 1936), 80–86.

[11]Faulkner, *The Hamlet,* pp. 309–367. This episode was originally published as "Spotted Horses," *Scribner's,* 89 (June, 1931), 585–597. The story is substantially revised and greatly expanded in the novel.

inspired, or with the sentimental sympathy which we might have had for them had they been presented as the culturally deprived. Neither Faulkner nor his reader regards most characters in the Snopes trilogy as on his own cultural level. The things which happen to them are seen as comic, rather than terrifying. Humor was among the major means by which Faulkner described his world and set it apart from the mainstream, while not denying its actuality. When Faulkner loses the distance which allows him to look without involvement at these characters (as happens in *The Mansion*), when he begins to move in close and understand Flem Snopes, and when he begins to follow Mink Snopes's determination to leave prison and seek revenge upon Flem with some admiration for his determination and persistence—at this point the comedy begins to weaken, and the trilogy begins to weaken as well. There is in Faulkner's Snopes trilogy vastly more than a mere redoing of the humor of the Old Southwest, but that kind of humor is one significant and very happy element in the novels. Faulkner could be—and, at his best, was —truly a master of the comic mode of story-telling. He used that mode to permit the realistic portrayal of characters and actions that might otherwise have overwhelmed us with their crudeness or their horror, as a means of achieving distance, perspective, and the redemption of detachment.

Certainly this treatment of Faulkner's Snopes trilogy is very incomplete, but I hope it suggests to those familiar with his work that Faulkner sometimes consciously wrote in the generally detached mode of the humorists of the Old Southwest frontier, the detached mode which I am maintaining is the most typical method of the writers of humor in the South. Such distance is always bought with a price and for a purpose. In Faulkner's case, the price is the lowering of his dark, tragic intensity; the purpose is the presentation of frail or ignorant or even rapacious people without converting them into devils. For example, in *Absalom, Absalom!* Thomas Sutpen looms vast and demonic over a blasted and monumental landscape, in large part because we see him through the eyes of those who are deeply involved with his tragic and demonic implications. Had V. K. Ratliff told the Sutpen story, Sutpen would have been greatly scaled down from his superhuman magnitude, and Wash Jones, who kills him with a scythe, would have appeared not as a fated Fury wielding the knife of time, but as a shambling poor white with a rusty blade. Comedy is the right mode for the realistic portrayal of people seen in terms of their weaknesses and limitations, particularly if one wants to portray their twisted selves without converting them into creatures of horror.

Now I wish to deal with two other southern writers who belong to this tradition of detached comedy, Erskine Caldwell and Flannery O'Connor. Both have produced distinctively humorous bodies of material, though in the minds of many readers neither should be thought of as a comic writer. In addition, the differences in their visions of the world are so great that, at first glance, they seem to share nothing except a landscape and a tendency to draw grotesque characters. Erskine Caldwell was overcome with the evil which grew out of the economic and agricultural deprivations associated with the South in which he grew up. Flannery O'Connor writes of the poor whites and the middle class in middle Georgia and Tennessee, the same people with whom Caldwell deals. But, being a profoundly religious person, she sees them under the light of eternity, and is deeply concerned with the spiritual deprivations which they suffer because of their unsatisfied hunger for God.

Perhaps the principal inheritor and, to some extent, exploiter of the frontier tradition in southern literature is Erskine Caldwell, whose world is largely populated by people who would have been thoroughly familiar to Johnson Jones Hooper, George Washington Harris, and Augustus Baldwin Longstreet. Indeed, since most of Caldwell's best work is centered in and around Augusta, Georgia, the locale of Longstreet's *Georgia Scenes,* to set Caldwell's portrayal against Longstreet's is to see what has happened to the same kinds of people under the impact of economic poverty, spiritual decay, and the collapse of the agricultural system. If Longstreet's Georgia denizens possessed an enormous zest and vigor, there are about the inhabitants of *Tobacco Road, God's Little Acre,* and *Trouble in July* a debilitation and weakness in which only hunger and sex remain forces that inspire any vigorous action. In this drab world, repetition becomes the dominant tone. Characters endlessly repeat the same actions—an aspect of *Tobacco Road,* for example, which the stage version caught very well by an almost stylized reiteration of characters and actions. These people are portrayed at the most elementary level, reduced to the level and the actions of animals. Social decorum is totally removed; public and private are interchangeable, and stimulus and response are automatic.

But Caldwell, in presenting these characters, differs significantly from the kind of exuberant extravagance which had characterized the Old Southwestern humorists. Where they had sought unusual and spectacular events, he uses seemingly endless repetition. Where they had used an extravagant style, capitalizing upon the rhetorical excessiveness of southern speech and action, he uses a plain, powerful, and direct style. Where they had portrayed the positive actions of their characters, Caldwell's people exist in the mental state of refusal. As Kenneth Burke pointed out in a brilliant essay, Caldwell "puts people into complex social situations while making them act with the scant, crude, tropisms of an insect."[12] Certainly Caldwell's characters should precipitate in the reader a sense of horror and shock, a revulsion at the skill with which he exploits their animal nature. Yet it is actually difficult to read about characters in wildly incongruous situations and stripped to the animal level without finding them ludicrous and ridiculous, rather than terrifying. It has been customary to think of Caldwell as having produced, in the early 1930's, a few important novels—*Tobacco Road, God's Little Acre, Journeyman,* and *Trouble in July*—and a group of short stories of great distinction, including "Kneel to the Rising Sun" and "Country Full of Swedes," and then having passed into a period of hack work and conscious pornography which renders him no longer a serious figure. Probably this view will be corrected with the passage of time, as James Korges has asserted with great vigor in *Erskine Caldwell.*[13] Whether Korges is correct or not, it is true that the comic strain present in the early novels is still very active in the ones Caldwell has written since the early 1950's, a number of which compare very favorably with his earlier works. Perhaps his funniest novel is *God's Little Acre* (1933), possibly his best is *Trouble in July* (1940), and *Georgia Boy* (1943) is his best nostalgic picture of childhood. But *Claudelle Inglis* (1968) is an almost flawless sexual comedy with the skill of story-telling and the exuberance of a

[12]Kenneth Burke, "Caldwell: Maker of Grotesques," *The Philosophy of Literary Form: Studies in Symbolic Action,* 2nd ed. (Baton Rouge: Louisiana State University Press, 1967), p. 354.

[13]James Korges, *Erskine Caldwell* (Minneapolis: University of Minnesota Press, 1969), pp. 5–8.

Chaucerian fabliau; *Miss Mama Aimee* (1967) is possibly his best novel since *Georgia Boy;* and *Summertime Island* (1968) is a treatment of a boy's initiation only slightly less important than his best work.

Miss Mama Aimee is based upon a whole series of comic reversals and contains some marvelous characters. The preacher Raley Purdy, when he sees a girl unclothed, worries about what Billy Graham would think if he saw him in such a situation. The girl asks, "Who's Billy Graham?" and Purdy replies, "I can't talk about Billy Graham when you're stark naked—he wouldn't want me to."[14]

At the heart of Caldwell's portrayal of his world is a sense of what the social system can do—indeed, has done—to people, and upon that basis he makes his strongest claims. In his autobiography Caldwell says of *Tobacco Road,* "I felt that I would never be able to write successfully about other people in other places until first I had written the story of the landless and poverty-stricken families living on East Georgia sand hills and tobacco roads. . . . I wanted to tell the story of the people I knew in the manner in which they actually lived their lives . . . and to tell it without regard for fashions in writing and traditional plots."[15] In that novel, which contained the essence of most of what he was to do best, Caldwell wrote with great simplicity and force, his clear, hard, clean, and forceful prose describing people whose lives are so stripped of economic and social hope that they become grotesque parodies of human beings; twisted by the simplest hungers, they are totally lacking in dignity and integrity. "All I wanted to do," Caldwell said, "was simply to describe to the best of my ability the aspirations and despair of the people I wrote about."[16]

Caldwell's people are twisted by social and economic deprivation, by the exhausting of the soil, by a cruel tenant-farmer system, by the absence of the most elementary aspects of culture. Tobacco Road and its environment is a soil depleted, a people washed out and drained and responding like animals to the forces around them. Yet Caldwell seems to be saying, "Fertilize the soil, return the price of cotton to a subsistence level, give them opportunity, and hope will follow, and in another generation something like the good life may

[14]Erskine Caldwell, *Miss Mama Aimee* (New York: New American Library, 1967), p. 79.
[15]Erskine Caldwell, *Call It Experience* (New York: Duell, Sloan & Pearce, 1951), p. 101.
[16]*Ibid.,* p. 132.

return." The system is wrong but remediable. Hence he can feel a social anger, and he can portray, through telling reductions to the animal level, the character and quality of life in this kind of world. But he knows that these characters, however misshaped, are people, and on them he lavishes much of his warmest attention. "It seemed to me that the most authentic and enduring materials of fiction were the people themselves,"[17] he said. To represent such people one must deal with them realistically on one level, and yet without contempt, while describing the system which makes them what they are. This is a difficult strategy, and one for which Caldwell successfully adapted the methods of the comic.

The world these people inhabit is one of cruel limitations and deprivations. To portray the products of such deprivation as monsters would be to misrepresent their human qualities, but to portray them as other than distorted and grotesque would be to ignore the effects of a cruel economic system. Comedy is the obvious answer, for it is the mode of limitations, the mode of hope. Above all, comedy gives the distance between reader and subject that allows grotesqueries to be seen with objectivity.

In recent years the southern writer most frequently discussed as a creator of grotesques has been Flannery O'Connor. A great deal of attention has been given to her portraits of poor whites in middle Georgia and Tennessee, and the key to her comic mode has often been sought. Although she is solidly in the tradition of southern detached humor, there is a crucial difference between her and most of her fellow southern writers, past and present, a difference which accounts for the special quality of her comedy. She was a Catholic writer in a Protestant world, and she saw the writing of fiction as a Christian vocation: "I see from the standpoint of Christian orthodoxy. This means that for me the meaning of life is centered in our Redemption by Christ and what I see in the world I see in relation to that."[18] What gives distance and comic perspective to her view of the world is fundamentally a religious distancing, resulting from her confidence of her own salvation in a world of those futilely seeking surety. As St. Augustine said, "Our souls are restless till they find rest in Thee." The world she portrays is made up of such restless, seeking souls, primitive in mind, Protestant in religion, sharing a

[17]*Ibid.*, pp. 101–102.
[18]Flannery O'Connor, "The Fiction Writer and His Country," pp. 161–162.

deep common and personal awareness of the awful and the awesome presence and power of God in the world. It is a power and a presence which they can recognize, but which they do not accept. Living in a world not ordered to an adequate sense of this power and presence of God, these characters become grotesque and unnatural when they seek to deny Him or to pervert their hunger for Him. From the perspective of one who has found peace and rests secure in the knowledge of herself, O'Connor can look out with a kind of amused pity upon a world that is still troubled and, though it knows it not, seeking salvation from its godlessness.

Though this perspective is religious and philosophical, in its aesthetic effect it is not greatly different from the distance of class or political position or economic status which has been, for a hundred and fifty years, essential to the kind of realistic humor fundamental to the South. And this assurance of hers, this sense that the ultimate reality transcends the physical world which she portrays with directness and hard clarity, makes all that happens within that world important only in what can come after it. Hence there occur repeatedly in her work those moments when not merely the humiliation of the flesh but the destruction of physical life proves to be an open door to a spiritual victory. People die with grace given them in their moments of expiration, as though death were, to the author, a triumph.

This perspective gives her an enormous freedom, which she consciously exercises as a comic writer. Of her novel *Wise Blood* she said, "The book was written with zest and, if possible, it should be read that way. It is a comic novel about the Christian *malgré lui,* and as such, very serious, for all comic novels that are any good must be about matters of life and death."[19] This kind of comedy, in one sense close to that which gives its title to Dante's great work, is a function of a tone which finds its basis in the author's own religious security, as Martha Stephens has persuasively pointed out.[20]

In the world of her fiction, Flannery O'Connor has dealt extensively with tortured, tormented, and distorted people and has treated them with both comic detachment and sympathy. The peculiar mixture of detachment and sympathy which O'Connor achieves

[19]Preface to Flannery O'Connor, *Wise Blood,* in *Three: Wise Blood, A Good Man Is Hard to Find, The Violent Bear It Away* (New York: New American Library, 1964), p. 8.

[20] Martha Stephens, *The Question of Flannery O'Connor* (Baton Rouge: Louisiana State University Press, 1973), pp. 3–42.

is most unusual in American writing. She herself suggested, "Whenever I am asked why southern writers particularly have a penchant for writing about freaks, I say it is because we are still able to recognize one. To be able to recognize a freak you have to have some conception of the whole man, and in the South the general conception of man is still in the main theological."[21] These "freaks" are such because they are far from whole.

As a writer of comedy O'Connor is best in the short story, and her most successful efforts here are in such stories as "Good Country People" and "The Life You Save May Be Your Own" in her first volume of short stories. Her method is exemplified very well in "Good Country People." Joy Hopewell, the daughter of a widow Mrs. Hopewell, regards herself as considerably above the simple people whom she sees about her and whom she calls "good country people."

Joy, who changes her name to Hulga to spite her mother and who has an artificial leg (one of her legs was shot off when she was a child), is thirty-two years old, has a Ph.D. in philosophy, a bad heart condition, and is living at home. She is an atheist, and proudly declares that she believes in nothing. A young Bible salesman —clearly from "good country people"—visits them, and Hulga sets out to seduce him into atheism. She leads him to the hayloft in the barn and there discovers that he is far from "good country people." One of his Bibles has been hollowed out and contains a bottle of whiskey, a set of cards with pornographic pictures on the back, and a package of contraceptives. He steals her glasses, removes her artificial leg and takes it with him, and leaves her alone in the hayloft, without her leg, declaring to her as he leaves, "Hulga you ain't so smart. I been believing in nothing ever since I was born!"[22] The story is both shocking and amusing; its amusement comes from the fact that Hulga has found in the young Bible salesman precisely what she has sought all her life, and it has betrayed her and left her without the means to move or to see.

On one level this story is a parable of the nihilism of atheism, but on another it is a comic masterpiece, primarily because of the wry, hard, and sardonic quality of Flannery O'Connor's style. A few

[21]O'Conner, "Some Aspects of the Grotesque in Southern Literature," p. 276.
[22]"Good Country People," in *The Complete Stories of Flannery O'Connor* (New York: Farrar, Straus and Giroux, 1971), p. 291.

examples from the story will illustrate: "Mrs. Hopewell had no bad qualities of her own but she was able to use other people's in such a constructive way that she never felt the lack."[23] "The large hulking Joy, whose constant outrage had obliterated every expression from her face, would stare just a little to the side of her, her eyes icy blue, with the look of someone who had achieved blindness by an act of will and means to keep it."[24] "The girl had taken the Ph.D. in philosophy and this left Mrs. Hopewell at a complete loss. You could say, 'My daughter is a nurse,' or 'My daughter is a school teacher,' or even 'My daughter is a chemical engineer.' You could not say, 'My daughter is a philosopher.' "[25] "As a child she had sometimes been subject to feelings of shame, but education had removed the last traces of that as a good surgeon scrapes for cancer; she would no more have felt it over what he was asking than she would have believed in his Bible. But she was as sensitive about the artificial leg as a peacock about his tail."[26]

O'Connor is aware of the caste structures that a relatively fixed social order can produce and that have fascinated many other southern writers. For example, in a very late story, "Revelation," she says:

> Sometimes Mrs. Turpin occupied herself at night naming the classes of people. On the bottom of the heap were most colored people, not the kind she would have been if she had been one, but most of them; then next to them—not above, just away from—were the white trash; then above them were the home-owners, and above them the home-and-land owners, to which she and Claud belonged. Above she and Claud were people with a lot of money and much bigger houses and much more land. But here the complexity of it would begin to bear in on her, for some of the people with a lot of money were common and ought to be below she and Claud and some of the people who had good blood had lost their money and had to rent and then there were colored people who owned their homes and land as well. There was a colored dentist in town who had two red Lincolns and a swimming pool and a farm with registered white-face cattle on it.[27]

These qualities of knowledge, sharp perception, and comic dis-

[23]*Ibid.*, p. 272.
[24]*Ibid.*, p. 273.
[25]*Ibid.*, p. 276.
[26]*Ibid.*, p. 288.
[27] "Revelation," in O'Connor's *Complete Stories*, pp. 491–492.

tance are mixed in all her work with zest and a stylistic precision so exact as to be almost overwhelming. Her religious attitude and sardonic voice give vivid pictures of her world shaped by her personal angle of vision. In the early stories collected in *A Good Man Is Hard to Find*,[28] the delight she takes in her "freaks" is greatest, although it is also present in *Wise Blood*,[29] a novel and her first published book. But *Wise Blood,* like *The Hamlet* (at least in this respect), was a novel parts of which had originally been written as short stories.[30] As O'Connor matured as a writer—she was only twenty years old when she submitted her first published story[31]— her themes deepened and her view of the world, although never losing its comic detachment, took on a more somber quality. In "Everything That Rises Must Converge," first published in 1961,[32] her sardonic portrait of Julian, the self-deceiving college graduate, is devastating, but the death of his mother does not have the comic distance which O'Connor had magnificently achieved in "A Good Man Is Hard to Find." "Parker's Back," posthumously published,[33] is a hilarious situation, but its theological meaning is impressed with a hand heavier than usual.

In these later stories and in the second novel, *The Violent Bear It Away* (1960), the basic comic method does not change. Although the seriousness of her intention deepens, she does not depart from her accurate portrayal of the literal world. Elizabeth Bishop properly observed of O'Connor's books, "They are clear, hard, vivid, and full of bits of description, phrases, and an odd insight. . . . Critics who accuse her of exaggeration are quite wrong, I think. I lived in Florida for several years next to a flourishing 'Church of God'. . . . After [this] nothing Flannery O'Connor ever wrote could seem at all exaggerated to me."[34] I have argued elsewhere that her portrayal of

[28]Flannery O'Connor, *A Good Man Is Hard to Find* (New York: Harcourt, Brace, 1955).

[29]Flannery O'Connor, *Wise Blood* (New York: Harcourt, Brace, 1952).

[30]These stories, now available in *The Complete Stories,* are "The Train" (*Sewanee Review,* April, 1948), "The Peeler" (*Partisan Review,* December, 1949), "The Heart of the Park" (*Partisan Review,* February, 1949), and "Enoch and the Gorilla" (*New World Writing,* April, 1952).

[31]Flannery O'Connor, "The Geranium," *Accent,* 4 (Summer, 1946), 245–253. It was submitted on February 7, 1946, forty-five days before her twenty-first birthday; see "Notes," *Complete Stories,* p. 551.

[32]In *New World Writing,* 19 (1961), and reprinted posthumously in *Everything That Rises Must Converge* (New York: Farrar, Straus and Giroux, 1965).

[33]*Esquire,* 63 (April, 1965), 76–78, 151–155; reprinted in *Everything That Rises.*

[34]Quoted by Robert Giroux in his introduction to *Complete Stories,* pp. xvi–xvii.

the southern region is accurate,[35] and I have asserted that "within two blocks of the Regency Hyatt [in Atlanta] you can find street evangelists extolling their primitive religions in tone and manner that make you think Hazel Motes of *Wise Blood* has come back to life."[36]

O'Connor's succinct, witty, and very direct prose is used with great success in picturing her segment of the South as a microcosm of the human lot. Like Hawthorne, she wanted to produce fiction "that should evolve some deep lesson and should possess physical substance enough to stand alone."[37] Her vision of man was not of a cloud-scraping demigod, a wielder of vast powers, but of a frail, weak creature, imperfect and incomplete in all his parts. To embody such a vision calls for either comedy or pathos, and pathos was alien to Flannery O'Connor's nature and beliefs.

Erskine Caldwell and Flannery O'Connor were the inheritors of a long southern tradition of detached humor; they employed it on the same kinds of people in many of the same locales, but for radically different purposes. Both sought salvation for the denizens of their worlds. In Caldwell's case, as Kenneth Burke observed, "In so far as he is moved by the need of salvation, he seems minded to find it in the alignments of political exhortation, by striving mainly to see that we and he take the right side on matters of social justice."[38] Flannery O'Connor, too, was seeking salvation, but the salvation she sought was transcendent, and was to be found only in God. She once said:

> The problem for [a southern] novelist will be to know how far he can distort without destroying, and in order not to destroy, he will have to descend far enough into himself to reach those underground springs that give life to his work. This descent into himself will, at the same time, be a descent into his region. It will be a descent through the darkness of the familiar into a world where like the blind man cured in the gospels, he sees men as if they were trees, but walking.[39]

For both Caldwell and O'Connor, the comic muse worked well, for it

[35] "Her Rue with a Difference," in Holman, *Roots of Southern Writing*, pp. 177–186; originally published in Friedman and Lawson, eds., *The Added Dimension*, pp. 73–87.

[36] C. Hugh Holman, "The View from the Regency Hyatt," in *Roots of Southern Writing*, pp. 96–107; originally published in *Southern Fiction Today: Renascence and Beyond*, ed. George Core (Athens: University of Georgia Press, 1969), pp. 16–32.

[37] Nathaniel Hawthorne, "The Old Manse," *Mosses from an Old Manse* (Boston: Houghton Mifflin, 1883), p. 13.

[38] Burke, "Caldwell: Master of Grotesques," p. 352.

[39] O'Connor, "Some Aspects of the Grotesque in Southern Literature," p. 279.

gave them the distance from which to see the world distorted and misshaped by its need to be saved.

To understand how this distancing comedy works, one may have to fall back on Randall Jarrell's judgment that "the best one can do with Mr. Caldwell's peculiar variety of humor is to accept it with gratitude."[40] But before one does so, it is well to listen to one more caveat from O'Connor:

> Even though the writer who produces grotesque fiction may not consider his characters any more freakish than ordinary fallen man usually is, his audience is going to, and it's going to ask him why he has chosen to bring such maimed souls alive. . . . In this country the general reader has managed to connect the grotesque somehow with the sentimental, for whenever he speaks of it favorably, he seems to associate it with the writer's compassion. . . . The kind of hazy compassion demanded of the writer now makes it difficult for him to be *anti* anything. Certainly when the grotesque is used in a legitimate way, the intellectual and moral judgments in it will have the ascendancy over feeling.[41]

Both Erskine Caldwell and Flannery O'Connor knew how to say "No!" in laughter.

[40]As quoted by Carvel Collins in the introduction to *Erskine Caldwell's Men and Women* (Boston: Little Brown, 1961), p. 7.

[41]O'Connor, "Some Aspects of the Grotesque in Southern Literature," p. 275.

CHARLES H. NICHOLS

Comic Modes
in Black America
(A Ramble through
Afro-American Humor)

Afro-American humor is a reaction to social reality as well as an exploration of the wit in our folk tradition. Forced to observe our society from the outside, the object of scorn and the butt of vicious attacks, black people have learned to survive behind the mask, to perceive the crude realities beneath shining surfaces, to express the contradictions of their lives in a language which cuts through stale speech and reveals rich varieties of idea and of feeling. The familiar comic modes are a traditional part of the colloquial speech and imaginative writing of the group: irony, paradox, exaggeration, innuendo, sarcasm, mirror-and-mask effects, protean roles, word play. The whole arsenal of satire. The incongruity at the center of wit and humor has become a way of organizing experience through protest, release, and self-assertion. The black writer is probably more keenly aware than most that he lives at the edge of a precipice, in constant danger of some bottomless abyss of chaos and destruction. This very consciousness heightens his wild joy. His art is his only real freedom, his mastery of the ludicrous his only redemption.

Friedrich Schiller insisted that "man plays when in the full meaning of the word he is a man, and he is only completely a man when he plays."[1] For Schiller, all art is an expression of this play instinct.

[1] J. F. Schiller, "Letters on the Aesthetic Education of Man," in *Modern Continental Literary Criticism* (New York: Appleton-Century-Crofts, 1962), p. 37.

Sigmund Freud revealed the unconscious meanings in our wit and humor, the repressed aggression and desire in our word play and slips of the tongue. Afro-Americans have had (historically speaking) too little to do with society's image of them. The comic Negro was defined in black-face acts, minstrel shows, and caste etiquette. The foolish darky appears in American authors from James Fenimore Cooper and Mark Twain through Irwin Russell, Joel Chandler Harris, and Harriet Beecher Stowe. White men boasted that the Negro was what they made him, and indeed, the creature presented in minstrelsy was a projection of the grotesques in the white mind. As Walter Hines Page said, "The Negro in America is a form of insanity that afflicts white men." But there has always been an in-group humor, as I shall shortly demonstrate. Since 1945, the rise of independent African states and the Black Power movement have spurred blacks to define more boldly their own identity and to create new images. Not the least of the contributions of Frantz Fanon in *Black Skin, White Masks* and *The Wretched of the Earth* was his attack on the spurious but widespread image of the Europeanized African, more often a fantasy than a person.

Like other Americans, blacks have been affected by the promises of American life, our tall tales and folk heroes, our breezy slang and attachment to what Tocqueville called "subjects of vast dimensions." The twentieth-century individual, especially, has been forced to live with the concentration camp and the constant threat of extermination, with anxiety and aggression. As Norman Mailer has pointed out, the American existentialist, the hipster, has emerged. "So it is no accident that the source of Hip is the Negro, for he has been living on the margin between totalitarianism and democracy for two centuries. But the presence of Hip as a working philosophy in the sub-worlds of American life is probably due to jazz, and its knifelike entrance into culture, its subtle but so penetrating influence on an avant-garde generation. . . ."[2] But in their creative modes of expression—spirituals, worksongs, blues, and jazz—African-Americans have not (as Mailer suggests) taken flight into psychopathology. They have learned to deal with soul-destroying reality. They have inverted the accepted forms with irony and satire which bare the absurdities of our relationships.

[2]Norman Mailer, "The White Negro," *Advertisements for Myself* (New York: Putnam, 1959), p. 305.

Jazz flouted all musical conventions yet conquered the world. By "changing the joke," as Ellison says, "they may slip the yoke."

The tradition of our humor in folk sayings and tales, in slave narratives and songs, in plantation jests and blues, in hipster and jive talk, is its keen unmasking of the stereotype, its piercing of the "master's balloons, of pride and folly." The slave could preserve some rag of honor and self-esteem by a witty retort. The high and mighty could be brought low by one-upmanship. Thus the master says to the servant, " 'You rascal, you ate my turkey.' 'Yes,' replies the slave, 'you got less turkey, but you sho' got mo' slave.' " Peter Randolph tells of an owner who dressed himself up for a fight and asked his favorite body servant how he looked.

> "Oh massa, mighty!"
> "What do you mean by mighty, Pompey?"
> "Why massa, you look noble."
> "What do you mean by noble?"
> "Why, sar, you look just like a lion."
> "Why, Pompey, where have you ever seen a lion?"
> "I seen one down in yonder field the other day, massa."
> "Pompey, you foolish fellow, that was a jackass!"
> "Was it, massa? Well, you look just like him"[3]

The humor of slaves employs a variety of such comic modes— sometimes directed aggressively against the slaveholder-boss- oppressor-landlord-owner, and often turned inward against the passivity, ineptness, or stupidity of their own fellows, but above all enjoying the incongruities of human experience. The Afro- American consciousness explores his marginal status with a kind of double vision: he expresses his outrage at oppression in critical attacks on the system, while unmasking the pretenses of his fellows by "playing the dozens." The folksongs of the alienated worker express his bitter determination with laconic humor:

> Dis is de hammer
> Kill't John Henry
> T'won't kill me, baby
> T'won't kill me.
>
> . . . .
>
> I got a rainbow
> Tied 'round my shoulder,

[3]Peter Randolph, *From Slave Cabin to Pulpit* (Boston: J. H. Earle, 1893), p. 199.

>   Ain't gonna rain baby
>   Ain't gonna rain[4]

The quality of these songs, the painful alienation of the blues, the hysterical cry of jazz gave authenticity to the language of the authors of the Harlem Renaissance. Especially Langston Hughes and Sterling Brown have left us a legacy of laughter in poetry and prose. Significantly, both immersed themselves in the language and rhythm of common folk. Langston Hughes created strikingly original poetry with blues and jazz rhythms, rhythms which, in their elements of surprise and improvisation, struck the listener with the electrical quality of paradox and wit. Hughes is the laureate of those nameless thousands who know the desperate need as well as the frantic joy of Harlem nights. His best-known Harlem street man is, of course, Jess B. Simple, who is as American as Huck Finn and has more horse sense than most of his betters. He works in a war plant making "cranks." "What kind of cranks? . . . Do they crank cars, tanks, buses, planes or what?—a woman asks. 'Aw, woman,' he responded, 'you know white folks don't tell colored folks what cranks crank.'"[5] The joke is not only in the sarcasm but in the *double entendre*.

Sterling Brown's Slim Greer ironically sums up segregation and discrimination in a single image:

>   Down in Atlanta
>   De white folks got laws
>   To keep all de niggers
>   From laughin' outdoors
>
>   . . . .
>
>   Cross my heart
>   It's de truth
>   Make de niggers
>   Do their laughin' in a telephone booth.[6]

For Slim has discovered "de place was *Dixie* dat I took for hell!"

George Schuyler created a memorable, if outrageous con man in the novel *Black No More*. His protagonist promotes and sells a nostrum which turns black people white, and then, himself transformed, marries the daughter of the Grand Imperial Wizard of the Ku

[4]Sterling Brown, Arthur Davis, and Ulysses Lee, *The Negro Caravan* (New York: Dryden Press, 1941), p. 446.

[5]Langston Hughes, *Best of Simple* (New York: Hill & Wang, 1961), p. viii.

[6]Sterling Brown, *Southern Road* (New York: Harcourt Brace, 1932), p. 88.

Klux Klan. Countee Cullen's epitaphs also attack white elitism, with
playful sarcasm couched in the common speech. This is "For a Lady
I Know":

> She even thinks that up in heaven
> Her class lies late and snores
> While poor black cherubs rise at seven
> To do celestial chores.[7]

Zora Neale Hurston collected much of the finest Negro folk humor
in her *Mules and Men* (1935) and employed the folk idiom to write
such lively plays and fiction as *Jonah's Gourd Vine* (1934) and
Moses, Man of the Mountain (1931). Like jazz musicians, she and
her fellow Harlem Renaissance writers used their native instruments
to improvise new and amusing sounds.

Since World War II, the number of Afro-American writers using
comic modes has grown considerably. The black writer has revived
the folk culture and humor of his people with a new pride; furthermore, as with all of us, his perception of the incongruities of the age
has deepened. Nuclear energy, automation, space travel, "wonder"
drugs, genetic engineering, missiles, flying saucers expanded the
world's imagination. Mind-boggling events glared at us from every
day's newspaper. As Afro-Americans enjoyed more freedom and
opportunity, their learning and creative capacities grew. Whereas
the writers of the Harlem Renaissance had read such authors as
George Bernard Shaw, H. L. Mencken, and Gertrude Stein, our
generation knows Nietzsche, Kafka, Orwell, Brecht, Sartre,
Camus, and Fanon. In their attack on the American tribal gods
(Christianity, democracy, and progress), Ralph Ellison, LeRoi
Jones, and Ishmael Reed dare much more than their predecessors.
They are sharp, bitter, and unrelenting. Everyone could laugh at
plantation humor, and even the master felt no threat to the status
quo. The Harlem Renaissance in its hedonism and wit caused some
raised eyebrows. But the impact of Jones, Reed, and Ellison is
iconoclastic. They know no sacred beliefs; everything is allowed.
What publishers would not print in 1930 because it was "obscene"
or "in bad taste" has become commonplace. Here is a humor which
shakes the very foundations of western humanism by attacking
science, profit, growth, and all forms of allegiance. It is sophisticated, yet primitive; traditional, yet innovative.

[7]Countee Cullen, *On These I Stand* (New York: Harper & Brothers, 1947), p. 33.

Ralph Ellison's *Invisible Man* (1952) is an ingenious union of conventional comic modes transformed by the keen intellect of an inventive, learned, and serious artist. The novel is a landmark in the history of American fiction, for its comic structure is built on irony, contradiction, and absurdity. Its language is rich: "a mixture of the folk, the Biblical, the scientific and political. Slangy in one stance, academic in another, loaded poetically with imagery at one moment, mathematically bare of imagery in the next."[8] Its levels of meaning are realistic, surrealistic, symbolic, mythic, existential. *Invisible Man* is an account of a young man's initiation into a disillusioning world; yet it is, at the same time, an account of the whole black experience of bondage, flight, resistance, struggle, discrimination, and self-discovery. The protagonist is a representative black man —an *underground* man in retreat from a hostile, absurd world, reliving the sardonic blues humor of his forebears: "What did I do, to be so black and blue?"

It is Ellison's achievement, furthermore, that he has written a novel about all Americans yet made the Manichaean struggle of black versus white the very dialectic of its comic structure, in a rising crescendo from the battle royal to the race riot. The bitterness of the humor here is not to be confused with the minstrel or the darky act. The Grandfather's deathbed speech makes that clear: " 'Son, after I'm gone I want you to keep up the good fight. I never told you, but our life is a war and I have been a traitor all my born days, a spy in the enemy's country ever since I give up my gun back in the Reconstruction. Live with your head in the lion's mouth. I want you to overcome 'em with yeses, undermine 'em with grins, agree 'em to death and destruction, let 'em swoller you till they vomit or bust wide open.' " American blacks wear a mask, but they know that whites, too, snatched their independence while dressed like Indians dumping British tea in Boston harbor. Indeed, in advertising we have created the masks which have robbed us all of whatever certainty we had.

The humor of *Invisible Man* is achieved by irony. Is the bronze statue of the founder raising or lowering the veil of ignorance? Meanings are enriched by parody—the sermon of the Reverend

---

[8]Ralph Ellison, *Shadow and Act* (New York: Random House, 1966), pp. 103–104. Ellison once asked the *Paris Review* interviewer: "Look, didn't you find the book at all funny?" He got no answer. *I* find the book *very* funny indeed.

Mr. Barbe (whose blindness is more than mere sightlessness), the speeches of trade-union organizers, Brotherhood leaders, and ranting Nationalists. The imaginative force of the action is in contradictions and absurdities; the wit and liveliness is maintained by the sense of timing. Ellison, the Jazz Musician, writes: "So under the spell of the reefer I discovered a new analytical way of listening to music. The unheard sounds came through, and each melodic line existed of itself." There are several levels of consciousness: "Beneath the swiftness of the hot tempo there was a slower tempo and a cave and I entered it and looked around. . . ." The wild confusion of the battle royal is punctuated by the naive hopes of the boy who later sees only the idyllic surface of the college at vespers. He tries to ignore the reality beneath the illusions by which he lives. "Here upon this stage the black rite of Horatio Alger was performed to God's own acting script, with millionaires come down to portray themselves; not merely acting out the myth of their goodness, and wealth and success and power and benevolence and authority in cardboard masks, but themselves, these virtues concretely! Not the wafer and the wine, but the flesh and the blood, vibrant and alive . . . (and who, in face of this, would not believe? Could even doubt?)"

The humor of the most striking chapters runs the gamut from slapstick and chaotic violence to absurdity and subtle wit. The outrageous indignity and nightmare horror of the battle royal is relieved by the panting lust and tense fear of these white members of a tinpot fraternal order at a stag party. A slip of the tongue ("social equality?" or "social responsibility?") can cause their world to tremble. The final irony of the hotel scene comes when the protagonist quotes the words of Booker T. Washington to these brutal boors who would destroy young black boys: "Cast down your bucket where you are . . . cast it down in making friends. . . ." The reality of his situation comes to the main character in a dream. His grandfather compels him to read that engraved document which has been for generations the law and the prophets to white America: "Keep This Nigger-Boy Running." Each scene is thus skillfully managed; nightmare violence, hysteria, absurdity, the grotesque, wordplay, and puns lead to a kind of epiphany—a revelation of his actual situation.

While the battle-royal scene is a fine paradigm of the underside of the white world, with its violent absurdity, the Golden Day unmasks the blacks. The philanthropist Norton is mesmerized by the incestuous Trueblood, who evokes Norton's inordinate attachment to his own daughter. Significantly, Norton brings together the dream world of the college, the madness of the insane asylum, and the wild chaos of the Golden Day bar. The protagonist encounters the range of "adjustments" which the educated ("successful") black veterans have made in the long battle for dignity: the cynical, the pompous, the aggressive, the hip, the mad ones are all there. The doctor has been almost lynched for attempting to heal others. The whole group is confined to the lowest levels of animal gratification. They are brutalized by their keeper, a "kind of censor" who is sent along "to see that the therapy fails." The turbulence is the natural consequence of this inhuman oppression and hopeless outlook. The chaos breaks out at every level, heightened by fighting, drink, sex, and psychoses. Yet there is a vestige of order, a sharp insight in the wildest moments. Norton and the protagonist are safer among these madmen than they are with Bledsoe, the president of the college. "We got whitefolks in the house" is said not without sarcasm, yet it heightens their consciousness of the absurdity and reality of their lives. When the "hero" meets the veteran again on the bus, he gets some sound advice: "Play the game, but don't believe in it—that much you owe yourself." The speaker only suspects how appropriate his words are. The protagonist, having been expelled from college with seven damning letters of recommendation, has been thrown overboard by Bledsoe. Bledsoe's total lack of principle makes him virtually a grotesque: "Why the dumbest black bastard in the cotton patch knows that the only way to please a white man is to tell him a lie!" he exclaims.

The protagonist assumes a more active role in his own affairs after he discovers the perfidy of Bledsoe. Having moved into the YMCA, he mistakes a fat preacher for Bledsoe and empties a spittoon on his head. Increasingly he assumes the identity of the street man, the rogue and con man: he lies his way into a job in a paint factory; trounces Brockway, the paranoid old man who becomes his overseer; and lands in a hospital where two doctors try unsuccessfully to make him their guinea pig. He joins a crowd in preventing the eviction of two old people from their miserable apartment and is taken up by Brother Jack, obviously a Communist. An apt student and active revolutionary (though skeptical of ideology), he is *too* successful in the Brotherhood and is denounced as egotistical and self-serving. Finally, he is pursued by followers of the Black Nationalist, Ras, the Exhorter. Our "hero" then learns that between invisibility and the con man, Rinehart, there are many possibilities. He dons a hat and dark glasses and in amused clownery plays out Rinehart's several roles. The name Rinehart suggests the man's inner (heart) and outer (rind) life.

Significant to the absurd and comic structure of the book is Ellison's frequent use of rituals of satire drawn from the protagonist's downhome, folk tradition. His most transforming contacts with Harlem are a series of ambivalent encounters with his ethnic past. The songs, blues, jazz, folk sayings of the culture that are the deepest part of his heritage provide him with the sense of spiritual freedom the group has always known. He writes:

I saw a man pushing a cart piled high with rolls of blue paper and heard him singing. . . . It was the blues, and I walked along behind him remembering . . . such singing at home. . . .

> "She's got feet like a monkey
> Legs like a frog—Lawd, Lawd!
> But when she starts to loving me
> I holler whoooo, God-dog!
> Cause I loves my baaby,
> Better than I do myself."

The man accosts the protagonist, establishing a common bond: "Oh goddog daddy-o . . . who got the damn dog." The play on words recalls Joyce's suggestion that GOD is dog spelled backwards. The man with the pushcart is struggling for survival and recognizes another outcast. *He's* pursued by a bear; "Cain't you see these patches where he's been clawing at my behind?" The protagonist still has some illusions: he will leave the oppressive, peasant black past behind him. He will not eat grits and pork chops in a restaurant or pass the time of day with semi-literate street peddlers. But their capacity to see through his facade becomes, at last, his refuge from the barbarism of the city, the paint factory, the hospital, the Brotherhood, and the Nationalists. Their language conveys with sharp insight their sophistication. They are not taken in by the elaborate charade of deceit, squalor, and deprivation around them: "All it takes to get along in this here man's town is a little shit, grit and mother wit." And "My name is Peter Wheatstraw, I'm the Devil's only son-in-law." The protagonist's final, bitter disillusionment with Bledsoe and his meeting with Emerson lead him back again to that rich folk past. "It was a joke," the same old joke: "Keep this nigger running." "I heard myself humming the same tune the man ahead was whistling":

> "O well they picked poor Robin clean
>
> . . . .
>
> Well they tied poor Robin to a stump
> Lawd, they picked all the feathers round from Robin's rump
> Well they picked poor Robin clean."

The paint factory, where the main character must labor in the bowels of the building with Brockway, serves as another source of satire. The *black* men use a *black* dope to make *white* paint. And the company's slogan is the contribution of the wizened old black man on whom the whole enterprise depends: *"If It's Optic White, It's the Right White."* Blacks have been saying sarcastically for generations:

> If you're white you're all right
> If you're brown, maybe you can stick around
> If you're black, stand back!

After the fight with Brockway and the "hero's" failure to seize the right valve, the explosion lands him in the hospital. Here again in his helplessness, straitjacketed in a machine designed to subject him to a frontal lobotomy, his subconscious mind reverts to folk memories:

Oh, doctor, I thought drowsily, did you ever wade in a brook before breakfast? Ever chew on sugar cane? You know, doc, the same fall day I first saw the hounds chasing black men in stripes and chains my grandmother sat with me and sang with twinkling eyes:

> "Godamighty made a monkey
> Godamighty made a whale
> And Godamighty made a 'gator
> With hickeys all over his tail. . . ."

His next important folk ritual marks a new level of consciousness, for he here embraces his past and savors the nourishment it gives him. On a cold day on the Harlem street he buys and eats hot buttered yams. The effect of these familiar things is to make him more human, to restore his identity: "I yam what I am," he exclaims, laughing. And the joke is not only in his newfound freedom but also

in his recognition of the strength in the formerly despised tradition.
"I let out a wild laugh." As a naive student, he had been taught that
"white is right," and that to gain status is to cast off the folk culture.
Now the joke is that a bloated and hypocritical ass like Bledsoe could
be destroyed by revealing his real past. "Bledsoe, you're a shame-
less chitterling eater! I accuse you of relishing hog bowels! . . .
Prominent Educator Reverts to Field Niggerism!"

Images like grits, pork chops, yams, and chitterlings are in striking contrast to the cast-iron bank he finds in his furnished room: the
rigid, red, smiling head of a Negro. Though he smashes it to pieces,
the invisible man cannot get rid of it. It is the cold, hard stereotype of
the African in the white mind. Like the battle royal, the briefcase,
Bledsoe's manipulating, the medical machinery, the dialectics of the
members of the Brotherhood, it symbolizes those systems which
thrive on chaos and paranoia surfeited with the arrogance of power.
It is not surprising, therefore, that his first public speech for the
Brotherhood displeases the doctrinaire revolutionaries. For he identifies with the ordinary people to whom he is speaking: "We share a
common disinheritance." His passionate exhortation is a call to
arms which may, of course, turn into a mob scene. Yet it brings him
closer to a sense of his own humanity. Soon the protagonist has
grown so much in his understanding of the social issues with which
he is dealing that he defies the Brotherhood and acts on his own
"personal responsibility." He comes at last to the recognition of his
invisibility. He has merely fulfilled the demands of those around him
without fulfilling himself. The picture of Brother Clifton selling
Sambo dolls on the pavement is, perhaps, the last ritual in the long,
absurd farce. Is Clifton a madman? Or is he consciously mocking
the Brotherhood, which has betrayed him as it has his friend? The
movement toward anarchy and destruction is accelerated by those
two grotesques: Rinehart and Ras, the Exhorter. Fittingly, the explosion of the mass in a race riot, the final act, is a series of rituals of
brutality, blindness, and illusion. In the confusion the "hero" falls
into an underground room—the room where he began his narrative.
It is a warm, light, secure place where there is power, where he
discovers the possibilities of his own mind and spirit. As Ellison
himself has pointed out, in keeping with the reverse logic of the plot,
his *falling* into a hole symbolizes his *rise* in the consciousness of his
own possibilities. "The final act of *Invisible Man* is not that of a

concealment in darkness in the Anglo-Saxon connotation of the word, but that of a voice issuing its little wisdom out of the substance of its own inwardness—after having undergone a transformation from ranter to writer."[9] He knows he cannot hibernate, that he loves and must love, that he must emerge once more into the human swarm and accept the moral responsibility for the world that he, too, has helped to fashion.

The humor of Afro-American authors is, despite its bitterness, a joyous embracing of life. LeRoi Jones (Imamu Amiri Baraka) sums it up: "The legitimate cultural tradition of the Negro in Harlem (and America) is one of wild happiness, usually at some black man's own invention—of speech, of dress, of gait, the sudden twist of a musical phrase, the warmness or hurt of someone's voice. But that culture is also one of hatred and despair. Harlem must contain all this and be capable of producing all these emotions."[10] Although he was briefly associated with some of the "Beat Generation" writers, Jones considers himself a revolutionary writer, a black leader in furious battle against "white cultural imperialism." This means that he rejects western humanism as well as our tawdry mass culture. He can dispose of much black writing as imitative and bourgeois in "The Myth of a Negro Literature" and employ the speech, jazz, blues, and consciousness of the black ghetto with a profoundly original (and at times learned) wit. Art for Jones is a vital process: "Hunting is not those heads on the wall." The revolutionary writer is engaged in the kind of black ritual art which raises the consciousness of his people, unmasks the hypocrisies and oppressiveness of a world endangered by the corrupt descendants of Europeans. LeRoi Jones is a master of comic modes, of mirror-and-mask effects, irony, sarcasm, and paradox—not only in plays like *Dutchman, The Toilet,* and *The Slave,* but also in his novel, *The System of Dante's Hell,* his stories, essays, and poetry. He, too, is profoundly influenced by the tone, rhythms, and form of the blues and of jazz. In his poem "In Memory of Radio" the choice of images, the joining of the sublime and the ridiculous, the sarcasm, the pace emphasize the deceptive emptiness and hucksterism of the mass media. His poem recalls some of the efforts of E. E. Cummings:

> What can I say?
> It is better to have loved and lost

[9]*Ibid.*, p. 57.
[10]LeRoi Jones, *Home: Social Essays* (New York: Morrow, 1966), pp. 92–93.

Than to put linoleum in your living rooms?
Am I a sage or something?
Mandrake's hypnotic gesture of the weak?
(Remember, I do not have the healing powers of Oral Roberts . . .
I cannot, like F. J. Sheen, tell you how to get saved and *rich!*
I cannot even order you to gaschamber satori like Hitler
    or Goody Knight
& Love is an evil word.
Turn it backwards/see, see what I mean?
An evil word. & besides
Who understands it?
I certainly wouldn't like to go out on that kind of limb.
                    . . . "Heh, heh, heh,
                      . . . .
Who knows what evil lurks in the hearts of men? The shadow
    knows"
Oh, yes he does
O, yes he does.
An evil word it is,
This Love.[11]

LeRoi Jones can achieve his comic effects with jazzy, staccato
rhythms and the selective use of the vernacular, as in "For Hettie":

                My wife is left-handed
                which implies a fierce de-
                termination. A complete other
                worldliness. ITS WEIRD, BABY.

                      . . . .
                    . . . & it shows
                in her work. Left-handed coffee,
                Left-handed eggs; when she comes
                in at night . . . it's her left hand
                offered for me to kiss. Damn.
                & now her belly droops over the seat.
                They say it's a child. But
                I ain't quite so sure.[12]

The persona in Jones's poetry is sardonic and bitter, frequently
sarcastic. Yet he is immensely sensitive. As in "An Agony: As Now"
("I am inside someone who hates me") the undertones, the rhythm,
the feeling convey an ineffable sense of the sacredness of the human

[11]LeRoi Jones, "In Memory of Radio," *Preface to a 20 Volume Suicide Note* (New York:
Totem Press, 1961), p. 12.
    [12]*Ibid.*, p. 13.

spirit virtually strangled by leeches, anger, hate, money-grubbing commercialism, and power politics. At bottom, Jones's faith remains: "The end of man is his beauty."

The best plays of LeRoi Jones, like *Dutchman* and *The Slave,* leap squarely into the terrifying madness of our race relations. *Dutchman,* which is acted out in the New York subway, is in every sense an underground play. The white prostitute, Lula, mocks the middle-class black man, Clay, for his bourgeois comformity and apparent apathy. But he is quick to point out that Uncle Tomism, the blues, jazz, are forms of adjustment and protest. Blacks have become a nation of neurotics to keep from being sane. If they were ever to act sanely, they would rise up and murder their oppressors. "Just murder! Would make us all sane!" *The Slave,* however, introduces another conflict in this absurd situation, for in the blood-letting of a black revolt blacks, too, would be swallowed up in oblivion. The art of the blues, jazz, the loud laughter and swaggering gait redeem us until our Messiah unshackles us. The incongruity of this situation, where madness and escape preserve what reason would destroy, is an outrageous joke.

Ishmael Reed will, perhaps, serve to illustrate how the folk tradition continues to be enriched and modified by craft, learning, and imagination to produce a strikingly original and often side-splitting humor in the living present. Reed is surely the most original and wide-ranging humorist writing today. We have, as one critic wrote, seen nothing like him since Mark Twain. Ishmael Reed has a "shrewd eye, a mean ear and a nasty tongue."[13] He is concerned not only with the conflicts of the individual's consciousness in our time, but with the many levels of meaning we derive from the cultures which have shaped our lives. A novel by Ishmael Reed is an excursion into politics, psychology, sociology, myth, anthropology, history, occultism, blues, and jazz—an amalgam of the real, the fantastic, and the absurd. Reed's humor is achieved by irony and contradiction, by "impossible" situations and the constant collision of the sublime and the ridiculous, the solemn and the lewd, the bitter and the joyous. The range of his imagination and the richness of his allusions are at times baffling. Yet it is clear that what concerns him ultimately is the condition of humanity in western civilization—our

[13]Robert Scholes, Review of *Last Days of Louisiana Red,* in *New York Times Book Review,* November 10, 1974, p. 2.

loss of the capacity for freedom, joy, and love, our substitution of artifacts for art, salesmanship for literature, imperialism for a sense of world community, private gain for humane values. As a black writer, he is steeped in African history, culture, and religion; he can make the historical leap from obeah and voodoo to jazz and rock without losing the social and emotional force they have brought to people's lives. When writing about Harding's administration or the Gross National Product or the numbers racket, Reed's satiric imagination and flair for language create marvelous wit. Clearly Ishmael Reed believes in the rich influence of African and Afro-American culture in a world where Africans are still despised, and he suggests that the redemption of the West lies in the animism, the harmony at the center of the African spirit. To illustrate the quality of Ishmael Reed's imagination, consider the poem "Railroad Bill, A Conjure Man: A HooDoo Suite."

> Railroad Bill, a conjure man
> Could change hisself to a tree
> He could change hisself to a
> Lake, a ram, he could be
> What he wanted to be. . . .

Railroad Bill "could change hisself" into a bird or a brook, a dog.

> Railroad Bill was an electrical
> Man he could change hisself into
> Watts. He could up his voltage
> Whenever he pleased
> He could, you bet he could
> He could, you bet he could.

Indeed, Railroad Bill, like the conjure man, personifies the long triumph of the race. Like Proteus and Antaeus, he represents the immortal creative spirit in the face of terror: he becomes a song, the blues. "Our Bill is in the / Dogwood flower and in the grain / we eat." Hollywood's script merely mocks and strips old Bill for "Railroad Bill was a star he could change / Hisself to the sun, the moon / Railroad Bill was free / Railroad Bill was free."[14] The rhythms, the language, the folk hero here are familiar. But to see the folk hero as a conjure man forces us to suspend our disbelief, while the humor disarms us: "conjure," "voodoo," "obeah" become words for that measureless dimension of possibility which we know

[14]Ishmael Reed, *Chattanooga* (New York: Random House, 1966), pp. 9ff.

we cannot comprehend or describe. Savor the compactness and beauty of such lines as these:

> Skirt Dance
> i am to my honey what marijuana is
> to tiajuana. The acapulco gold of her
> secret harvest, up her lush coasts i
> glide at midnight bringing a full boat.
> (that's all the spanish i know.)[15]

The images in a love poem like this bubble up with a wit and freshness we can only savor with delight; ah, "the acapulco gold of her secret harvest"!

The novel, however, seems to be Ishmael Reed's proper métier, for in fiction he opens the mythic and historical—indeed, the allegorical—possibilities of the popular culture. The four novels, *The Free-Lance Pall-Bearers* (1967), *Yellow-Back Radio Broke Down* (1969), *Mumbo Jumbo* (1972), and *The Last Days of Louisiana Red* (1974) employ conventional modes for comic effect, shift rapidly from farce to satire, from historical fact to surrealistic fantasy, from scholarly allusion to obscene jive talk.

A closer look at *The Free-Lance Pall-Bearers* and *Mumbo Jumbo* will reveal the extraordinary range of his comic imagination. Reading Ishmael Reed brings to mind Hieronymous Bosch, Hogarth, Rabelais, or Swift. *The Free-Lance Pall-Bearers* has, at different times, a nightmarish fantasy, a Kafkaesque absurdity, the horrible prophesy of some new version of 1984, the violence, squalor, and realism of ghetto life. The novel operates on several levels, each in maddening tension between outrage and parody, contradiction and satire, lunacy and disarming sanity. The narrator's first sentence is: "I live in Harry Sam. Harry Sam is something else." At the end of the novel, he comes to "The hollow of an abysmal throat." On one level Harry Sam is Uncle Sam, and the personae in the book are swallowed up in the corruption, vermin, and excrement of this monster—a fate too grotesque for mere words. At the same time, the main character, Doopeyduk, is a hospital orderly (who calls himself a psychiatric technician) married to Fannie Mae and living in a dictatorship where "the Screws" are everywhere in evidence. Doopeyduk is not very bright; he is the "last one on the block to know" that his civilization is doomed. But he recognizes that the

[15]*Ibid.*, p. 19.

world around him is filled with dope pushers and disappearing children, vampire bats, graft and deception, "belching foghorns" and incredible filth. It is a society that is totalitarian, yet subversive, criminal, and chaotic. The main conflicts of this mad world appear in the headlines:

"Actor Calls for Guerrilla Warfare Against Sam
    Calls Dictator A Barn Burner"
"Pope Gives Up as Bingo Crisis Escalates. Take God–Damned
    Cards, Weary Pontiff Says."
"Chinese Escape Through Dumbwaiter"
"M/Neighbor and Nosetrouble Demand Parley on Missing Tots."

A confused and manipulated populace is dominated by the Nazarene religion, the mass media, the black nationalists, and a ruthless, God-like dictator who devours little children. Their daily lives are relieved only by drink, drugs, movies, and military parades. A HooDoo epidemic has them in thrall. And Reed's imagery is replete with numerous cloacal references: every old man has his colostomy bag. Doopeyduk's father-in-law is "devoted to thumb sucking and once kissed Calvin Coolidge's ass." The greatest treasure is a golden spittoon; Doopeyduk's days are spent emptying bed-pans. Everywhere the plumbing seems to be constantly backing up. The animal imagery is especially loathsome, even while it may evoke a laugh. There are "furry creatures in the theater." A character is described by another thus: "Porkchop got bubble gum in his brain." An actor is a "hip kitty and a cool, cool Daddy-O." Such jive talk is as effective a parody as the political and religious speeches. The devout sing repeatedly: "It's going to be all right by and by in the sky." The social satire spares no one. Ishmael Reed's barbs are directed also at pussyfooting white liberals, at those who have prostituted their art for "hoopla hoops," at the cultural empti-ness of our commercial market society. Here is the decline of the West as even Spengler and Orwell could hardly have imagined it. Doopeyduk is hanged at the end, and as he expires, he notes:

Helicopters bounced up and down on its roof and the sign of the new regime blinked on and off:

Eats—Save Green Stamps—Bingo—Wed—Eats—Save Green
    Stamps. . . . etc.
Written in Chinese—no Less!

The cycle of brutal inhumanity goes on, unrelieved by the next conqueror.

Mumbo Jumbo is an even more remarkable ritual satire with Reed's fine ear for living speech, his imaginative use of the frenetic lunacy of our popular culture, his witty unmasking of folly, violence, and pretense. Mumbo Jumbo is the "magician who makes the troubled spirits of ancestors go away." Yet for the average Westerner it suggests mere gibberish. Here jazz is the large symbol of the Afro-American culture; the novel explores the historical backgrounds of our heritage and its startling impact on the joyless plastic white world which threatens the life of the spirit. The rationalistic, Puritanical, power-mad, militaristic, exploitative world we celebrate as western civilization's finest achievement is the focus of Reed's attack. The action begins when the mayor of New Orleans, shacked up with "a slatternly floozy" and "a bottle of bootleg gin," is interrupted by an urgent telephone call: "What was once dormant is now a Creeping Thing." *Jazz* is spreading like the plague—the magic of African animism, music, dance, spontaneous joy is everywhere. The year is 1915 and it is reported that even a priest has been "carrying on like any old coon wench with a bass drum." Even at St. Louis Cathedral they are dancing the "Eagle Rock" and "The Sassy Bump." Consternation grips the "respectable" white middle class. Harding (whom the underground called the "He-Harlot" and "The Black Babylonian") exhorted the righteous: "Let's be done with the Wiggle and the Wobble!" But there is no stopping the psychic epidemic of what comes to be called "Jes Grew." Ishmael Reed thus produces a hilarious, imaginative farce on the growth of ragtime, blues, and jazz as well as the drama, poetry, fiction, and criticism of the Harlem Renaissance. His satire includes both blacks and whites in a new dimension of conflict and creation—a searching look at western civilization. As one critic has described Reed's intention: "Western civilization, it seems, is the deliberate creation of Atonism, the rationalist, monotheistic, militarist creed dedicated from the dawn of history (its symbol is the sun) to the suppression of animism, the natural magic figured in music, dance, and generative rhythms that reasserts itself periodically, as in the cult of Osiris, The Dionysian mysteries, and Jazz." [16]

[16]Thomas R. Edwards, "News from Elsewhere," *New York Review of Books*, October 5, 1972, p. 23.

The enemy of Jes Grew is "The Wallflower Order" led by "The Grand Master," Hinckle Von Vampton, the "fourth horseman of the Apocalypse." The Wallflower Order has long been banning books and putting apostates and heretics in the dungeon. "Due to the domination of their senses by Atonism, [they] were robbed of any concerns other than mundane ones." They had tortured the IWW in 1947 and deported "Reds" in 1920. Their creed is well known: "Lord, if I can't dance, No one shall." In Ishmael Reed's fantasy (a cloak-and-dagger parody as well as a historical allegory and *roman à clef*) our hero is Papa La Bas, detective and high priest of animism who knows that Jes Grew is not a plague but an anti-plague. He has what Freud would call "a feeling of an indissoluble bond, of being one with the external world as a whole." Papa La Bas is in contact with the vital source of African religion—voodoo and obeah. There is another secret society, the *Mu'tafikah,* whose members are bent on restoring the art stolen from Africa. Their cleverest adversary, however, is Hinckle Von Vampton, formerly of *The New York Sun,* now editor of the *Benign Monster.* Hinckle scorns the strong-arm methods of the Wallflower Clan and attempts to infiltrate Harlem as a Negrophile, mingling with black poets and musicians. Von Vampton strongly resembles Carl Van Vechten, and Reed's book directs withering barbs at some of the tendencies of the Harlem Renaissance.

Here is a novelist whose book creates a genre of its own. (It is significant, perhaps, that Reed includes at the end five pages of his "partial bibliography.") His weapons against Atonism are where he finds them. Carl Jung, for example, had written: "The catastrophe of the first World War and the extraordinary spiritual malaise that came afterwards were needed to arouse a doubt as to whether all was well with the white man's mind." Reed's mocking wit can characterize that mind more succinctly. Whether it is the war against Haiti or the campaign against Jes Grew, the Americans are determined "to knock it, dock it, co-opt it, swing it, bop it or rock it." Jazz and sex must not prevail: "plastic will prevail over flesh and bones." In the merry-go-round of argument over black identity, "The Negro Past," nationalism, and militancy, *Mumbo Jumbo* teaches us more about the black man's plight than Harold Cruse's *The Crisis of the Negro Intellectual.* It is instructive, entertaining, inventive in its use of language and symbol. It is a hilarious introduction to the deep imprint of the Afro-American imagination on American civilization. "Cab Calloway had startled a Cotton Club audience by announcing his candidacy for President on the strange Jes Grew ticket." The intellectual and emotional battles of the 1960's are seen here through a broad perspective, and the reader awakens to a sense of participation in the long struggle of the human race toward its humanity. "Time is a pendulum. Not a river. More akin to what goes around comes around."

Although Ishmael Reed's most recent novel, *The Last Days of Louisiana Red*, strikes this critic as less impressive than *Mumbo Jumbo*, it is a dazzling achievement, especially in its satire and in the pyrotechnics of the style. Here Papa La Bas, the private eye and HooDoo man, appears again to unmask the moochers, and the struggle between good and evil is framed in a kind of satirical allegory. *The Last Days of Louisiana Red* is an extraordinarily many-sided view of the cultural revolution and political upheaval of the 1960's and early 1970's. The setting is Berkeley, California. The personalities are two groups pitted against each other: Ed Yellings, a worker who has built the gumbo business searching for a way to end Louisiana Red (the modern malaise), and the "Moochers," a variety of parasites preying on the population.

> Louisiana Red was the way they related to one another, maimed and murdered one another, carving one another while above their heads, fifty thousand feet, billionaires flew in custom-made jet planes equipped with saunas, tennis courts, swimming pools, discotheques and meeting rooms decorated like a Merv Griffin show set. . . .
> When Osiris entered Egypt, cannibalism was in vogue. He stopped men from eating men. Thousands of years later when Ed Yellings entered Berkeley, there was a plague too. . . . Men were inflicting psychological stress on one another. Driving one another to high blood pressure, hardening of the arteries, which only made it worse, since the stabbings, rapings, muggings went on as usual. . . .

The bitter lives of the workers have not changed. They are still being manipulated by politicians and business tycoons—"whose political campaigns amounted to: 'Get the Nigger.' " Nothing new in that. What distinguishes the Moochers of our time is their ingenuity. Everybody can get into the act. There is Minnie the Moocher, who is enrolled in the Ph.D. program in rhetoric at the University of

California; there's Street Yellings, who "had his consciousness raised in prison and was immediately granted asylum in an 'emerging' African nation." There is the Reverend Rookie of the Gross Christian Church, who always talks in capitals—a psychedelic preacher. There is Maxwell Kasavubu, a white critic who is about to make a reputation by resurrecting the convicted Bigger in a new interpretation of *Native Son,* and who later has hallucinated that he is a blond about to be raped by Bigger. There's Big Sally, with her Ph.D. in "Black English." There are hosts of others—the usual small-time gamblers, pimps, crooks—rich and poor. "The highest order of this species of Moocher is the President who uses the taxpayer's money to build homes all over the world where he can be alone to contemplate his place in history when history don't even want him." The bitterest satire is directed against blacks—men and women who oppress, humiliate, manipulate, and murder one another. Reed can shock us into outrage even as we laugh at our folly. We need a solid Gumbo as an antidote to the insolence, the sloppiness, "the sounds from the reptilian brain" infected by Louisiana Red. The laughter hangs in midair while the shades descend on our mad world.

Ellison and Reed suggest the need for a value system which recognizes the worthiness of each individual. The moochers "cooperate with their oppression for they have the mentality of the prey who thinks his destruction at the fangs of the killer is the natural order of things and colludes with his own death." The Workers, on the other hand, have learned from Ed Yellings to turn "from manual to mind, that is, everything the Business required was inside of each worker. They had gotten rid of Louisiana Red but maintained its pungency."

LeRoi Jones can speak of "the holiness of life." Ellison revives the hope in an enlightened spirit, self-motivating and responsible. It would appear that the black revolution has come full circle, rejecting mere protest, violence, revolution, and nationalism and embracing what used to be called the eternal verities—the divinity of the individual. In any case, the satire of the black writer since 1945 is a revival not only of the spontaneity, improvisation, and intensity of the African-American's folk humor. This satire also restores reason and faith, even in the midst of the violence and absurdity of our world. Reed's Word is in the spirit of the spirituals, the blues, and jazz:

> ... i
> am moving into a new age. today
> i broke the ice. My pulse begins
> to move across a new world.[17]

[17]Reed, "The Last Week in 30," *Chattanooga*, p. 48.

ALLEN GUTTMANN

Saul Bellow's
Humane Comedy

For more than three decades now, ever since the publication of
Dangling Man in 1944, Saul Bellow, Nobel Prize winner, has been
fascinated by ideas. At moments he has seemed enthralled by them,
the lion-tamer helplessly caught in the commanding gaze of his
dangerous partner, but no American novelist since Melville has
dared more successfully than Bellow to dramatize the intellectual
life. Berating Bummidge, the clown turned psychiatrist in *The Last
Analysis*, lawyer Winkleman complains, "The suckers had their
mouths open for yucks—he fed them Aristotle, Kierkegaard,
Freud."[1] Bummidge proves Winkleman wrong. When he offers his
closed-circuit televiewers Aristotle, Kierkegaard, and Freud, a marvelous transformation takes place. They journey with him into the
depths of the unconscious, they tremble and grow fearful, they
undergo catharsis and are renewed. They laugh. Of the play, Bellow
remarks, "Its real subject is the mind's comical struggle for survival
in an environment of Ideas" (p.vii). One can go further and say that
the mind's comical struggle with ideas has been Bellow's real
subject since the turn of his career, marked by the appearance in
1953 of *The Adventures of Augie March*.

Bellow did not begin as a comic writer. Although fascinated from
the first by ideas, he began with Kafka's grim humor. Laughter

[1] Saul Bellow, *The Last Analysis* (New York: Viking Press, 1965), p. 10.

would be a churlish if not a sadistic response to *Dangling Man* (1944). Laughter would be an equally inappropriate response to the labyrinthine ironies of *The Victim* (1947). The former novel is nothing if not an ironic study in marginality. The alienation is more severe than in any of Bellow's other books; the Durkheimian anomie shows forth with case-study clarity. To dangle is, metaphorically, more extreme than to be rootless. The situation is classically simple: Joseph resigns his job in order to make positive use of the time left him before induction into the army. All eagerness and expectation, he creates for himself the equivalent of Erik Erikson's "psycho-social moratorium." He enters a period of suspension between his now-abandoned ordinary life and the new roles of his future "profession." With his freedom, Joseph optimistically imagines that he can become the earnest huntsman of the Self, the introspective voyager into the undiscovered realms of Identity. The joke is on him, and on us. Small wonder that no one laughs. But what is the joke? Simply that the self is no transcendental entity, no center or node of organizing energy which acts upon the world. The self is merely the intersection of social sets, the fabric woven by the tediously repeated crisscross of social roles. To withdraw from society and to look within is to discover the abyss.[2]

Dangling Man is devoted rather single-mindedly to the irony of Joseph's ontological wild-goose chase. *The Victim* is a more optimistic and more complex orchestration of two ironic themes—first, the relation of the victim to the victimizer; then the somewhat chagrined acceptance of an ethnic identity which seems to escape efforts at explanation and definition. Although Asa Leventhal begins with the indignant rejection of Kirby Allbee's accusations, he must eventually acknowledge a measure of complicity in Allbee's downfall. Leventhal and Allbee are twinned by fate, *Doppelgänger* who metaphorically undergo simultaneous deaths and rebirths. Victim and victimizer are one and the same. Similarly, Leventhal's own uncertainty about his identity as a secular Jew makes him hypersensitive to Allbee's rather mindless version of cultural pluralism, whereby each of us is required to live within the bounds of our inherited ethnic or racial identities. Leventhal's inconsistent attitudes are occasionally comical—there is no reason why a Jew

---

[2]For a somewhat more detailed discussion of both *Dangling Man* and *The Victim*, see my book, *The Jewish Writer in America* (New York: Oxford University Press, 1971), pp. 178–189.

shouldn't sing ballads and spirituals; there are, on the contrary, good reasons to insist that Benjamin Disraeli was really an Italian Jew; there is no reason why Jews shouldn't write books about Emerson and Thoreau—but he attains an acceptance of himself and is finally content to leave the question of ethnic identity unanswered.

The Victim is a marvelous technical achievement, a skillful weave of the two related themes of complicity and identity, an exemplary version of what we have come to think of as modern (as contrasted to contemporary) fiction. But it was an achievement that left its author unsatisfied. Bellow felt constricted, too closely bound by a great tradition which took its ideas *too* seriously. The modernists have tended to irony. Except for James Joyce, they have produced little that might be called *comic* literature. Bellow's own comments are important:

> My first two books are well made. I wrote the first quickly but took great pains with it. I labored over the second and tried to make it letter-perfect. In writing *The Victim* I accepted a Flaubertian standard. Not a bad standard, to be sure, but one which, in the end, I found repressive—repressive because of the circumstances of my life and because of my upbringing in Chicago as the son of immigrants. . . . Those books . . . did not give me a form in which I felt comfortable. A writer should be able to express himself easily, naturally, copiously in a form which frees his mind, his energies.[3]

In the six years that separated *The Victim* from *The Adventures of Augie March,* Bellow began to publish pieces of a comic nature, like "Sermon by Doctor Pep" and "Address by Gooley MacDowell to the Hasbeens Club of Chicago." Secure now in his sense of himself as a writer, Bellow was ready to indulge himself as an unsurpassed comedian.

The themes of *Augie March* are variants of the familiar ones, but the style is transformed. Augie March is the picaresque hero who tells his own story with a gusty eloquence far beyond that of Bellow's previous characters. It is, moreover, a *joyful* noise that Augie makes. ". . . I got very tired of the solemnity of complaint," says Bellow, "altogether impatient with complaint. Obliged to choose between complaint and comedy, I choose comedy. . . ."[4]

The first paragraph is characteristic of Bellow's new style:

[3]Alfred Kazin, ed., *Writers at Work,* 3rd ser. (New York: Viking Press, 1967), pp. 182–183.
[4]*Ibid.*, pp. 187–188.

> I am an American, Chicago born—Chicago, that somber city—and
> go at things as I have taught myself, free-style, and will make the
> record in my own way: first to knock, first admitted; sometimes an
> innocent knock, sometimes a not so innocent. But a man's character is
> his fate, says Heraclitus, and in the end there isn't any way to disguise
> the nature of the knocks by acoustical work on the door or gloving the
> knuckles.[5]

The language is loose, colloquial, with parenthetical inserted remarks rather than clauses of subordination and superordination. The
metaphors are drawn "free style" from the many realms traversed,
vicariously or actually, by the much-traveled and much-read (but
decidedly unschooled) narrator. The allusion to pre-Socratic philosophy is tossed into the paragraph amidst a scatter of images
from sports, business, and engineering. "The most ordinary Yiddish
conversation," wrote Bellow in an article also appearing in 1953,
"is full of the grandest historical, mythological, and religious allusions. The Creation, the Fall, the Flood, Egypt, Alexander, Titus,
Napoleon, the Rothschilds, the sages and the Laws may get into the
discussion of an egg, a clothes-line, or a pair of pants."[6] It is easy,
however, to overemphasize the Yiddish contribution to Bellow's
language, and thus to minimize the encouragement received from
Emerson and Thoreau, who also mingled the marvelous with the
ordinary, who jumbled the siege of Troy and Persian poetry into their
accounts of life in Concord, Massachusetts.

There is another aspect to the style which brings American literary
analogs and precedents to mind. Emerson wrote that America is a
poem to our eyes, and Whitman labored manfully to realize
Emerson's optimistic metaphor. Bellow followed suit. A room, a
street, or an elevator cage is suddenly transformed into a microcosm
of Chicago, which is already Bellow's microcosm of America.

Life is, for Augie, a game, one well worth the candle. He wants to
be cut in on life's deal. What's in the cards? He may not be great, but
he can recognize greatness in others, can understand and respond to
the extremes of heroism and humiliation, can be moved to laughter
and to tears by the gestures and speeches fixed forever in history and
in literature. Augie likens his crippled patron, Einhorn, to Socrates
and himself to Alcibiades; he insists that such comparisons are

[5] Saul Bellow, *The Adventures of Augie March* (New York: Viking Press, 1953), p. 3. All
other references to the novel are cited in the text.
[6] Saul Bellow, "Laughter in the Ghetto," *Saturday Review*, 36 (May 30, 1953), 15.

legitimate and even necessary if we are to maintain our pride. Augie is an unrepentant and even boasty Plutarchian whose parallel lives of illustrious men match obscure Chicagoans to the mighty names that stride through Greek and Roman history. Augie is stubbornly egalitarian, but he is not foolishly enthusiastic. Unlike his older brother Simon, who was dazzled by Tom Brown's schooldays, Augie lacks the illusions that are prerequisite to disillusionment. He writes with an eye to perfection, but also with an awareness of the gap that separates the actual from the imagined. Like Asa Leventhal, Augie March accepts the conditions within which we live—but Augie makes a good deal more of them.

Augie is the comic hero who looks at his own misadventures and grins, "That's the *animal ridens* in me . . ." (p. 536). His response is important. One of the recurrent figures of comic literature is the type whose education costs him dearly in buffets and shakings and tongue-lashings. Augie blunders, and pays for his blunders, too, but he—and not some aloofly distant third-person narrator—describes, comments, and sets in perspective. The *animal ridens* can laugh at himself. The laughter is reflective.

Thematically as well as stylistically, the novel is a contrast to *Dangling Man*. Joseph's moral collapse followed upon his partly voluntary, partly helpless isolation from others. Deprived of his customary roles, he falls apart. Augie, however, goes through life *evading* fixity and permanence. If our identity derives from the parts we play in the social drama, why not let us play as many parts as possible! Expand the repertory! Metaphorically, Augie is an orphan. "People have been adoptive towards me, as if I were really an orphan" (p. 103), he remarks. The irony is that he is more at home in the world than those who wish to adopt and thus to define and limit him. It is, moreover, possible to see the entire novel as a series of episodes in which families and individuals attempt to adopt Augie while he, always tempted by the attractions of stasis, manages nonetheless to evade them all.

The family into which he is literally born is no family at all. His father has deserted his mother long before the narration commences. Mrs. March is a kind but nearly helpless creature under the domination of "Grandma" Lausch, who is actually no relative of the Marches. The old woman is the first of many who try to wrest Augie to their will. With her pretensions and her passions, she dominates the first chapter. Her irreverence reminds Augie of his own minimal Jewishness.

Although Grandma Lausch never attends the synagogue, eats bread on Passover, and loves canned lobster, she still burns a candle on the anniversary of her husband's death. She is not quite an atheist. She practices a "kitchen religion" that "had nothing to do with the giant God of the Creation who turned back the waters and exploded Gomorrah but it was on the side of religion at that." Augie's relationship to the Law is even more peripheral: ". . . sometimes we were chased, stoned, bitten, and beaten up for Christ-killers, all of us, even Georgie, articled, whether we liked it or not, to this mysterious trade. But I never had any special grief from it, or brooded, being by and large too larky and boisterous to take it to heart . . ." (p. 12). Augie confronts the question of Jewishness more directly than Asa Leventhal was able to, and more conclusively. The metaphor from the era of apprenticeship is significant; there is a strangely contractual quality to the relationship. It is, however, a contract that Augie breaks effortlessly and almost without thought. "It wasn't my nature to fatigue myself with worry over being born to this occult work" (p. 12). It cannot be said that he does this "occult work" at all; he dismisses his status as a Jew as one might dismiss theosophy or the heresies of the Hindu. The contrast between Augie and the doomed-to-suffer Jews of Bernard Malamud could scarcely be greater. He is not one who has been chosen. Among the myriad factors that condition choice, he will pick and choose for himself.

Much of the time, his choice is simply the refusal to let others choose for him. The second chapter sets him in the midst of the Coblin family, his relatives. The milieu is described in great detail. As powerful new personalities rush upon the state—Anna Coblin's boastful brother, "Five Properties," for example—one tends to forget Grandma Lausch and her concerns. Now Anna Coblin sees Augie as an inadequate replacement for her son, who has run off to the Marines, and as an appropriate husband for her daughter. She greets him with the announcement of her plans: "Hear, Owgie, you'll be my son, my daughter's husband, *mein* kind!" But Augie resists such blandishments: "Even at that time I couldn't imagine that I would marry into the Coblin family" (p. 17).

In the fifth chapter, Augie moves into the orbit of William Einhorn, a crippled manipulator of men and money, "the first superior man I knew" (p. 60). Once again, Bellow creates a whole new world of Einhornism to replace the environments from which Augie has come. A plethora of Einhorns rush onstage and push the Marches and the Coblins into the wings. Einhorn's father, half-brother, son—they all play important parts. Each is amply characterized. Einhorn wants Augie not as a son and heir but as a retainer, servant, and disciple. He is the Sun King of South Chicago, and Augie is his chamberlain. There is no doubt that the crippled Einhorn's compensatory energy attracts Augie. His rhetoric is so similar to Augie's that certain speeches might have been made by either of them. He, too, broods on Socrates and Alcibiades. He begins to quote Shakespeare and ends in Yiddish: "What a piece of work is a man, and the firmament fretted with gold—but the whole *gescheft* bores him" (p. 75). He, too, is an assimilator, a lover of images and episodes, an almost insane collector of commercial samples, come-ons, offers, odds and ends. Einhorn becomes almost a parody of Augie's *Weltanschauung,* a pathetic figure carried to a brothel on Augie's back in complicated mythological reverberations of Aeneas and Anchises and the demanding prostitute that medieval legend placed on the back of love-stricken Aristotle.

From Einhorn's sphere of influence, Augie moves on to that of the Renlings. Mrs. Renling, a haberdasher, outfits Augie in a version of English style, arranges for riding lessons, sends him on excursions. Mrs. Renling takes him as a companion to the resort at Benton Harbor, plans for his education, and formally proposes legal adoption; but Augie refuses, partly because he is now in love with beautiful Esther Fenchel, whose sister Thea loves him (and will return to carry him off to Mexico).

Between Benton Harbor and Mexico, however, Augie passes through a maze of adventures and avoids every *cul de sac.* At one point, he becomes the organizer of a union and begins an affair with a chambermaid, Sophie Geratis, but Thea Fenchel quickly reappears to prove that Augie's political commitments are superficial. How could they be otherwise? When Thea knocks on the door, Sophie rises and departs in as good a humor as can be expected in such circumstances. The union forgotten, Augie turns to Thea as Ishmael turned to crazy Captain Ahab. Thea's plan is to train an eagle to hunt iguanas. The fiery hunt of which Ishmael spoke is now with, rather than for, the symbolic animal. Augie bewails his own weakness and foolishness. He protests half-heartedly, "Do we have to go to Mexico?" (p. 323), but against her he is as ineffectual as Starbuck against Ahab. Off they go.

The Valley of Mexico blazes with blue as it did for D. H. Lawrence, and Augie is soon excited by Thea's impetuous prospect. The situation is richly comic in ways that Bellow had not previously ventured upon. There are plays on words, as when the Spanish boys see the eagle and shout *"El aguila, el aguila!"* Not knowing the language, Augie and Thea name the bird Caligula, with comic overtones of that mad emperor. Still more unusual for Bellow at this stage of his career is the slapstick which characterizes the whole sequence in Mexico. The great bird perches in the bathroom and seems to menace Augie in his least heroic moments.

The comedy takes an ironic turn when Caligula begins to hunt iguanas. The eagle is a coward. Bitten by a lizard, he flees; in the face of opposition, he gives up. Thea is furious; Augie is sympathetic. He identifies wholly with Caligula's lack of valor.

Augie is, of course, immediately out of favor with Thea, but there is always someone in the wings, waiting to adopt him. Enter Stella, who asks him to help her evade a lover. The flight is comic. It begins with Thea's attempt to halt them, leads to the brink of disaster when the car nearly goes over a cliff, and ends with the "one appropriate thing" (p. 390). They make love. The whole scene resembles an escapade in a comic movie. Augie returns for the moment to Thea, but it is Stella whom he will eventually wed, for reasons which she sees clearly at this time: ". . . one of things I thought is that you and I are the kind of people other people are always trying to fit into their schemes. So suppose we didn't play along, then what?" (p. 384) What, indeed?

Before Augie realizes that Stella is the perfect match for his restless adventurousness, he pursues Thea, returns to Chicago, and launches several new rounds of picaresque episodes replete with assorted exotic personages. Eventually he settles down, more or less, but his acceptance is not despair. "Why, I am sort of Columbus of those near-at-hand and believe you can come to them in this immediate *terra incognita* that spreads out in every gaze. I may well be a flop at this line of endeavor. Columbus too thought he was a flop, probably, when they sent him back in chains. Which didn't prove there was no America" (p. 536). Augie is the Columbus of the commonplace, another Whitman, in open shirt and Panama hat. Although persistent efforts have been made to connect Augie with the archetype of the *schlemiel,* who never gets anything right, his breezy confidence, his appetite for experience, his extraordinary self-awareness, and his obvious delight in the gamut of the American language relate him to the speaker of "Song of Myself," rather than to the plaintive protagonists of Yiddish literature. For Augie, marginality is possibility, an occasion for exuberance and not for the ironies of Jewish humor.

A dozen years after the publication of *Augie March,* Bellow judged that he had changed his style too quickly, had removed restraints recklessly. "I had just increased my freedom, and like any emancipated plebeian I abused it at once."[7] The book is, indeed, too long, the language sometimes suggestive to the point of confusion, but the excesses were necessary. Without the comic outburst of *Augie March,* Bellow might never have written any of his subsequent comedies.

Between *Augie March* and *Henderson the Rain King* (1959) came the novella, *Seize the Day* (1956), a somber work of puzzling popularity. Although the work is stylistically akin to the richly allusive *Augie March,* the themes carry one back to the dark ironies of *Dangling Man.* Wilhelm Adler, a young man of no remarkable ability or talent, changes his name to Tommy Wilhelm and seeks his fortune. He discovers, amid the ruins of his hopes, that he has made himself into a metaphoric orphan. Estranged from his father, his wife, and himself, he stands before a coffin, looks upon his alter ego—a corpse—and weeps. He is a cautionary rather than an exemplary figure.

Henderson the Rain King remains Bellow's most purely comic work. At the time of its publication, it was generally condemned, and it remained undervalued until the late 1960's. It may be that reviewers and critics still imagined that *The Victim* and *Seize the Day* were somehow authentic products of Bellow's imagination, while *The Adventures of Augie March* and *Henderson the Rain King* were aberrations which ought not to be encouraged.[8] It is hard now to understand why recognition came as slowly as it did.

The book is generally parodic, irreverent, and zany. The targets

[7]Kazin, ed., *Writers at Work*, p. 182.

[8]For a discussion of the book's reception and poor reputation, see *The Jewish Writer in America*, pp. 201–202.

for satire vary—Romantic writers take their lumps, along with humorless anthropologists; Bellow seems, moreover, ready to exaggerate Romantic themes to the point where he begins to parody himself.

Henderson begins where Jay Gatsby would have ended, if only he could have had everything the green light across the water symbolized—wealth and status, money and love. Of Henderson, the envious say that "His great-grandfather was Secretary of State, his great-uncles were ambassadors to England and France, and his father was the famous scholar Willard Henderson who wrote that book on the Albigensians, a friend of William James and Henry Adams."[9] From his famous father, Henderson inherited three million dollars and a country house designed to flush the countenance of a Jamesian observer. But the money is useless. The first great image of the book is Henderson in the library, literally pursuing wisdom in words read and forgotten. Seeking wisdom and finding only the money his father used as book marks, Henderson is the ironic hero of an age of affluence. He is a comic rebuke to solemn moralists whose work earnestly portray the sad fates of those who sacrificed youthful idealism at the altar of Mammon.

The fact that Henderson is in his fifties and suffers from poor teeth rather than consumption may seem to disqualify him as Romantic hero (as does the possession of wealth rather than wisdom), but Henderson is driven by an inner need, by a voice which repeats its demand, "I want, I want, I want!" The novel is, therefore, a quest. What is it that the voice wants? What *is* "his heart's ultimate need"? Henderson is determined to find out.

He marries a girl of his own social class: "A remarkable person, handsome, tall, elegant, sinewy, with long arms and golden hair, private, fertile and quiet" (p. 4). Unsatisfied, Henderson moves from bourgeois to Romantic love, from Frances to Lily. The courtship, rife with quarrels and reconciliations, takes place amid a dozen digressions (like all the actions in a novel filled with anticipations and remembrances).

Important among the digressions is the confrontation of Henderson and an ominous octopus, who swims in relation to Henderson very much as Theodore Dreiser's lobster and squid swim in relation

[9]Saul Bellow, *Henderson the Rain King* (New York: Viking Press, 1959), p. 7. All other references to the novel are cited in the text.

to young Frank Cowperwood in *The Financier*. Within the presence of the octopus emitting "cosmic coldness," Henderson felt he was dying. He then abruptly starts to tell us why he is going to Africa.

However, Henderson's reasons for his African safari are delayed for another twenty pages of Shandy-like digressions. The marriage with Lily fails to still the voice within, and Henderson throws himself into a Thoreauvian vocation. Perhaps the pastoral mode will turn the trick. Thoreau tells us in *Walden,* with a characteristic play of wit, that he was determined to know beans. Henderson does him one better and attempts to know pigs. In defiance of his outraged neighbors, he makes his estate "a pig kingdom, with pig houses on the lawn and in the flower garden" (p. 20). He empathizes with pigs and thinks of the prophecy of Daniel to Nebuchadnezzar: "They shall drive thee from among men, and thy dwelling shall be with the beasts of the fields" (p. 21). Pigs are the wrong beasts.

And art is as useless as money, love, and labor. With Lily at Chartres Cathedral, where Henry Adams found a world of radiant significance, Henderson threatens suicide. Alone in the basement of his house in Connecticut, he tries the violin and seeks thereby to reach his father: "I played in the basement to my father and my mother, and when I learned a few pieces I would whisper, 'Ma, this is "Humoresque" for you,' or, 'Pa, listen—"Meditation" from Thais.' " Most important, Henderson plays from *The Messiah,* "He was despised and rejected, a man of sorrows and acquainted with grief" (p. 30). The voice of his griefs ("I want") is louder than the music.

The Messiah introduces still another comic parallel. Henderson's daughter Ricey comes home from Danbury on the morning of the winter solstice, bringing a colored baby she had found, she says, in a parked car. Although a virgin has come home with a newborn child, the much put-upon father does not rejoice. This episode is but one of many parodies on biblical events. Two pages later, the references are pagan: "In her yard [Miss Lenox] had an old catalpa tree of which the trunk and lower limbs were painted light blue. She had fixed little mirrors up there, and old bicycle lights which shone in the dark, and in summer she liked to climb up there and sit with her cats, drinking a can of beer." (p. 39). Miss Lenox, unlike Virgil's Cumaean sibyl, is mortal. One morning she starts Henderson's breakfast for him, and dies. He finds breakfast on the stove and Miss

Lenox on the floor. He doesn't know what else to do and pins a note to her skirt: DO NOT DISTURB. Death, however, means as little as birth to Henderson's inner voice. Appalled by the wasted life visible in the old woman's testamentary half-century of accumulated rubbish, Henderson decides to go to Africa.

It is an Africa that no explorer and no anthropologist ever visited. Reviewers who found this a fault missed the point of Bellow's burlesque. The story, fantastic from the beginning, now becomes increasingly fabulous, a series of adventures richly imagined in themselves and doubly effective as ironic parallels to Old Testament parables and anthropological data lifted from *The Golden Bough*. Reaching the Arnewi in company with a Queequegesque guide named Romilayu, Henderson performs his first Old Testament miracle: "Without waiting for Romilayu's advice I took out the Austrian lighter with the drooping wick, spun the tiny wheel with my thumb, and immediately a bush went flaming almost invisible in the strong sunlight." But the American millionaire is clearly not Moses. "The embers of the bush had fallen by my boots" (p. 48).

Although reluctant to fight ("Your Highness, I am really in a kind of quest"), he wrestles ceremonially with Prince Itelo of the Arnewi and, like an inverted version of the angel who vanquished Jacob, digs his thumbs into the African's thigh and throws him down. "I felt almost as bad as he did" (p. 68). Itelo's aunt, to whom Henderson is introduced by the felled prince, has no store of primitive wisdom to impart. She asks instead, Who are you? That is indeed the question: "Who—who was I? A millionaire wanderer and wayfarer. A brutal and violent man driven into the world. A man who fled his own country, settled by his forefathers. A fellow whose heart said *I want, I want*. Who played the violin in despair, seeking the voice of angels. Who had to burst the spirit's sleep, or else" (p. 76). For Queen Willatale and her sister Mtalba, he sings the thematic aria from *The Messiah;* from them he receives a bit of advice which Bellow presumably recognizes as a cliché from the fiction of E. M. Forster and D. H. Lawrence: "Grun-tu-molani. Man want to live" (p. 85). In gratitude for this perception, he sets out on another misadventure. The land is stricken by a drought and the cistern is clogged with frogs. With a do-it-yourself bomb constructed of a flashlight case, a shoelace, and a Band-Aid, he is a Connecticut Yankee in the Court of the Fisher King, a Rube Goldbergized Grail

Quester, a utilitarian Moses fanatically turned against the plague of frogs. The bomb destroys the cistern and leaves the stricken Arnewi worse off than before. Mtalba's comment is, in Romilayu's translation, "Goo' by Fo'evah" (p. 111). (How Romilayu acquired a Mississippi accent is never explained.)

The travelers move on, with echoes now of Joseph's voyage to Egypt. They reach the land of the Wariri and spend their first night moving and removing a corpse left in their hut. With such preparation, Henderson attempts to move the gigantic idol Mummah, which no native has been strong enough to move. Henderson succeeds and becomes the Rain King. Thereupon the Amazons chase him through a cloudburst and pound him and throw him into the mud and leave him, finally, "in my coat of earth, like a giant turnip" (p. 202). Are we to take Mummah as Mama and look for a Freudian significance here? Who knows?

Henderson is now ready for the descent into the Underworld that all the mythic parallels have prepared us for. Dahfu guides Henderson downward to the cage of the lion Atti. Comparisons with Melville's emblematic whale and Faulkner's symbolic bear (and Augie March's meaningful eagle) are inescapable. The contrasts are greater than the points of similarity. Ahab hunts in order to destroy the visible symbol of an invisible and intolerable malignity. Ike McCaslin divests himself of the implements of civilization in order to be initiated into the realms of primeval nature existing before man and after him. Henderson seeks only to quiet the voice "repeating, *I want,* raving and demanding, making a chaos, desiring, desiring, and disappointed continually, which drove me forth as beaters drive game" (p. 210). In fear and trembling, Henderson fulfills the thrice-quoted prophecy of Daniel. He gets on all fours, stares the lion in the face, and does his best to follow Dahfu's instructions (given in a slightly stiffened Oxbridge English). Henderson must become a lion, he must roar. But his vocal cords "seemed stuck together like strands of overcooked spaghetti" (p. 266), and his noises are porcine rather than leonine. He does his best, but the voice is unstilled. "When I could do no more I fell flat on my face" (pp. 267–268). Once recovered, he is ready for Dahfu's praise of the creative imagination: "Imagination, imagination, imagination! It converts to actual. It sustains, it alters, it redeems!" (p. 271) So it does. Romantic poets from Coleridge to Wallace Stevens have all but deified the shaping spirit of the imagination, and literary critics have marched like acolytes to worship. Bellow, too, believes in the imagination, but his comic qualifications are an acknowledgment of the painful triteness of truth. He lampoons his own convictions and mocks those whom possibility makes solemn. Let the praise of imagination be, at the very least, imaginative.

One further step leads Henderson to the most common discovery of all: we must love one another or die. Inspired, he writes a long letter to Lily and asks her to enroll him in medical school (under the name of Leo E. Henderson) so that he can follow the course of Albert Schweitzer. He tells her: "I had a voice that said, I want! *I* want? I? It should have told me *she* wants, *he* wants, *they* want. And moreover, it's love that makes reality reality" (p. 286). The movement is from verb to verb, from *want* to *imagine* to *love;* the movement is from pronoun to pronoun, from *I* to *they*. And Henderson is as good as his grammar. He joins Dahfu in the hunt for the lion Gmilo, Dahfu's father reincarnated. The terrible hunt ends as Dahfu falls from his frail platform into the reach of the lion.

In the conventional philosophical terms that Henderson himself uses in an early colloquy with Dahfu, Henderson embraces the world as Becoming and rejects the world of Being. He *had* longed for Being: "Being people have all the breaks. Becoming people are very unlucky, always in a tizzy. The Becoming people are always having to make explanations or offer justifications to the Being people" (p. 160). He has now painfully learned what Augie March seems to have known from the beginning. He accepts himself as one of the Becoming people. He can play the roles of Rain King and leonine roarer *de profundis* and aide-de-camp in Dahfu's campaign to trap his father's transposed spirit, but he cannot *be* a lion or a king. He grabs up a lion cub, whom he names Dahfu, and flees.

The book ends with two magnificent scenes, one remembered, one enacted. Henderson remembers Smolak the bear, with whom he had, as an adolescent, ridden a roller coaster in an amusement park: "By a common bond of despair we embraced, cheek to cheek, as all support seemed to leave us and we started down the perpendicular drop. I pressed into his long-suffering, age-worn, tragic, and discolored coat as he grunted and cried to me" (p. 338). Henderson then employs the biblical metaphor that was one of Melville's favorites:

"Smolak was cast off and I am an Ishmael too" (p. 338). Henderson follows the reference to Ishmael with a Transcendentalist's interpretation. "Nature," wrote Emerson, "is the symbol of spirit. . . . Particular natural facts are symbols of particular spiritual facts." This perception maddened Ahab, for whom "all visible objects" were but "pasteboard masks" which mocked the demand to know what lurked behind them. Ahab's effort was to strike through the mask in a frenzied effort to destroy whatever it was that lay behind the natural fact. But Emerson's perception is turned by Henderson to happier uses: "If corporeal things are an image of the spiritual and visible objects are renderings of invisible ones, and if Smolak and I were outcasts together, two humorists before the crowd, but brothers in our souls—I enbeared by him, and he probably humanized by me—I didn't come to the pigs as a tabula rasa" (pp. 338–339). Who but Bellow would mix references to Melville, Emerson, pigs, and John Locke?

In the final scene, Bellow dramatizes love and imagination. While the plane bringing him home refuels in Newfoundland, he grabs up still another outcast, an American boy born in Persia and bereft of parents and mother tongue. With the orphan in his arms and the cub in the plane, he runs in the cold morning air, round and round the plane. Kindred spirit now to Walt Whitman, who contained multitudes and rejoiced to imagine himself "stucco'd with quadrupeds and birds all over," Henderson leaps with joy that men can love airplanes and orphans and lion cubs. The world is, as again and again in American literature, newly found (i.e., Newfoundland) in the renaissance of dawn. ("There is more day to dawn," wrote Thoreau characteristically, "The sun is but a morning star.") The world lies white and silent all about, not with the terror of ambiguity, as in Poe's *Narrative of Arthur Gordon Pym* or Melville's "Whiteness of the Whale," but with the joy of possibility. After all, American writers have traditionally sought a transcendence based on freedom. Emerson, Whitman, and William James, in their very different ways, wrote of human freedom in lovely imagined worlds ever various and new. Today we find it difficult, if not impossible, to sustain their enthusiasm. Bellow was forced to acknowledge, through the ironic hyperboles of the comic mode, that there is always a Hawthorne or a Melville to remind one of the tragic. Nonetheless,

Bellow mastered art's paradox and reproduced in written language the excited, disorderly buzz and bloom of life itself. One must, even in an age of anxiety, leap with joy as best one can.

Henderson the Rain King is Bellow's most purely American comedy, the book in which he comes closest to Walt Whitman and Mark Twain. *Herzog,* published in 1964, is his most extended performance in the tradition of Jewish humor. If American humor is largely the product of the frontier, Jewish humor is to roughly the same degree the result of the socio-economic situation of European Jews. In the ghetto and in the *shtetl* of Eastern Europe, the nineteenth-century Jew was forced to take an ironic view of himself. In his own eyes, in the traditions of Orthodoxy, he was one of the Chosen People, a man set aside by God to perform a sacred task; in the eyes of his neighbors, he represented the stubbornness which had rejected Jesus and the greed which thrived upon the exploitation of others. The contrast between the glory of one's religious mission and the misery of one's earthly situation led to the creation of *schlemiel,* the righteous unfortunate.[10] Moses Herzog is not quite a *schlemiel*—he is, after all, a man with considerable status, a successful professor—but there is nonetheless a gap between his grandiose intellectual pretensions and the ignominious muddle of his private life. He himself sees his kinship with the *schlemiel* of Yiddish literature; perhaps it is this ironic perception which saves him.

Constructing the novel, Bellow proved once again his familiarity with the tradition of modernism. "If I'm out of my mind, it's all right with me, thought Moses Herzog,"[11] whose point of view dominates the novel. The justification of his acceptance of self is technically complicated by flashbacks, swift transitions in time and in topic, and the digressive opportunities of the epistolary form. To understand *what* happened to Moses Herzog is in itself a difficult enterprise, but one can undo the tangled skein and summarize in a paragraph the events that Bellow is at such pains to scramble.

Moses Herzog was born in Montreal in about 1917, was taken to Chicago as a child (like Saul Bellow), graduated from college in about 1938, served briefly in World War II, received his Ph.D. in

---

[10]For a discussion of Jewish humor, see my essay in Louis Rubin, ed., *The Comic Imagination in America* (New Brunswick, N. J.: Rutgers University Press, 1973), pp. 329–338.

[11]Saul Bellow, *Herzog* (New York: Viking Press, 1964), p. 11. All references to the novel are cited in the text.

about 1950, married Daisy, published *Romanticism and Christianity* in about 1954, fathered a son, also about 1954, divorced Daisy, married Madeleine Pontritter in about 1956, moved to the Berkshires to work on his magnum opus, fathered a daughter in about 1959, moved to Chicago in 1962, was divorced in the fall of 1963, traveled in Europe that winter, experienced a time of confusion and then a return to stability in the summer of 1964. At this moment, at the time of Herzog's tentative recovery, the narration begins.

What happened is simple enough (if one reads the book three or four times). But *why?* The answer is complex, of course, but the root of the matter lies in Herzog's romantic desires to be more than human. Like Tommy Wilhelm, Moses Herzog sinned against the moral law as laid down by old Schlossberg. He comes to realize how foolish he had been in his desire to become "a *marvelous* Herzog." All around him, men attempted to reduce human freedom to historical necessity or to the dictates of the unconscious. Marxists and Freudians conspired to insist that man must sacrifice his "poor, squawking, niggardly individuality. . . . But of course he, Herzog, predictably bucking such trends, had characteristically, obstinately, defiantly, blindly but without sufficient courage or intelligence tried to be a *marvelous* Herzog" (p. 93). For these ambitions, he has been punished, but he remained reluctant to renounce them: "What if he failed? Did that really mean that there was no faithfulness, no generosity, no sacred quality? Should he have been a plain, unambitious Herzog? No" (p. 93). Better to have striven and failed than never to have striven at all.

How did he come to have such dreams of grandeur? In Aunt Zipporah's view, Herzog's mother was already the victim of illusions: "You got used to putting on style, in Petersburg, with servants and coachman. . . . Why must your children go to the conservatory, the Baron de Hirsch school, and all those special frills? Let them go to work like mine" (p. 142). In Herzog's memory, his father was grand, powerful, kingly. That impractical man was actually a bootlegger, a cheerful faker of whisky brands. "Well, children," he called out, "what shall it be—White Horse? Johnnie Walker?" (p. 146) When his truck is hijacked, when he is beaten and humiliated, he is still, to his adoring son, "a father, a sacred being, a king" (p. 147). Of such love are illusions born.

Among Herzog's illusions was the typically academic ambition to change the world with a book. His first monograph had been a scholarly success which whetted his appetite. His efforts had been heroic: Herzog, responsible to civilization in his icy outpost, lying in bed in an aviator's helmet when the stoves were out, "fitted together Bacon and Locke from one side and Methodism and William Blake from the other" (p. 127). Encouraged by the reception of his first book, he deemed himself ready for the ultimate intellectual effort. He wanted to stun the world, to save the world, to change the course of history: "The progress of civilization—indeed, the survival of civilization, depended on the successes of Moses E. Herzog" (p. 125). In comparison to his enormous intellectual vanity, his preening before the mirror and his pride in his physique were foibles. Compared to the wild promiscuity of his ideas, his affairs with Wanda and Ramona and Sono Oguki were bourgeois imitations of romantic love.

Such were his hopes. How did the Herzog whom we meet in Chapter One arrive sanely—more or less—in the pastoral landscape of the Berkshires? Credit must be given, and Herzog gives it, to those whom he calls "reality instructors" (p. 125). Chief among those who punish him with "lessons of the Real" were Sandor Himmelstein, Valentine Gersbach, and Madeleine Pontritter Herzog. Sandor Himmelstein ("stony heaven"?) insisted that "facts *are* nasty" and delivered the bad news about the husband's chances in a divorce proceeding: "They'll kill you. . . . Put you over a barrel. Tear your hide off. . . . Tie your guts in knots. Sonofabitch. They'll put a meter on your nose, and charge you for breathing. You'll be locked up back and front. Then you'll think about death. You'll pray for it. A coffin will look better to you than a sports car. . . . They'll throw the book at you in court. She's the mother—the female. She's got the tits. They'll crush you" (pp. 86–88). That Sandor Himmelstein displayed his own measure of sentimentalism when he discussed his daughter annoyed Herzog, but it offered him no license to ignore the hard truths and nasty facts that Himmelstein used to bombard Herzog's maudlin, indiscriminate, naive "potato love." Betrayal by Valentine Gersbach, friend turned cuckolder, was another lesson in reality instruction, a lesson rendered all the more painful by the fact that Gersbach is a parody of Herzog. The most comic sections of the novel are those in which Herzog roars out his vengeful characterizations of gimpy Gersbach's intellectual vulgarity and opportunism: "He sold tickets to a reading of his poems. Five dollars for the front seats, three bucks at the back of the hall. Reading a poem about his grandfather who was a street sweeper, he broke down and cried. Nobody could get out. The hall was locked" (p. 196). Herzog complained about Gersbach's uncanny ability to ride the wave of fashion: "With pinochle players he plays pinochle, with rabbis it's Martin Buber, with the Hyde Park Madrigal Society he sings madrigals . . ." (p. 217). How can the world *be* this unfair? How can people listen to a fraud like Valentine Gersbach peddle his popularized versions of ideas that are already outmoded before he hears of them, when Moses E. Herzog has the real McCoy? How can Madeleine Pontritter Herzog spurn the man who fathered her daughter in order to set up domestic shop with a sweetheart named Valentine?

Herzog eventually realizes that he had asked the wrong questions. Better to have wondered how he came to marry anyone as unsuitable for him as Madeleine. The answer is not simply that she was a woman of "great charm, and beauty of person also, and a brilliant mind" (p. 5); it was also that she was a great actress. She was able to play the parts that Herzog assigned her; she was able to reinforce his belief in his own marvelousness. Too late, he realizes her theatricality. Her first important appearance in the book is the remembered scene in which she announced her desire for a divorce. She dressed for the part, she staged it perfectly. In retrospect, he can see how she shared his own weaknesses; he can understand her extravagance and wastefulness, her love of intellectual display, her refusal to play second fiddle in the stirring philosophical symphony of Herzog's *Weltanschauung*. No, a woman of her dramatic ability needed the starring role. Valentine Gersbach and she were well matched.

Before Herzog arrived at this perception, he nearly made the same mistake himself. In New York, killing time while waiting to talk to a lawyer, he observed a courtroom scene in which an impassive female defendant was found guilty of impulsively killing her son by smashing him against the bedroom wall. Horrified, Herzog decided on the spot to rush off to Chicago, to confront Madeleine and Gersbach, to bring his own drama to a grand climax. In Chicago he took his father's old revolver to Madeleine's apartment, watched Gersbach bathing Herzog's daughter, and realized that he had been tempted by whatever theatrical impulse it was that impelled the defendant to kill: "To shoot him!—an absurd thought. As soon as Herzog saw the actual person giving an actual bath, the reality of it, the tenderness of such a buffoon to a little child, his intended violence turned into theater, into something ludicrous. He was not ready to make such a complete fool of himself" (p. 258). Although the plot leads Herzog through several more detours, he is now on the road to recovery. The reality instructors have taught him a lesson.

The lesson was quite unintentional, at least in Gersbach's case. One of Herzog's profoundest insights is into the dangers of ideas. The reality of Gersbach bathing little June shattered the theatrical idea of murder. Similarly, Herzog's painful experiences bring him finally to reject the regnant ideas of contemporary Romanticism, to reject, that is, the varieties of existentialism which have run rampant through much of the literature and philosophy of the last fifty years. The most difficult aspects of the novel are those which call upon the reader's knowledge of twentieth-century intellectual history. For those who have wrestled with the same questions that Herzog has, these aspects are precisely what set *Herzog* aside as a uniquely Bellovian achievement. There is a truly savage humor in Herzog's root-and-branch assault on Spengler, Heidegger, Buber, Sartre, and their American disciples. Writing to Madeleine's psychiatrist, Herzog complains,

> I'm sure you know the views of Buber. It is wrong to turn a man (a subject) into a thing (an object). By means of spiritual dialogue, the I-it relationship becomes an I-Thou relationship. God comes and goes in man's soul. And men come and go in each other's souls. Sometimes they come and go in each other's beds, too. You have dialogue with a man. You have intercourse with his wife. . . . And somehow it is all mysteriously translated into depth. [p. 64]

Writing to Shapiro, his rival, Herzog goes out after Spengler, T. S. Eliot, Sartre, Heidegger, and the *Frankfurter Institut für Sozialforschung* (which turned Marx's concept of alienation into a philosophical pass-key): "The canned sauerkraut of Spengler's 'Russian Socialism,' the commonplaces of the Wasteland outlook, the cheap mental stimulants of Alienation, the cant and rant of pipsqueaks about Inauthenticity and Forlornness. I can't accept this foolish dreariness. . . . It was easy for the Wastelanders to be assimilated to totalitarianism" (pp. 74–75). By the "Wastelanders" Herzog means not the allegedly "banalized" masses of industrial society, but the intellectuals—Eliot, Pound, Lawrence, Wyndham Lewis—whose scornful elitism belittled the humanity of modern man. Writing much later to Mermelstein, another rival, Herzog condemns again "safe, comfortable people playing at crisis, aliena- tion, apocalypse and desperation." His humane response to existen- tialist bombast is the now-familiar dictum of old Schlossberg: Be human. "I am simply a human being," cries Herzog, "more or less" (pp. 316–317).

As such, he turns for help to others who can return his love. He turns to Ramona, not as his Romantic salvation but as another human, with faults as real as his own. Early in the book Ramona brings forth from Herzog a deeply irrational response which he refers to as "Quack! A sexual reflex that had nothing to do with age or subtlety, wisdom, experience, history, *Wissenschaft, Bildung, Wahrheit.* In sickness or health there came the old quack-quack- at the fragrance of perfumed, feminine skin" (p. 23). Big Latinate words are followed by small Germanic ones. Large philosophical thoughts are followed by small physical stirrings. So be it.

The book ends where it begins—as a narrative structure—with Herzog alone in the Berkshires, sharing his pastoral retreat with field mice and the stars. He is content, without a want. To Mrs. Tuttle, who raises too much dust while she cleans the house, he calls, "Damp it down" (p. 341)—which is, after all, what he has said in response to Heidegger and Sartre. He is of a piece, complete.

Herzog appeared in the same year as Bellow's two-act comedy, *The Last Analysis,* of which the revised version was published in 1965. The play dramatizes another time of troubles which comes to a happy end. In this case, the central figure is Philip Bummidge, once a clown, now a philosopher-psychiatrist about to demonstrate to a closed-circuit TV audience his method of therapy through reenact- ment. The comedy is twofold. In the first place, there is the spoof on Sigmund Freud. Bummidge's acceptance of psychoanalytic dogmas seems to be complete. Only his attempts to act them out make them seem ridiculous; this gives the comedy its intellectual bite. In addi- tion, there are the rather conventional complications of plot as Bummidge's friends and relatives converge on him in the hour immediately prior to his videocast. Their ridiculous desires combine with his rather absurd purpose to produce pandemonium. One need only name the *dramatis personae* to imagine the farcical occasion:

Bummidge the clown-philosopher-psychiatrist, his estranged wife, his estranged son, his estranged sister, his estranged cousin, his estranged girl-friend, his devoted secretary, his devoted assistant (formerly a rat-catcher), and several other characters. All take part in Bummidge's televised Existenz-Action-Self-analysis, which Bummidge's querulous relatives assume to have been a fiasco. But Fiddleman the promoter arrives with a handful of checks. Bummidge's reenactment of the birth of a soul has been a thundering success: "Everybody in New York from caveman to egghead. What excitement! Since Valentino's funeral, I haven't seen such a spontaneous mob. Women kissed the television screens. And strangers were hugging and dancing. They wept with laughter, or else they grinned as they were sobbing—sometimes it's hard to tell. The place was like the deck of the *Titanic*" (p. 103). When Bummidge recovers from his strenuous efforts, he spurns Fiddleman's millions in order to dedicate himself to good works, first of which will be the metamorphosis of the Kalbfuss Palace of Meat into the world headquarters of Bummidgean therapy. A funny play, no doubt; but scarcely a profound one.

Mr. Sammler's Planet (1970), the novel that Bellow wrote after *The Last Analysis,* is a profound work, the novel which many believe to be Bellow's finest achievement. However, its comedy is limited. Sammler, in his seventies, is a half-blind survivor of the Holocaust. With one eye, he sees more clearly than most, but his vision is nonetheless impaired. Bellow undoubtedly stands behind Sammler, as he stands behind Asa Leventhal, Augie March, Eugene Henderson, and (much more closely) Moses Herzog, but Sammler is an older, narrower, more crotchety and opinionated Saul Bellow. Sammler's sorrowfully witty condemnations of modern society are based upon a humanistic belief in a moral sense which tells us, even when we err, what it means to be human. To temper the earnestness of Sammler's moral sense, Bellow surrounds his hero with comic examples of human folly, his wacky extended family who continually interrupt his philosophizing. But the action of the novel is, finally, tragic. Sammler mourns the loss of cultural and spiritual values. He laments the death of his nephew, a good man whose fate he soon must share.

Interviewed in the *New York Times* on the occasion of the publication of *Humboldt's Gift* (1975), Bellow described that novel as an attempt to deal with modern American society. It is a social comedy in the sense that it dramatizes Bellow's wonder and amazement at the richness, variety, delights, and horror of contemporary America. There are a thousand pleasurable recognitions in the book. It's a crazy world we live in. And yet . . . Charles Citrine, the successful writer, says about Von Humboldt Fleisher—his model, friend, burden, enemy, benefactor—that he was "the Mozart of conversation. . . . His monologue was an oratorio in which he sang and played all parts." Bellow is still, at sixty plus, the Mozart of American literature, but the lyrical prose and the leading parts have suddenly become predictable. This is a painful criticism to make. Bellow's weakest work contains moments beyond the reach of most of his rivals, but *Humboldt's Gift* is, unfortunately, his weakest work. That the novel received the very award which Humboldt richly ridiculed—the Pulitzer Prize ("for the birds—for the pullets . . . given by crooks and illiterates" [p. 3])—confirms Humboldt's ridicule.

We know the music. The prose is inventive, allusive, capable of sudden shifts in tone and reference. With Bellow behind him, Humboldt can move "easily from the tabloids to General Rommel and from Rommel to John Donne and T. S. Eliot. . . . And this rained down on me with references to Polish socialism and football tactics of George Halas and the secret motives of Arnold Toynbee, and (somehow) the used-car business"[12] It's grand, it's witty, it's fun—but it's also familiar, all too familiar. Citrine's voice isn't Augie March's, and it isn't Moses Herzog's, but it is undoubtedly the voice of a character by Saul Bellow. We've heard the voice; we know the lyrics.

What is worse, we know the parts. The characters and situations are too close to those in *Herzog*. Humboldt resembles Moses Herzog. Of course, there are differences. In biographical details, Humboldt is drawn largely from the poet Delmore Schwartz, while Herzog's features are plainly those of Saul Bellow. But the Herzogian megalomania is there, the desire to be marvelous, the *chutzpah*, and, especially, the professional rivalry. Parallels abound. Herzog composes letters to great men, living and dead; Humboldt imagined that he might become an influential advisor to

[12]Saul Bellow, *Humboldt's Gift* (New York: Viking Press, 1975), p. 31. All other references to the novel are cited in the text.

Adlai Stevenson. The rhetorical resemblances are frequently precise. Herzog liked puns: "Lead us not into Penn Station," he prays. Von Humboldt Fleisher is obsessed by puns: "Two is company, Three is a Kraut" (p. 333). Citrine is infected, too: "To air it is human, to bare it divine" (p. 337). Is this Bellow's parody of Heller-Vonnegut humor? Other Herzogian traits appear in Charles Citrine, whose girlfriend, busty Renata, is reminiscent of Herzog's Ramona. More serious is the parallel between vindictive Madeleine Herzog and vindictive Denise Citrine. Again the husband suffers through a divorce, persecuted by the revengeful wife. Again lawyers are portrayed as selfish, hardened men whose cannibalism serves to instruct the naive writer in the realities of modern *mores*. There are repetitive details as well. When Shapiro discusses existentialism with Madeleine, he betrays his crassness: ". . . she opened the jar of pickled herring. Saliva spurted to Shapiro's lips. Quickly, he pressed his folded handkerchief to the corners of his mouth. Herzog remembers him as a greedy eater" (p. 73). Consider Citrine's brother Julius: "The fish which he was supposed to bring home was eaten. We sat with him under a tree sucking at the breast-sized, flame-colored fruit. The juice spurted over his sport suit, and seeing that it now had to go to the cleaner anyway he wiped his fingers on it as well" (p. 397).

Charles Citrine's involvement with the petty mafioso, Rinaldo Cantabile, is the liveliest and at the same time the most overdone part of the book. Here, too, one suffers from a sense of *déjà vu*—what does Cantabile owe to Augie March's gangster pals, Joe Gorman and Sailor Bulba? What does he owe to the Negro pickpocket who menaces Mr. Sammler? How different is proud Cantabile's humiliation of Citrine—whom he forces to climb out on the girders of an unfinished skyscraper in order to fling money to the winds—from the black man's demonstration of genital power? Sandor Himmelstein's tough-guy tirade ended with a pathetic plea for Herzog's help with his daughter Carmen. Similarly, Rinaldo Cantabile's display of hoodlum pique leads to his request that Citrine help his wife with her Ph.D. dissertation.

There is, finally, Citrine's absorption in the mystical theories of Rudolf Steiner. The parallel here is to Sammler's fascination with the work of Meister Eckhart.

No doubt, there are many splendid moments in Bellow's latest comedy. The reversal at the end, where Humboldt's legacy of a wild manuscript he and Citrine had once worked on suddenly becomes a valuable piece of film property, is a fine irony. The once-popular poet who fell into neglect rises again as a master of the newest media. There are, en route to the Happy Ending, a hundred scenes and a thousand turns of phrase that make the book an essential part of Bellow's canon. But the triumphs of *Henderson the Rain King, Herzog,* and *Mr. Sammler's Planet* have not been equaled. Nobody's perfect.

SHELDON GREBSTEIN

The Comic Anatomy
of *Portnoy's Complaint*

In the surge of Jewish-American fiction that began about twenty-five
years ago—a body of writing comprising perhaps the most significant and visible movement in American literature since World War
II—three novels occupy a special eminence. Bernard Malamud's
Assistant remains, after two decades, its most powerful moral statement of the basic Jewish-American theme of redemptive suffering,
as well as a superlative example of the ethnic style which fuses
Yiddish and English. Saul Bellow's *Herzog* stands as the Jewish
movement's leading novel of ideas, as well as perhaps its most
accomplished work of art in the richness and variety of craft and
materials. Philip Roth's *Portnoy's Complaint* must be recognized as
the comic masterpiece of this body of writing, and a remarkably
funny, irreverent, daring book by any standards.

Humor is hardly Roth's exclusive domain. From its inception the
Jewish movement has been characterized by a strong component
of comedy: often dark, as in Malamud's story "The German
Refugee," which mixes the death camps, suicide, and hilarious
mimicry into a peculiar but compelling synthesis; frequently
naughty, as in the long passage in *Herzog* which recounts the hero's
after-dinner seduction by the delectable Ramona; sometimes man-
ifestly self-hating and anti-Semitic, as in Bruce Jay Friedman's
Stern. But until *Portnoy's Complaint* no single literary work had

treated the subject of being Jewish in modern America with such brutal candor and comic genius. The major topics of *Portnoy's Complaint*—sexuality, family life, and Jewish self-hatred —frequently inspire comic treatment in the work of Bellow, Malamud, Singer, Friedman, Herbert Gold, and other Jewish-American writers, but nowhere with Roth's concentration, intensity, or profane gusto.

To approach *Portnoy's Complaint* as a "literary work" seems a little artificial and pretentious. The word "performance" appears to be much more appropriate. No voice quite like Portnoy's had ever spoken to us from the pages of an American book. What is immediately evoked for most readers is the "live" performance of stage and nightclub, the attractive-repulsive, brilliant-neurotic, awful-hilarious, aggressive-self-destructive Jewish stand-up comedian, perhaps epitomized in Lenny Bruce, who also exploited sexuality, obscenity, the burden of being Jewish, and the display of his tortured ego for painful laughs. Indeed, one interviewer, writing soon after the novel's appearance, asserted that "the first few pages of Bruce's autobiography, *How to Talk Dirty and Influence People,* is like the archetype of *Portnoy's Complaint* both in the manner in which the bits are strung together and in the kind of material used."[1] Certainly Jewish comics are a factor in Portnoy's consciousness, as he begs to be released from his "role . . . of the smothered son in the Jewish joke." In the same passage, as evidence of his sensitivity to media influence, Portnoy cites Sam Levenson, Myron Cohen, Henny Youngman, and Milton Berle, not as mere entertainers but as "black humorists" whose "macabre" evocation of laughter depends upon a world of unbearable Jewish family relationships.[2]

Viewed in the light of Irving Howe's acute observations on the prominence and significance of the host of Jewish comedians who flourished in the 1950's and 1960's, it becomes easier to understand both the affinity of *Portnoy's Complaint* with some aspects of popular culture and one factor in its enormous success. I speculate that *Portnoy's Complaint,* published in 1969, capitalized on the

[1]Howard Junker, "Will This Finally Be Philip Roth's Year?" *New York Magazine,* January 13, 1969, p. 46. On the similarity of *Portnoy's Complaint* to live comedy, see Irving Howe, "Philip Roth Reconsidered," *Commentary,* 54 (December, 1972), 69–77; and Sanford Pinsker, *The Comedy That "Hoits"* (Columbia: University of Missouri Press, 1975), pp. 55–71.

[2]Philip Roth, *Portnoy's Complaint* (New York: Random House, 1969), p. 112. All other references to the novel are cited in the text.

"Yiddishization of American humor," represented not only by Levenson, Cohen, Berle, and Youngman, but also by Sid Caesar, Woody Allen, Shelly Berman, Jack Carter, Jan Murray, Jackie Miles, Buddy Hackett, Jack E. Leonard, Mort Sahl, Mike Nichols and Elaine May, Alan King, Jackie Mason, etc. No longer limited to New York, Miami, or Borscht Belt audiences but promulgated nationally by television, American comedy became dominated by performers whose styles and routines, however varied, relied heavily on ethnic materials and Yiddishisms. As Howe points out in his magisterial *World of our Fathers,* these comedians at once aggressively asserted and abused their Jewish identity. Instead of the sentimentalism or dialect comedy exploited by such earlier entertainers as Al Jolson, Fanny Brice, and Eddie Cantor, these postwar comics were satirical. If for a moment we think of Alexander Portnoy as a stand-up comic of the new generation, Howe's analysis applies with extraordinary accuracy:

> . . . the stand-up comics of the fifties and sixties knew that they might milk a laugh out of a snarling return to Jewish mothers and other shared embarrassment. Embarrassment was an important element in this humor, as it had been in the humor of Jewish entertainers thirty or forty years ago; but now it became more needling, less innocent, given to malice and savage abrasions—the self-contempt of Jews embarrassed not so much out of the culture from which they had emerged (or, as some felt, escaped), but about the shame they could still feel at their own ethnic denials and evasions.[3]

Even Portnoy's manner of delivery resembles that of the stand-up comic: the *shpritz* (literally "spray" or "outpouring"), which has been defined as "the spontaneous satire that gathers momentum and energy as it goes along, spiraling finally into the exhilarating anarchy of total freedom from inhibition."[4] Of course, this release is never obtained by Portnoy as a psychological condition; rather, it is expressed as the bravado to open up dark and fetid cellars of experience and to utter words forbidden to respectable folk.

The kinship between the routines of popular Jewish comedians and Roth's performance in *Portnoy's Complaint* may be documented further. Theodore Solotaroff, who knew Roth from graduate school days at the University of Chicago, recalls the comic

---

[3]Irving Howe, *World of Our Fathers* (New York: Harcourt Brace Jovanovich, 1976), p. 569.

[4]Albert Goldman, quoted, *ibid.,* p. 571.

gift Roth often displayed at parties in recounting "Jewish jokes and caustic family anecdotes" with "fantastic mimicry and wit." For Solotaroff, who published two of the episodes of *Portnoy* in *New American Review* before the novel was completed, "the comedian of those Chicago sessions of nostalgia, revenge, and general purgation had landed right in the middle of his own fiction." Solotaroff also remarks on the similarity between the novel's method and that of the stand-up comic: "the contemporary winging art and humor of improvisation and release."[5]

Paradoxically, Roth himself denies the direct influence of popular comedy. In the series of interviews and essays collected in *Reading Myself and Others*, a body of commentary which constitutes the fullest dossier on *Portnoy's Complaint* and in some respects its most illuminating criticism, Roth at once affirms his admiration for such performers as Bruce and the Second City group for "that joining of precise social observation with extravagant and dreamlike fantasy," and rejects them as his primary inspirations. Instead, Roth pays homage to "a sit-down comic named Franz Kafka." For Roth, "guilt as a comic idea," an idea derived from Kafka, provided the momentum he needed to release himself from the more conventional concerns of his earlier work. There is an element of self-contradiction in Roth's denial, however, for elsewhere in his observations on *Portnoy's Complaint* he refers to his hero's life as "drama, or vaudeville skit," and to the hero himself as "babbling sinner/showman seeking absolution/applause." Who has not conceived the same thought while watching some driven, demonic comic or emcee lash himself into ever more frenetic and vulgar self-revelations as the audience howls, part in laughter, part in shame? Roth has also taken care to fend off too autobiographical and personal a reading, insisting that his private *Weltanschauung* remains undisclosed: "Imbedded in parody, burlesque, slapstick, ridicule, insult, invective, lampoon, wisecrack, in nonsense, in levity, in *play*."[6]

Roth's attribution of the Kafka influence is intriguing, but not so

---

[5]Theodore Solotaroff, "Philip Roth: A Personal View," in *The Red Hot Vacuum* (New York: Atheneum, 1970), pp. 313, 323, 326.

[6]Philip Roth, *Reading Myself and Others* (New York: Farrar, Straus and Giroux, 1975). The quotations are, respectively, from pp. 21, 22, 94, 31–32. Henceforth all criticism of Roth should begin with his own critical expositions and *apologia*, collected in *Reading Myself and Others*.

much for the form of *Portnoy's Complaint*. Suffice it to say that Kafka could use the monologue with consummate skill, as in "A Report to the Academy" and "The Burrow," and Roth may have learned something from them; but Kafka's method is cool, his language spare, taut, understated, his diction genteel, his allusions to sexuality and Jewishness carefully repressed. Only in the letter to his father does Kafka's own voice speak with the naked intensity of Portnoy's, and in that, of course, Kafka was not writing fiction for an audience. In sum, whatever the impact of Kafka's example upon Roth's imagination—and there is no reason to doubt it—the direct influence is neither structural nor stylistic. In contrast, the debt to Kafka in Roth's next novel, *The Breast*, hardly requires explanation.

The literary affiliations of *Portnoy's Complaint* have provoked considerable critical attention. By consensus, it belongs to the tradition of the *Bildungsroman*. Strong similarities are evident between Portnoy's attempts to break free of his family and culture, and the protagonists' ordeals in *A Portrait of the Artist* and *Sons and Lovers*. Like Paul Morel, Alexander Portnoy is entrapped in an Oedipal situation from which he escapes physically but remains confined and crippled psychologically. Like Stephen Dedalus, Portnoy aspires "to forge in the smithy of my soul the uncreated conscience of my race." Like Stephen, Alex rebels against received opinion and unexamined practice, risking exile in an awareness almost too acute to be tolerable. As a comic-ethnic version of the archetypal scheme of quest and initiation, the hero is bereft of his innocence somewhat earlier than most. He is wounded at home, rather than in the world (except here the world is the home), and he struggles against improbable antagonists, i.e., mother and father, rather than hostile strangers. Nevertheless, the hero sets out to seek a worthy goal, self-acceptance, and persists in it despite the vicissitudes of circumstance and self-administered rebuffs. The problem is that the good quest for the Self becomes confused with another no less intriguing but perhaps ideally less worthy quest: for the perfect lay.

One student of *Portnoy* has also suggested interesting sources and analogs in *The Satyricon* and *Tristram Shandy*, especially the latter. Both *Portnoy* and *Shandy* use the nose as a source of humor and sexual symbolism. Both heroes suffer from castration complexes; both struggle with family heritage and personal identity; both have impaired fathers disappointed in their sons. In both novels the plot is episodic and circular. Patricia Meyer Spacks, in an admirable essay, places *Portnoy's Complaint* in the picaresque mode by dint of the novel's loose structure and its hero's roguery and solitude.[7]

These are all fertile suggestions, but they do not much help us to place Roth's technique. For this we can look to a native American tradition. Perhaps the most immediate and pertinent source or analog for *Portnoy's Complaint,* one which melds *belles lettres* with popular entertainment, is the colloquial seriocomic monologue and tall tale, originally developed by the Old Southwestern humorists a century ago and perfected by Mark Twain in written and "live" performance.[8]

The vaudevillian's or stand-up comic's routine is itself indebted to this tradition, while its earlier twentieth-century literary practitioners—for example, Ring Lardner and Sinclair Lewis—developed it into an effective comic and satiric mode. Indeed, Lewis's *Man Who Knew Coolidge,* published some thirty years before *Portnoy's Complaint,* is a direct predecessor of Roth's work. Although Roth was undoubtedly familiar with such major novels as *Babbitt,* and thus cognizant of the self-exposing monologues omnipresent in Lewis, I do not mean to suggest that Roth consciously borrowed from Lewis. I am trying to establish a line of succession, rather than a case for attribution. From that perspective, there are a number of interesting parallels between *Portnoy* and *Coolidge.*

Lewis's work, like Roth's, consists of a book-length satirical monologue spoken by a single protagonist to an identified but silent audience. Like Roth's, it is divided into a series of parts or sections which fit neatly into a sequence or totality, yet could stand as self-contained entities. By a striking coincidence, each book has six such sections. Portions of both works originally appeared in periodicals, although in Lewis's case the book-length work developed from

[7]Pinsker, *Comedy,* pp. 61–62, for example, comments on the novel's place in the *Bildungsroman* tradition, and on the affinities with Lawrence and Joyce. See Robert Dupree, "And the Mom Roth Outgrabe Or, What Hath Got Roth," *Arlington Quarterly,* 2 (Autumn, 1970), 175–189, for the *Portnoy, Satyricon, Shandy* analogies. Patricia Meyer Spacks, "About Portnoy," *Yale Review,* 58 (Summer, 1969), 623–635, deals with the picaresque and offers many other stimulating observations.

[8]Although he does not treat *Portnoy's Complaint,* Bernard F. Rodgers, Jr., "*The Great American Novel* and 'The Great American Joke,' " *Critique,* 16 (1974), 12–29, establishes illuminating connections between Roth's work and native American humor.

a single episode published in H. L. Mencken's *American Mercury*. Both books emphasize the protagonists' social circumstances and backgrounds as determinants of attitude and psyche, and in both the characters are obsessed by the behavioral norms established for the group to which they belong. Lewis's figure, Lowell Schmaltz, yammers as maddeningly about his professedly All-American conduct (the subtitle of the book is "Being the Soul of Lowell Schmaltz, Constructive and Nordic Citizen") as Portnoy relentlessly worries his Jewishness. Concomitantly, both heroes are highly conscious of such matters as status, reputation, and "face," although Schmaltz is apt to consistently bluster and bluff where Portnoy vacillates between arrogance and abasement.

Each novel depends essentially on its writer's mimetic abilities. Lewis reproduces a banal, colloquial, standard midwestern American, replete with current slang and catch phrases, yet decorated with purple patches borrowed from advertising, popular literature, patriotic addresses. Roth's idiom is that of the educated eastern-urban Jew with humble origins. Both writers, keen observers and skilled chroniclers of manners, particularize their narratives with names, signs, emblems, products, and topical references which are instantly suggestive to their contemporary audiences. Conversely, foreign readers or those removed in time would require a glossary and footnotes to understand the dense detail, and even then much of its purport would be lost. A good many allusions in *Coolidge* are already recondite, and I can imagine the same fate befalling *Portnoy* a generation hence. In fact, Lewis has anticipated the future and heightened his satire by providing sardonic footnotes identifying such notables as Mrs. Rinehart, Peter B. Kyne, Arthur Brisbane, Dr. Frank Crane, and Gene Tunney (whom he lists as "Another celebrated athlete, much influenced by G. Bernard Shaw").[9] Yet the elements of timeliness and specificity of detail are intrinsic to satire, which is a form of history, a deliberately exaggerated chronicle of attitudes and manners that achieves a sort of truth through its very distortions of reality. To illustrate, here is a sample of Lowell Schmaltz's utterances:

[9]Sinclair Lewis, *The Man Who Knew Coolidge* (New York: Harcourt, Brace, 1928), p. 47. Stanley Cooperman, "Philip Roth: 'Old Jacob's Eye' with a Squint," *Twentieth Century Literature*, 19 (July, 1973), 203–216, makes a passing comparison of Roth and Lewis but with no specific Lewis novel.

I've learned a lot here lately. I've been studying and delving into psychoanalysis. Know anything about psychoanalysis?

Well, I do, and say, it certainly is a revelation. I've read almost clear through a manual on it—a very authoritative book written by a lady, Miss Alexandrine Applebaugh, that's a great authority on the subject, because she studied with a man that was a pupil of one of the biggest pupils of old Freud, and it was Freud that invented psychoanalysis.

Well, now I'll explain what psychoanalysis is. It's like this:

Everybody ought to have a rich, full sex-life, and all human activities are directed toward that. Whenever a guy is doing something, it's directed toward making himself attractive sexually, especially if it's something big and important—no matter whether it's painting a picture or putting over a big deal in Florida Town-Lots or discovering a new eclipse or pitching in a World Series game or preaching a funeral sermon or writing a big advertisement or any of them things. On the other hand, when fellows like us do put over something, we want to be appreciated, and we got a right to expect it, and if we don't get appreciated at home, we ought to find new mates, see how I mean?

Only you get into so doggone many complications and trouble and all that maybe it ain't practical, even with a cute girl like this one in New York I was speaking about—Ain't really worth it.[10]

This is, of course, ridicule through a parodic representation of American popular speech and of the level of public mentality, 1920's vintage, on such arcane matters as psychoanalysis. It is not characterization, but caricature: the cartoon achieved is Mencken's version of Swift's Yahoo—the "Boobus Americanus." Like virtually all of Lewis's creations, Lowell Schmaltz is simultaneously flat and vivid, grotesque and easily recognizable. The method of humor here is essentially that of tastelessness or *reductio*. Alexandrine Applebaugh, Freud, sexual fulfillment, art, real estate speculation, scientific discovery, professional athletics, funeral sermons, and advertising are all perceived on the same level of value. Unfortunately for Lewis, by the time he wrote *Coolidge* the performance of his mimetic skill had become its own sufficient reason. There are no delayed revelations in the book, no tension, suspense; it's all brilliant surface—Babbitt's speech before the Zenith Real Estate Board expanded *ad infinitum*. One sketch is amusing and memorable; three

[10]Lewis, *Man Who Knew Coolidge*, pp. 172–174.

hundred pages of it verges on the intolerable. However, to Lewis's credit, we must recall that no one in America before him had created this particular kind of *tour de force*.

As a comic writer and craftsman, Roth surpasses Lewis considerably. The blatant irony of Lewis's subtitle is that Schmaltz has no soul, or at least Lewis permits him none. The reader remains too aware of Lewis as ventriloquist and puppeteer, despite the use of the subjective voice whose greatest literary asset is its immediacy and aura of verisimilitude. Everything in Lewis's performance is contrived to make us despise Schmaltz as he is, without allowing us to care or understand how he became as he is. In contrast, not only is Roth's approach to characterization psychoanalytic, but so is its method, its very style and voice. The overt situation of Portnoy's addressing himself to a listening but (until the end) silent psychiatrist is not merely a convenient stratagem or situation for the monologue; it functions as necessary or organic form. Portnoy's tirade is most coherent from a clinical standpoint, as a series of hysterical outpourings which are a mimesis of the stream-of-association unburdening of patient to doctor. The incredible rapidity and intensity of the language attempt to re-create the reality of hysteria, as the patient relives in his reminiscences those traumas responsible for his present condition. But that condition cannot be relieved until the traumas are re-experienced, in effect, re-expressed, in their original force and agony. Thus, the language itself must be the vehicle for the reenactment of the past. It cannot merely be said; it must be *felt*. The style of *Portnoy's Complaint* is the rhetoric of hysteria, or perhaps the rhetoric of neurosis.

Moreover, style correlates with structure. The thematic structure is governed by two kinds of logic. First, there is the simple and superficial logic of chronology, as the narrator moves from his earliest memories to the present moment, or the "now" of his speaking voice, finally revealing in the closing pages the "illness"—his impotence—which has brought him at age thirty-three to the psychiatrist's couch. Second, and far more important, there is the logic of psychoanalysis, the deeper and deeper delving into the experiences which have produced the malfunction of what, for this particular hero, is the most vital part of his anatomy. In the simplest sense, Portnoy's complaint is his *schlong*.

The logic of psychoanalysis can also account for the novel's formal organization. Each of the various sections could be described not only as a phase in Portnoy's unburdening to Dr. Spielvogel, but as actual sessions or visits.[11] Although the book is hardly a model of tight or symmetrical form, there is a kind of architectonic proportioning in the length and arrangement of the separate parts, an order of increasing intensity and climax suggested by the first three gradually building and lengthening sections, a long middle, then two concluding sections of decreasing length.

Of course, none of these patterns of arrangement or logic is pure. Purity would be an anomaly; order and consistency are not Portnoy's strengths. As in life, the patient's account of his problems does not fit into perfectly tidy compartments. Past cannot be clearly separated from present; motive is subsumed by act; instinct is filtered through concept. All are inextricably and incongruously intertwined, especially in a highly educated, keenly intelligent, acutely sensitive Jew—for whom act and idea, event and feeling, are rarely separate. In fact, these confusions and juxtapositions are at the center, the root, so to speak, of Portnoy's problem. They also engender much of the novel's humor. Nevertheless, the thematic logic or continuity does persist enough so that we can understand Portnoy's impotence as deriving directly from the affair with the Monkey, with its erotic climax in the Rome hotel, soon followed by his abandonment of her. Both the orgy of group sex and the abandonment have stricken him in the conscience, which, in turn, descends into his being and becomes localized in the agency of his manhood. Since Portnoy's impairment or crippling is psychological and self-induced, we can afford to laugh.

There is yet a subtler logic of argument. As the book progresses, the weight of blame for what the child has become, at first placed on the parents, is shifted to the child-now-man. True, the Oedipal involvement with Mother persists from start to finish; it supplies the novel's frame and one of its major ideas. As frame, the Oedipal motif is introduced at the very beginning, in that the young Alex's

[11]The whole matter of Portnoy and psychoanalysis has hardly escaped critical attention. Bruno Bettelheim, in an admirable and insightful spoof, has provided a visit-by-visit diagnosis of Portnoy's complaints in "Portnoy Psychoanalyzed: therapy notes found in the files of Dr. O. Spielvogel, a New York psychoanalyst," *Midstream*, 15 (June/July, 1969), 3–10. See also Lois G. Gordon, " 'Portnoy's Complaint': Coming of Age in Jersey City," *Literature and Psychology*, 19 (1969), 57–60; and Mark Shechner, "Philip Roth," *Partisan Review*, 41 (1974), 410–427. Shechner deems *Portnoy* "the most spectacular attempt at Freudian fiction in recent American literature."

first idea of sexuality is formed upon his mother's flesh, with her silk-stocking routine; for him she becomes the total female. At the end, he is prostrate and beaten—like a child before its mother—by a strapping woman, Naomi, who not only apotheosizes the total female, but even *looks* like Portnoy's mother. She stands for a higher culture and stronger values than he possesses; she is herself without sin; she rejects him for his faults. Even her size—just as the child visualizes his parent—is gigantic. At the end, as at the beginning, he is locked out of his "home," a bad boy who fancies himself an authentic criminal.

To return to some earlier considerations of *Portnoy's Complaint* as "performance," the novel's organization can also be seen as analogous to a series of improvisations. Just as no patient can prepare and follow a precise script in a visit to the analyst, the novel proceeds by the loose association of what Roth himself called "blocks of consciousness."[12] The very randomness and unpredictability of what is narrated, the sudden shifts in time, locale, and situation, create exactly that ambience of fluidity and surprise which is most congenial to the genre of low comedy. Central to this is an incessant stream of dramatizations or skits, with Portnoy playing all the roles as well as that of commentator.

There are three basic kinds of skits in *Portnoy's Complaint:* elimination (bathroom) skits, eating (kitchen) skits, and sex (bedroom) skits. These physical functions are, of course, fundamental and archetypal sources of comedy, especially slapstick and burlesque. In his unrestrained imagination, Roth often intermixes all three. For example, in the series of masturbation skits which provide the novel's raunchiest and most daring comedy, the adolescent Portnoy barricades himself in the family bathroom—purportedly in the throes of digestive upset, which his intolerably solicitous mother blames on the gorging of bad food *(chazerai);* actually, he is frantically relieving his lusts. For better or worse, this epic masturbation skit, which features the whole family—constipated father and worried mother alternately pounding on the bathroom door, while young Portnoy strives to bring himself off into his sister's bra— is unique in the annals of comic writing. Or Portnoy makes love to various comestibles: e.g., a cored apple, or a piece of liver later

[12]Roth, *Reading Myself and Others,* p. 15.

served as the family's dinner. The latter are not actual skits but outlines or scenarios, sketched in a few lines of evocative prose.

As boy becomes man, masturbation-food skits develop into oral sexuality. The first encounter with the delectable Monkey begins with this form of sexual gusto, and such intimacies continue to characterize their torrid relationship. In the background of this food-sex association there hover Jewish injunctions against both Gentile girls and non-kosher food. As dramatizations of Portnoy's case history, masturbation, pursuits of the forbidden *shikse,* and the predilection for giving and receiving oral gratification interweave and contrast with the childhood recollections of home and kitchen ruled by mother. As Mark Shechner has pointed out, "Food is to Jewish comedy and Jewish neurosis what drink is to the Irish."[13] In the comic logic of the novel, the food skits are Jewish—as in Mrs. Portnoy's dramatic rendition of her perilous encounter with lobster—while the sex skits are *goyish.* Father Portnoy suffers the worst fate that can befall a decent Jewish man, constipation. For the son, as he imagines in a characteristically funny and awful juvenile fantasy, the worst fate is the loss of his organ: transformed by venereal disease (contracted beyond the Pale) into a petrified object which disengages itself from Portnoy's body and drops with a clink to the kitchen floor.

These materials, particularly the vivid re-creations of Portnoy's sexual adventures, border on the pornographic. Certainly the affair with Monkey, in its emphasis on the orgiastic, on her easy readiness and lubricity, and on Portnoy's own redoubtable virility, resemble some of the formulaic elements of porn. It is a risk deliberately taken by Roth, this teetering along the edge of the grossly obscene. But if many of his readers were offended—especially those with presuppositions about what was fitting for a Jewish writer and his creations—others were delighted by Roth's skill. If the novel's skits and situations are often crude, the presence of phenomenal wit, inspired wackiness of invention, and dazzling turns of language deflect our attention from the vulgarity. As in the richest comedy, we respond not so much to what is happening in front of us (which may be quite awful), but to its mode of happening.

The language of *Portnoy's Complaint,* as of all comic fiction, is

[13]Shechner, "Roth," p. 416.

essential to its mode of happening. While the skit and the incongruous juxtaposition of ideas and values are important, language is more
important. The live performer has gesture, voice, timing, facial
expression, and group dynamics to work with, and often the drum-
beats and sound effects provided by a musical back-up; the writer has
only the written language and the limited resources of typography. In
fact, with these relatively sparse means Roth attempts to transform
the visual medium into the aural, to imitate the distinctive voice so
crucial to the delivery of the stand-up comic. For example, a series of
exclamatory sentences, often interspersed or in combination with a
series of interrogatives that are really declarations, convey the rising tone, rhythm, and effect of the build-up to climax, a type of
accelerando which requires either a scream or a laugh to release. I
quote a relatively innocuous and "clean" passage to illustrate this
speed-effect and necessary comic discharge:

> I am something called "a weekend guest"? I am something called
> "a friend from school"? What tongue is she speaking? I am "the
> *bonditt*," "the *vantz*," I am the insurance man's son. I am
> Warshaw's ambassador! "How do you do, Alex?" To which of
> course I reply, "Thank you." Whatever anybody says to me during
> my first twenty-four hours in Iowa, I answer, "Thank you." Even to
> inanimate objects. I walk into a chair, promptly I say to it, "Excuse
> me, thank you." I drop my napkin on the floor, lean down, flushing,
> to pick it up, "Thank you," I hear myself saying to the napkin—or is
> it the floor I'm addressing? Would my mother be proud of her little
> gent. Polite even to the furniture! [p. 220]

The most intense passages, which aspire to a roaring and painful
hilarity, are skits or bursts of mimicry conducted at peak volume, as
conveyed by sentence patterns, italics, exclamations, capital letters,
and a chorus of impersonated voices dubbed in by that expert
ventriloquist, Alexander Portnoy. Portnoy's favorite impressions
are, of course, of his parents, especially Mother, as in this brief
example: "'DON'T RUN FIRST THING TO A BLONDIE, PLEASE!
BECAUSE SHE'LL TAKE YOU FOR ALL YOU'RE WORTH AND THEN
LEAVE YOU BLEEDING IN THE GUTTER! A BRILLIANT INNOCENT
BABY BOY LIKE YOU, SHE'LL EAT YOU UP ALIVE!" (p. 189)
But the zaniest and most feverish of these full-blast episodes are
the events and imaginings devolving from the visit to Bubbles
Girardi, Portnoy's first adolescent sexual encounter. In a fantasy

sequence Portnoy returns home blinded; the scene concludes with a frantic torrent of questions to Ba-ba-lu Mandel, summarizing Alex's boyhood erotic flights. In another fantasized episode the Devil (another ghost from Portnoy's puberty, Rabbi Warshaw) indicts Portnoy for sexual selfishness, chains him to a toilet bowl, and condemns him to masturbate for eternity.

Another sort of mimicry dependent on high-volume, high-speed techniques is the interjection of imagined newspaper headlines that evoke the tabloid approach. The screaming banner, a subhead, and a photo contain most of the story worth telling (i.e., the *New York Daily News* method). Portnoy tends to visualize his fate, particularly his sexual fate, in a series of these catchy headlines:

ASST HUMAN OPP'Y COMMISH FOUND HEADLESS IN GO-GO GIRL'S APT. [p. 161]
INSURANCE MAN'S SON LEAPS TO DEATH. [p. 171]
ASST HUMAN OPP'Y COMMISH FLOGS DUMMY, Also lives in Sin, Reports Old School Chum. [p. 175]
JEW SMOTHERS DEB WITH COCK, Vassar Grad Georgetown Strangulation Victim; Mocky Lawyer Held. [p. 240]

Or, as a variation of the banner headline, Portnoy will issue a slogan reminiscent of advertising or political campaigning, for example, LET'S PUT THE ID BACK IN YID!

Although the jargon and technique of advertising are much less important to Roth than to Sinclair Lewis as a source of humor, it does sometimes appear in skit or dramatized form as one aspect of Portnoy's hyperactive media consciousness, a heightening of his tale to comic excess. For example, Portnoy stages the imagined suicide of the Monkey as though he were an advertising director. He concludes the acutely visual scene with a series of resounding epithets, undercutting the poetry and elegance of the suicide tableau, and supplying the painful surprise twist of death. (Reflect on the impact of a lingerie ad employing a *dead* model.)

> Only what about the dead girl back at the hotel? For she will have accomplished it by now, I'm sure. Thrown herself off the balcony in her underpants. Walked into the sea and drowned herself, wearing the world's tiniest bikini. No, she will take hemlock in the moonlit shadows of the Acropolis—in her Balenciaga evening gown! That empty-headed, exhibitionistic, suicidal twat! Don't worry, when she does it, it'll be photographable—it'll come out looking like an ad for

ladies' lingerie! There she'll be, as usual in the Sunday magazine
section—only dead! [p. 249]

In addition to his adaptation of newspaper and advertising styles for
comic purposes, Roth exploits radio and film. Profuse allusions to
radio shows and popular movies are augmented by skits, dramatizations, and fantasized scenes. Such bits have long been staples in the
patter of stand-up comics.

Portnoy has several favorite radio voices; among his expert imper-
sonations are those of sportcasters such as Red Barber and the
patriotic narrators of Norman Corwin's dramas. Portnoy uses these
voices early on to establish his adolescent ideals of sports hero or
super-citizen and achiever, then later juxtaposes them comically
against his lowered adult ethnic and sexual preoccupations. Again,
this is just the kind of routine we can easily imagine witnessing in a
nightclub, rather than in a book; the impersonated voice helps
transmute it from the literary sphere to the live. Here Portnoy stages
a bedroom encounter in the manner of a prizefight announcer
—suggestive also of the serious business of sexual combat which
lurks behind the burlesque:

> In the black pubic hair, ladies and gentlemen, weighing one
> hundred and seventy pounds, at least half of which is still undigested
> halvah and hot pastrami, from Newark, N.J., The Shnoz, Alexander
> Portnoy! And his opponent, in the fair fuzz, with her elegant polished
> limbs and the gentle maidenly face of a Botticelli, that ever-popular
> purveyor of the social amenities here in the Garden, one hundred and
> fourteen pounds of Republican refinement, and the pertest pair of
> nipples in all New England, from New Canaan, Connecticut, Sarah
> Abbott Maulsby! [pp. 234–235]

Many of Portnoy's boyhood fantasies of romantic conquest of
Gentile girls are cast as film scenes, as asexual and All-American as
the actual movies of the 1940's which inspire him. In these fervid
imaginings, which combine dreams of assimilation with the first
rites of adolescent passage, we have the sardonic paradox of a young
American Jew trying to hide his Jewishness because of the propaganda of Hollywood films produced in Jewish-dominated studios.
Portnoy's pubescent American Dream of Success thus provokes as
much pathos as it does laughter: "O America! America! It may have
been gold in the streets to my grandparents, it may have been a
chicken in every pot to my father and mother, but to me, a child

whose earliest movie memories are of Ann Rutherford and Alice Faye, America is a *shikse* nestling under your arm whispering love love love love love!'' (p. 146).

It is interesting, as well as amusing, that although Portnoy savagely berates his parents and his Jewish origins for warping his personality and denying him freedom from guilt, he obviously takes great pleasure in exploiting his meager though vivid vocabulary of Yiddish terms. It is also significant that Roth supplies no glossary, obviously on the assumption that the general audience has become familiar with these terms, largely via Jewish comedians. *Goy, shikse*—repeated dozens of times throughout the novel—everyone knows, of course. Many of the others are almost equally familiar: *kishkas, chazerai, shvartze, shmattas, kvetching, meshuggeneh, shlepped.* Most of the rest are obscene, especially synonyms for the male sexual organ: *putz, shlong, shmuck, shvantz.* For the one Yiddish sentence the novel contains, that familiar folk epigram which is also a simple diagnosis of Portnoy's complaint—*Ven der putz shteht, ligt der sechel in drerd*—Roth supplies an accurate but awkward translation. The same wisdom has sometimes been rendered into apocryphal Latin: *penis erectus non conscientiam habet.*

The Yiddish terms serve a range of stylistic and comic functions. Primarily they are a constant reminder of character, one of Portnoy's basic "languages" or voices. The paucity of his vocabulary, yet the persistence, even obsessiveness, with which he uses some of these terms, form a paradigm of his divided self. He knows his heritage and identity poorly and tries to escape it, but he cannot. Its voice breaks through, not only in vocabulary but also in syntax and sentence rhythms. This voice is Roth's able version of that dialect style developed and perfected by Malamud and Bellow. However, where the older writers use this style for serious or even epic effects, as well as for comedy, Roth largely turns it back to the original functions of American dialect styles: local color, satire, and humor. But Roth's skill prevents the dialect style from culminating in reductive stereotype or mere mockery. It combines with standard English, even rather formal English at one extreme, and pungent street argot at the other. The result is great fluency, constant modulation, considerable variety, and frequent surprise, as we saw above in Monkey's suicide-scene fantasy. I am tempted to offer a formulaic analysis: that Portnoy talks "Jewish" only when he speaks of his parents or his home experiences; otherwise he talks like a lawyer, or, on the subject of sex, like a street tough. But formulas do not apply. In fact, the language is unpredictable. It soars, swoops, swerves, wanders as often as his memories. Notice this crafty sentence, which suddenly dives from the elegantly belletristic to the vulgate "dork": "What strength she has stored in that slender frame—the glorious acrobatics she can perform while dangling from the end of my dork" (p. 194). With less artistry—or, to say it otherwise, with fewer voices—Roth could never hold our attention for 274 pages, nor could we bear to reread the novel. On this I must disagree with Irving Howe, who said: "The cruelest thing anyone can do with *Portnoy's Complaint* is to read it twice."[14] Even after one knows all the jokes and skits, it does support rereading on the basis of virtuosity, *performance*.

Here is one delicious sample of linguistic variety in which Roth plays off the Gentile-Jewish antithesis that is everywhere the source of humor in the novel, and simultaneously establishes subtle contrasts of language that subliminally score and record the associations suggested:

> Our eight-grade class visits the courthouse to observe the architecture. Home and in my room that night, I write in my fresh new graduation autograph album, under YOUR FAVORITE MOTTO, "Don't Step on the Underdog." MY FAVORITE PROFESSION? "Lawyer." MY FAVORITE HERO? "Tom Paine and Abraham Lincoln." Lincoln sits outside the courthouse (in Gutzon Borglum's bronze), looking tragic and fatherly: you just know how much he cares. A statue of Washington, standing erect and authoritarian in front of his horse, overlooks Broad Street; it is the work of J. Massey Rhind (we write this second unname-like name of a sculptor in our notebooks); our art teacher says that the two statues are "the city's pride," and we head off in pairs for the paintings at the Newark Museum. Washington, I must confess, leaves me cold. Maybe it's the horse, that he's leaning on a horse. At any rate, he is so obviously a *goy*. But Lincoln! I could cry. Look at him sitting there, so *oysgemitchet*. How he labored for the downtrodden—as will I! [p. 247]

Perhaps the easiest way to analyze Roth's method is simply to list the associations separately attached to Washington and Lincoln, although one must also *listen* to the words:

[14]Howe, "Philip Roth Reconsidered," p. 74.

Washington	*Lincoln*
standing	sitting
erect and authoritarian	tragic and fatherly
J. Massey Rhind	Gutzon Borglum
cold	cry
leaning on a horse	sitting
goy	*oysgemitchet*

After thoroughly discrediting the *goy* Washington—upright, bossy, horsey—Portnoy zings in the punch line, that marvelous word *oysgemitchet,* for which there is no English equivalent. "All pooped out" is fairly close, but too crass. "All worn out" is accurate but banal. "All struggled out" is just about right. With that word, culminating the subtly Yiddish syntax and diction of "But Lincoln! I could cry. Look at him sitting there . . .", an irresistible conception of a dark, bearded, Hebraic, rabbinically thin and struggled-out Lincoln jumps into the reader's head. Not Lincoln—LinCOHEN!

Roth does so well with what Yiddish he has in *Portnoy* (about fifty words, the minimum supply for a Jewish comic), it's a shame he doesn't have more. Perhaps the same could be said about Roth's Jewishness. Certainly Roth's hostile critics, and especially those who cried out against what they saw as the anti-Semitism and shameful filth of *Portnoy's Complaint,* would wish him a larger and more satisfying share of his ethnic heritage. Yet, paradoxically, the portion he does claim, and has chosen to work with, yields him a distinctive place in the Jewish movement. In a sense, the major line of development of Roth's career—as well as his reply to all the attacks from the Jewish establishment—can be summarized in this Portnovian declaration: "Jew Jew Jew Jew Jew Jew! It is coming out of my ears already, the saga of the suffering Jews! Do me a favor, my people, and stick your suffering heritage up your suffering ass,—*I happen also to be a human being!*" There can be no doubt about Roth's own awareness of his role in this movement, and his consciousness of his relationship to Bellow and Malamud.[15] Yet from the beginning of his career, and most notably in *Portnoy,*

---

[15]See esp. Roth's essay "Imagining Jews," in which he reviews his own career as a "Jewish" writer in the context of Bellow, Malamud, Grace Paley, and Norman Mailer; *Reading Myself and Others,* pp. 215–246. It is also clear from this indispensable essay that Roth has been stung by those who have attacked him for defaming Jews and Jewishness. For a sample of a typically virulent assault on Roth and *Portnoy,* see Harry Roskolenko, "Portrait of the Artist as a Young Schmuck," *Quadrant,* 1970, pp. 63–68.

he has stubbornly followed his own calling. Obviously more remote than Bellow and Malamud from Judaism as a total lifestyle
and worldview, Roth is more directly concerned with personality
than with fate. Unlike their work, his reflects no glimmers of transcendence, metaphysics, superstition, awe. For Portnoy, as for
most of Roth's protagonists, the most intense experiences are
through human love. In these respects his work is intrinsically closer
to comedy.

But none of these comparisons intend to discredit the novel's
Jewish authenticity. Roth's cultural value is precisely his difference
from the other writers. His is the "inside view," the exposé of the
contemporary quasi-assimilated Jew. Thus *Portnoy* gives us the
most comprehensive, graphic, and detailed account of the texture of
the Jewish-Oedipal family experience and the results of that experience, mainly guilt. The book also presents the clearest and most
vivid statement of how Jewish righteousness, intellectual superiority, and ethical sensitivity—as represented by Portnoy—are engen-
dered by his very guilt. As part of this exposé of Jewish character and
personality, Roth gives us the most explicit account to date of how
Jews despise Gentiles while slavishly imitating and pursuing them.
Still another kind of revelation, one strangely resembling Portnoy's
attitude toward Gentiles, is that of Jewish misogyny. What may be
perceived as far back as Abraham Cahan, and running through
Bellow and Malamud as a latent attitude and motif, is at last made
manifest by Roth. In *Portnoy,* as elsewhere in Jewish-American
fiction, women are man's chief temptation and source of misery.
Roth is the first to say it blatantly, humorously, and at length.
Finally, *Portnoy's Complaint* renders explicitly another recurrent
suggestion in Jewish-American writing, one only whispered elsewhere: that to be Jewish is to be neurotic.

The compensation for these bitter messages is less uplifting in
Portnoy's Complaint than in those other remarkable books, *Herzog*
and *The Assistant,* but it is far funnier. Because Jews have absorbed
so many cultures, it would be difficult to prove the existence of a
specifically Jewish humor, irrespective of time and place. Two
elements do persist, however, and they are both superbly exemplified in *Portnoy:* marginality (i.e., the Jew's sense of the precari-
ousness and strain of his status in any given society), and the
anti-heroic figure of the *schlemiel,* who is an incarnation of Jewish

destiny—the archetypal Jew.[16] I would define the *schlemiel* as an aware loser, who complains as he loses but doesn't quit. Alexander Portnoy, who breaks a leg pursuing *shikses,* ejaculates into his own eye as the climax to his first big sex experience, and finds himself at last inert in Israel, is surely a *schlemiel.* But at least he is the funniest of his kind in American literature. True, his *shpritz* can be messy and discomfiting, as any *shpritz* will be if it happens to hit you. But a really good *shpritz* can also be refreshing, even liberating.

[16]Allen Guttmann, "Jewish Humor," in Louis D. Rubin, ed., *The Comic Imagination in American Literature* (New Brunswick, N.J.: Rutgers University Press, 1973), pp. 329–338, treats Portnoy as a prime example of American-Jewish *schlemiel* humor.

SARAH BLACHER COHEN

The Jewish Literary
Comediennes

Jewish-American humor has openly flourished in fiction and the
entertainment arts since the 1950's. In the past, however, a Jack
Benny never capitalized on his own Jewish identity for laughs;
instead, he invented a grotesque stereotype called Schlepperman
for his comic scapegoat. Arthur Miller did not identify his
schlemiel-salesman, Willie Loman, as Jewish, but made him an
outer-directed, secular everyman. In the years after World War II,
however, American Jews felt more accepted. They had received
sympathy from the Gentiles for the loss of their people in the
Holocaust. They had been admired for helping create the state of
Israel. No longer ashamed of being greenhorns and interlopers, they
now showed pride in their individuality. No longer compelled to be
public relations men, they now revealed what was not most choice
about the Chosen People. Such gifted comedians as Lenny Bruce,
Shelley Berman, Mel Brooks, Milton Berle, and Woody Allen
made their Jewish identity paramount and, without fearing what the
Gentiles would think, joyfully exposed the *schmaltz, schmutz*, and
meschuggas of their heritage. The most distinguished Jewish-
American novelists—Saul Bellow, Bernard Malamud, Philip Roth,
and those they influenced, Herbert Gold, Bruce Jay Friedman,
Stanley Elkin—derived much of their comic material from Jewish
culture—its manners, folkways, values, and language. Though their

humor was not as frenzied and sustained as that of the comedians, they, too, benignly mocked the Jews for their minor lapses and sardonically censured them for their major offenses.

But where were the women comics and novelists who could find humor in the Jewish-American experience? Were they too busy quieting the tumult in their family's lives to be the *tummlers* themselves? Were they, as homemakers and Hadassah ladies, unwittingly serving as objects of satire, rather than acting as satirists themselves? One reason why women have not developed a rebellious sense of humor, according to psychologist Naomi Weisstein, is that the option has not been available to them. "A funny nasty clown doesn't go along with the definition of woman that gets us our provider," the woman who is "beautiful, passive, accepting and mute." "An independent, mocking humor is too active for the objectified role"[1] the woman is meant to fill.

This holds true for the Jewish woman. In biblical times she was expected to be as submissive as Eve, who, created out of Adam's rib, would not dare rib others. Out of gratitude for her creation, she is the nurturer. In Proverbs 31:10–31 she is likened to a "merchant ship" bringing food from afar to her family, and a "lamp" that stays lit during the night. She works in the field, weaves and sells garments so that her husband can sit at the gates with the elders. The only laughter she engages in is laughter at the time to come, since she has spent such a dutiful life.

During the Talmudic period the Jewish woman's frailty, rather than her virtue, was stressed. In rabbinic sayings she is depicted as sexual demon, tale-bearer, and numbskull. Judged too frivolous for studying the Torah, she is instructed to marry, cultivate her purity, and preserve the sanctity of the home. Denied exposure to the circuitous wit of biblical commentary and the jocular exchanges of Yeshiva students, she can be only a creature of levity, not an originator of it.

This was not the case with the Eastern European *shtetl* woman of the nineteenth and twentieth centuries. She was viewed not as "temperamentally light-headed,"[2] but as a shrewd businesswoman who greatly contributed to the support of her family. Though she did

[1]Naomi Weisstein, "Why We Aren't Laughing Anymore," *Ms.*, November, 1973, p. 89.

[2]The saying "Women are temperamentally light-headed" is from *Ta'anith* 7a of the Talmud, quoted in Charlotte Baum, Paula Hyman, and Sonya Michel, *The Jewish Woman in America* (New York: Dial Press, 1976), p. 4.

not share in the subtle humor of the academy, she often functioned as the lively comedienne of the marketplace. Exaggerating the worth of her wares, she gleefully outwitted the peasants. A perfecter of the comic curse, she tongue-lashed any who wronged her. At times a *yente* or busybody, she engaged in character assassination with gusto. In earthy Yiddish she exposed affectation and hypocrisy. She invented satiric epithets for family and friends. She mimicked idiosyncratic speech and imitated awkward mannerisms of vocational and class types. Her one-woman comedy of castigation amused herself, as well as others. But she never did find time to write down her wry impressions. Her talent for mockery and savory demotic language were instead transmitted to her American-born sons and grandsons, who often made her the most unforgettable character in their comic routines.

When the *shtetl* woman immigrated to America, she lost her spirited sense of humor. As her husband abandoned his studies to earn a living in the New World and became more monetarily successful, she no longer had to be his economic helpmate. She could retire to the home to make it a stylish American dwelling for her rapidly assimilating family. Initially, she was ill equipped for the task. Used to being "robust and direct, energetic and independent" in the world at large, she found it difficult to acquire "female charm in the recognized American sense."[3] She lacked what Hutchins Hapgood in *The Spirit of the Ghetto* described as "the subtle charm of the American woman, who is full of feminine devices, complicated flirtatiousness, who in her dress and personal appearance seeks the plastic epigram, and in her talk and relation to the world an indirect suggestive delicacy."[4] As the Jewish woman became more "Yankeefied" in the ensuing years, however, she became more adept at being feminine. She learned to be more passive, narcissistic, and indirect. Imitating the high-toned Christian woman, she raised her daughter to be refined and enjoy what Veblen calls the duties of "vicarious leisure and consumption." She taught her not to be candid, speak loudly, or possess *chutzpah,* a male perogative. Certainly she was not to challenge authority, or (even more heretical) ridicule it. And if she were privileged to marry, she was to be a *balebusta,* not a big-mouth; a woman of virtue, not of vituperation.

[3]*Ibid.,* p. 189.

[4]Hutchins Hapgood, *The Spirit of the Ghetto* (New York: Funk and Wagnalls, 1902), p. 71.

With the revival of the feminist movement in the late sixties, Jewish women did speak up and challenge authority. In the forefront of the movement, they were theoreticians, organizers of consciousness-raising groups, workers for legislative reform. They also wrote feminist novels, but their heroines had no tell-tale Jewish characteristics. They were striving to achieve full personhood, but this full personhood was nondenominational. The protagonists of Lois Gould, Alix Kate Shulman, Sue Kaufman, and Sandra Hochman may have been born Jewish, but their matrimonially beleaguered lives were no different from those of their Gentile sisters. Up from connubial slavery was the goal which consumed them all. Even the clever bitching about their plights was devoid of ethnic accent.

There were a few novelists, however, who felt it kosher to mix their Jewishness with their feminism and had the *chutzpah* to be funny about it. Gail Parent's *Sheila Levine Is Dead and Living in New York*[5] is representative of this kind of novel. Though *Newsweek* described it as "sometimes heartbreaking, mostly hilarious, always full of life," the novel is seldom hilarious, seldom profound in its depiction of the Jewish-American woman. Jewish-sounding in a pop-urban sense, it is like that fiction which novelist Norma Rosen claims was written "with the eyes alone"—and, I might add, with the ears alone. Referring to the paucity of her own and her contemporaries' knowledge of Jewish ideas and values, Rosen states: ". . . it was still possible for a 'Jewish writer' to write a 'Jewish book' merely because of living in New York, or Cleveland, or similar places. One had inherited, literarily speaking, a trust fund. Without even trying, one had certain speech rhythms in one's head —colloquialisms that were inherently funny, relationships always good for a cutting down by wit, and a large, energy-radiating store of culture-abrasions."[6] Such is the case with Gail Parent. An urban Jewish novelist, she writes about a Jewish heroine, Sheila Levine, a thirty-year-old overweight, oversexed girl-woman whose sole desire from infancy on has been to get married. Because there are no prospects and spinsterhood seems assured, Sheila decides to kill herself. The novel proper is an extended first-person suicide note and life history. A nonstop confessional, it overflows with mock self-pity and recrimination, all with Jewish intonation and syntax. Since

[5]Gail Parent, *Sheila Levine Is Dead and Living in New York* (New York: Bantam, 1973).
[6]Norma Rosen, "Writing about the Holocaust," *Midstream*, 20 (October, 1974), 56–57.

the author is compelled to keep the reader laughing on every page, Sheila Levine often resembles an unsuccessful stand-up Jewish comic trying desperately to amuse the audience with rapid-fire, second-rate gags.

Sheila's physical appearance, her basic inferiority and concomitant bungling provide the sources for the novel's humor. She has a nose that needs bobbing, hair that needs straightening, and fat that needs rendering. She chooses female roommates who exploit her, men who betray her, and jobs which degrade her. She cannot even commit suicide successfully. Such humor flaunts Sheila's inadequacies and reinforces the commonly held conception of woman as ludicrous object. Sheila has been so brainwashed by society that she uses the weapon of laughter against herself. Unable to employ her humor as a means of protection and survival, she cannot "turn what is defined as a ridiculous state of being into [her] own definition of the ridiculous, to take control of the quality of the absurdity, to turn it away from [herself]."[7] Sheila Levine is essentially a female *schlemiel* figure without the *schlemiel's* humor of verbal retrieval, his ability to transform chaos into comedy through rhetorical skill and emotional resilience. She also lacks the affectionate regard which the *schlemiel*, primarily a male breed, receives in Jewish folklore and literature. She is simply a maladroit woman who relishes and deserves her masochism. Unlike the *schlemiel*, whose Jewish traits are his most endearing ones, Sheila Levine's flippant attitude toward her Jewishness discourages sympathy with her plight. The chief villain in her life, she claims, is her mother, whose Jewishness resides in her obsession to marry her off before thirty. Sheila can't abide a prospective suitor because he resembles her ineffectual Jewish father. She resents a new organizational rabbi for his exorbitant fee to deliver her self-created funeral eulogy. She abhors a Jewish funeral director for requiring her to purchase a double cemetery plot. Such is the extent and depth of the novel's Jewish references.

In the absence of any spiritual dimensions, the book is devoted to the somatic. What most absorbs Sheila is the revulsion for and attempted sacrifice of her body. Since we don't get a very full and vivid sense of the Jewish woman whose body it is, we wish Sheila, a one-dimensional figure of a lonelyhearts burlesque, a speedy suc-

[7] Weisstein, "Why We Aren't Laughing," p. 89.

cess in her disappearing act. But Sheila does not disappear. Her mother rescues her before her overdose of sleeping pills takes effect. The novel ends with Sheila being revived by a number of handsome interns whom she immediately views as possible husbands. Devoid of any anagnorisis, she is still the comic type, ignorant of her true needs and vainly pursuing her family's conception of the ideal mate.

More perceptive is Isadora Zelda Wing, the heroine of Erica Jong's *Fear of Flying*,[8] and more wide-ranging and complex is the novel's humor. Isadora is the picaresque heroine satirically commenting on the foibles and pretensions of the educated and affluent in America and Europe. Impatient with systems and systematizers, she reserves her greatest mockery for psychiatrists of every size, shape, nationality, and sexual prowess. Also prime objects of her raillery are creativity-destroying English professors, demented suitors, adulterous Arabs, and her philistine family. But unlike the conventional rogue who observes more of the world's folly than his own, Isadora wryly scrutinizes herself and candidly reveals her comic eccentricities. By confessing all the gamey details of her physiological responses, she enables us to laugh with her. She is seldom the butt of the joke the way Sheila Levine is with her habitual criticism of anatomy. Any weakness Isadora acknowledges, she describes in the most clever and imaginative fashion so that she has some control over the reaction to her inadequacy. Hers is not the nervous laughter of the self-despiser, but that of the woman who likes herself for her ready wit.

What is particularly Jewish about Isadora, and what is the connection between her Jewishness, her humor, and her being a woman? In one of her many interviews Erica Jong suggests an answer to this question:

> You see, I had never been particularly conscious of being Jewish. My family was cosmopolitan; nobody cared much about being religious. I had never been to a synagogue. All my life I have had friends who were not Jewish—lovers, husbands, even. But in some way, that German experience changed something inside me, in that I came to understand what it means to have an identity you would fight for, and I began to burrow into those feelings. I wrote a lot of poems in Germany, and many of them dealt with the idea of being a victim and with rage. And from that I moved into writing about female rage and

---

[8]Erica Jong, *Fear of Flying* (New York: New American Library, 1973). Other references to the novel are cited in the text.

all those unexpressed negative feelings I had about family, about men and so on.[9]

Similarly, Isadora's three-year stay in Heidelberg with her psychiatrist army husband, and her subsequent return to Vienna, contributed to her identification as a victimized Jew. Unlike the Jews of the Holocaust, who couldn't openly express their rage and resorted to the camouflaged humor of the insulted and injured, Isadora responds with an undisguised, feisty humor. She turns her devastating wit against those same oppressors who persecuted her fellow Jews because of some crazed notions of Aryan superiority. Of the Austrians who host the psychoanalytic congress and are overly friendly to the analysts they banished in 1938, she writes: "The people who invented *schmaltz* (and the crematoria) were going to show the analysts how welcome back they were. Welcome back! Welcome back! At least those of you who survived Auschwitz, Belsen, the London Blitz and the co-optation of America. *Willkommen!* Austrians are nothing if not charming" (p. 5).

By employing such vindictive irony to attack a common enemy, Isadora is on safe ground. She has the approval of the Jewish community for comically belittling former and potential destroyers. But Isadora also thinks there are forces within this same community undermining her worth as a Jewish woman and preventing her from realizing her full potential. At the risk of being a renegade to the faith and finding herself ostracized from the group, she directs her fractious humor against her own people. Angered by the excessive demands placed upon the Jewish woman, she hyperbolically describes what is expected of her:

> Somewhere deep inside my head . . . is some glorious image of the ideal woman, a kind of Jewish Griselda. She is Ruth and Esther and Jesus and Mary rolled into one. She always turns the other cheek. She is a vehicle, a vessel, with no needs or desires of her own. When her husband beats her, she understands him. When he is sick, she nurses him. When the children are sick, she nurses them. She cooks, keeps house, runs the store, keeps the books, listens to everyone's problems, visits the cemetery, weeds the graves, plants the garden, scrubs the floor and sits quietly on the upper balcony of the synagogue while the men recite prayers about the inferiority of women. She is capable of everything except self-preservation. [p. 210]

[9] "*Playboy* Interview: Erica Jong," *Playboy Magazine,* September, 1975, p. 70.

The fact that Isadora can originate such iconoclastic humor to shatter the domestic idols of the Jewish tribe suggests that she might have found a more acceptable Jewish female role for herself. But the role she adopts for the greater part of the novel resembles the Thomas Wolfean stereotype of the sensual, gross Jewess. This is not, however, the image Isadora would like to project. At moments of high esteem and effervescence, she thinks of herself as a Hebrew hedonist, a Nietzschean Jewish superwoman—beyond good and evil. In her fantasies she rallies to Portnoy's battle cry of "put the id back into Yid" and has pleasure-filled "zipless fucks" with strangers on trains. In real life, she attempts to be the "Matron Saint of Adultery," swapping her Chinese psychiatrist husband for an English one, but her guilt feelings interfere with her sexual rites (rights). Once again she blames the Jews for her unliberated state. In tones of mock whining, she, like Portnoy, complains of what a dubious blessing it was for the Jews to be given the Ten Commandments. She comically exaggerates the painful consequences of such a gift:

> What did Moses do for the Jews anyway by leading them out of Egypt and giving them the concept of one God, matzoh-ball soup, and everlasting guilt? Couldn't he just have left them alone worshipping cats and bulls . . .? Is it any *wonder* that everyone hates the Jews for giving the world guilt? Couldn't we have gotten along nicely without it? Just sloshing around in the primeval slush and . . . fucking when the mood struck us? Think of those Egyptians who built the pyramids for example. Did they sit around worrying about whether they were Equal Opportunity Employers? [p. 245]

Though Isadora blames her Jewish heritage for her "hypertrophied superego" (p. 245), clearly her fear of flying and her fears of being an artist, a wife, and mother are her own. She doesn't know who she wants to be: "Isadora Duncan, Zelda Fitzgerald, or Marjorie Morningstar" (p. 140). But at least she can see the comic limitations of each of these exclusive identities.

A Jewish writer not preoccupied with her characters' gender identity and more sure of her artistic identity is Cynthia Ozick. Finding the designation "woman writer" too confining and essentially discriminatory, she regards the entire range of human experience as the fit subject matter for her fiction. Exploring the consciousness of both male and female characters, she doesn't mind being considered a betrayer to the feminist cause or a trespasser in male territory. What does concern Cynthia Ozick is that her fiction retain an authentically Jewish nature. At the American-Israel Dialogue of 1970, she described the characteristics of a genuine Jewish literature in the American diaspora. Its language, though written in English, will be "New Yiddish." "Centrally Jewish in its concerns," the literature will be "liturgical in nature." By "liturgical" she does not mean "didactic or prescriptive," but "Aggadic, utterly freed to invention, discourse, parable, experiment, enlightenment, profundity, humanity." As for its potential for humor, this "New Yiddish" literature, Ozick claims, "will be capable of genuine comic perception in contrast to the grotesqueries of despair that pass for jokes [in the literature of] current Gnostics and aestheticians."[10]

Cynthia Ozick's "Envy; or, Yiddish in America,"[11] is an excellent illustration of this liturgical "New Yiddish," since it is a parabolic comedy in which morality and humor are inextricably linked. Edelshtein, the central figure of the story, is a sixty-seven-year-old Yiddish poet desperately striving for forty years to have his talents recognized in America. In one respect he is still the fearful little man of the *shtetl* who has a Chaplinesque sense of himself as the accidental and insignificant creature barely surviving in the hostile world. In another respect he has the hauteur of the high priest of Yiddish culture, censuring superficial Jewish-American writers and a slickly translated Yiddish author, Yankel Ostrover, who have made financial killings in the literary marketplace. Edelshtein's feelings of extreme inferiority and extreme superiority incur Ozick's humorous treatment. When he is the insecure *shtetl* figure, she compassionately views him as a saintly fool in his valiant efforts to keep Yiddish alive for American Jews. She sympathizes with him when at the first Yiddish word in one of his lectures, "the painted old ladies of the Reform Temples would begin to titter from shame, as at a stand-up television comedian" (p. 43). She acknowledges the ruefully comic incongruity of his mourning the death of Yiddish in

[10]Cynthia Ozick's address at the American-Israel Dialogue of 1970 was published as "America: Toward Yavneh," *Judaism*, 19 (Summer, 1970), 264–282. This quotation appears on pp. 279–280.

[11]"Envy; or, Yiddish in America" was originally published in *Commentary*, 48 (November, 1969). It later appeared in Cynthia Ozick's collection, *The Pagan Rabbi and Other Stories* (New York: Alfred A. Knopf, 1971). Citations to "Envy" are from this collection.

synagogues which have become Cecil B. DeMille amusement parlors and fancy catering halls. Like other Jewish-American novelists, she ridicules the gastronomic Judaism and edifice complexes of *nouveau riche* American Jewry. But she also harshly mocks Edelshtein when he becomes the supercilious Yiddish purist. This is not to suggest that Ozick totally disagrees with his assessment of American Jewish literature. With the exception of Saul Bellow, whom she respects as the "most purely and profoundly ideational"[12] of the Jewish-American novelists, she generally shares Edelshtein's belief that they are largely ignorant of their Jewish heritage, yet reviewers praise them for their ethnic wit and perception. Indeed, much of the story's amusement stems from the fact that Edelshtein acts as the stringent literary critic who, often expressing Ozick's views, employs the quaint accent and syntax of Yiddishized English to pronounce his unkind judgments. He deplores, for example, the cheap way Jewish-American novelists add Yiddish local color to their work: "Their Yiddish! One word here, one word there. *Shikseh* on one page, *putz* on the other, and that's the whole vocabulary. . . . They know ten words for, excuse me, penis, and when it comes to a word for learning they're impotent" (pp. 79–80). Edelshtein is just as merciless in his lampooning of Yankel Ostrover, the third-rate Yiddish writer who enjoys national and international acclaim because his modernist English translators freed him of the "prison of Yiddish" (p. 47). Edelshtein both ridicules Ostrover for his graceless Yiddish style and comically exaggerates the perversities of his characters' behavior: "boys copulating with hens, butchers who drank blood for strength behind the knife" (p. 47). Clearly Ostrover, whose fiction about imaginary Polish villages reeks of the occult and pornographic, is a caricature of Isaac Bashevis Singer. Since Ozick abhors the violations of taste committed by such a caricature, she has Edelshtein dwell upon what an obscene literary faker Ostrover is, thus exposing the idiocy of the literary establishment for considering Ostrover a universal genius.

What Ozick finds most objectionable and worthy of satire about Edelshtein is his hypocrisy. Much as he mocks Ostrover, he prefers to be like him. He, too, would like to escape from the "prison of Yiddish" (p. 47), if he could achieve fame. He pretends to lament the waning of Yiddish when he actually laments the waning of an

[12]Ozick, "America: Toward Yavneh," p. 266.

audience to appreciate his creativity. His hypocrisy is attacked, however, not by the author but by a twenty-three-year-old Yiddish-reading woman whom Edelshtein implores to be his translator, though she is a devotee of Ostrover. Refusing to give life to Edelshtein's dying poems, she heartlessly lashes out at him: "You jealous old men from the ghetto. . . . You bore me to death. You hate magic, you hate imagination, you talk God and you hate God, you despise, you bore, you envy, you eat people up with your disgusting old age—cannibals, all you care about is your own youth, you're finished, give somebody else a turn!" (pp. 94, 97–98). We are not to side with the young woman, however. Her diatribe shows the limitations of American-born Jewish youth who would readily sacrifice the parochial for the universal and, in so doing, lose their claim to any distinctiveness. Because Yiddish is an indigenous part of Edelshtein, and because Christians and anti-Semitic Jews alike won't allow him to forget this fact, he can't give up Yiddish. Since he has the misfortune of living at a time when Yiddish "died a sudden and definite death, in a given decade, on a given piece of soil" (p. 42), Ozick sympathizes with his desire to communicate and be understood in an alien land. She can even forgive his envy of those who achieve a spurious kind of communication.

Satiric indictment and sympathetic acquittal of petty Yiddish writers is not Ozick's primary concern in "Envy." The story allows her to express her affection for Yiddish, the *mamaloshen,* the mother tongue, in which childhood endearments, *shtetl* solidarity, and a closeness with God are conveyed. Moreover, she laments the American Jews' abandonment of Yiddish for English, a language they consider more secular and thus more aesthetic. Abandonment of the Jewish sources for creativity in pursuit of more worldly fame is also the theme of "Virility,"[13] the next short story Ozick wrote after "Envy." On the surface, "Virility" appears to be a feminist comedy of literary manners revealing the double standard in the world of letters. Edmund Gate, born Elia Gatoff, has come to America from Czarist Russia via Liverpool to make his literary fortune. His first attempts at poetry are marred by contrived alliteration and polysyllabic diction. Though his work is continually rejected, he is a confident male and still believes in his talent. After several years of

[13] "Virility" was originally published in *Anon,* February, 1971. It later appeared in *The Pagan Rabbi.* Citations are from this collection.

persistence, his poems miraculously improve and appear in the best magazines. Promoted by a married woman with whom he has had two illegitimate children, he publishes five volumes of poetry, each entitled *Virility*. The critics, more impressed with the title of the poetry than with its substance, single out what they consider its masculine virtues and overpraise them: "If Teddy Roosevelt's Rough Riders had been poets, they would have written poems like that. If Genghis Khan and Napoleon had been poets, they would have written poems like that. They were masculine poems . . . [like] superbly controlled muscle . . ." (p. 257).

It turns out, however, that Edmund Gate is not the author of these poems. They have been written by Tante Rivka, his spinster aunt who cared for him in Liverpool. Soon after his arrival in America, he has been passing off as his own the eloquent poems she sent him in her letters. Three years after her death, he has nearly exhausted the supply of her poetry and faces artistic sterility. A Jamesian mentor convinces him to confess his plagiarism and do right by Tante Rivka. Her remaining poems, which were to comprise Gate's *Virility VI*, are published under her own name as *Flowers from Liverpool*. This collection contains Tante Rivka's finest poetry, yet the reviewers are unimpressed. Employing phallic criticism, they find her book to be "Thin feminine art," "Limited as all domestic verse must be. A spinster's one-dimensional vision" (p. 266). Yet Gate's poetry they acclaimed as "Seminal and hard," "Robust, lusty, male" (p. 254).

This flagrant example of male critical bias which Cynthia Ozick describes with bitter humor could be straight out of Victorian England. Elaine Showalter mentions a similar occurrence concerning the publication of George Eliot's *Adam Bede*. Since the book was thought to be too good for a woman's work, the critics hastily found the male whom they assumed to be the author, a clergyman named Joseph Liggins, who readily accepted credit for the book. When the real George Eliot could not abide the homage paid to the fraudulent author and revealed her identity, the reviews changed. "Where critics had previously seen the powerful mind of the male George Eliot . . . they now discovered feminine delicacy . . . a disturbing unladylike coarseness."[14]

---

[14]Elaine Showalter, "Women Writers and the Double Standard," in *Woman in Sexist Society*, ed. Vivian Gornick and Barbara K. Moran (New York: New American Library, 1972), p. 476.

"Virility," however, is not exclusively an attack upon male parasites and male supremacists. Ozick includes an element of the ludicrous within Edmund Gate's treachery for the purpose of jest and symbolic import. Since he has appropriated a woman's talents, Ozick has him fear he has acquired a female's gender as well. Clutching his genitals to confirm his sex, his last words to the narrator are: "I'm a man" (p. 266).

Gate's uneasiness about his anatomy is symptomatic of his uneasiness about being a Jew. He readily saps the creativity of Tante Rivka, Ozick's allegorical figure representing Judaism, but he is reluctant to acknowledge his indebtedness to her. Once in America he ceases to communicate with her and lets her starve to death. If he had provided nourishment for her, she would have survived many more years and prolonged Gate's poetic career. Instead, Tante Rivka, productive until the end, died with dignity, whereas Edmund Gate, disaffected Jew and poet manqué, committed suicide.

In a recent novella, "Usurpation (Other People's Stories),"[15] Cynthia Ozick mocks herself as author for pilfering other writers' fiction. That the novella's narrator-protagonist is a woman writer who has plagiarized from the works of male writers is not at issue. Her prime concern is not the invasion of the males' literary domain to redress the wrongs perpetrated against her sister writers. Rather, she is an asexual spinner of tales who jests about the snags in her narrative technique and the literary larceny she commits.

She informs us that at a public reading she heard a famous writer read a story which she had already composed in her own mind. That story is unmistakably Bernard Malamud's "Silver Crown." Filled with the same envy which Edelshtein had for the successful Ostrover, she is bent on winning her own fame. She rewrites the ending of Malamud's work by incorporating a story which she filches from a young writer, David Stern, and further modifies it by including a parable she has stolen from Agnon. Unlike Edmund Gate, she does not try to conceal that she is a literary purloiner. She openly admits her crimes, applauds herself for her cunning, and instructs neophyte writers to adopt her questionable practices.

One of the purposes of "Usurpation," other than providing the

---

[15] "Usurpation" was originally published in *Esquire*, May, 1974. It later appeared in Cynthia Ozick's collection, *Bloodshed and Three Novellas* (New York: Alfred A. Knopf, 1976). Citations are from this collection.

true confessions of a story thief, is to ridicule the writing of fiction itself. It is revealed not as a miraculous process whereby the finished product emerges fault-free from the divinely inspired head of the creator. Rather, it is shown to be a suspect art, relying on counterfeit experience, dubious techniques, and contrived language to achieve its lifelike effects. Ozick also mirthfully punctures the inflated position of the writer. Her narrator-protagonist is a vain, short-tempered opportunist who values public renown over the perfection of her craft. For her, no edifying relationship exists between tradition and the individual talent. She is too busy exploiting the talent of others to appreciate tradition and to cultivate her own creativity.

Ozick disapproves of the art of fiction not only on aesthetic and ethical grounds. For the Jewish writer, fashioning a make-believe reality through words is an idolatrous act, in direct violation of the Second Commandment. Story-telling is too Christian an activity as well, since it reminds her of the "Eucharist, wherein the common bread of language assumes the form of a god."[16] But her greatest objection to story-telling is its usurpation, since the author appropriates from God the role of creator. To prevent readers from missing the theological meaning of "Usurpation," Ozick further explains it in a preface to the collection in which it appears: " 'Usurpation' is a story written against story-telling; against the Muse-goddesses; against Apollo. It is against magic and mystification, against sham and 'miracle,' and, going deeper into the dark, against idolatry. It is an invention directed against inventing—the point being that the story-making faculty itself can be a corridor to the corruptions and abominations of idol-worship, or the adoration of magical event."[17]

Ozick herself claims to "dread the cannibal touch of story-making," yet continues to "lust after stories."[18] Similarly, the narrator-protagonist of "Usurpation" is aware of the evil consequences of story-telling, yet continues to "moon after magical tales" (p. 131). When the ghost of the Jewish poet Tchernikhovsky asks her to choose between the "Creator or the creature. God or god. The Name of Names or Apollo" (p. 176), she unhesitatingly selects the pagan deity and becomes the prolific transmitter of pagan narratives: "Stories came from me then . . . none of them of my own

---

[16]Ozick, "Preface," *Bloodshed*, p. 11.
[17]*Ibid.*
[18]*Ibid.*, p. 12.

making, all of them acquired, borrowed, given, taken, inherited, stolen, plagiarized, usurped, chronicles and sagas invented at the beginning of the world by the offspring of giants copulating with the daughters of men" (p. 177).

Ozick here suggests that as long as the Jewish storyteller writes in this world, where he is exposed to an alien culture and must employ a secular language, he will be an idolatrous fiction-monger. And if he chooses to write about the heathen rather than the holy in the next world, then the pagan inhabitants of Paradise, like Hitler in this world, will not allow him to forget that he is a Jew. He will be caged and instructed: "All that is not Law is levity" (p. 177).

Fortunately, Cynthia Ozick has not been caged, and she writes about levity and Law. Of the Jewish women writers discussed, she has shown the most *chutzpah*. She has not taken refuge in the hackneyed jokes of Jewish masochism or mocked things Jewish with a self-advertising bravado. Her humor does not confine itself to stereotypes, nor does she exploit ethnic externals for ready laughter. Steeped in the Jewish tradition and aware of its conflicting viewpoints, she deftly reveals its wry paradoxes. A comedienne of ideas, she transforms the farcical into the philosophical. But because of her wit and imagination, her "philosophical stories" do not "make excellent lullabies."[19] They keep her readers awake and amused.

[19]Ozick, "Usurpation," p. 143.

WENDY MARTIN

The Satire and
Moral Vision of
Mary McCarthy

Mary McCarthy's writing chronicles the modern American woman's struggle for selfhood during a period of rapid social change. At the same time, her work exposes the patriarchal certainties which undermine reverence for life in both private and public spheres. Exploring the implication of sexual politics and the opposition of patriarchy to feminism, her satire provides perspective on the tensions between women and men in the twentieth century.

McCarthy's work evolves from the personal and private to the public and political. Her moral vision remains the same, whether she focuses her satiric lens on her cruel Uncle Myers, who bullied her as a child, or on John Ehrlichman, who tried to hoodwink a nation into believing in his honesty. However, her scope enlarges to include international events as in *Vietnam, Hanoi, and the Watergate Portraits,* as well as the autobiographical experiences of *Memories of a Catholic Girlhood, The Oasis,* and *The Company She Keeps.* Through McCarthy's satire, we discover that as a nation we have our collective Uncle Myers in Colonel Corson, a military strategist in Vietnam, and in the Watergate villains—Maurice Stans, John Mitchell, and John Ehrlichman.

In a series of portraits in the tradition of Juvenal, Martial, Pope, and Swift, her penetrating and uncompromising wit explodes ludicrous and dehumanizing sexual stereotypes. Her humor, though often painful, functions as a moral corrective, following the traditional purpose of satire, which is to illuminate the follies and foibles of the times. As Gilbert Highet observes, "the purpose of satire is, through laughter and invective, to cure folly and punish evil; but if it does not achieve this purpose, it is content to jeer at folly and to expose evil to bitter contempt."[1]

Because McCarthy spares no one, not even herself, from her corrective gaze, she has been described as "cold, steely, merciless" by critics who are discomfited by her piercing vision; dismissing her as unfeminine, bitchy, and shrewish, they call her "raging Mary" or "lady with a switchblade."[2] But McCarthy uses her switchblade deftly as she slices with skillful precision through the pretensions of a patriarchal society. It is unfortunate that her work has been undervalued by critics who have been unable to accept the validity of her anger, or to acknowledge that the rage fueling her invective is as significant and as artful as the fury or disdain in the satire of Pope, Swift, Huxley, and Orwell.

Satire has been described by Highet as "the literary equivalent of a bucket of tar and a sack of feathers";[3] David Worcester notes that satire corrects what "is out of proportion," often using exaggeration to deflate, as in the case of the elevation of Belinda's toilet rituals to a major military strategy in *The Rape of the Lock*.[4] Alvin Kernan also points out that satire corrects excesses resulting from the loss of order and proportion; he observes that the staples of satire —periphrasis, macrology, hyperbole, diminishing figures, tautology, and noble comparison—are techniques of inflation and deflation which expose human failings.[5] Similarly, McCarthy says that satire "invites exaggeration. You can't have it without some sort of distortion." Furthermore, she adds, "the best satire seems to spring from hatred and repugnance . . . I suspect it is usually written by powerless people; it is an act of revenge."[6]

It is significant that McCarthy comments on powerlessness and revenge as motives for writing satire. As a woman writer, she

[1]Gilbert Highet, *The Anatomy of Satire* (Princeton: Princeton University Press, 1962), p. 156.
[2]"Editorial," *Life*, September 20, 1963, pp. 61–62.
[3]Highet, *Anatomy of Satire*, p. 155.
[4]David Worcester, *The Art of Satire* (New York: W. W. Norton, 1940), pp. 21, 43.
[5]Alvin Kernan, *The Plot of Satire* (New Haven: Yale University Press, 1965), pp. 30–31.
[6]Quoted in Doris Grumbach, *The Company She Kept* (New York: Coward-McCann, 1967), pp. 146–147.

understands and is affected by the oppression of women in a society dominated by men; at the same time, she perceives the self-indulgence and frailty of the modern woman along with the excesses of the patriarch. This double-edged perspective makes McCarthy's satire more complex and varied, and her writing brilliantly conveys the convoluted aspects of women's experience in the twentieth century.

The women in Mary McCarthy's novels, essays, political and personal narratives are very much affected by the problems created by modern social and sexual mores. Improved methods of contraception permit them to be sexually liberated, but they are constrained by the very real fears of loss of reputation, inadequate performance, or being exploited; increased opportunities in the job market permit these women to be economically self-sufficient in theory, but the realities of unequal pay and lack of opportunities for advancement prevent them from discarding the dream of the gallant knight who will rescue his princess from life's rigors. With their distorted definitions of femininity, these women are frequently the target for McCarthy's satire. Lacking traditions to teach them autonomy and self-reliance, MCarthy's women, like their counterparts in real life, flounder in confusion; they do not perceive their options, or are paralyzed by them. Convinced of their powerlessness, they look for salvation in a man: "There was no use talking. *She knew*. The mind was powerless to save her. Only a man . . .," laments Margaret Sargent in *The Company She Keeps*.[7]

In spite of unprecedented freedom, McCarthy's heroines are still bound by the nineteenth-century ethic of true womanhood which is based on self-sacrifice.[8] Margaret Sargent marries, divorces, lives alone, travels alone, works, is a Trotskyite, marries again, is psychoanalyzed, but never really escapes male dominance. In each episode of her picaresque adventures, she ultimately chooses to play Florence Nightingale, nurturing men who are morally, psychologically, or sexually handicapped. "All my efforts were bent on keeping Mr. Sheer in a state of grace, and I stood guard over him as fiercely, as protectively and nervously, as if he had been a reformed

[7]Mary McCarthy, *The Company She Keeps* (New York: Harcourt, Brace, 1942), p. 302. All other references to the work are cited in the text.

[8]Barbara Welter, "The Cult of True Womanhood: 1820–60," *American Quarterly* (Summer 1966), 151–162, 173–174, provides an excellent discussion of this feminine ideal based on "piety, purity, submissiveness, and domesticity."

drunkard. And, like the drunkard's wife, I exuded optimism and respectability" (p. 55), says Margaret Sargent about a charlatan who spends his life selling fake *objets d'art* and who doesn't even pay her the salary he owes her. However, McCarthy's satire is double-edged: it undercuts Margaret Sargent's selflessness by revealing the arrogant egotism and frustrated need to dominate that is the other side of the redemptive impulse. Sargent's efforts to attain moral superiority through the salvation of these unregenerate men are often foiled; hoping to give the man in the Brooks Brothers shirt "back to himself . . . these fits of self-assertion on his part discouraged her by making her feel there was nothing very good to give" (p. 94). Disturbing her script, he spoils her vision of herself as the romantic heroine whose love transforms the toad into a prince—but what is she to do if he persists in his toad-like ways?

Trapped by her scenario, Margaret Sargent is unable to recognize her own feelings, nor can she acknowledge her fundamental aversion to her seducer: "The attraction was not sexual, for, as the whiskey went down in the bottle, his face took on a more and more porcine look that became so distasteful that she could hardly meet his gaze" (p. 95). In spite of her repulsion, she is more worried regarding his impression of her and the possibility of losing face than she is about her own responses: "she felt bitterly angry with the man for having exposed her—so early—to this supreme test of femininity, a test she was bound to fail, since she would either go into the compartment, not wanting to (and he would know this and feel contempt for her malleability), or she would stay out of the compartment, wanting to have gone in (and he would know this too, and feel contempt for her timidity)" (p. 87). False pride, a concern for her performance in this romance, eclipse her self-knowledge and erode her self-respect.[9]

In McCarthy's dissection of the charade of seduction, it becomes clear that Margaret Sargent's role requires that she adjust every gesture, every facial nuance to affirm and support her leading man: "She found that she was overextending herself to please him. All her gestures grew over-feminine and demonstrative; the lift of her eyebrows was a shade too arch: like a passée belle, she was overplaying herself" (p. 137). Unlike Marilyn Monroe, the sex goddess of the

[9]Excellent background for this subject can be found in Karen Horney, *Neurosis and Human Growth* (New York: W. W. Norton, 1950), and *Feminine Psychology* (New York: W. W. Norton, 1967).

1950's whose face continually quivering in expectation of the cue which would command the appropriate response, Margaret Sargent premeditates her coy gestures and then waits to see what happens. However, since she is not a *femme fatale,* she ultimately wounds only herself. Margaret Sargent's vision of sacrificial womanhood obscures her own self-hate, and her self-mockery expresses her powerlessness:[10] "the glow of self-sacrifice illuminated her . . . quickly she helped him take off the black dress, and stretched herself out on the berth like a slab of white lamb on an altar." Her self-abnegation is complete as she "waited with some impatience for the man to exhaust himself, for the indignity to be over" (p. 114).

Even in her mortification, she waits for prince to emerge and thinks, "Perhaps at last she had found him, the one she kept looking for, the one who could tell her what she was really like" (p. 101). Yet, her desire for this midwestern businessman to define her life for her, in fact to give her to herself—and this is the final irony, *she* is the one who waits to be redeemed—cannot blind her to her humiliation: "Waves of shame began to run through her, like savage internal blushes, as fragments of the night presented themselves for inspection" (p. 106). And here "white crepe-de-chine pants, many times mended, with a button off and a little brass pin in its place" (p. 107), which she retrieves from the floor, only remind her that she feels not like a carefree modern adventuress, but more like a fallen woman of an earlier generation.[11]

Drifting in a sea of social and romantic possibilities, the modern heroine has not yet learned to steer her course. After divorcing her first husband, Margaret Sargent remarries, this time to an architect, "the perfect compromise candidate, something halfway between a businessman and an artist" (p. 284). She begins to understand that "it is some failure in self-love that obliged her to snatch blindly at the love of others, hoping to love herself through them, borrowing their feelings, as the moon borrowed light. She herself was a dead planet" (p. 302). Psychoanalysis helps her to realize that the persona

---

[10]Elaine Showalter observes that McCarthy's heroines are very masochistic; "Killing the Angel in the House: The Autonomy of Women Writers," *Antioch Review,* 32 (1973), 339–353. Also see Clara Thompson, "Some Effects of the Derogatory Attitude toward Female Sexuality," *Psychiatry,* 13 (August, 1950), 349–354, for a discussion of relationship between low self-esteem and the sacrificial ethic, especially in sexual relationships.

[11]For further discussion of this subject, see Wendy Martin, "Seduced and Abandoned in the New World: The Fallen Woman in American Fiction," in *The American Sisterhood,* ed. Wendy Martin (New York: Harper and Row, 1972), pp. 257–272.

of "the beleagured princess in the fairy tales" (p. 302) conceals her own self-loathing. Though the psychoanalyst, in McCarthy's view, is part shaman, part exorcist, and psychoanalysis is a secular religion, "Freud would have labored in vain if she had not ended up sobbing on a psychoanalyst's blue couch" (p. 262). The process of therapy reduced Margaret Sargent's psyche to shards, and from these fragments comes the possibility of a new order. McCarthy's detachment and aloof analysis of her heroine's traumas suggest new versions of reality for the modern woman; the satire of *The Company She Keeps* destroys the defenses Margaret Sargent uses to shield herself from taking responsibility for her own life, and she is left with the possibility of changing her life.[12]

While the satiric rendering of Margaret Sargent results in a restructuring of her world in which eros and responsibility are connected, the portraits of the patriarchs are static. These men are perceived to be fixed; their egotistical, narrow perception of the world is a permanent failing, deserving patronizing laughter, if not ridicule and scorn. Mr. Sheer, the dealer in fake antiques, "worshipped any kind of ingenuity: boxes with false bottoms, cuckoo clocks, oval miniatures of the school of Boucher that opened if you pressed a button and disclosed a pornographic scene" (p. 35). Pflaumen (which means prunes in German), the genial host, is a social middleman; his price for a dinner invitation is that he "should never be left out of anything" (p. 161). Lacking self-awareness, Sheer and Pflaumen are infantile and self-indulgent, but the Yale man, Jim Barnett, is pernicious. He hates Margaret Sargent for making him aware of his limitations: "He had never been free, but until he had tried to love the girl, he had not known he was bound. It was self-knowledge she had taught him; she had showed him the cage of his own nature. He had accommodated himself to it, but he could not forgive her. Through her he had lost his primeval ignorance, and he would hate her forever as Adam hates Eve" (p. 246). In this portrait, masculine certainties are destroyed as the feminist exposes the inflated self-esteem and exaggerated self-importance of the glamorous, liberal intellectual who is used to patriarchal mastery.

Memories of a Catholic Girlhood (1946) provides much of the

---

[12]This view of satire is defined and explored by Northrop Frye in *Anatomy of Criticism* (Princeton: Princeton University Press, 1957).

early background of McCarthy's concern with the excesses of patriarchy and absurdities of redemptive womanhood. This autobiographical work is the reconstruction of an early childhood in which she was orphaned and sent to live with relatives who, she felt, humiliated her. McCarthy's early understanding of patriarchal absolutism is the result of her frequent clashes with her Uncle Myers, who beat her if she disobeyed him. He is the original rogue in her gallery:

> [Myers sits] in a brown leather armchair in the den, wearing a blue work shirt, stained with sweat, open at the neck to show an undershirt and lion-blond, glinting hair on his chest. Below this were workmen's trousers of a brownish-gray material, straining at the buttons and always gaping slightly, just below the belt to show another glimpse of underwear, of a yellowish white. On his fat head, frequently, with its crest of bronze curly hair, were the earphones of a crystal radio set, which he sometimes, briefly, in a generous mood, fitted over the grateful ears of one of my little brothers.[13]

McCarthy reports that "we were beaten all the time, as a matter of course, with the hairbrush across bare legs for ordinary occasions, and the razor strap across the bare bottom for special occasions" (p. 64). These early experiences with Uncle Myers's arbitrary power left her with a conviction not only of her basic unworthiness and sinfulness, but also of the essential depravity of all human beings. Much of the force of McCarthy's satire is the direct result of her early lessons of human frailty; social pretention, sham, and arrogance do not pass unnoticed in her work, and her penetrating vision reveals the truth behind the social act. Her portraits reveal the base natures of those who attempt to construct a self which hides their essential unworthiness. Her technique is to present men like Uncle Myers as flesh without redeeming spirit, thereby reducing them to brutes or beasts without intelligence.

At the same time, she parodies the ideal of spiritual womanhood. In an effort to atone for her own sins, she dreamed of "being a Carmelite nun, cloistered and penitential; I was also much attracted by an order for fallen women called The Magdalenes" (p. 18). But, finally, the aesthetics and sensory appeal of "the Mass and the litanies and the old Latin hymns, in the Easter lilies around the al-

[13]Mary McCarthy, *Memories of a Catholic Girlhood* (New York: Harcourt, Brace, 1946), p. 56. All other references to the work are cited in the text.

tar, rosaries, ornamented prayer books, votive lamps, holy cards stamped in gold and decorated with flower wreaths and saint's picture" (p. 18) attracted her more than martyrdom. McCarthy's irreverent attempts to become a cloistered nun undercut the tradition of sacrificial femininity, and the resulting self-knowledge frees her from the confining polarization of the male and female into flesh and spirit.

In the collection of stories, *Cast a Cold Eye* (1944), life is depicted as a Hobbesian power struggle—marriage and friendship are constructs which barely conceal the predatory nature of social life. McCarthy's "correcting tendency" sometimes takes the form of excessive didacticism, she does succeed in bringing familiar social these sketches of alienated domesticity are considered misanthropic by many critics. However, as Elizabeth Hardwick observes, "A career of dissent isn't easy for any woman . . . very few writers can resist the temptation of feminine sensibility; it is there to be used as a crutch." Praising McCarthy for her skill in writing about the comedy of sex from a woman's point of view, Hardwick adds, her "daring of self assertion, the brashness of the correcting tendency fills us with nervous admiration and even with the thrill of an exploit."[14] Though McCarthy's "correcting tendency" sometimes take the form of excessive didacticism, she does succeed in bringing familiar social types to life in these stories. While she baldly pronounces, "What passes for love in our competitive society is frequently envy: the phlegmatic husband who buys up the stock of a rival corporation in order to kill it,"[15] she also creates such characters as Francis Cleary in "The Friend of the Family," who embodies the unctuous, self-centered parasite:

> In the old days Francis was always prompt to shut off one of his anecdotes when his companions' interest slightly wavered away from him; indeed, much of his conversation seemed to be constructed around the interruption he awaited. Gradually, however, he has become more adhesive to his topics. He may be interrupted by the arrival of a newcomer, the host may excuse himself to fetch somebody's coat, or the hostess may go in to look at the baby—but Francis has put a bookmark in his story. "As I was saying," he resumes, when the distraction has passed. [p. 50]

[14]Elizabeth Hardwick, *A View of My Own* (New York: Farrar, Straus and Giroux, 1962), p. 43.

[15]Mary McCarthy, *Cast a Cold Eye* (New York: Harcourt, Brace, 1944), p. 11. All other references to the work are cited in the text.

An equally vitriolic domestic portrait can be found in "The Weeds," a story of an unhappily married woman who masks her hatred of her husband and rationalizes her inability to leave him by immersing herself in domestic details: "She remembered all the times she had thought of leaving him before. But there had always been something—the party Saturday night she did not want to miss, the grapes blue on the vines waiting to be made into jelly, the new sofa for the living room that Macy's would deliver next week, the man to see about the hot-water heater" (p. 9). When the wife finally does leave her husband briefly, she discovers that she "had exchanged the prison of the oppressor for the prison of the self, and from this prison there was not even the hope of escape" (p. 19). These stories are important in tracing the development of McCarthy's satiric skills because they document her ability to remain aloof from the compunction to be sociable, to be "a good girl."

Very few women writers have been able to free themselves from the supportive, nurturing role assigned to females in patriarchal society. Although Virginia Woolf implored her readers to "kill the Angel in the house,"—that is, the self-sacrificing part of themselves—most women are not sufficiently strong to resist the rules of decorum which mire them in passivity and self-abnegation. Satire requires aggression, the willingness and ability to be detached from convention, the perspective to remain aloof from sentimentality as well as the skill to turn anger into invective or parody. Northrop Frye associates satire-irony with winter, a cold, withering season which McCarthy evokes in her title.

In *The Groves of Academe* (1952), McCarthy presents a gallery of portraits of academics which dispels all illusions about the nobility of the life of the mind. Prefaced with a quotation from Horace—"And search for truth amid the groves of academe"—the novel exposes the characters' follies and affectations, which are inadequately camouflaged by intellectual posturing. The plot revolves around the impending dismissal of Henry Mulcahy "when he was halfway to tenure," and the political machinations and endless committee meetings which follow are no less complicated or underhanded than a corrupt corporate scheme. This novel approaches moral allegory as outer appearances are connected with inner being—the soul is reflected in the face, a person's spirit embodied in gesture and demeanor. Mary McCarthy creates these portraits to exemplify the putrefaction of the spirit. The description of Mulcahy, for example, leaves the reader with no doubt that Mulcahy's mind is as flaccid as his body: "A tall, soft-bellied, lisping man with a tense, mushroom white face, rimless bifocals, and graying thin red hair, he was intermittently aware of a quality of personal unattractiveness that emanated from him like a miasma; this made him self-pitying, uxorious, and addicted to self-love, for he associated it with his destiny as a portent of some personal epiphany."[16]

In contrast to Mulcahy, who capitulates to the political and social forces which cause physical and moral sagging, his female colleagues are determined to triumph over moral fallibility by transcending their bodies altogether. One succeeds in refining herself to the point of abstraction; the other is beset by physical ailments. "Domna Rejnev was the youngest member of the literature department, a Radcliffe B.A., twenty-three years old, teaching Russian literature and French . . . her finely cut, mobile nostrils quivered during a banal conversation as though, literally, seeking air. . . . Her very beauty had the quality, not of radiance or softness, but of incorruptibility; it was the beauty of an absolute or a political theorem" (p. 37). The other female colleague is described as suffering "from intermittent eczema, asthma, shingles, and all the usual disorders of the repressed female brain-worker. Her neck, as she spoke, reddened and she coughed, from time to time, awkwardly" (p. 117). David Worcester comments that "satire probes the open sores of society with the same unholy joy that a doctor feels over an unusually 'interesting' case."[17] As McCarthy probes and pokes the bodies of Mulcahy and his colleagues for evidence of spiritual disease, she takes great delight in examining the tissue of arrogance and selfishness exposed by her verbal scalpel.

Marya Mannes asserts that McCarthy "claws her characters to ribbons"[18] in *A Charmed Life* (1955), a novel about unsuccessful writers and painters who live in New Leeds, an exurban New England village. But, in fact, McCarthy continues the process, begun in earlier novels, of carefully stripping layer after layer of psychic and spiritual armor to reveal the underlying hubris and greed: Martha Sinnott's spiritual pride, the infantilism of her present

[16]Mary McCarthy, *The Groves of Academe* (New York: Harcourt, Brace, 1951), p. 6. All other references to the work are cited in the text.

[17]Worcester, *Art of Satire*, p. 69.

[18]Marya Mannes, "The Cat and the Mice," *The Reporter*, December 15, 1955, p. 13.

and former husbands obscured by their intellectual and moral posturing, are laid bare.[19] One of the devices McCarthy uses to expose their excesses is the inflation of trivial domestic details to explode the absurdities of the pompous domesticity of the inhabitants of New Leeds. For example, by magnifying the importance of the cocktail ritual, McCarthy ridicules Martha Sinnott's bourgeois materialism disguised as love: "Martha's Old-Fashioneds were a sign of love. She did them with bourbon, no fruit, and a half a lump of sugar, in their best glasses, rubbing the rims with orange peel and putting them in a silver muddler" (p. 115).

Martha Sinnott is at the center of the moral drama of *A Charmed Life;* with her second husband, she has moved back to the small town on Cape Cod where she lived with her first husband, who has since remarried, having remained there to write. After briefly resuming a sexual relationship with her first husband, Martha discovers she is pregnant but is unsure whether her present or past husband has fathered the child. Unable to live with the ambiguous paternity, she decides to have an abortion; however, her efforts to redeem the past are in vain—she dies in a car accident caused by a woman who was driving on the wrong side of the road. Irwin Stock observes, "Martha wants honor and she wants her love, she wants both together as if her one lapse had never occurred; and in the world of Mary McCarthy, such a wish has to be in vain."[20] But McCarthy says in a *Paris Review* interview that Martha Sinnott—her last name reveals her deepest wish—cares enough about atoning for her lapse to "put up a real stake," believing that "the past *could* be undone, in certain conditions. It could be bought back, paid for by suffering. That is, it could be redeemed."[21] Nevertheless, there is some smug self-congratulation in Martha Sinnott's anguished decision: "Yet all the while the moral part of Martha knew that she would have to have an abortion because her inclinations were the other way. The hardest course was the right one; in her experience, this was almost an invariable law. . . . She would not have guessed that she had so much integrity. In the midst of her squirming and anguish, there was a sensation of pleased suspense" (pp. 262–263). Once again, female

[19]Mary McCarthy, A Charmed Life (New York: Harcourt, Brace, 1954), p. 24. All other references to the work are cited in the text.
[20]Irwin Stock, *Mary McCarthy* (Minneapolis: University of Minnesota Press, 1968), p. 34.
[21]Elisabeth Niebuhr, "The Art of Fiction," *Paris Review,* 27 (Winter-Spring, 1962), 63.

suffering is glorified, and at the same time it is proof of moral superiority. This strange combination of masochism and false pride prevents Martha from knowing what she really wants.

The occasion of Martha Sinnott's probable impregnation deserves closer scrutiny because it allows us to understand the essential structure of the sexual and social comedy which is played at again and again in McCarthy's fiction. The strategies and maneuvers of the men and women to outwit each other in and out of bed illuminate the battle between the sexes which is at the core of McCarthy's satire. This time the skirmish between Martha and Miles begins with a mild flirtation and ends as an assault. Essentially, the renewed sexual contact is the result of Martha's fatalistic curiosity, as well as her careless and frightened passivity, and of Miles's need to dominate and to claim her once again as his.

Martha is uncertain and confused about what to do, but she is drunk and Miles, who has also been drinking heavily, takes advantage of her. Actually, this is a scene of rape:

> She had struggled at first, quite violently when he flung himself on top of her on the sofa. But he had her pinioned beneath him with the whole weight of his body. She could only twist her head away from him, half-burying it in one of the sofa pillows while he firmly deposited kisses on her neck and hair. . . . He was much stronger than she was, besides being in good condition, and he did not let her little cries of protest irritate him as they once might have done. [p. 199]

Armed with the weapons of reason, logic, and analysis, Miles thinks, "she was too ironic a girl not to see that one screw, more or less, could not make much difference, when she had already laid it on the line for him about five hundred times" (p. 201).

In their struggle—which is very real, even if disguised by a veneer of polite gentility—he is no longer erotically involved, and she simply endures him. She complies because she has no choice: "Her movements subsided; her limbs became inert. It occurred to him, with a start, that she was actually very drunk, though she had not showed it especially. Compunction smote him; he ought not to have done this, he said to himself tenderly. Tenderness inflamed his member. Clasping her fragile body brusquely to him, he thrust himself into her with short quick strokes. A gasp of pain came from her, and it was over" (pp. 202–203). The arrogance, the blind impulse to dominate, to assert mastery, revealed in this scene is the core of patriarchy, and this need to control and dominate is the primary focus of McCarthy's satire in her later works. The rape of Martha by Miles becomes a metaphor for oppression of women by men, or, in her later works, of the domination of underdeveloped nations by industrial-technological countries.[22]

The Group, a best-seller published in 1963, is a novel about classmates at Vassar whose lives are dominated by men. In spite of their illusions about being self-determining, these women discover that they must depend on men for their economic and social survival, that they are defined by men. Again, McCarthy's satiric narrative mercilessly exposes the social and political values which shape these attractive women who are an American elite—most of them have wealthy parents, social privilege, and have attended the most prestigious schools.

This study of a generation of modern American women begins, as McCarthy herself points out, with the inauguration of Roosevelt and ends with the inauguration of Eisenhower; McCarthy says "it was conceived as a mock chronicle novel. It's a novel about the idea of progress really, seen in the female sphere; the study of technology in the home, in the playpen, in the bed."[23] In *The Group* progress is based on the promise of technology, which is male territory: nutrition becomes a matter of recipes and availability of canned goods; sex, a matter of contraception; childbearing and rearing, a matter of methodology. The women are simply pawns in a male world where even their most basic biological functions of conceiving, bearing, and nurturing children are regulated and controlled by men.

In a *Partisan Review* essay, "The Kingdom of the Fathers," Adrienne Rich defines patriarchy as "The power of the fathers: a familial, social, political system in which men—by force, direct pressure, or through ritual, tradition, law and language, customs, etiquette, education, and the division of labor—determine what part women shall or shall not play."[24] The relationships of women and men in *The Group* conform to Rich's definition. Dick deflowers Dottie, orders her to get a diaphragm at Margaret Sanger's, and then decides not to see her again. Instead of being angry, she is alternately grateful to him for having been her lover and guilty about her own

---

[22]Susan Brownmiller, *Against Our Will: Men, Women and Rape* (New York: Simon and Schuster, 1975), argues that rape is at the core of our social and political institutions.

[23]Niebuhr, "Art of Fiction," p. 29.

[24]Adrienne Rich, "The Kingdom of the Fathers," *Partisan Review,* 43 (1976), 17.

lack of experience which, she is convinced, turned him off. Libby spends hours adorning herself and perfecting her feminine charms and is incredulous when Nils, a ski instructor, tries to rape her when she resists his seductive approach. Polly takes Gus as a lover only to be incorporated into his fantasy life; she provides the sympathy that his wife and analyst fail to give him, and when he no longer needs her, he leaves. Priss marries Sloan, and he takes charge of the birth and breast-feeding of their child as if directing a play in which she has a walk-on part. Immediately after graduation, Kay marries Harold, a philanderer and failed playwright, who commits her to a mental hospital after a violent argument; however, she does not leave him, because "if I did, everyone would know it's a failure."[25] The only two women in *The Group* who are not dominated by men are Helena, who seems like a freckled little boy, and Lakey, a lesbian. Moreover, only Lakey emerges in command of her energy and power at the end of the novel.

The Group is a thorough chronicle of the lives of daughters of the professional and upper classes who, because of their socio-economic advantages, should be autonomous and self-directing, but who, in reality, are slaves of fashion or convention, or who pursue freedom by rebelling against tradition only to find themselves easy prey for unscrupulous men like Harold or Dick. The novel contains a series of satiric vignettes which are peppered with chatter about clothes, recipes, affairs, household furnishings. McCarthy carefully constructs her characters in their own settings, and, through these glimpses of what seem to be the surfaces of their lives, we understand the truths of two decades of American life:

> Her scrutiny veered to Kay, who was wearing a pale-brown thin silk dress with a big white *Mousseline de soir* collar with a wide black taffeta hat wreathed with white daisies; with her glowing cheeks, vivid black curly hair, and tawny hazel eyes, she looked like a canny lass on some old tinted postcard; the seams of her stockings were crooked, and the backs of her black suede shoes had worn spots, where she had rubbed them against each other. Pokey scowled. "Doesn't she know," she lamented, "that black's bad luck for weddings." [p. 11]

McCarthy's ability to present her characters in their own terms,

[25]Mary McCarthy, *The Group* (New York: Harcourt, Brace, 1954), p. 344. All other references to the work are cited in the text.

using their language to construct the details of their lives, gives the novel its power. Many critics object to its gossipy, trivial, breathy approach, but this accurate rendering of the traditional feminine style effectively exposes the cultural contradictions and absurdities with which this class of women lives. They have been confined to domestic and decorative spheres, and thus their energies are directed toward etiquette and clothes.

In "The Woman Writer and the Novel," written in 1922, H. L. Mencken asserts that women novelists have been hindered by a "lingering ladyism—a childish prudery inherited from their mothers." Women will succeed in the novel as they "gradually throw off inhibitions that have hitherto cobwebbed their minds."[26] In *The Group,* McCarthy certainly succeeds in shredding inhibitions when she writes about sex, birth control, and childbirth. In *Cast a Cold Eye,* she succeeds in "killing the angel in the house" as she discusses the private lives of her heroines from their college days to their lives as young matrons, wives, and mothers. *The Group* is the novel which Mencken forecasts will be written by the woman of the future: "If I live to the year 1950, I expect to see a novel by a woman that will describe a typical marriage under Christianity, from the woman's standpoint. . . . That novel, I venture to predict will be a cuckoo. . . . It will seem harsh, but it will be true. And, being true, it will be a good novel. There can be no good one that is not true."[27]

In addition to exploring taboo subjects and presenting a view of the other side of patriarchy—a view of the world behind dominant men—the novel deflates romantic illusions based on the mythology of love as a benevolent force, and exposes the limitations and absurdities of bourgeois individualism. The novel enraged reviewers who dismissed it as trivial or bitchy. But it is Norman Mailer who complained most bitterly, insisting that McCarthy is insufficiently daring: "She simply is not a good enough woman to write a major novel. . . . She suffers from a lack of reach. She chooses not to come close enough to the horror of the closet . . . nice girls live on the thin, juiceless crust of the horror beneath"[28] Yet, *The Group* contains the essentials of life; it begins with a wedding and ends with

[26]H. L. Mencken, "The Woman Writer and the Novel," *Prejudices: Third Series* (New York: Knopf, 1922), p. 103.

[27]*Ibid.,* p. 104.

[28]Norman Mailer, "The Case Against McCarthy: A Review of *The Group,*" in *Cannibals and Christians* (New York: Dial Press, 1966), p. 82.

a funeral. In the course of the novel, free love, adultery, cruelty, divorce, insanity are confronted squarely—the horror beneath social surfaces *is* exposed, and McCarthy's courage to examine these issues gives the novel its power. *The Group* is the pivotal point in McCarthy's career: in this work, she successfully fuses private lives with political issues.

In general, McCarthy's writing evolves from personal subjects, such as her childhood memories, to public events, such as the Vietnam war and the Watergate trials. But when her whole work is viewed in its totality, a distinction between private and public cannot be made—what happens to individuals happens to social groups, as well as to nations. *Birds of America* (1965), dedicated to Hannah Arendt, is a novel about the difficulty and dangers of allowing an idea to dominate perceptions so that it obscures the diversity and variety of nature and impairs the capacity for virtue and vice. It is also a satire about the rape of nature by technological society. Peter Levi and his mother attempt to ignore or sidestep the mushrooming standardization, mechanization, plastification of their world. They move to a New England seacoast town where he watches birds and she plays the clavichord and cooks Fanny Farmer dishes which are at least one hundred years old. Although their reactionary responses are frequently absurd, not a day goes by that they aren't forced to confront the fact that their world is shrinking. Loss pervades the novel: The great horned owl disappears; the library-benefit cake sale no longer offers "potato salads and chicken pot pies and clam pies. Rice, salad, lobster salad, macaroni salad . . . baked beans and home-made ice cream. Peppermint . . . Boston brown bread. Oatmeal bread. Date bread"; instead, commercial ice cream and hot dogs are sold.[29] There are no longer flowers in the gardens; Peter muses, "'Old Mother Nature seemed to have taken the pill'" (p. 80), while Mrs. Levi remembers: "'Those old New England gardens could be marvelous. . . . Old-fashioned roses. White double narcissus and poppies that bloomed every year on Memorial Day. Spicebush, lemon lilies, a kind of Persian lilac that smelled of Necco Wafers. . . . Beauty Bush . . . sensitive plant . . . heliotrope and verbena and pinks. Hollyhocks. . . . A great deal of honeysuckle, privet and box. Sundials, arbors, trellises, an occasional gazebo"

[29]Mary McCarthy, *Birds of America* (New York: Harcourt Brace Jovanovich, 1965), p. 74. All other references to the work are cited in the text.

(p. 77). At every turn, the variety of life is diminished as people narrow their existences for the sake of convenience. Nature is no longer appreciated, and Peter and his mother are anachronisms.

In spite of the fact that the two are essentially sympathetic people who are dedicated to values which respect life and the nurturing ethic, McCarthy does not conceal their occasional lapses. Like Martha Sinnott, Mrs. Levi is fond of playing the purer-than-thou game, but McCarthy's irony makes it clear that Mrs. Levi is also dependent to a considerable extent on technology: "She was always trying to draw the line, her personal high-water mark, across the history of achievement and avoid being a total reactionary: in the home, she said, a good place to stop would have been the flush toilet and the vacuum cleaner. In front of Peter, she did not add Tampax, but he had heard her say it to her sister" (p. 167). Peter, a very sensitive, introspective young man, sometimes suffers from the rigors of his conscientiousness, as when he ends up cleaning the communal toilet of his Paris apartment house. (This was a particularly odious task, since many of the users were not in the habit of flushing it.) Nevertheless, the absurdities created by an overzealous super-ego are innocuous when compared to the crimes of politicians and military men who rape and pillage the earth in the name of progress and peace. *Birds of America* concludes with the bombing of Hanoi and with Peter's understanding that, just as God died in the nineteenth century, so nature has died in the twentieth.

In "One Touch of Nature," which appears in *The Writing on the Wall and Other Literary Essays* (1962), McCarthy observes that nature has become a "photogenic setting, and has nothing to say, one way or another, in determining values or revealing truth."[30] She goes on to say that along with the total devaluation of nature, in the name of scientific control of the environment through fission and fusion, modern physics threatens "the species and perhaps most other forms of organic life on earth."[31] When the principles of science are applied to weapons of warfare such as napalm, defoliants, and antipersonnel bombs, the result is Vietnam, our first pushbutton war.

McCarthy's essays on Vietnam and Hanoi chronicle the ravaging

[30]Mary McCarthy, "One Touch of Nature," *The Writing on the Wall and Other Literary Essays*: (New York: Harcourt, Brace, 1962), p. 212.
[31]*Ibid*.

of a civilization by technological warfare and, at the same time, document the arrogance behind the war. Her descriptions of American military leaders are very much like the same portraits in her fiction. In *Vietnam* (1967), her description of Colonel Corson, a Marine commander and pacification officer, is another portrait in her gallery of patriarchs: ". . . The ironic colonel sitting like an unintelligible Socrates among his disciples with a model Vietnamese village on the table—struck me with wonder. . . . Colonel Corson was playing God and the Devil up there in the hills behind Da Nang. . . . He held the little country of Vietnam—where people wore conical hats and lived in bamboo thickets—like a toy in his hand."[32] This description of Corson is an example of satiric distortion which focuses on the imbalance created by the aggrandizing ego of the patriarch. Colonel Corson toys with the fate of a country the way a little boy plays with a new game, and he never questions his right to do so. This same loss of proportion occurs earlier in McCarthy's fiction, with her description of Taub in *The Oasis:*

> Standing alone on the peak . . . he laughed aloud to himself in sheer victorious contentment. His mind explored sensuously the realm of possibility that lay outstretched at his feet: across the valley, a herd was grazing on a knoll; smoke came from the chimney of a farm house; fences, the barking of a dog, a ploughed field cut neatly into sections gave a sense of the human scale, reduced by distance to miniature, like a toy agricultural set. . . . All this Taub's eye appropriated . . . he felt like Utopia's discoverer and an impresario to Nature.[33]

In *Hanoi* (1968), she continues her study of the war and its effects. Documenting the remarkable resilience and life force of the Vietnamese, her sketches contain descriptions of food, clothing, interior furnishings which are every bit as detailed as those of *The Group:* "To return from a shelter to a disarrayed table where the tea has grown cold in the cups and resume a conversation at the precise point it had left off ('You were saying . . .?') is a daily, sometimes an hourly, occurrence in the North. . . . Hospitality requires that tea should be served at the beginning and end of any visit: tea, cigarettes, candies, and long slender little cakes that taste of ba-

[32]Mary McCarthy, *Vietnam* (New York: Harcourt, Brace and World, 1967), p. 80.
[33]Mary McCarthy, *The Oasis* (New York: New American Library, 1944), pp. 148–149.

nanas."[34] Once again, enlargement of trivial domestic details
enables the reader to make moral judgments: tea, cigarettes, candies, and cakes that taste of bananas are juxtaposed with bomb
shelters, and the incongruity of hospitality and a military battle
forces the reader to experience the effects of war in Vietnam. In
this study of a war-torn country, McCarthy merges her sensitivity
to domestic details, her private sensibility, with an astute political
analysis of public issues. Because her perspective is personal as
well as political, the reader is able to comprehend the war's effects
on the human life of an entire country. In McCarthy's study, military strategy, casualty statistics, and details of weapon manu-
facture are correlated with their effects—charred fields, hills
stripped of foliage, dead and wounded civilians and soldiers. Just
as her early works trace the evolution of modern woman, her later
works chart national history.

In *The Mask of State: Watergate Portraits* (1973), the corrective
impulse in the form of social satire is a necessary and healthy
response to greed and corruption in public life. Viewing national
politics with the same discerning judgment she uses in *Memories of a
Catholic Girlhood,* she untangles the threads of a national scandal
just as she puzzled through the confused memories of her childhood.
Instead of satiric portraits of Uncle Myers, the Man in the Brooks
Brothers Shirt, the Yale Intellectual, Mr. Sheen, or Mulcahy, there
are biting descriptions of Maurice Stans, Jeb Magruder, Mitchell,
Haldeman, Ehrlichman, John Dean, and Gordon Liddy. Again,
McCarthy uses the technique of correlating moral qualities with
physical appearance, and the Watergate Group is ridiculed for being
as self-indulgent, arrogant, domineering as any of their fictional
counterparts in Mary McCarthy's rogues' gallery: "With his white
fluffy celebrity sideburns, small well-cut features, smart suit acces-
sorized with tie-clasp and cuff links bearing the presidential seal,
Maurice Stans resembled a successful actor, a combination of
Claude Rains in *Caesar and Cleopatra* and Claude Dauphin."[35]
Mitchell is described as "sour, old, rancid, terse," and the portrait of
Ehrlichman vividly recalls her description of the ape-like Uncle
Myers: "Everything about his features and body movements is

[34]Mary McCarthy, *Hanoi* (New York: Harcourt, Brace, and World, 1968), p. 19.

[35]Mary McCarthy, *The Mask of State: Watergate Portraits* (New York: Harcourt Brace
Jovanovich, 1973), pp. 9–10. All other references to the work are cited in the text.

canted, tilted, slanting, sloping, askew. The arms swing loosely; the left hand with a big seal ring, like a brass knuckle, moves in a sweeping gesture. The broad head is too round—pygmyish" (pp. 94–95).

These men are self-important, bombastic, and pompous, and McCarthy's portraits of them as unthinking beasts expose them to public ridicule. Stripping away illusions of their reliability and competence as public leaders, her satire does not remedy the underlying pathology of their lives, but it does reveal the effects of their distorted values on a nation.

Like the satire of her eighteenth-century counterpart, Jane Austen, McCarthy's writing judges as well as chronicles a complex social and economic reality, exposing the pretensions of men and the illusions of women in patriarchal society. Finally, McCarthy's work substantiates the effort of the modern woman to erode the encrusted traditions which prevent her from being heard. She is our contemporary Ann Hutchinson, who looks her judges in the eye and refuses to let them tamper with her reality.

GEORGE GARRETT

Ladies in Boston
Have Their Hats: Notes
on WASP Humor

> I felt a little heavy-hearted about
> the gang, but not much, for I reckoned
> if they could stand it, I could.
> —Mark Twain, *The Adventures*
> *of Huckleberry Finn*

A man I know who lives in suburban Philadelphia bought a piece of furniture. It was delivered by a cheerful man with an Italian surname. Who looked around and commented that it was a very nice house.

"This house is almost two hundred years old," my friend told him.

"Well,"said the furniture mover, genuinely sympathetic, "don't feel bad about it. Nobody would ever know unless you told them."

That, ladies and gentlemen, is a double-barreled WASP joke. Right out of real life. Pretty thin, slim pickings. But it shows and tells a good deal when looked at from all sides.

Probably the funniest thing is the whole idea, the outrageous subject matter of this piece. (And maybe, too, the image of someone trying to wrestle with that subject.) WASPs may be funny, indeed are commonplace figures of fun in a great deal of contemporary literature. But the notion that there are distinctive, characteristic tropes of ethnic humor, forms of wit, comedy, jokes even, which are created by WASPs and may be in some way an influential part of our large and various culture, seems outlandish, absurd enough in and of itself to qualify for a couple of quiet chuckles.

Many of our notions of WASPs and their lives come to us through literature, including theater and film. Much of it is the testimony of witnesses from other ethnic groups for whom the WASP, in abstraction, is at best baffling and most often foolish. The trouble with abstract imagining (a contradiction in terms we all have to live with) is that it assumes an artificial uniformity. In abstraction all WASPs tend to look and act alike. Take former Mayor John Lindsay. For much of the popular press he was the very embodiment of WASP virtues and vices. A great many WASPs found Lindsay funny, a comic character in both style and substance. For others, especially those who may have shared his apparent political persuasion, he was a considerable embarrassment. But for almost nobody in the WASP world was he an adequate or accurate representative of themselves.

To consider the possibility of WASP humor in contemporary American literature, we have to start with their ideas of virtue and vice. And to do that we have to agree on who the WASPs are, what has happened to them, and some of the things they believe or assume. White Anglo-Saxon Protestant covers a lot of territory, literally. There are distinct differences between the eastern and New England WASP and the others, scattered all up and down and across the continent. All are white, to be sure, though the southern WASP shares much, more than he might admit, with the southern black. All are not necessarily, not strictly Anglo-Saxon, again particularly in the South. In the sense of Protestantism, the religious background and affiliation, the definition has to be wide and broad enough to include the whole range of sects and splinter groups, from the pure and simple Holy Rollers, say, through the maze of middle denominations, to the Episcopalians. Who, though relatively small in numbers (roughly 3.5 million), remain influential by means of the weight of tradition, social position, and the vague general power of their slowly dwindling old wealth. And who, also, within their own very flexible limits of doctrine, offer an almost complete variety of service and liturgy, from witnessing, healing, and speaking in tongues to the last examples of the full-scale Latin Mass in America. Similarly, the whole spectrum of Protestantism would also have to include those sects which are not strictly Christian in detail or doctrine but are, nevertheless, clearly Protestant—the Quakers, for example, or the Unitarians. Any honest picture of the religious variety of the WASPs, particularly those of the South, would have to take account of other and different ethnic groups with whom the WASPs have joined closely in a more than casual ecumenical embrace—the Lutherans, Scandinavian and German, for example, the Dutch Reformed Church, and (perhaps curiously) the Greek Orthodox Church, with which the Episcopalians have often shared churches and services.

About an hour's drive north of Charleston, South Carolina, off the main traffic route and built beside the broad red clay and dust of the King's Highway, among tall pines and silence, stands the old church of St. James Santee. St. James Santee can stand as a symbol for the relatively easy interchange among Protestants of various sects and ethnic groups. Though nominally built as an Episcopal church, it also served all the Protestants in that part of the lonesome Santee Delta, including not only Anglo-Saxons, but also the Welsh, Scotch-Irish, Dutch, Germans, and the French Huguenots. From the beginnings, in that part of the country, there was a great deal of intermarriage and assimilation among all these groups. Family trees in the Charleston area, and elsewhere in the South, usually contain them all and often, too, a sprinkling of the refugee Jews from Spain in the seventeenth century. The separate Protestant sects have mostly remained separate and, in fact, have, as if by some natural law, continued to subdivide and proliferate; but there has always been considerable freedom of movement among them.

The first point, then, and probably the crucial one in the definition of the imaginary abstract WASP, is the recognition that Protestantism, in all its multiplicity and contradictions, is the key to understanding the WASP character. There are, of course, some separate social forces which have worked to create a sort of hierarchy and to put the chiefly Anglo-Saxon Episcopalians at the top of the heap; but the central element of any definition is the common heritage of Protestantism. The Protestant is always a creature of mixed feelings, or paradox. His faith, essentially heretical, individual, and anarchic, is in constant conflict with the very institutions he has created to preserve and foster it. All Protestant groups are basically democratic, if only in the sense of the equality of all believers. Even the grandest of Episcopal bishops is no prince of the Church, but a representative in a way that his Roman Catholic equivalent is not. The emphasis upon faith, an inner state of being and a mystery, eliminates much of the weighing and judging of outward condition and behavior as a *spiritual* matter. That is to say, the often and justly cited WASP habit of conformity is, by definition, purely a social and secular matter. There is, therefore, a continual warfare within each Protestant between the demands of the secular world and the rigors of his religious experience. At best it is an uneasy marriage. If good works in the world will not guarantee salvation and if apparent wickedness is not necessarily a one-way ticket to eternal perdition, then it follows that the secular and social world is greatly reduced in real significance. Since freedom of the spirit is assumed, then one is liberated to live in the social world with contempt or indifference for it and with as much convenience, comfort, and conformity as conscience will allow. Theoretically, you pay your taxes to Caesar without a big hassle, tip your hat, and go on your joyous way toward the Delectable Mountains. Seen one Caesar and you've seen them all.

Of course, from time to time—in Calvin's Geneva, post-Reformation Scotland, the Massachusetts Bay Colony, for example—the accidental coupling of Protestantism with power or influence has resulted in extraordinary secularization, or at least an unusual identification with secular movements or ideas. Inevitably this breeds rebellion and reforming zeal among the faithful. Witness fairly recently (*Newsweek,* September 29, 1975) the "Appeal for Theological Affirmation" signed by prominent Protestant theologians which, as described by *Newsweek,* "attacked the church's 'surrender to secularism' and to other worldly 'diseases' from the activist 1960's. 'People were equating Esalen with theology, a marijuana high with a religious experience, and calling masturbation a sacrament,' says co-author Peter Berger, a Lutheran sociologist. 'There was a readiness for a sobering word.' " From the beginning Protestants have been ready with sobering words against the secularization of their spiritual experience, even if, as is the case, there is a strong and continual urge to transfer perceived spiritual values into the social and political (and transitory) realm of the world, the flesh, and the Devil.

Products of Reformation, Protestants can be very serious about reform and even rebellion. Revolution, however, is mostly meaningless, does not engage passionate attention. The American Revolution was, in fact, a rebellion carried out by Protestant reformers; the French Revolution was a more Catholic enterprise. A WASP will be the first to ask you which one worked, which one really accomplished anything. That secular order is best which best protects the freedom of the Protestant to cultivate his faith and follow the promptings of faith and the dictates of conscience. Therefore that government is best which, while allowing this freedom, maintains the maximum possible degree of order, peace, and quiet. The secular order must be as reasonable as possible. Caesar gets respect, to be sure, often more than he deserves. But behind all that is the absence of any passionate commitment. For the WASP the end never justifies the means, because, in the secular world, by definition, the end is trivial.

Philadelphia again. Why not? W. C. Fields and all that . . .

I am riding East on a train from Chicago. Breakfast in the dining car with two Chicago businessmen, neither a WASP, as the train pulls into Paoli.

"Jesus," one says. "The recession must be really bad over here."

What has prompted this observation is the parking lot at the Paoli station, the cars left behind for the day by the commuters on the Paoli Local. Through his eyes I can see that it looks like a junkyard. Rows of cars which are shabby and old without the ostentation of being antique.

"It's a damn shame what the economy is doing to some people," his buddy adds as the train moves on, right down the string of expensive jewels which is the Main Line.

Nothing to say. Nod and sip my coffee. They cannot conceive of the classic WASP custom of non-conspicuous consumption. Not for them, ever, the patched and cuff-frayed tweed jacket, the button-down shirt with a turned collar.

What we are talking about, when we talk about the comic, is vice and virtue and the limits of the flawed human imagination. Presumably the WASP whose reality is inner should possess a full and rich imaginative life. And to a degree this is true, bounded, however, by the simple fact that the WASP must (as must we all) imagine all others as more or less like himself. Therefore deviations from his own code are either examples of deliberate and savage nihilism, or are the result of some defect, some missing element or defective part. In the latter case the WASP conceives that he is dealing with folly. Mostly, then, those who do not behave like him are comic figures.

Take "fair play," one of the English ideals which has survived the long separation from the homeland. The WASP still believes in "fair play" or, anyway, the appearance of it. He applauds examples of apparent "fair play" and either laughs at or detests and condemns its absence. He is not likely ever to recognize, except intellectually, which (as indicated) means superficially to the WASP, that others coming from different ethnic and racial groups are so disadvantaged in the context of our culture that any rules of "fair play" are, *de facto,* unfairly loaded against them. "Fair play" prevents WASPs from being efficient and successful muggers. Urban mugging, since it is generally a group or team enterprise in which the victim is, among other things, outnumbered, is particularly offensive to the sensibility of the WASP. The argument that any mugger would be a fool to risk personal safety or efficiency in the name of "fair play" won't wash with WASPs. The WASP admires Robin Hood and the highwayman straight out of Alfred Noyes, but condemns the muggers as both cowardly and subhuman. Vince Lombardi's passionate declaration, that winning is the only thing, is at once meaningless, vulgar, typical, and a little sad to the WASP, who sees the game, any game, as an idle, perhaps amusing recreation, mainly an orderly form of physical exercise. Certainly not as something in which anything of value can be won or lost. WASPs make wonderful losers. For one thing, they are trained by tradition and heritage never to quit or to slack off, not even when further effort is senseless and destructive, until some final official gong or whistle sounds. At which point they will gather and give a jolly cheer for the opposing team and then walk away, having gained or lost . . . exactly nothing. Frustrating to the opposition since, because of that, the WASP cannot be thoroughly defeated or humiliated. He won't admit—it never occurs to him—that defeat or victory have changed anything. It should be added that there remains among American WASPs at least the pale ghost of one old-country emotion. Novelist Mary Lee Settle (in *All the Brave Promises*) has described Britain as "a nation whose deepest emotion is embarrassment." Though a WASP may not be truly defeated or humiliated, he can be subtly embarrassed. Which is almost the same thing.

The Civil War was, essentially, the great WASP war. Nothing in modern history, neither World War, equals that war (in a relative and proportional sense) for sustained military savagery. At the war's end one out of ten males of military age in the northern population was dead or disabled. In terms of military casualties that is more severe than anything we know about, including France in the First War, Russia in the Second. In the South the ratio was one out of four, which is worse than anything we know about except perhaps the Roman destruction of Carthage. The truly remarkable thing, in spite of the real or imagined rigors of Reconstruction, is how very swiftly and easily hatred and rancor faded. As if that war had been a kind of game.

Though the American WASP has long since discarded the characteristic English habit of reserve, he retains a deep admiration for something closely related to it. Open or public display of emotion is clear evidence of a defect of character. The sight of Edmund Muskie weeping in snowy New Hampshire, never mind why, was disturbing if not disgusting to WASPs. Nixon's appeals to cheap sentiment were wasted on the WASPs. Truth is, most WASPs voted for Nixon because they thought he was wicked and shrewd, and they believed that was what we needed. It wasn't his wickedness, but his stupidity that turned them against him. The black runningback who crosses the goal line, raises his arms in a victory V, and does the little dance, is amusing. It's the way They are. Not so much naturally uninhibited as lacking some requisite gear or governor of self-control.

When Robert E. Lee was president of Washington College, after the War, he was asked by a parent to pass on some words of wisdom to his child. "Teach him to deny himself," Lee said.

Another familiar WASP characteristic, the emphasis on personal conformity to certain social amenities, to what the WASP defines as good manners, is rooted in Protestantism. For, if we cannot ever truly weigh and judge the motives and mysteries of others or, indeed, much comprehend the motives and mysteries of ourselves, we acknowledge this fact by and through a rather formal code of good manners which protects us from the temptation. Alienation is a kind of social goal, which is, itself, another paradox. On the one hand it salutes and celebrates the ineffable mystery at the center of every other human soul. On the other it denies the possibility of ever being truly honest and open with each other in this world. (Try to imagine a completely WASP consciousness-raising group.) Some common results of the WASP emphasis on manners are, in the best contemporary sense, "counterproductive." There is the usual and regular danger that manners will freeze into the rigidity of the simply genteel. There is the undeniable fact that most others perceive the WASP code of manners as mostly insincere and usually hypocritical. Similarly, WASPs tend to interpret minor violations of the code as much more meaningful than they are. When you speak rudely (if impersonally) to a WASP, when you cut in front of a WASP in a queue, you are denying, in the deeper language of the spirit, that he is a human being with an immortal soul. In effect, you are wishing him dead. Just so, WASPs take the angry rhetoric of militants (coming from anyone but blacks, and sometimes taking blacks seriously, too) as (a) meaning exactly what is being said, and (b) a violation of their own humanity, their honor. In self-defense, the WASP assumes that only subhumans would be guilty of such behavior. So, under appropriate circumstances, the WASP will take you at your word. Given the right circumstances, now or later, he will punish you for it. WASP folktales and myths are replete with stories of revenge exacted for what others might perceive as minor slights.

Politically the WASP is also a bundle of contradictions. The eastern urban and New England WASP (upper class only) is seen by most people, especially other WASPs, as the classic model of the elitist reformer, the "limousine liberal." The great majority of WASPs, in all other regions, are better described and understood as populists. This stance serves to make them inconsistent, uneasy, and conservative. Socially, politically, and above all religiously, they distrust human authority and view all government (Caesar again) as an adversary. Even when, sometimes, they may share a general social goal with their liberal cousins, WASPs are habitually dismayed by the usual means of its accomplishments—the use of the power of government, especially the power of the federal government. The WASP perceives the federal government as distant, alien, and hostile. (See Edmund Wilson's angry introduction to *Patriotic Gore*.) To the populist WASP, the more distant a secular authority may be from his direct and individual involvement, influence, and responsibility, the less that authority deserves more than rudimentary, minimal acceptance. (See Baker's and Blotner's biographies of Hemingway and Faulkner for the attitude of these two masters toward the Internal Revenue Service.) Local issues, or *very* distant ones, are more likely to arouse passion in a WASP than are state or national affairs.

Economically the WASP may be, as his pioneer ancestors were, adventurous, but never truly speculative. The WASP takes a dim view of speculation. For the WASP, the building of an estate (if any) is a slow and cumulative matter. Very conservative. Which may explain why so many WASPs are successful bankers. It also illustrates yet another way in which the WASP has been out of touch with the mainstream of American corporate life in the past fifty years. American business has been chiefly based upon speculation, serious gambling for the Big Hit. The WASP, rich or poor, has been more baffled observer than active participant in this process.

In a literary sense, one should note that very few WASP writers of any kind, moderately successful or clearcut candidates for the Tomb of the Unknown Writer, have managed even to stumble into a Big Hit. WASP writers of three generations—Faulkner, Wright Morris, John Updike, for example—have had cumulative careers just like WASP businessmen and professionals. This certainly has put them out of touch with the modern American publishing business and, to a large extent, with fellow writers (see Norman Mailer) of other religious and ethnic groups, who comprehend that to succeed in a speculative society you have to gamble constantly and that, in any case, there is small value and little return in a slowly built, long-term reputation. Their answer to the WASP is that reputation and a quarter may buy you a cup of coffee, but it won't pay bills and earn a living, and it isn't likely to gain you attention or one of the prizes until you're too old to care one way or another.

The WASP view of American history is fairly simple and straightforward. His ancestors—and, like certain African tribes and Oriental peoples, the WASP is constantly conscious of the presence of his ancestors—settled the wilderness, made the colonies, fought and won the Revolution, created the Constitution and the Bill of Rights, protected and expanded the United States, and settled its federal form, for better or worse, with the Civil War. (A spinoff of this latter was the emancipation of the slaves, to whom the WASP sincerely believes his debt was paid once and for all in the spilled blood of a large part of his male population.) After the Civil War ended, there began the great surging waves of immigration to this country. Not many came to the defeated agricultural South, which, once cosmopolitan, was rendered, by comparison, more homogeneous than the rest of the changing country. The immigrants came, from *everywhere*. And the nation was never to be the same. Deep down, however, feeling much like the American Indian whom he dispossessed, the WASP considers all these others as, at best, interesting guests in his country. After all, he feels, though by the exercise of self-control he might not allow himself to say it, the United States is now the second-oldest nation in the world. (Britain, the old homeland, is appropriately the oldest.) He has the deepest roots here. Those who came along later (ignoring the blacks, who certainly arrived among the first), whether a hundred years ago or late last night with wetbacks over the Rio Grande, have their real roots elsewhere. Whatever he might allow himself to think or to say, the WASP was truly baffled that, for example, Earl Warren, child of immigrants (albeit decently Scandinavian ones), would presume to interpret the Constitution of the United States for them. And when, say, a William Kunstler invokes the Bill of Rights in defense of someone, a Yippie named Abbie Hoffman, before a judge on the bench with the same kind of name, well . . . that's another example of WASP humor.

It is not entirely a matter of pure prejudice. For the WASP, like the original Angles and Saxons and the Japanese, is wonderfully assimilative. (Some would say acquisitive.) At least since World War II he has put garlic in the salad and wine on the table. An improvement, most WASPs would agree, over marshmallows and iced tea. Chinese restaurants thrive throughout the heartland. Even lox and bagels and cream cheese are not scorned. The WASP enjoys Jewish comedians, black singers and dancers, Chinese ping-pong players. But he is more than puzzled that a foreigner (at this writing, Henry Kissinger) should represent his country as secretary of state. He shrugs like a man with a heavy invisible yoke at the incredible slow dissolve of history which has somehow replaced John Marshall with Thurgood.

On the other hand, severely inhibited by his distrust of, if not full-fledged contempt for, the active, secular world, the WASP is more or less resigned to the mutability ("downward mobility") of his worldly fortunes. He shrugs at the prospect of a continuing diminution of WASP power and influence, thus confirming, by chronic apathy, his own bleak prophecy. Faith has given the WASP the strength to endure, but at a price. He loves his country but has no great hopes for it.

> The "Gentile" era was ending—Fitzgerald
> was dead, Hemingway and Faulkner in decline—
> and the Jewish one beginning.
>> —Richard Gilman, review of
>> Saul Bellows's *Humboldt's Gift*,
>> in *New York Times Book Review,*
>> August 11, 1975.

> The arts, you know—they're Jews, they're
> left wing—in other words, stay away.
>> —Nixon to Haldeman,
>> June 23, 1972.

Here is another primary WASP paradox, another raging and rumbling visceral contradiction. Not so much anti-intellectual as indifferent to or, more accurately, evenly disinterested in intellectual concerns, the WASP is to be known chiefly by his feelings. They matter. Yet how are they to be known by anyone, since control of the expression of real feelings is an essential element of the WASP social character? This means that one need not pay much attention to what a WASP seems to *think* about things. Integrity and honor rank very high in the WASP catalogue of ideal virtues. But intellectual integrity and consistency are rare and don't count for much. Was Thomas Jefferson a model of intellectual consistency? Most intellectual activity is trivial to the WASP. The passionate and committed intellectual is seen as belonging more or less to the same order of being as, say, a very tall (and most likely black) man who earns his bread and keep by bouncing basketballs and trying to shoot them through a hoop. In a pinch, the WASP prefers the ballplayer. Intellectual structures, be they ever so elegant, are on the level of the things kids make with their Erector sets. Freud was funny. Marx was some kind of a crackpot. WASPs enjoy Einstein anecdotes (which I'll spare you) that show him as a befuddled human being just like everyone else. They couldn't care less about relativity or the whole intricate course of modern physics. Except as a game. Matter of fact, one system (Copernican or Ptolemaic) is about as good and faulty as any other. Einstein was a gifted clown, a sort of a lovable panda bear with a knack for arithmetic. He sure came in handy when we needed that Bomb, but you couldn't count on one of them to drop it.

Because of the profound place of inner feelings in WASP life and of all the tensions created by the tug-of-war between secular ideals and spiritual reality, you might conclude that the WASP would be drawn strongly and naturally to art. Not quite. The creation of art is a good thing, of course, a good outlet for women and troubled adolescents and for funny people with funny names. Finger painting and potting, that's about the size of it. If it keeps them happy, no harm done. WASPs aren't oblivious to the appreciation of art. They support museums and orchestras. But they have a fixed and firm disinclination to keep up with contemporary fashions in the arts. Our grandchildren can in leisure enjoy whatever may survive from what is fashionable now. Meanwhile we can get along just fine with what William Faulkner called (on more than one occasion) "the old verities."

Literary art is something of a minor exception. It has always been more or less respectable in the WASP world to be a writer, especially a poet, male or female, if you can afford the habit. Maybe it is not as worthwhile, all things considered, as being a professional or a maker and doer of *real things,* but writing is at least not a dishonorable avocation. (Which may explain, by the way, why there have always been so many more WASP poets and writers than WASP painters, sculptors, dancers, musicians.) WASPs read a good deal, but, again, they do not read much that is contemporary except for nonfiction and the purely practical. Since the earliest days of settlement, WASPs habitually have read a generation or so behind the times. Edmund Wilson noted the great popularity of the works of Scott among the southern soldiery. And WASPs are just now getting around to Faulkner, Fitzgerald, and Hemingway, and are rather enjoying the experience.

One of the things all this means to the contemporary WASP writer is that he knows that, barring some extraordinary accident, he will not be read very much by anyone. The audience, if any, will not be composed of WASPs. It is possible that a serious WASP writer may gain either or both of the rational goals of writing, described briskly by Tolkein as "cash or kudos," but neither of these is likely to mean much, measured by the standards of his own group. This built-in disappointment is a thread, a whole theme, running through John Berryman's *Dream Songs* (342):

> Fan-mail from foreign countries, is that fame?
> Imitations & parodies in your own,
> translations?
> Most of the relevant prizes, your private name
> splashed on page one, with a photograph alone
> or you with your lovely wife?

All of which can liberate the WASP writer (again, if he can afford the pleasure) in a number of ways. One of which is the freedom to be funny even at the expense of his own group if he chooses. As long as he is working in some recognizably comic mode, he is relatively immune from severe critical reaction from his own group or any other. Dealt with directly and seriously (solemnly), WASP attitudes appear to be offensive to most other people. Case in point: James Gould Cozzens, a very fine novelist who, because he dealt with the WASP consciousness of his central characters from the inside, dramatically, allowing them to feel, think, speak, and act for themselves, has found himself very roughly treated by literary critics—as if he not only shared, but also seemed to subscribe to, to advocate their stance and quirks. (This reaction is a little strange. No one has successfully accused Shakespeare of advocating the ideas and actions—"Put money in thy purse"—of Iago or, for that matter, Othello.) Because the customs and habits of WASPs strike others as absurdly quaint when not genuinely reprehensible, reviewers and readers wanted to be reassured, by clear lines of demarcation of authorial distance, that Cozzens wasn't speaking for himself. There is a good deal of wit and irony in Cozzens's work, but his central characters do not usually see themselves as funny. Faulkner has had the same problem—the attribution of character viewpoint to the author, the "mouthpiece" theory—even when the situation and context were obviously comic. Most notably there is the critical reaction to the lawyer, Gavin Stevens, who appears in a number of works. Stevens is not wicked or hateful by any means; but he is often wrongheaded and, as a result, often hopelessly ineffectual in thought, word, and deed. He is a classic WASP example of the farcical effects of over-education and over-intellectualization. Jason, in *The Sound and the Fury,* is genuinely wicked (and Faulk-

ner, in published interviews, so identified him), but he is also a
clearly comic figure, an archetype of many WASP prejudices and
preconceptions. He seems to be acceptable to critics because he is
so completely wiped out in the events of the story—gets what he
deserves, and with no danger of authorial sympathy. It's worth
noting, though, that Faulkner's treatment of Jason is mixed. Jason's
burning of the circus tickets was cited by Faulkner as the example of
wicked, gratuitous cruelty. Jason's ideas and illusions—for instance, his rages against "the Jews of Wall Street"— are seen as
funny. Harmless enough and typical.

Mixed feelings are at once the raw material and the mode of
WASP comedy. As a literary form, it could not really begin until
American writers found a language and a way to support the expres-
sion of the mixed feelings at the center of WASP consciousness.

> I don't trust anybody who isn't capable of nonsense
> and moments of collapse into ridiculousness.
> —Richard Wilbur,
> *The Writer's Voice*

Poetry is something of a special case. It begins by being special to
the imaginary general WASP who, though he may neither write nor
read poems, assumes that poetry is the highest (therefore more
important) form of literary art. One might note that this assumption
has not been seriously questioned by the WASP poets of our time.
Poetry is serious, and most of our WASP poets have been modestly
respectable, not only in the social world, but also in the literary
scene. The extremely influential American masters of the earlier part
of this century were WASPs—Eliot, Pound, Stevens, Frost, Ransom, and Tate, even William Carlos Williams, despite a slight touch
of the Spanish tarbrush of which he was proud. These men were
(typically) highly personal, individual, eccentric (in terms of immediate fashions and conventions), idiosyncratic in thinking, simply
superb at the expression of mixed feelings, mixed reactions, mixed
states of being. Their highly personal views of human and American
history are conventionally Protestant, even in their singularity; and
this characteristic remains evident in the work of different and later
poets growing out of their tradition. See, for instance, Lowell and
Wilbur, and Berryman's *Dream Songs,* perhaps starting with
217—"Some remember ('Pretty well') the Korean War."

Though none of these earlier masters of American modernism is

usually regarded as a comic poet, each, in his own way, made rich
and various use of the rhetorical devices of poetic humor, wit, irony,
and the comic juxtaposition of mixed, often indecorous feelings.
Stevens did so most often and most explicitly, but even Frost, in his
darkest poems, is seldom far from a cosmic grit of teeth which might
be called a grin.

These masters cast long shadows and remain powerfully influential. The next two generations of American poets, including the
present one, are more ethnically and racially inclusive; but plenty of
WASPs are still found in the front ranks—Warren, Wilbur, Lowell
(despite his period of Catholicism), Jarrell, Merrill, Meredith, Brin-
nin, William Jay Smith, Dickey, Mark Strand, etc. Each, again, is
often funny, willing and able to indulge in nonsense and in
"moments of collapse into ridiculousness"; but the tradition and
reputation of poetry as a proper form for high seriousness, the
respectability of it, limits still, for the WASP poet, the complete
range of comedy. Raw and rowdy comedy, slapstick and pratfalls,
laughing and scratching have come along from people like the Beats.
Who, however, except for the father figure, Charles Olson, did not
claim the allegiance of significant numbers of WASPs. Some of
these later WASP poets may have affected fashionable beards and
love/worry beads, armed themselves with bows and arrows and
cowboy hats in real life; but their clowning around in poems has been
fairly mild, reasonably proper. These later WASP poets (like the
earlier) tend to be well born, well educated; some are quite wealthy;
you'll even find some in *The Social Register*. Which is to say that
most American WASP poets have been and continue to be establishment children whose principal, and perhaps sufficient, act of
rebellion was to follow the vocation of poetry in the first place. They
are often witty, sometimes funny, and are very lively in comparison
with contemporaries like Robert Bly and Denise Levertov. But their
major concern has been conservative; to preserve and to purify the
poetic language of the tribe against continual waves of pollution.
Exceptions? Well, sometimes the late Charles Olson was cheerfully
slangy in a professorial sort of way. Major exception: John Berryman clowning in the *Dream Songs;* he managed to create a language
as mixed and various as his feelings and the subjects and occasions of
the poems, but always through the mask of Henry, "an imaginary
character (not the poet, not me) named Henry, a white American in

early middle age sometimes in blackface,'' who is a traditional figure out of that vanished WASP form—the minstrel show.

There are some WASPs in the new generation of poets, at present fashionably dominated by a loose group which poet Brendan Galvin has satirically named "The Iowa City Mumblers"; but none of these highly serious young men and women would seem to be very interested in public or intentional displays of humor. I am thinking of the likes of Charles Wright or Stanley Plumly, for example, whose dedicated (if sometimes surreal) solemnity precludes any joking or fooling around in verse. On the other hand, some of the younger WASP poets, including some of the youngest and freshest, like Leon Stokesbury and Frank Stanford, show signs of developing and exploiting a real sense of humor in their poetry. Time will tell if they are able to keep laughing.

With exceptions granted, then, you will find examples of certain kinds of WASP humor, deriving from the inevitable confusions of being both a WASP and a poet, in the poetry of our age. However, the overall strategy of the WASP poets, singly or seen collectively, is very seldom strictly comic.

You must go to prose to look for that.

> There have often been literary Establishments of those with similar tastes and backgrounds who touted each other's work and disparaged that of the outsider. The Yankee Establishment in Concord had no use of Walt Whitman, disapproved of Poe, and shed no tears over Melville's decline. Concord has long since been replaced by Manhattan, where the literary Establishment takes very good care of its own. But as tastes change, Establishments change.
> —Edward Weeks, "The Peripatetic Reviewer," *Atlantic Monthly,* August, 1975.

And now, following a digressive route, we take you to Boston, where, according to the tedious old WASP joke, the ladies do not buy their hats (like other people) because, you see, they already *have* their hats. And where, once upon a specific time, WASP humor was introduced into serious American literature.

Early in the *Green Hills of Africa* (a book with a good deal of genuine comedy in it, by the way), the character-narrator named Hemingway and called Papa makes his much-quoted assertion to the

Austrian interrogator Kandinsky: "All modern American literature comes from one book by Mark Twain called *Huckleberry Finn*. . . . All American writing comes from that. There was nothing before. There has been nothing as good since." True or false (and it's worth remembering that Hemingway's ideas and certainties are much modified by the pattern of experience in the rest of *Green Hills*), the generalization is a good enough starting place. The New England crowd was the literary establishment of America. Uncontested, it seemed, certainly unchallenged since they had succeeded in destroying the South. Where the few writers who survived either wrote for northern publishing houses or, more honorably and obscurely, wrote for the expendable pages of their own local newspapers. Both Melville and Hawthorne wrote some humorous material. Cosmic humor you might call it. Even Emerson, Thoreau, Longfellow, Whittier, Holmes, and Lowell occasionally lapsed into intentional comedy.

Wherever modern American literature comes from, the beginning of modern WASP humor in serious literature can be precisely dated—the eve of December 17, 1877, in the Brunswick Hotel in Boston, at the dinner given by the editors of the *Atlantic Monthly* in honor of Whittier's birthday. It was on that auspicious occasion that William Dean Howells cautiously introduced Mark Twain to the distinguished assemblage, which included such as Whittier, Emerson, Longfellow, Oliver Wendell Holmes, Charles Eliot Norton, and Henry O. Houghton. Twain, on the verge of being accepted as a sort of junior member of the club, blew it all with his rough and ready story of the miner in the western mountains, "a jaded melancholy man of fifty, barefooted" who had been visited by three literary types calling themselves Longfellow, Emerson, and Holmes. Describing the speech (after all these years) in *Mark Twain: The Development of a Writer*, Henry Nash Smith tells us: "He is reducing exalted personages to a low status and is incidentally concocting a literary burlesque. . . . It is clearly an act of aggression against the three poets as representative of the sacerdotal cult of the man of letters."

Twain had already started *Huckleberry Finn* (in 1876) and, for the time being, had put it aside. After rising to blow his harsh kazoo in the halls of high culture (the gesture itself being typically WASP and one which any WASP, except the victims, would love him for), he went back to it, together with other things—*The Prince and the Pauper, A Tramp Abroad, Life on the Mississippi*—and finished it in 1883. And, if Hemingway is right, modern American literature had begun.

Mark Twain's stance in the notorious speech in Boston, and as well in the ways and means of *Huckleberry Finn,* is exemplary, a model of what to look for in WASP humor. It is a satirical stance first, its special barbs being aimed at the WASP establishment. Which, in the gentle glow of worldly honor and repute, had lost sight of the fundamental and requisite Protestant contempt for Caesar and his rewards. It is characterized also by self-satire, a saving self-mockery. It is often vulgar and vernacular, violating conventions of decorum with a free-ranging style, using the living lingo in surprising contexts. At heart it is populist, not merely announcing us all as the fallen sons and daughters of a fallen Adam and Eve, but simultaneously celebrating the intelligence, sensitivity, and wisdom of the ordinary, often painfully uneducated human being. Who is set off against the pride and authority (ignorance and folly) of the pointy-headed intellectuals. Beneath and behind laughter and absurdity, it is always deeply serious. The reforming spirit is zealous, if disguised. And finally it strives to be joyous (if darkly so), constructed upon the solid rock assumption that this world, the social and the secular world, as distinct and divorced from the individual, invisible, and spiritual world, is flawed beyond repair and well lost.

Its literary antecedents are to be found in the whole Augustinian, patristic tradition, ranging backward, as Augustine himself did, to include Ovid and the great Latin satirists, Juvenal and Horace. In English its masters are the lonely likes of Chaucer, Fielding, Swift, and Byron.

I find myself talking with a gifted and popular writer of nonfiction, author of any number of excellent *New Yorker* "Profiles." Somebody (maybe me) mentions the work of Tom Wolfe.

"I can forgive that guy everything except his insane attack on Shawn and *The New Yorker*. That was really uncalled for. That is really unforgivable."

> He saith among the trumpets, Ha ha; and he smelleth the battle afar off, the thunder of the captains and the shouting.
>
> —Job 39:25

Where are we to look for the satiric spirit of Mark Twain among the WASP writers of our own time? Probably not among the reasonably well known and honorable "serious" writers of North or South or any other region. Perhaps a modest case could be made for some of the work of John Updike, who, though seldom funny by any standards, is often an amusing writer. But crucial to Twain's comic stance was the deliberate cultivation of the embarrassing and the inelegant. This stance is almost entirely absent from Updike's work. There may be many personal and artistic advantages to the strict and slick schooling of *The New Yorker,* but comedy, especially of the raw and rude tradition, is not one of them. Except for the uniformly marvelous cartoons, the ghost of comedy does not haunt the haughty pages of *The New Yorker.* Updike's work can be best and most accurately described as a superior and representative example of contemporary establishment WASP writing, his fiction being frequently threaded and laced with humor (especially with little chuckles at others who stand outside the charmed circle) but always also being far too serious for the author to accept the risk of being laughed at. At no point is John Updike secure enough to dare the risk of being taken as . . . *plebeian.* He would be much more likely to be found as a member in good standing of that distinguished audience at the Brunswick Hotel than to be mistaken as an ally of the artist who was willing to play the fool (and to pay the price for it) in order to make serious fun of them.

Wright Morris still stands tall as a master of comedy, following in the grand tradition of Twain at least in the quirky, screwball eccentricity of his plots and characters and in the special language and style he has developed and magically refined, exploiting the living American cliché until, thus transformed and renewed, it approaches the edges of poetry. And Morris once chose, critically at least, to define his art and aims precisely in terms of *Huckleberry Finn* in *The Territory Ahead* (1958). Of course, none of Wright Morris's novels—not even the wildly funny ones like *Love among the Cannibals* (1957) and *In Orbit* (1967)—is purely and simply comic. All are masterworks of mixed feelings; and, just so, all, even the most persistently serious, contain sharp and clear comedy, splendidly evoked absurd moments. His most recent work, *The Fork River Space Project,* offers, in addition to a very funny plot and situation (As the jacket copy describes it, it's "about an almost abandoned town and its suddenly vanished population. Were they taken away by a spaceship or a tornado?''), a narrator who is a WASP writer named Kelcey, writing under the name of Serenus Vogel. But most of the characters, the principals in Kelcey's life, as we know it, are genuine ethnics with names like Dahlberg and Taubler and Tuchman. And a good deal of the good humor of Kelcey is based upon fundamental WASP bemusement at the habitual eccentricities of alien cultures: "He had a Brooklyn accent, a cheerful, blue-jowled smiling face. 'You're American?' I asked him. 'Me?' he wheezed at me, 'I'm Tuchman. Wait till he hears this one.' ''

But all along the way Morris has also been very strongly influenced by the art and artifice, the imaginative *maturity* of the European novel as he takes it and understands it. The result is mixed feelings about the American tradition. In his most recent critical work, *About Fiction* (1975), Morris devotes considerable time and space to exploring the American "vernacular," with all its emphasis on "true-to-life" experience. In this context, and contrasted with the traditions of Europe, the line of development from Huck Finn is seen as severely limiting to American fiction. "Boys who tell us all —from Huck Finn to Portnoy—we believe tell us the most about ourselves. The coinage of a language suitable to a boy is at the headwater of our literature. Portnoy merely reports to us further downstream, where there is more muck and pollution. Only the vernacular would prove to be equal to this awesome task." *About Fiction* concludes with "A Reader's Sampler," a section of brief comments on some twenty-one works of recommended fiction. The majority of these are by foreigners—Rilke, Mann, Joyce, Lawrence, Italo Svevo, Isaac Babel, Céline, Elizabeth Bowen, Malcolm Lowry, Camus, Max Frisch, and Gabriel Garcia Marquez. And only one writer in the "Sampler," William Faulkner, is specifically cited and praised for his sense of humor. Morris's own humor and his mixed feelings are conventionally WASP-like, even as is his emphatic stressing the high culture of the Europeans over the vernacular crudities of the natives. And, incidentally, all the American writers in the "Sampler," with the exceptions of Gertrude Stein and Theodore Dreiser, are themselves WASPs. Even in 1975 Morris appears (with the exception of some kind words, in passing, about Saul Bellow) to be not very much interested in the so-called urban Jewish novel or, indeed, any of the currently fashionable ethnic taxonomies.

The South would seem to be the best place to look for a supply of WASP humor. There is, in fact, a good deal of WASP humor in contemporary southern writing, but it does take some searching for. The whole fugitive/agrarian school and tradition, from Ransom and Tate and Gordon and Davidson on through Brooks and Warren to Jarrell and Dickey and Madison Jones, is, with the notable exception of some of Ransom's sly and wry little jokes, characterized by an almost urgent solemnity, and by a passionate attempt to avoid the possibility of being accused of vulgarity. Of course, some of the issues professed and defended by the fugitives/agrarians have been serious enough and traditional WASP concerns as well, particularly their distrust of urban and ethnic culture as against the sturdy ideal of an agrarian WASP yeomanry. But the distinct absence of humor is as much the result of specific social situations as anything else. One situation is the result of the relationship of the southern writer to the North, especially to the northern literary and publishing establishment. Even before the Civil War ended serious publishing in the South, it was clear that the southern writer, to be accepted and respected in the North, whether WASP or ethnic, had to live up to certain preconceptions about Southerners. These assumptions are extensive, subtle and complex; but it is safe to assert that among them is neither the privilege of taking a truly comic satiric stance, at least on many sacrosanct issues which must be approached on reverent tiptoes, nor the easy right to vulgarity. To achieve success in the North, and most of these did so and most of them moved North as well, it was necessary to cultivate an image far removed from that affected by Twain in Boston; all the more so since the basic *ideas* of the fugitives/agrarians were and are, despite the disguises of civility and the patina of learning, antithetical to the prevailing consensus of liberalism among the intellectuals of the North. You may find professions (do they protest too much?) of a certain outward and visible liberalism in the works of expatriate Southerners like Willie Morris and Larry King; you may even find some jokes here and there; but they will be very safe jokes at very safe targets. The expression of basic WASP feelings and prejudices may well appear, but usually in a context of clear attribution to the consciousness of a character who still has a lot to learn from his betters. Take, for example, this reaction of Robert Penn Warren's Bradwell Tolliver, early in *Flood* (1964): "The remarks about her mother were made in connection with an easy reference to her own psychoanalysis, a reference which came to Bradwell Tolliver with as much shock as had her use of the vulgar word for excrement. He knew, he thought, what psychoanalysis was, but what he knew was totally abstract. It was something that happened to people in Austria or London, usually to Jews. Everybody knew that Jews like to suffer anyway.'' Most WASPs remain extremely suspicious of psychoanalysis and, indeed, the whole discipline of psychiatry, treating both as passing intellectual fads. No psychiatrist will engage WASP admiration as, for instance, a good surgeon does. In this joke, Warren brings together a pair of primary WASP prejudices, the one against all intellectual systems, the other against Jews. But it should be noted that the joke is at the expense of Bradwell Tolliver and is addressed to, accessible to, a different and presumably more sophisticated audience than southern WASPs.

A second social condition which has been at least mildly inhibiting to the growth and development of a sense of humor among the agrarians/fugitives is their singular social position within the society and culture of the South. At the time of the Civil War, Tennessee and Kentucky and most of the land west of the Appalachians (with the notable exceptions of New Orleans and the civilized plantation country of the Mississippi Delta) were not unreasonably perceived by other Southerners as being at best a backwoods where it was not still rude frontier country. In the eyes of Southerners with roots in the earlier-settled East and the Deep South, this middle South, home country for the agrarians, is *still* somewhat raw and new. Home for hicks and hillbillies. And so you will not find, for example, such highly regarded writers as Andrew Lytle or Peter Taylor taking the least chance of confirming that image by risking much broad humor. These writers insist on being taken as to the manner and the (mythical) manor born. Which very insistence may well be amusing to other southern WASPs, who, rightly or wrongly, view Peter Taylor's Jamesian Southerners as, in truth if not in fiction, only one generation removed from bare feet and bib overalls and thus more than a little ludicrous for their pretensions to aristocracy; but which will not serve as the structure for much of a joke outside the confines of the Old South.

For parallel reasons, one would not turn to the works of such reputable southern writers as William Styron or Reynolds Price or

William Humphrey, each of whom has been justly celebrated for the high gloss of a *lyrical* talent, for the pleasures of anything that resembles rowdy comedy or hard-knuckled satire. It would be extremely disadvantageous to any of these three writers to introduce much WASP humor of the Twain variety into their works, even if they felt naturally inclined to do so. On the other hand, comedy and satire are richly and elegantly displayed in the fiction of Calder Willingham, especially in the brilliant novel *Eternal Fire,* and in his collection of stories and short pieces entitled *Gates of Hell.* In *Eternal Fire* Willingham adds a functional element of humorous self-parody which is almost indescribable, but might be compared to the art of singing a well-known operatic aria *just* off key. . . . This wedding of comedy and satire, including, as in Willingham's example, an echo of Twain's disarming self-satire, is also a vital quality in the fictions of a number of gifted and diverse southern writers such as William Price Fox, Guy Owen, James Whitehead, and Lee Smith. These writers may not yet be so well known as their more solemn peers, but they are certainly more firmly rooted in the traditions of WASP humor.

So is the work of Truman Capote, when he wishes to be funny. His work-in-progress, *Answered Prayers,* so far appears to be a classic and savage WASP satire on the Gomorrah-like manners and morals of the "beautiful people."

> "We are," she said, tenderness and sorrow and love all informing her quiet voice, her brown eyes drowning in tears, "we are all moral octoroons."
> —R. H. W. Dillard, "The Road: A Story of Social Significance"

I am thinking here of two working contemporary writers, with many things in common and with some clear, sharp differences between them, who can be taken as exemplary of the best of present-day WASP humor and the range of it. These two are R. H. W. Dillard and Tom Wolfe. Near enough in age to be of the same generation, though Dillard is a few years younger, they are both native Virginians of old and honorable bloodlines; each is a practicing Protestant Christian; both are WASPs and comic satirists among other things. Both hold Ph.D. degrees, and they spent their undergraduate years in small colleges not many miles apart in the Shenandoah Valley—Dillard at Roanoke College, Wolfe at Washington and Lee. And each has developed a perhaps surprising (and certainly not widely advertised) area of academic interest and expertise—Wolfe in classical and Renaissance rhetoric, Dillard in bibliography. Despite much in common, there are significant differences between them. Perhaps the most fundamental difference lies in the fact that Dillard comes out of a family tradition which has long been strongly Democratic and populist. His father was for many years the mayor of Roanoke and, for example, was instrumental in helping John Kennedy to carry southwest Virginia in 1960, just as Dillard himself worked vigorously and effectively for Jimmy Carter in the same area in 1976. While Tom Wolfe has not (yet) been counted as openly active in politics, it is clear enough from his works and his known affiliations that his views are much more profoundly conservative and that his kind of populism—for there is always a populist strain in the WASP Southerner—is more paternal than political. The political differences between them, the distinction, may be seen in their attitudes toward Lyndon Johnson. One of the best pieces of writing about the war in Vietnam is Tom Wolfe's "The Truest Sport: Jousting with Sam & Charlie," collected in *Mauve Gloves & Madmen, Clutter & Vine* (1976). It is unusual in taking as its subject the extraordinary courage of carrier-based pilots flying missions over North Vietnam, in particular, one WASP pilot named Dowd; but one of the principal villains is "the Johnson Administration," which forced these pilots to take terrible and often unnecessary risks. Which stance may be surprising enough and WASP-like in its indifference to the prevailing (and, to the WASP, alien) intellectual consensus. But Dillard goes a step farther, goes on record, in *The Experience of America: A Book of Readings* (1969), edited by himself and Louis D. Rubin, Jr., celebrating Johnson as one of the most important of our presidents, asserting that "the first year of his administration in his own right saw the enactment into law of more important pieces of social legislation than any similar time in the history of the republic. . . . The pace may have been slowed by the demands of war and the tone may have been different, but the social revolution of 1932 was restored to full and real vitality in 1964."

For Wolfe's view of the domestic effectiveness of the Johnson years, see *Radical Chic & Mau-Mauing the Flak Catchers* (1970).

Of course the primary, if paradoxical difference between the two lies in the forms they work in. Wolfe, though he may speak as an unreconstructed elitist, writes in the more popular form of nonfiction, specifically in the terms of "the new journalism" which he at once helped to create and define. Dillard, the populist, is a poet, with three published collections, and a writer of fiction with the artistocratic artistry of Borges and Nabokov, both of whom have recognized his work. Dillard's work is frankly difficult. Of his novel, *The Book of Changes,* Wright Morris wrote: "I do believe you have written one of the goddamnest books I have ever read from front to back. The writing is a delight. The fancy elegant and resourceful. I have only one question. Should I read it from the back to the front?"

The range of Dillard's WASP comedy, as revealed in his poetry, short stories, and especially in *The Book of Changes* (1974) and *Mysteries: Three Extravagant Tales* (scheduled for publication in 1978), is wide. On the one hand, he is fond of one-liners, wacky allusions, puns good and bad, and of wonderfully dimensionless cartoon characters with funny names—Sir Hugh Fitz-Hyffen, the eccentric and defective detective; Pudd, the executioner (" 'Pudd,' he hissed, tears of anger on his cheeks, his bald head flashing, 'you are through. As an executioner, you are a nothing!' ") who eventually turns into a magazine; Winslow "Puke" Guffaw, Klansman and (long before Brother Billy Carter) cheerful proprietor of the Honk-E-Tonk; Rastus Coon, who changes his name to Royal Crown and becomes a militant civil rights leader; Cosmo Cotswaldo, scientist and author of *Darwin's Bassoon;* Sara Band, sexy scientist who looks and acts suspiciously like a praying mantis; a cheerful group of strippers with memorable names like Holly Cost, Tricia Vixen, Miss Hurry Cane, Ottavia Rima, Pristine Peeler. At the other end of the spectrum, the jokes are much more complex, based on literary parodies (including a constant element of self-parody) on elaborate narrative and symbolic patterns which, even as they function, satirize many of the basic tropes and techniques of contemporary fiction. And, above all, in the development of what he half-in-jest defines as his "post-Einsteinian fiction," Dillard loves to use and to abuse the big ideas, the intellectual clichés and counters of our times. Darwin, Hegel, Marx, Fabre, Freud, Einstein, Husserl, Schrödinger, Emerson, and William James are familiarly referred to; but then, so are Mayor Richard J. Daley, Fu Manchu, and critic

Stanley Moss. The juxtapositions of high and pop culture, of the serious and the facetious, are sudden and violent. The aim, in part at least, is to evoke the familiar WASP reaction of amusement at the intricate predicaments of intellectual life. Take, for example, Cosmo Cotswaldo's explanation, in "The Bog: A Naturalist's Notebook," of the thinking behind his monumental *Darwin's Bassoon:*

> The key, I asserted in my book, to the darkness and despair of our lives for the last century was that bassoon, for it literally shook the fine mind of Charles Darwin into madness and produced the theory of random selection which continues to this day to deny the place of mind in the movement of nature. Think as you will, says Darwin (or rather Darwin's bassoon speaking through Darwin), but for all your effort, all your subtle thoughts, you are of no more value or significance than the ringing of a buoy bell on a rising sea, ringing and ringing, random and mad, or a cattail reed nodding pointlessly in a winter wind, or one of those hideous little dogs with its head bobbing up and down and up and down in the rear window of a battered automobile.

Neither Dillard nor Cosmo (though he is slowly disappearing in quicksand throughout the story) is a nihilist. The key to Dillard's good humor, often bordering on glee and described by one critic as "joyous existentialism," lies not merely in his deep WASP certainty that neither art (his own or anyone else's) nor intellect, any more than good works, shall be our salvation, but also in his firm adherence to the Augustinian tradition of aesthetics and of meaning in literature. St. Augustine is often cited as his touchstone of truth, never in jest. Excepting that Augustine himself viewed the truth of scripture, literature, and the world as joyous, and the alienation of man from that joy most often as a matter of folly rather than tragedy. All of which means that, despite the apparently trendy surface of his fiction, Dillard is in fact closer to Chaucer than to writers like Barthelme or Vonnegut or Pynchon. In a very serious sense, his fiction is satirically critical of the work of these fashionable writers and many others. It is therefore not likely to be very popular with them or their fans. But this does not seem to trouble Dillard very much. He seems to share Mark Twain's courageous willingness to attack the enemy boldly and on his own home ground.

"Te rog să-mi aduci încă o pătură," he says,

his voice fading and falling, "mi-a fost frig."
"An Inca, eh?" says Sir Hugh. "And far from home."
—R. H. W. Dilllard,
The Book of Changes

From among the uneven ranks of the new journalists, Tom Wolfe seems to me to be a powerful example of the persistence of WASP humor and comedy in our own times and in many ways Twain's lineal and natural descendant. Wolfe is "well known," more popularly so than most of our novelists. But the particular comic characteristics of his work, and the attitudes behind his comedy, do not yet seem to have been much noticed by either his admirers or his critics. With six books published in a decade, beginning with *The Kandy-Kolored Tangerine-Flake Streamline Baby* (1965)—and all of them, to the envy of any novelist, still in print—he is certainly to be reckoned with. With *The Painted Word* (1975), dealing satirically with the sacred cow of contemporary art in the New York gallery and museum scene ("Cultureburg"), he has managed to touch a painful nerve, to evoke from reviewers cries of outrage, angry catcalls from the otherwise reserved guardians of high culture. The camouflage of comedy in *The Painted Word* is familiar—short-fused jokes, caricatures, the sparkle and dazzle of the language of the speaker, composed half of shards of the latest slang and half of a parodic inflation of classical rhetoric, and all blithely indecorous; the shifty stance of the narrator, at times the wise naif, plain and pragmatic as Huck Finn, and at the next moment a kind of shrewd Tom Sawyer with his imaginative capacity to transform the ordinary into the grandly romantic; and above all the burlesque of treating a serious and complex subject as if it were simple and trivial, as if it were inherently funny. Behind and within the comedy stands a firm framework of WASP assumptions. Most reviewers have not noticed that *The Painted Word* is funny, perhaps because they sensed the ghostly presence of these assumptions without being able to identify them. It is hard to recognize a profoundly conservative writer who wears such a stylish, thoroughly modern disguise. The general reaction, like the reaction to his series of articles on *The New Yorker* (as yet uncollected in book form), was that this time he had gone too far.

In fact, from the beginning Wolfe has been going "too far." There is nothing new in *The Painted Word* except its single-minded focus on one limited subject. All he had lacked was the right subject for his satire, something the Establishment really cared enough about to take offense where it has always been intended. One might have supposed that *Radical Chic & Mau-Mauing the Flak-Catchers,* a paradigm of WASP attitudes on race, society, and politics, would have raised a chorus of critical objection. But there, somehow, Wolfe was on safer ground; for his ridicule of the radical chic of Leonard Bernstein and others came after the fact of strong, if deadly serious, editorial criticism by the *New York Times.* Significantly, *The Painted Word* takes as its point of departure a solemn critical article on contemporary art by Hilton Kramer, identified by Wolfe as "the *Times'* dean of the arts" and "critic-in-chief." The target of his satire is the thriving industry of art criticism, personified in a trio of influential critics—Clement Greenberg, Harold Rosenberg, and Leo Steinberg, "the big fish" of "Cultureburg," all three shown (like Post Office "wanted" posters) in solemn ethnic splendor in carefully selected photographs in the book. This is, incidentally, not overtly and exactly anti-Semitic; WASPs since John Calvin have prided themselves on not wholly sharing the long-prevalent and active Roman Catholic prejudice against Jews. It is, then, a more secular than theological prejudice. But the point is clear enough: these critics, like Freud and Marx, are intellectual gamesmen and hustlers, an alien if amusing group, not to be taken seriously or at face value. You won't find many of us, of *ours,* making a buck and a reputation out of the latest fashions (shades of the garment industry!) in modern art. The artists themselves, though shown to be exploited by these entrepreneurs, are also depicted as (just like everyone else) greedy, hypocritical, eager to "make it," hungry most of all for success. Both artists and critics are, then, seen to be hypocrites. To satirize these critics, all Wolfe needed to do was to build upon the WASP assumption that most art is trivial and that all modern art is suspect and probably fraudulent anyway, that serious grownups do not produce it and that those who profit from it are, at best, confidence men (like the Duke and the Dauphin).

But Wolfe's satire is more serious than that, more deeply protesting and Protestant. It is clearly populist. In the second chapter, "The public is not invited (and never has been)," he reduces "the art world" to a minimal elitist group: "That is the art world, approximately 10,000 souls—a mere hamlet!—restricted to *les beaux mondes* of eight cities." The view of American history is, at least implicity, solidly WASP. He cites, not in this context with any clear disapproval, the reaction of conservative critic, Royal Cortisoz, to the arrival of European modernism in America in the 1920's: "Writing in 1923, at the time of a national debate over immigration (which led to the Immigration Act of 1924), he compared the alien invasion of European modernism to the subversive alien hordes coming in by boat." The narrator is too sophisticated to assert such a thing himself, but it echoes a deep WASP feeling. More to the point, however, are the pictures of human motivation and duplicity among these foolish artists and critics. The WASP assumption of the flawed and divided self is precisely defined in this statement about the intense desire of the artists to be chosen, picked to be lifted from obscurity to the joys of success—"By all means, deny it if asked —what one knows, in one's cheating heart, and what one says are two different things!" The artist, too, like every other "soul," is a creature with a "cheating heart." Finally there is the scene itself, New York, treated traditionally as Babylon suffering under the delusion of being the new Jerusalem.

Whatever Wolfe himself may or may not believe, it is clear that consistently throughout all his work he has at any rate *used* WASP attitudes as the standard against which to measure and to satirize the contemporary scene. Like Twain, he can be savage in the exposure of the forms of stupefacient pretension and hypocrisy that he finds, special lashes being reserved for all the forms of moral hypocrisy. As a divided self, a creature made of mixed feelings, the WASP is extremely sensitive and alert to signs of hypocrisy in the self. It is, therefore, a fairly simple act of WASP imagination to detect and recognize those signs in others. But, like all good satirists, Wolfe has a core of positive standards, usually implicit, against which the behavior of deviants can be compared. There are even some heroes. Among them are people like Marshall McLuhan; George Barris, the artist of custom car design, "absolutely untouched by the big amoeba god of Anglo-European sophistication that gets you in the East"; and Junior Johnson ("The Last American Hero"), the good old boy and racing driver who is presented as admirable for, among other things, his courage, generosity, independence, honesty, lack of secular and social ambition, and the absence of hypocrisy in his social character. These are classic WASP virtues. Wolfe's moral indignation, like Swift's, is tempered into comedy because there is always at least the possibility of reform. "The old verities" endure and, measured by them, most human vices are more a matter of folly than of crime.

Manners have always been important to Wolfe. In such essays as "Tom Wolfe's New Book of Etiquette" and "O Rotten Gotham —Sliding Down into the Behavioral Sink" (from *The Pump House Gang* [1968]) and in the earlier piece, "The Big League Complex," he is particularly severe with the absence of good manners among the citizens, high and low, of New York/Babylon. Manners mean, in these pieces, what they mean to the WASP—first, the self-recognition of the flawed self which should lead to humility and, second, the recognition of the divine in others (thus also in oneself) which should lead to charity.

A spy in Babylon, Wolfe has found his place and the subject for his WASP comedy. He can be cheerful enough in recording the decline and fall of New York/Rome/Babylon because the Augustinian image of Jerusalem, the shining city of faith outside of time and human history, is always there for at least his WASP readers. What he may do next remains to be seen. Perhaps the reactions to *The Painted Word,* like the reaction of Twain's audience in Boston, will serve to liberate him and lead him toward wider subjects and deeper comedy. Meantime, however, the work is there, and in it the traditions of WASP humor burn bright and steady like a small pilot light.

> Then was our mouth filled with laughter, and our tongue with singing; then said they among the heathen, The Lord hath done great things for them.
>
> —Psalms 126:2

In summary: WASP humor, such as it has been, is, will be in our literature, is, on the one hand, inhibited by a complex cluster of beliefs and assumptions deeply held by most WASPs. Yet, on the other hand, it has been and can be liberated by the intensely Protestant spirit which is at the heart of WASP culture. By definition this spirit is rare and lonely, often incommunicable, rooted in faith rather than in works in any form. And a general WASP disregard for works of intellection and art—these seen and felt by the WASP as being a vanity of lesser breeds—works against the production of much WASP humor. When it appears, however, it is apt (like Twain's humor, its finest example) to be complex, incorporating many of the primal WASP assumptions and attitudes (for it is the purest expression of these) even as it ridicules much that is most characteristic of WASP society. Even as it always seems, to one degree or another, not to spare *itself* whipping and ridicule.

WASP humor is, then, a humor based on paradox and born out of painful conflict. It should not be forgotten that the first Anglo-Saxon poet (therefore the true archetype for the WASP literary artist) comes to us as a humorous figure, an illiterate cowherd at the dinner table (like Twain?) ashamed of his inability to play and sing. Who stole away to the barn. Where an angel came to him and bade him sing and even taught him how. An art not so much beyond as *aside from,* separate from all the power and status of Caesar, all the intellectual brilliance of Plato and Aristotle. An angel visits an illiterate, untalented cowherd. It's a funny idea. What the WASP writer, who is true to his heritage, aspires to is the condition of Caedmon, of faith. Here is how it is expressed by R. H. W. Dillard, in the last words of Cosmo Cotswaldo as he slowly sinks to his death in the bog: "I am walking on water. I am sinking in sand. In either case, both cases, I shall be, late or soon, swimming in air."

EARL ROVIT

College Humor and
the Modern Audience

Even the most minimal humility should lead me to preface my
observations on contemporary humor with apologetics, qualifications, and pedagogically pious disclaimers. After all, the literary-
critical road to humor is securely fenced by slapsticks and treacher-
ously paved with prat-falls, and nothing is more certain in this
uncertain world than the pathetic ignominy that awaits the brash
expert who would analyze the muzzle velocity, trajectory, and
effective killing range of laughter. But while it is undeniable that
humor is too volatile a subject to suffer the heavy-handedness of
literary criticism, it is even more true that humor is too deeply
embedded in the moral fabric of a society's sense of itself for it to
be left entirely under the purview of those who manipulate it for
their own purposes. Even though we know that laughter is largely
an involuntary response which is incited by impulses that we are
frequently unconscious of and that are expressive of attitudes of
superiority/inferiority, sadism, and masochism that we prefer not to
recognize in ourselves, still *homo sapiens* has some obligation to try
to understand himself as *homo ridens*. We may have little control
over our laughter while it is going on, but we can surely attempt to
examine what that laughter has exposed or concealed in ourselves
and our society after its cessation. As I write, the current fads of
humor include *Monty Python's Flying Circus, Crawdaddy,* obscene

and/or silly T shirts, Mel Brooks, Woody Allen, and TV "roasts" of well-known entertainment personalities. My concern will be to trace some of the currents in the last fifty years that have led our society to these curious giggling ways.

As everyone knows, literary humor generally exploits a situation of radical disproportion—some grotesque discrepancy from an established norm or ideal state of affairs which has been tacitly or explicitly embodied in the philosophic and ethical perspectives of one's time. Conditioned to expect a certain predictably reasonable pattern of behavior, the reader is subjected instead to an abrupt disturbance in rhythm—a sudden deviation from his legitimate anticipations. One of the possible responses to such a shock is that gradual or explosive release of energies which is most dramatically expressed in laughter, and this physical reaction is the essential target of all deliberate humor. I have no doubt, of course, that the dynamics of the comic transaction are a good deal more complicated than this, but for my purposes I will assume such a model as a minimal description of what evokes risibility in literature.[1]

The difficulty of dealing with contemporary humor is, as I see it, at least threefold. First, we can no longer take for granted any real consensus on what constitutes a "reasonable pattern of behavior." Contemporary psychology, modern physics, and current history—to point to only three areas—have succeeded in partially legitimizing the once-considered qualities of the bizarre and the outrageous within the most familiar texture of our lives. As psychology has learned to ignore morality in its examination of behavior and personality (B. F. Skinner, R. D. Laing et al.), and as theoretical science has come to accept the uncertainty principle in what had been the impregnable fortress of objective surety, recent events (ranging from genocide and global international bungling to political assassinations, Watergate, etc.) sometimes seem to suggest that the very notion of reasonable behavior has become the wildest of our contemporary fantasies. Without a general agreement on the nature of reasonable behavior, however, how can the writer and his audience be expected to recognize those deviations which evoke laughter?[2]

---

[1] In all fairness I should declare my indebtedness to Arthur Koestler's discussions of humor, especially those in *Insight and Outlook* (New York: Macmillan, 1949). His attempt to synthesize the views of Aristotle, Freud, and Bergson with the physiological experience of laughter is, I believe, extremely useful to the student of humor.

[2] One reason for the generally impoverished quality of literary humor in the past decades

Second, we can no longer count on a conditioned social or religious sense of decorum which will enable us to distinguish between those extreme events which may shock us into laughter, and those which should elicit from us emotional paralysis, disgust, or religious awe. The traditional targets of the humorist's critical venom—affectation, hypocrisy, and complacently administered injustice—are mercurical abstractions which are pragmatically cogent only when their opposites are firmly fixed in the collective experience of a culture. When the weight of the supposed moral virtues relaxes on one side of the scale, the vices draw to an even level, and the two categories tend to become blurred and without emotional urgency. Or, to view it in a different way, *taste*—our traditional arbiter of fine gradations in the quality of experience—has been assiduously invited to become polymorphously perverse, to become—at least in theory—all-accepting, and hence to surrender the judgmental stance which the humorous response requires.[3] Both of these factors are enormously complex and susceptible to endless analysis and interpretation, but in this brief essay I should like to examine a special facet of a related third factor, one that might be called

---

may be our grudging realization that "reasonable behavior" is not an objective "given" to be discovered in the human condition, but a collectively shared fabrication of a particular ethos. Those eras like the eighteenth century, which seem so fertile in producing brilliant satire and ebullient comedy, are eras in which "reasonable behavior" and corresponding moral imperatives are secure enough in their claims to existence that they can be healthily criticized without being squeezed into amorphousness. Our century's elevation of the grotesque may indicate the degree to which we have lost a spontaneous belief in the objective existence of reasonableness and rationality. For me, the pivotal figure in this development is Kafka, whose work is brilliantly defined by Thomas Mann as that of "a religious humorist." Those writers who have followed in his mode have done so either without his moral intensity (Borges) or without his sense of humor (Céline, Hesse), or without both. Three novelists who seem to be his legitimate successors in balancing humorously the imperatives of both self and society—and thus who refer back through Kafka to such novelists as Dostoevsky, Melville, and Dickens—are Faulkner, Günter Grass, and Gabriel Garcia Marquez.

[3]Newspaper photos of self-immolating monks and documentaries of bulldozers filling in mass graves have been known to elicit responsive titters from contemporary viewers; and the theater of the absurd (Ionesco, Beckett, Albee) has prepared audiences to see *King Lear* and the crucifixion as spectacles of "hip" or grotesque comedy. When *taste* abrogates its responsibility to prescribe the rules of etiquette, we should not be surprised at the emergence of such temporary sophomoronic successes as *MacBird, Doctor Strangelove,* Lenny Bruce, a variety of ephemeral rock superstars, etc. *Taste* used to be under the partial dominance of a loosely connected group of publishers, editors, critics, religious representatives, academics, and the like; what they lacked in intelligence, sensitivity, and courage—and this was substantial—they partly made up in the simple fact of their visibility. Now, measured by Nielsen ratings, box-office receipts, and volume of paperback sales, taste has become an economic function of the marketplace, rather than an arguable moral judgment. It is curious, and not a little humorous, that a certain kind of temperament will interpret this development as an expansion of freedom and a strengthening of individualism.

more specifically "sociological"; namely, the composition of the humorist's audience.

The effectiveness of literary humor hinges crucially on the establishment of an assumed channel of understanding between the writer and his selectively restricted readership. That is, in order for there to be those who are "in" on a joke, there must also be those who are, by definition, outside of it. In this sense, the humorous transaction deliberately seeks partiality rather than universality, and strives to develop a tenuous connection between writer and reader through which may be formed a kind of fluid, semi-secret membership whose adepts will find a specific literary style or vision laughable.[4] By the same token, all those for whom the humorous text is written in an undecipherable code are clearly excluded. Thus, of all literary strategies, humor is especially needful of a very concrete (and commercially viable) social definition of its potential audience —who they are, what values and interests they share, what they are willing to believe in (at least for the duration of their laughter), and what moral and ethical considerations they may be induced to discard temporarily as irrelevant or of expendable importance.

As our culture has moved steadily in the direction of some variety of homogeneity since World War I, many of our traditional social demarcations have become significantly blurred and, consequently, less and less useful as sources of tension in the production of humor. The conventional antagonisms of rural and urban, vulgar and genteel, poor and rich, newly arrived and well established, ignorant and educated have grown appreciably less marked as our population—or

---

A trivial enough example of the kinds of literary-critical problems which the taste vacuum forces upon the student of humor may be seen in the ambiguous reception of Mailer's *American Dream*. While nothing in the novel clearly indicates that the book is to be read under the broad rubric of humor, some of its more eloquent advocates have insisted that its humorlessness, its melodramatic sensationalism, its structural incoherence, its cartoon characterizations, and its failure to project a clear thematic position constitute compelling evidence that the novel is intended to be read as a parody. This procedure, I must confess, reminds me of the art dealer who successfully sold a very badly proportioned portrait by entitling it "A Lady with a Big Head." Similarly, novels like those of Jerzy Kosinski—which seem, to me, simple cases of art failure—are boosted as examples of courageous and cunning satirical craftsmanship; this suggests that when formal *taste* disappears, "bad taste" becomes automatically valuable. Cf. *Hair, Jesus Christ Superstar, Let My People Come, Portnoy's Complaint, Play It As It Lays*.

[4]As George Bernard Shaw suggested, there is no laughter in heaven; a comedy with truly "universal" appeal would be a comedy devoid of humor—a *Divine Comedy* consisting only of the *Paradise*. Or, more accurately, we can conceive of angelic laughter only when it is being contemptuous of mankind—as at the conclusion of Chaucer's *Troilus*. An interesting variation of this—laughter in heaven which *mocks* the angels—is seen in Peretz's "Bontche the Silent."

at least our official image of it—attains a greater degree of socio-economic uniformity. At the same time, and in spite of the recent emergence of various group consciousness-raising movements, there has been a considerable decrease in the capacity of regional, religious, and some ethnic identifications to serve as an automatic means of isolating and addressing specific audiences. Accordingly, while it is probable that black, Hispanic, Chicano, and homosexual writers should be able to expand and intensify their rapport with their respective constituencies for some time into the future, it seems safe to suggest that most of the rest of our contemporary humorists or would-be humorists—including Southerners, Jews, and Catholics—are faced with a serious difficulty in discovering or creating groups of like-minded people to whom they can comically address themselves.[5]

Possibly the largest definable audience in our society at the present time—the consumer group most readily identifiable in terms of values, interests, and lifestyles—is one which cuts a wide swathe across regional, economic, sociological, ethnic, and religious categories. If we consider the ambiguous concept "adolescence" in a somewhat broader context than that of either the merely psysiological or the sheerly psychological—if we think of it as a flexible state of responsiveness which can be indulged in by people of almost any age, sect, or sex—we may be able to discern a surprisingly pervasive and consistent focus for humor in contemporary culture. In other words, and to place it in a purposely oversimplified perspective, what was with some just condescension regarded as "college humor" in the period between the two World Wars—a highly exclusive in-group product of a very sheltered upper-middle-class WASP minority—has become the ubiquitous style and attitude of our contemporary media and one especially prominent in contemporary fiction. Or, to put it even more succinctly, John Barth's metaphor of the world-as-college-campus in *Giles Goat-Boy* may possess an accuracy of definition which many of us have regarded as mere poetic license.

[5]The extent to which the partly or wholly liberated female composes a distinct interest-group, and the degree to which the female sex-experience provides material for an exclusive kind of humor suggest problems which I am incompetent to pursue. Talented female writers with keen senses of humor (Cynthia Buchanan, Erica Jong, etc.) exist in abundance, but I do not know of any for whose work the sexual adjective is a militantly restrictive definition. If there are some, I would expect their work—humorous or non-humorous—to run the danger of taking the form of special pleading, either as self-indulgent propaganda or as pornographic monologue.

Let me, at any rate, project a fanciful line of development that may illustrate this generally unremarked shift and growth of audience. We might begin with our quintessential collegiate talent, Scott Fitzgerald—perhaps with his recurrent gag about sawing waiters in half, or maybe with Jake Barnes and Bill Gorton's smart-aleck conversations about pity and irony, or the cost of stuffed dogs *(The Sun Also Rises)*. We would have to pay careful and respectful attention to the 1925 founding of *The New Yorker* magazine, its casual but powerful relationships—partly through the Algonquin group—with Broadway and Hollywood, and the incalculable influence wielded for the next fifteen years or so by such ex-college humorists as Robert Benchley, S. J. Perelman, James Thurber, and E. B. White. (One might contrast the satirical techniques and tones of their humor with that of Ring Lardner, Damon Runyon, and Sinclair Lewis to appreciate the distinction I have in mind.) The 1930's would contain Henry Miller's two *Tropic* extravaganzas and might be conveniently bracketed by Nathanael West's *Dream Life of Balso Snell* (1931)[6] and *The Day of the Locust* (1939); and, with Hollywood in mind, we should note that these were the years when writers like Perelman and George S. Kaufman were contributing scripts to the Marx Brothers' great film productions. And then we might pause for a breath of reflection on a novel like Max Shulman's *Barefoot Boy with Cheek* (1944). Commercially popular—in fact, over thirty years later it is still in print—this book might be considered emblematic of the audience and style shifts I am trying to delineate. As far as I know, *Barefoot Boy* has never been discussed in terms of existential, black, sick, grotesque, absurd, or apocalyptic humorous strategies. It is a simple first-person narrative, ingenuous, silly, parodic, safely irreverent, repetitive, enamored of funny names like Yetta Samovar, Asa Hearthrug, Lodestone La Toole, casually digressive and dedicated to the device of the pointless meandering anecdote. Dealing with a young man's first encounter with college, it is almost a textbook illustration of college humor, professionally crafted for an extramural readership in much the same way that Notre Dame football teams used to attract a vast working-class subway alumni. The novel is devoid of any but a slight

---

[6]After writing this, I was gratified to find my judgment supported by Ezra Pound, who called West's first novel "the sort of thing we should get off our chests by the beginning of sophomore year in college." Cited by Robert McAlmon in *McAlmon and the Lost Generation,* ed. R. E. Knoll (Lincoln: University of Nebraska Press, 1962), p. 305.

historical interest, yet it contains in full the materials that critics have found so beguiling in the fiction of Vonnegut, Brautigan, Wurlitzer, and others.[7]

Continuing and accelerating along my fanciful line, however, we might mark off such cultural events as the meteoric success of the San Francisco "Beats" (particularly *Howl*), the fantastic circulation of *Mad* magazine, the popularity of the stand-up nightclub comedians of the 1950's, the relentless ardor of the J. D. Salinger cult, and the 1959 publication of Burroughs's *Naked Lunch*. Is it not clear, in retrospect, that in some wildly proliferating way pre–World War II "college humor" had managed to create or discover for itself an audience that went far beyond the old campus-subsidized burlesque skits and humor magazines, at the same time that our college populations and their burgeoning alumni were swelling prodigiously in number?[8] And still proceeding toward the present—toward Pynchon, Ishmael Reed, Sukenick, McGuane, DeLillo, Barthelme, Elkin et al.—we would cite such mixed-media marketing achievements as the widespread growth of poetry readings, *Playboy* magazine, *Catch-22*, Kurt Vonnegut, Woody Allen, Mel Brooks, *M*A*S*H**, Neil Simon, and the innumerable "underground" pub-

---

[7]Shulman's symbolic position as college humorist emeritus is supported by his career after *Barefoot Boy,* not so much with his subsequent novels as in the regular syndicated column which he produced, under the sponsorship of Philip Morris, for distribution to college newspapers all over the country. The direct and indirect influence of these *Ski-U-Mah* (the University of Minnesota humor magazine) snippets on some ten years' worth of American college students (through the 1950's) cannot be discounted.

It is also instructive to note the very different roads taken by Shulman and his classmate-rival for honors in humor, Thomas O. Heggen. The latter, the author of *Mr. Roberts,* grounds his novel and the stage version (in which he collaborated with Joshua Logan) on a solid realistic acceptance of social and psychological limitations. Apparently the Logan production was preceded by an abortive play version produced by Heggen and Shulman. It would be interesting to compare the Shulman script with both the novel and the Logan version to try to isolate the differences between "college humor" and non-college humor. For material on the Shulman-Heggen relationship, see John Leggett, *Ross and Tom* (New York: Simon and Schuster, 1974).

[8]I have had, necessarily, to slight the crucial and concomitant development of the advertising and public relations industry which takes place within the time period of our concern. From its amateurish Ivy League beginnings in the 1920's, it was to become the highly efficient, incalculably wide-ranging communications grid of the late 1960's, and it would embrace an interlocking network of radio, TV, theater, movies, newspapers, magazines, and publishing houses whose main staples of concern—equally interlocking—would be news, education, and, above all, entertainment. McLuhan's heralded equation of "medium" and "message"—whatever its other shortcomings—accurately expresses the relationship between the communications industry and its insatiable demand for entertainment—a demand for which college humor has become a major supplier. A careful study of the humorous content in major forms of advertising between 1920 and 1970 would be enormously useful.

lications associated with the drug culture, rock, student rebellion, liberated sex, back-to-naturism, and a general dissatisfaction with middle-class manners and mores.

Perhaps a heroic attempt at a definition may contribute some clarification at this point. What I have been cavalierly pointing toward as "adolescent" or "college" humor is something like this: at its most characteristic, it is of an elephantine subtlety, deliberately grotesque and meant to be shocking in its obsessive concern with creature functions and body orifices (eating, sweating, evacuating, fornicating), defiantly irresponsible and buoyantly paranoid in its absolutistic assaults on whatever is not itself, usually impatient or clumsy with the devices of wit, inexperienced or inept with language, but desperately dependent on the machinery of parody. Further, it tends to be fanatically imbued with a righteous zeal to equate its own moral position with that of the angels; it consistently projects an amorphous sentimentality that upholds goodness, naturalness, spontaneity, and freedom as though these were inalienable properties of humankind capable of thriving like magic weeds in everyone's garden, except that—for reasons that are never quite clear—they are under continual psychotic attack by the forces of crippled and diseased evil. Or, perhaps even more clarifyingly, it is interesting to note what this kind of humor does *not* concern itself with. It almost always avoids those strategies of satire and ridicule which pay their respects to the social determinations of personality and behavior.[9] It has an inherent disposition to distrust the rational and the intellectual—although it may very well be lavish in its own pretensions of bookish grandiosity (cf. William Gaddis's *Recognitions,* Barth's *Sotweed Factor,* Pynchon's *V.* and *Gravity's Rainbow* as examples). It consistently oversimplifies the human condition, straining itself toward the extreme and the surreal rather like a verbal cartoon; it is terrified of and preoccupied with death, and desperately fearful of birth, continuity, tradition, the historic past, and, above all, the future. When faced with the challenge of making a real moral commitment, it is likely to retreat into jejune irony or ingenuously to award itself the unmerited plum of an untested and irrevocable innocence—and, frequently, it will do both of these

---

[9]This, it seems to me, is what distinguishes comic novelists like Saul Bellow and John Updike from many of their peers—namely, their concern to understand the relationship between character and formative environment as a reciprocal one.

things at the same time.[10] Where the traditional processes of satire are aimed at exposing and ridiculing hypocrisy and affectation in an educative effort to reassert social and psychological harmonies, the adolescent comic spirit seems curiously unanchored in any practical conception of society or selfhood, unfocused on any goal beyond its immediate *yuk* or pratfall or put-down, and blithely directed on a path of pure and aimless destructiveness when it is not being just plain silly.[11] One would not ordinarily think of the delicate Narcissus as a humorous character, but his seems to me the archetypal figure that best illustrates the emotional valences of the adolescent comic spirit.

Because of its ivied isolation, college humor of the twenties and thirties could easily afford the lugubrious and morally irresponsible gestures of apocalypse. It was, after all, the luxurious product of a pampered class that was impeccably secure, elegantly well favored, and safely impotent within the restraints of the outside "real" world. And its style could not but be attractive to the fledgling writer—who was normally an apprentice not only in his craft, but in his pursuit of maturity as well. As the boundaries of the campus become coterminous with our entire culture, and as the older arbiters of taste and ethics disappear, to be supplanted by the impersonal marketplace-

[10]A brilliant example of that kind of masterful juggling between sentimentality and irony in which the positive elements of both are cancelled out is, I think, Vonnegut's *Cat's Cradle*—a novel which tends to diffuse like a puffball under the barest breath of critical analysis. This is, of course, a dangerously subjective area for the critic to cavort in, but it seems to me useful to try to compare a novel like *Cat's Cradle* with Heller's *Catch-22* and Salinger's *Catcher in the Rye*. Besides the alliteration which their titles share, they have all been massive publishing successes, each of them has served as a cult object for readers below the age of thirty, and each of them—in different ways—establishes a precarious balance between the indulgences of sentimentality and the strictures of irony. While all three novels exhibit powerful elements of what I have been describing as "college humor," only *Cat's Cradle* goes over the line into sheer frivolousness. Whether it is the artist's concern for language or the humanist's grudging acceptance of the experienced reality of social and psychological structures, Heller's and Salinger's novels succeed in becoming *responsible* metaphors in a way that *Cat's Cradle* does not.

[11]It is only fair, of course, to recall Philip Roth's comments on the difficulties of being a modern humorist, and to reemphasize the possibility that our time—with its strong sense of civic impotence—is, in many ways, singularly unsuited for satire. T. R. Henn has suggested some of the reasons for this: "partly because our society is too diffuse, partly because of the law of libel, partly because most of us are too busy to hate violently and long, but most of all because our hatred has so little effect" (*The Apple and the Spectroscope* [New York: W. W. Norton, 1966], p. 87). One might add also that while there is a plethora of material to excite our disgust, irritation, and contempt, there seem to be few personalities who are worthy of our hatred. One of the more depressing elements in the Watergate affair was the revelation of the drab seediness of those who might have been considered villains. Part of the conditioning of our time is to perceive "the banality of evil" in human affairs—a perspective that may be too realistic to incite great satire.

statistics of corporate management, the contextual restraints within and against which humor operates are drastically altered. The adolescent style of comedy has come to pervade our entire culture; it is indiscriminately targeted at all ages (from *Sesame Street* to *Let's Make a Deal*), at every socio-economic level, at all interest groups. It is the standard comic ingredient in advertising and public relations, in radio and TV talk shows, in news reportage which aims at "human interest," as well as in the more traditional forms of entertainment. But since this extraordinary audience shift has occurred in combination with a wholesale relaxation of moral/ethical standards within all our social agencies, it becomes questionable whether the critical edge of that humor can be wielded against anything other than itself. In other words, its dominant aim tends to be self-congratulation rather than clarification, and its overall effect is to invite a resigned acceptance of a demonstratedly absurd status quo.

Ultimately, the comic spirit draws its strength from the realm of possibilities, rather than from limitations. Its most profound and healthy appeal is to that creative and destructive explosion of energies which offers men a renewed promise of themselves and a recognition of the realistic options that are open to them in their lives. On this level, the humorous response is precisely parallel to the traditional religious response—a life-oriented and life-redeeming underwriting of the present, and an ungrudging acceptance of a promissory note on the future. Adolescent humor can, of course, mature into such a humanistic attitude, even as adolescence itself can struggle toward adulthood. But it is at least equally disposed to avoid the painful ambiguities of maturity—to move in the direction of sick or black or purely farcical humor which is, at best, a kind of holding action or a nervous giggle signifying one's self-pitying impotence and despair in the face of presumed disaster. Serving almost entirely as a defense mechanism, it can very easily become in league with the very forces it is built to defend against. Narcissus, terrified, makes faces at his own grotesque reflection in the pool, and is as prone to slip into suicide out of self-fear as out of self-love. Every bit as inherently characteristic of adolescent or college humor as its natural strengths—its ebullience, its rebelliousness, its willingness to experiment, its courageous desire to appraise the stale familiar world with fresh eyes and an uncorrupted heart—is this narcissistic invitation toward melodramatic writhing and indulgent self-immolation. And at this parlous time in our history, I worry whether the latter tendency may not be the one which is more seductive to the contemporary humorist and his audience, as well as the one that we must most stringently guard our fatigued and world-sated sensibilities against.

SANFORD PINSKER

The Urban Tall Tale:
Frontier Humor
in a Contemporary Key

In a delightful piece of showmanship, Josh Billings, the nineteenth-
century humorist, would have a glass of milk solemnly placed on the
podium before he delivered his famous lecture on "milk."[1] Epi-
grams of every sort blended into disgressions and then into lengthy
asides, but milk per se was never mentioned. One is tempted to write
about the urban tall tale in a similar mode, by circling the subject
endlessly but never quite touching the thing itself. Unfortunately, an
analysis of comic elements cannot—and probably should not—be a
comic performance. Besides, what example of the urban tall tale
could be as portable, as clear, or as subliminally funny as a glass of
milk? Nevertheless, having announced my subject—the urban tall
tale—I will, temporarily, abandon it. Which is to say, in a spirit
more akin to General MacArthur than to Josh Billings, I promise
to return.

Ours is an age with good reasons for insisting upon the universality of humor. A world more willing to laugh at itself might also be a
world able to survive the considerable dangers of our century. But
humor, like all art, begins in gritty particulars. American humor is
characterized by bigness and swagger—or some folksy combination
of the two. Exaggeration was a necessary component of the Ameri-

---

[1]Willard Thorp, *American Humorists* (Minneapolis: University of Minnesota Press,
1964), p. 19.

can imagination, and we have retained a national fondness for it ever since. For example, when England claimed that the colonies could not provide even one pair of stockings for each inhabitant from the wool produced in America, Benjamin Franklin answered as follows: "The very Tails of the American Sheep are so laden with Wooll, that each has a little Car or Waggon on four little wheels, to support and keep it from trailing on the ground."[2] Thus, long before things were "bigger in Texas," they were fair-sized in Philadelphia.

But Franklin's ingenious falsehood about the biology of American sheep is more than just a good retort; it is the very essence of the tall tale, albeit in an embryonic form. Exaggeration is, after all, closely aligned with overcompensation, with those mechanisms which metamorphose apparent inferiorities into stunning boasts. Tall tales are a version of this psychology. That is, they build themselves upon "exaggerations" of a very special sort, ones which insist that environment is less a naturalistic determiner than an occasion for wry embellishment. In effect, imagination turns the tables on quotidian reality. If the confirmed hand-wringer believes he has been beaten *a priori,* defeated by what James T. Farrell once described as "a world I never made," the folk humorist brings the ground conditions of his universe into birth with one hand while he engineers his savvy victories over them with the other. He is, in short, a fabulous artist of the endlessly possible. As his version of the Cartesian equation would have it: Things rendered bigger than life *are* Life.

In talking about even the folksiest of tall tales, we are, ineluctably, talking about Art. The exaggerated stories associated with, say, Davy Crockett or Mike Fink depend as much upon the teller's stance as they do upon an audience's willing suspension of disbelief. For all its rough edges, the tall tale is sophisticated enough to know that the line separating that boasting which charms and that which merely grates is a thin one indeed. *Style* separates a confirmed boaster like Nimrod Wildfire from those who generate more opposition than good cheer. As Mark Twain put it: "The humorous story is told gravely; the teller does his best to conceal the fact that he even dimly suspects that there is anything funny about it. . . ."[3] Something of

---

[2] From Benjamin Franklin's 1765 letter, as quoted in Thorp, *American Humorists,* p. 6.
[3] From Mark Twain's essay "How to Tell a Story," included in *American Literature: The Makers and the Making* (New York: St. Martin's Press, 1973), p. 1292.

the same aesthetic applies to the ring-tailed roarers who populate the tall tale. When Nimrod Wildfire boasts that he is "half horse, half alligator and a touch of the airthquake—[that he's] got the prettiest sister, fastest horse, and ugliest dog in the district, and can out run, out jump, throw down, drag out and whip any man in all Kentuck!"[4] he suggests that the obverse of the Delphic oracle's "Never too much!" may be a Blakean faith in "Never too little!" A seemingly endless barrage of colorful language—riddled with fanciful metaphor and outrageous comparison—creates the proper atmosphere and, by extension, the desired effect.

Contemporary modes of bragging employ similar techniques, but apply them to the other end of the stick. That is, they tend to emphasize the protagonist's ineptness rather than his accomplishment, his inferiority instead of his swaggering confidence. The result is a heroic *schlemiel*hood, one which substitutes the nebbish for the backwoodsman, the man who can do nothing right for the man who could do nothing wrong.

At least part of the radical alteration in psychology is the result of shifting one's locale from an expansive frontier to a claustrophobic city. Urban tall tales reflect the faster, hipper rhythms of city life, but they also insist upon creating zany brands of good cheer not unlike those fashioned by their comic ancestors. As the term itself implies, *all* tall tales are a matter of artfully stretching the facts until the landscape that results is bigger, richer, funnier or grimmer than the mundane life surrounding it. By focusing upon a hybrid like the urban tall tale, I am trying to suggest not only something about the transfer of a literary imagination from the comic gusto of the frontier to the comic brands of paranoia currently generating from our cities, but also something of the dynamics involved when folk materials are incorporated into the structure of a novel.

Let me begin with the latter point. In roughly the same way that we have learned to distinguish between "pure" and "impure" poetry, the tall tale generally functions as an element within a larger fictional canvas. A novel composed of tall tales strung together like beads on a string would be not only unsatisfying to read, but virtually impossible to write. Once again, Mark Twain provides the clearest

[4]Walter Blair, *Horse Sense in American Humor* (Chicago: University of Chicago Press, 1942), p. 36.

index for that delicate balancing required when frontier humor turns, almost imperceptibly, into high art. I am referring, of course, to *The Adventures of Huckleberry Finn.*

As Huck's opening speech would have it, Mr. Mark Twain ". . . told the truth, mainly. There was things which he stretched, but mainly he told the truth. That is nothing. I never seen anybody but lied one time or another, without it was Aunt Polly, or the widow, or maybe Mary. Aunt Polly—Tom's Aunt Polly, she is —and Mary, and the Widow Douglas is all told about in that book [*The Adventures of Tom Sawyer*], which is mostly a true book, with some stretchers, as I said before." To be sure, one generalizes about Huck's saga at his own peril, but nothing seems closer to its essential spirit than the spectre of "stretchers" expanding ominously. That is, what begins as those small embellishments separating the "plain-speaking" voice of Huck from the more literate one of Mr. Twain quickly mushroom into exaggerations of a darkling stripe. The result calls the imagination itself into question, balancing the assets of illusion against the liabilities of reality.

The dichotomy receives its clearest expression in the Tom Sawyer who superimposes "A-rabs and elephants" onto the fabric of an unsensational realism, and in the Huck Finn whose skeptical horse sense declares, "It had all the marks of a Sunday School." Such are the twin faces of boyhood's charm: the good "bad boy" in search of a sustaining fiction, and the bad "good boy" who refuses to outgrow his subversive rebelhood. The one turns life into compulsive theater; the other is obsessed by the truth lying just beneath illusion's layers. Unfortunately, the former—that Tom Sawyer destined, despite himself, to become the charismatic president of, say, a Moose lodge —carries the day in ways the latter never can. Which is to say, the seductions of romantic adventure will always have a greater appeal than the clarity of vision which brings us bad news. *Both* have more than a touch of the artist in their bones, but Tom will write the best-sellers, crack up the talk-show crowd. Huck, on the other hand, finds himself cursed into a "seeing" he cannot avoid or alter. Huck's temperament pushes at those edges beyond which fiction, at least for Twain, could not go.

In a novel where "lies" turn inexplicably into dark truths, where Huck *becomes* Tom in both name and essential character, illusions are as problematic for critics as they are troubling for the innocent

Huck. Consider, for example, the following bit of deadpan commentary about things that "seem" and those that are:

> . . . and by and by a drunken man tried to get into the circus ring-
> —said he wanted to ride; said he could ride as well as anybody that
> ever was. . . . So, then, the ringmaster he made a little speech, and
> said he hoped there wouldn't be no disturbance, and if the man would
> promise he would let him ride if he thought he could stay on the horse.
> So everybody laughed and said all right, and the man got on. The
> minute he was on, the horse begun to rip and tear and jump and cavort
> around, with two circus men hanging on to his bridle trying to hold
> him, and the drunken man hanging on to his neck, and his heels flying
> in the air every jump, and the whole crowd of people standing up
> shouting and laughing till tears rolled down.[5]

But slapstick humor is only the initial attention-getter. Granted, drunks are a staple item in the repertoire of comic grotesquerie and incongruous action which strikes the rubes as knee-slappingly "funny." The idea is at least as old as Aristotle's notion that comedy is an imitation of men who are inferior but not altogether vicious. As the poor drunk bobs and weaves, we give expression to our own sober superiority. That is, until the "snapper" reverses the tables:

> But pretty soon he struggled up astraddle and grabbed the bridle,
> a-reeling this way and that; and the next minute he sprung up and
> dropped the bridle and stood! and the horse a-going like a house afire,
> too. He just stood up there, a-sailing around as easy and comfortable
> as if he warn't ever drunk in his life—and then he begun to pull off his
> clothes and sling them. He shed them so thick they kind of clogged up
> the air, and altogether he shed seventeen suits. And, then, there he
> was, slim and handsome, and dressed the gaudiest and prettiest you
> ever saw, and he lit into that horse with his whip and made him fairly
> hum—and finally skipped off, and made his bow and danced off to the
> dressing-room, and everybody was just a-howling with pleasure and
> astonishment.

To be sure, the calculated piece of theater quoted above depends upon visual double-take, rather than on shrewdly restrained narration. But in a novel where the Duke and King exploit human weaknesses via con games, or Jim brings minstrel antics to his own tall tale about the "witches" riding him around the world, frontier humor provides Twain with methods of satiric attack and, then, with strategies of necessary psychic defense. Huck can function as the

[5]Mark Twain, *The Adventures of Huckleberry Finn*, Ch. 22.

traditionally naive persona who expresses the deadly absurdities lurking behind chivalric codes, or the mores which make slavery legally right and morally proper; but he also threatens to move beyond sensitive "boyhood" to that realm just a little higher than the angels.

Ironically enough, however, at the point when Huck seems to have learned what mythic journeys of initiation would teach, Twain introduces a highly disturbing snapper. In this sense, the episode at the circus is emblematic of those larger vacillations between illusion and reality which characterize life on the Phelps's plantation. Good cheer—rather than grim recognition—is the note on which Jim is sadistically "rescued" and the novel itself is resolved.

Put another way: characters in a traditional tall tale are spared the anguish of existential reality. Unlike the protagonists of a novel, they do not have to wake up the next morning, worry about how much a loaf of bread costs and what they will do to earn some ready cash. Created bigger than life already, they live in all the comfort of legend, secure in the house their teller's rhetoric built. Dovetail these colorful characters into the world of a novel and they change shape, becoming an index of the continual warfare between harder-headed claims about reality and the energy which would stretch that "truth" into grotesquely comic shapes.

If *The Adventures of Huckleberry Finn* demonstrated a technique for blending folk material into the larger concerns of a "serious" novel, J. D. Salinger applied the lessons to an urban milieu and to that avatar of Huck whom he called Holden Caulfield. Granted, the movement I am suggesting from Twain's classic to *The Catcher in the Rye* is neither surprising nor thrillingly revisionist. After all, critics have been pointing out the parallels (mythic and otherwise) between the Mississippi and the Hudson for some time now. I reopen the case merely to link one brand of shape-stretching exaggeration with another.

In effect, Holden's wild romp through New York is the "madman stuff" of which tall tales, frontier and urban, are made—albeit rendered in ways which simultaneously conceal his unhappy loneliness and reveal its darker underpinnings. Holden's obsessive "stretchers"—his pointless lie to Mrs. Morrow about her "sensitive" son Ernest ("Sensitive. That killed me. That guy Morrow was about as sensitive as a goddam toilet seat."), or his offhand remark about "this tiny tumor [he has] on the brain"—allow him to maximize control without the baggage of consequence. Too, Holden's flair for the melodramatic provides a brief respite from the novel's ongoing confrontations with evidences of mutability. Tom Sawyer took his cue from the pages of *Don Quixote,* as Mark Twain laughed sardonically from the wings; Holden, apparently, knows better: "The goddam movies. They can ruin you. I'm not kidding."[6]

One talks about such parallels easily (perhaps *too* easily), confident that the bridges between Huck and Holden have been buttressed by dozens of previous articles. At this point, however, I would like to suggest that something akin to the comic energy of frontier humor permeates an ever-widening arc of contemporary American fiction. Granted, the signposts are not as clearly marked as they were with *The Catcher in the Rye,* and some surface characteristics get lost in the translation, but the essential component of grotesque stretching remains.

Viewed conservatively, the tall tale achieved its literary apotheosis in a work like *The Hamlet* (1940), where yarns about spotted horses or hidden treasure kept the rubes scurrying across Faulkner's Yoknapatawpha County. Approached more broadly, however, the tall tale is adaptable enough to encompass everything from a folkloric novel like Ralph Ellison's *Invisible Man* to the apocalyptic visions of Thomas Pynchon's *V.* What these radically different novels share is a sense that the contours of urban life require funhouse glass, rather than realistic mirrors.

In this latter sense, Franz Kafka—rather than William Faulkner—has made the influential difference to novelists like Bruce Jay Friedman or Philip Roth. To be sure, the "Kafkaesque" includes a wide range of territory. For some, his name invokes the nightmare of our century's bureaucratic history; for others, he represents the starkly alienated man pitted against authorities allegorically defined as father, God, or some Freudian combination of the two. But as Philip Roth has pointed out, it was not "until I had got hold of guilt, you see, as a comic idea, did I begin to feel myself lifting free and clear of my last book [*When She Was Good*] and my old concerns."[7] Whatever else *Portnoy's Complaint* might be, it is a

---

[6]J. D. Salinger, *The Catcher in the Rye* (New York: Bantam, 1964), pp. 55, 58, 104.

[7]Philip Roth, *Reading Myself and Others* (New York: Farrar, Straus and Giroux, 1975), p. 22.

book which makes it clear that the traumas of an American-Jewish (which is to say, *urban*) childhood were, in Roth's own words, "so *funny,* this morbid preoccupation with punishment and guilt."

In Kafka's world, the corridor turns, almost predictably, into a labyrinth or *cul-de-sac;* vague guilts exert a constant, disorienting pressure. One lives in a surrealistic dream, with the uneasy sense that "surrealism" may have outlived its usefulness as a literary term and become, instead, a fairly accurate way of describing the conditions of daily life. Yet it is at this point in Kafka's fiction, when ill-defined terrors threaten to reach the breaking point, that the collective excess begins to take on comic dimensions.

"The Metamorphosis" is such a fiction. It suggests in bold relief the kind of transference endemic to the urban tall tale. The essential "seriousness" of the story must be set against the contrapuntal rhythms of its deadpanned narration. The result is a species of *Galgenhumor,* at once morbid and outrageously comic. If frontier heroes imagined themselves as "half horse, half alligator," the antiheroic protagonists of urban tall tales suffer a very different fate: "As Gregor Samsa awoke one morning from uneasy dreams he found himself transformed in his bed into a gigantic insect." The *Zeitgeist* may have altered radically, and overcompensations may have become *under*compensations, but "stretching" itself remains intact.

As a character in Ken Kesey's *One Flew Over the Cuckoo's Nest* exclaims: "It isn't happening. It's all a collaboration of Kafka and Mark Twain. . . ."[8] His assessment is a deadly accurate appraisal not only of life within the mental asylum of Kesey's novel, but also of much which has been centrally important to contemporary American literature. And it is a good working description of the urban tall tale. In a novel like Bruce Jay Friedman's *Stern*, the ethos of Kafka's Prague is transported to an affluent American suburbia, where it provides a conducive atmosphere for floating paranoia. In Philip Roth's *Breast*, Kafkan influences are felt more directly, as David Kepesh is metamorphosed into a female breast.

To be sure, not *all* the influences upon architects of the urban tall tale are so unabashedly "highbrow." If a folk artist like Mark Twain transposed the idiom of inveterate storytellers into the more demand-

[8]Ken Kesey, *One Flew Over the Cuckoo's Nest* (New York: Viking, 1963), p. 254.

ing stuff of literature, something of the same process occurs when the centers of popular culture shift from the campfire to the cinema, from platform orators to stand-up comedians. Too, the psychodynamics of a contemporary "boast" depend upon this time, this place. Legends about Davy Crockett insisted that he was "watered with buffalo milk and weaned on whiskey," that his family "used his infant teeth to build the parlor fireplace," and that he once "escaped from an Indian by riding on the back of a wolf which went like a streak of lightning towed by steamboats."[9]

For all its playful exaggeration, this was the quintessential hero as the frontier storyteller imagined the term. The urban tall tale also aspires toward a version of herohood, but one which understands that "boasting" can be the province of the meek as well as the mighty. Thus Alexander Portnoy describes his special constituency as ". . . the sad and watery-eyed sons of Jewish parents, sick to the gills from rolling through these heavy seas of guilt . . . cry[ing] out intermittently, one of us or another, ' Poppa, how could you?' 'Momma, why did you?' and the stories we tell, as the big ship pitches and rolls, the vying we do—who had the most castrating mother, who the most benighted father."[10]

In such stories, macho protagonists are replaced by sensitive flops. The ante of inverted boasting keeps being raised until only those players with an inexhaustible supply of psychic defeats can stay in the game. No single figure epitomizes this shift from the exaggerations of two-fisted swagger to those of neurotic whining better than Woody Allen. In "Play It Again, Sam" (Broadway play, 1969; film version, 1972), Allan Felix (surely an avatar of the public Mr. Allen) is juxtaposed against the ghostly presence of Humphrey Bogart. As "Casablanca"—with its romantic idealization of stoical suffering and ersatz Hemingway codes—flickers in the background, the sad-sack effects that triumph which film buffs dream about: He *becomes* his favorite film in a contemporary, "real-life" remake of the famous airport departure.

Moreover, it is a victory of the vulnerable over the hard-boiled, the bespectacled over the broad-shouldered. For Allen, the comic mode is a way of deflecting that hostile fist which may be a set of

---

[9]Blair, *Horse Sense,* p. 26.
[10]Philip Roth, *Portnoy's Complaint* (New York: Random House, 1969), pp. 117–118.

very literal knuckles, but which generally arrives in more figurative forms: nagging parents, imploring rabbis, bitchy women, bullying men, self-appointed czars of the intellect, authorities in general.

As the title of Allen's first collection of essays makes clear, *Getting Even* is a central concern—and the parodic mode is how you do it. Here, for example, is Woody Allen's version of those gang-land histories which pretend to be scholarly tomes:

> In 1921, Thomas (The Butcher) Covello and Ciro (The Tailor) Santucci attempted to organize disparate ethnic groups of the underworld and thus take over Chicago. This was foiled when Albert (The Logical Positivist) Corillo assassinated Kid Lipsky by locking him in a closet and sucking all the air out through a straw. Lipsky's brother Mendy (alias Mendy Lewis, alias Mendy Larsen, alias Mendy Alias) avenged Lipsky's murder by abducting Santucci's brother Gaetano (also known as Little Tony, or Rabbi Henry Sharpstein) and returning him several weeks later in twenty-seven separate mason jars. This signalled the beginning of a bloodbath.[11]

In Woody Allen's comic vision, metaphysical jargon coexists with the abruptly local reference. The net effect is absurdity with a very cosmopolitan stamp. A course description of Philosophy 1 reads as follows: "Metaphysics: What happens to the soul after death? How does it manage?"[12] or this entry from an essay entitled, significantly enough, "My Philosophy": "Can we actually 'know' the universe? My God, it's hard enough finding your way around Chinatown." In short, it is the sort of middle-brow wit designed to gladden the hearts of *New Yorker* readers. They vaguely remember terms like "categorical imperative" from a survey course in Western Ideas.

Allen, on the other hand, came to the sophomoric relatively late in life. Both NYU and City College dumped him during his freshman year. I mention this (a) because pompous discussions of Woody Allen as an intellectual giant are not only a bit silly; they also violate the essential spirit of his work, and (b) because such "failures" solidify his credentials as a contemporary version of Chaplin's Little Tramp. Let me amplify my second point in ways that will no doubt smack of heresy to the *Sight and Sound* crowd. Films like "City Lights" and "Sleeper" not only share a sense of common enemies

[11]Woody Allen, *Getting Even* (New York: Random House, 1971), p. 17.

[12]One has the sinking feeling that one has read descriptions like those in Woody Allen's "Spring Bulletin" before—and, worse, that one has *written* them.

(modern technology in general; the absurd irritations of urban life in particular), but, more important, they also share an infectious lovability which replaces rancor with gentleness, the clenched fist with the ludicrously tipped hat. However, the essential differences between Charlie Chaplin and Woody Allen are those which separate the pioneering artist from the compulsive film buff. Allen's work suffers all the ravages of postmodernism, all the liabilities which result when too much of one's art is propped against the work of too many predecessors. Parody cannot avoid being self-conscious; it comes with the territory.

And yet, for all the assorted borrowings, Woody Allen's work retains a uniquely personal stamp. In a recent film like "Love and Death," Tolstoy's *War and Peace* may meet Bergman's "Seventh Seal," but it is the clash of disparate languages—all the earnest double-talk about ethics or the flights into overblown, quasi-lyrical poetry—which get the big laughs. Woody Allen has a delightful habit of breaking through the parodic mask, of dropping a gratuitous allusion to Ratner's dairy restaurant on one hand or adding cheerleaders to an epic battlefield on the other. In this sense, "Love and Death" is less about Mother Russia than it is a version of the urban tall tale, one filled with comic swipes at the affectations of what passes for sophisticated culture.

Granted, Woody Allen is not the only practitioner in the art of comic boasts about one's inferiority. Stanley Myron Handleman affects a similarly bedazzled stance, Rodney Dangerfield "gets no respect," and David Brenner reconstructs all the anguishes of growing up ugly in South Philly. Belly laughs are merely the tip of their collective icebergs; larger reservoirs of hostility, anger, and frustration lie just underneath. And yet, for all the talk about contemporary comedy as aggression rechanneled or painful rejection metamorphosed into nervous energy (that sense of *shpritz* which Albert Goldman reverently describes in his biography of Lenny Bruce), the prevailing style of our most popular stand-up comedians is built upon the psychodynamics of failure. This is especially true when their monologues brighten the late-night talk shows, following a day marked by fierce national competition and all the gloomy stuff of the eleven o'clock news. Avatars of the *schlemiel*, whether they come off as fashionably hip (George Carlin) or warmly nostalgic (Bill Cosby), reduce the level of urban threat by a process of comic defusing. In this guise the urban tall tale comes closest to the style developed by platform humorists like Artemus Ward, Josh Billings, and Mark Twain.

Unfortunately, even the best comic monologue can make only limited inroads where a complicated national sensibility is concerned. Freed from those restraints which govern socially approved behavior, the spinner of urban tall tales, like his frontier progenitor, creates his pithy observations in a hit-and-run fashion. The sterner demands of fiction necessarily complicate the process. However much he might agree with the stand-up comedian's assessment of our cultural situation, the novelist must deepen those local observations into a more comprehensive vision of life, one tempered by art and integral to itself. The unbridled play of a zany imagination must be balanced by a search for an appropriate structure.

With a writer like Bruce Jay Friedman, the anxieties of urban living are linked to scenes which generate that Kafkaesque flavoring I touched upon earlier. By way of expanding this point, a few examples may be helpful. The following scene from *A Mother's Kisses* is disturbingly representative of a wide range of contemporary American novels in which versions of the urban tall tale play a significant part: "A long line had formed in the men's room, leading to a single urinal, which was perched atop a dais. When a fellow took too long, there were hoots and catcalls such as 'What's the matter, fella, can't you find it?' As his turn came near, Joseph began to get nervous. He stepped before the urinal finally, feeling as though he had marched out onto a stage. He stood there a few seconds, then zipped himself up and walked off. The man in back of him caught his arm in a vise and said, 'You didn't go. I watched.' "[13] In *Stern,* fears about being cuckolded produce ulcers and darkly comic fantasies in which Friedman's protagonist imagines his wife "dropping him off at the [rest] home, then going immediately to a service station and allowing the attendant to make love to her while her feet kept working the pedals so that she could always say that she had driven all the way home without stopping." Philip Roth is even shriller about the comic possibilities of a self-generating urban *angst*. In *Portnoy's Complaint* projections cut from a similar bolt of cloth take on frighteningly public dimensions: "What if he blabs to the *Daily*

[13]Bruce Jay Friedman's *A Mother's Kisses* (New York: Simon and Schuster, 1964), p. 184.

News? ASST HUMAN OPP'Y COMMISH FLOGS DUMMY, *Also Lives in Sin, Reports Old School Chum.* "

And, as Thomas Pynchon would have it, even the lovable bungling of a character like Benny Profane is inextricably tied to the larger apocalyptic convulsions of our century. Complications lurk amid the smallest, most banal activities. When Profane merely wants to take a shower, he discovers (as a *schlemiel* must) that "the handles wouldn't turn. When he finally found a shower that worked, the water came out hot and cold in random patterns. He danced around, yowling and shivering, slipped on a bar of soap and nearly broke his neck. Drying off, he ripped a frayed towel in half, rendering it useless. He put on his skivvy shirt backwards, took ten minutes getting his fly zipped and another fifteen repairing a shoelace which had broken as he was tying it . . . being a *schlemiel,* he'd known for years: inanimate objects and he could not live in peace. "[14]

Other examples suggest themselves cancerously, until one has the uneasy feeling that (to paraphrase Mark Schorer on "technique"), in speaking about the urban tall tale, we are speaking about *everything*. The problem here is not unlike that faced by Irving Howe in his introduction to *Politics and the Novel*. As critics, we are trained, first, to fashion definitions, and then to revere them above all else. Howe shrewdly takes another tack: "When I speak of the political novel, I have no ambition of setting up still another rigid category. I am concerned with perspectives of observation, not categories of classification. . . ."[15] To be sure, a focus upon what I have been calling the urban tall tale is not *quite* the same order of business as an investigation of the relationship of politics to the novel, and I am surely *not* Irving Howe. Nonetheless, much of the spirit one feels in contemporary American fiction can be better understood by establishing lines of continuity between a frontier sensibility and its Protean configurations in an urban setting. The humor generated by the need to establish that masculine swagger we all associate with the American grain persists in our collective imagination. Generally speaking, urban tall tales are more confined than sprawling, more likely to emphasize comically exaggerated weaknesses than comically inflated strengths. Curiously enough, a novel like Ken Kesey's

[14]Thomas Pynchon, *V*. (New York: Bantam, 1964), pp. 27–28.
[15]Irving Howe, *Politics and the Novel* (New York: Horizon Press, 1957), p. 16.

One Flew Over the Cuckoo's Nest seems to be fashioned from aspects of both. The locale is a mental asylum in the Far West, but its inmates are very urban casualties indeed. It makes for an appropriate note on which to conclude.

As Kesey imagines it, the matriarchal crunch is directly responsible for the resulting "cartoon world, where the figures are flat and outlined in black, jerking through some kind of goofy story that might be real funny if it weren't for the cartoon figures being real guys" Big Nurse may be emblematic of this highly efficient unmanning, but her avatars are everywhere. As Chief Bromden puts it: "All of us here are rabbits of varying ages and degrees, hippity-hopping through our Walt Disney world. Oh, don't misunderstand me, we're not in here *because* we are rabbits—we'd be rabbits wherever we were—we're all in here because we can't *adjust* to our rabbithood. We need a good strong wolf like the nurse to teach us our place."[16]

Into this world of grotesque automatons (at once symbolic Waste Land and the urban situation thrown into exaggerated relief) comes R. P. McMurphy—raconteur, con man, and spinner of tall tales extraordinaire. And with him comes that sense of laughter which becomes increasingly desperate as battle lines are drawn and psychic weapons bared:

> "I never saw a scareder-looking bunch in my life than you guys . . .
>
> "[You're] even scared to open up and *laugh*. You know, that's the first thing that got me about this place, that there wasn't anybody laughing. I haven't heard a real laugh since I came through that door, do you know that? Man, when you lose your laugh you lose your *footing*. A man go around lettin' a woman whup him down till he can't laugh any more, and he loses one of the biggest edges he's got on his side. First thing you know he'll begin to think she's tougher than he is and—"[17]

In this sense, the urban tall tale may produce a laughter more embittered and nervous than that of frontier humorists, but it is hardly a radical innovation. Like that glass of milk I mentioned at the beginning of this essay, it has been staring us in the face all along.

[16]Kesey, *Cuckoo's Nest*, p. 61.
[17]Ibid., pp. 65–66.

PHILIP STEVICK

Prolegomena to the Study of Fictional *Dreck*

Like so many Americans, she was trying to construct a life that made sense from things she found in gift shops.

> —Kurt Vonnegut, Jr.,
> *Slaughterhouse-Five*

You know what a drugstore is? A temple to the senses. Come down those crowded aisles. Cosmetics first stop. Powders, puffs, a verb-wheel of polished nails on a cardboard, lipstick ballistics, creams and tighteners, suntan lotions, eyeshadows, dyes for hair—love potions, paints . . . shampoos, all the lotions and hair conditioners proteined as egg and meat . . . sun lamps, sleep masks, rollers . . . the Venus Folding Feminine Syringe . . . supporters, rupture's ribbons and organ's bows . . . diarrhea's plugs and constipation's triggers.

> —Stanley Elkin,
> *The Dick Gibson Show*

We like books that have a lot of *dreck* in them.
. . .

> —Donald Barthelme,
> *Snow White*

Much new fiction in the United States which is innovative in form and sensibility is also comic. Writers like Barthelme, Barth, Pynchon, Coover, Gass, Elkin, Brautigan, Vonnegut, Hawkes, and a multitude of others achieve their most unconventional effects while inducing laughter. And the common reader who could not make anything of the form of *Gravity's Rainbow* would have to be remarkably unresponsive to some broad and perfectly intelligible comic appeals not to be hugely amused at individual passages of Pynchon's book. Readers of American fiction, in fact, may well be so accustomed to thinking of experimental motives and forms as being consistent with comic appeals that they may find it inevitable that the two should coexist. It is not, of course, inevitable at all.

Most of the great works of Modernism are comic only incidentally, if at all. Nobody laughs at *To the Lighthouse* or *Swann's Way* or *Nausea* or *The Sound and the Fury*. Nor is it even true that most "postmodern" experimental fiction is comic. The French have given a whole generation in mid-twentieth century to certain kinds of fictional experimentation, most of it relentlessly serious. Much of Robbe-Grillet is played out against the very edge of lunacy; yet for the most part the only reader who laughs while reading a Robbe-Grillet novel is the reader who laughs at Robbe-Grillet. John Berger's novel *G,* for an English example, has all of the techniques that persuade us of its implicit claim to kinship with the most innovative narrative of our time; but it is not funny. Although an American reader can find his way around in its sensibility and its techniques of verbal collage, he will wait a long time for a laugh. Which brings us back to my premise: that American narrative literature which is nontraditional and anti-realistic in the last twenty years is most often comic, but that one is not a necessary condition of the other. Most innovative art of other times and places has been serious in motive and execution, asking of its readers respect, understanding, intermittent ironic amusement, and a willing adjustment of expectations, but not laughter.

Experimental fiction is, by its very nature, uncircumscribed and anti-conventional, so there must always be a range of effects at work in such fiction that defies orderly explanation. Yet there is a center to the comedy of experimental fiction, a common concern, set of images, or metaphor for the experience of the 1970's as that experience is rendered in new fiction. This shared characteristic derives from certain attitudes toward, and treatments of, the shared mass-cultural objects of our world, especially the ephemeral objects, the floating junk, the jingles and slogans of advertising, the clichés of our common cant, the songs of forgotten hit parades, the faded movies, the throw-away plastic things, the names from the news-papers, the receding but still talking faces from the TV screen, the disconnected items of shlock merchandise bought and unused, the brand names lusted for and cherished, the mounting trash—in a word, the *dreck* of our lives.

It is not self-evident how the use of *dreck* should be comic. A beer can by the highway is not funny, nor is an old shoe on a trash heap, or coffee grounds in the garbage. Neither is it self-evident what any of this has to do with the innovative, anti-realist, experimental motives of the writers I have cited. Nor is it self-evident that such material is new to fiction, since we tend to think of realist fiction from Defoe as being defined by the prominence it gives to sharply realized, com-paratively insignificant details. Yet the use of trash is, in a certain context, all of these—funny, "experimental," and new, as I hope to illustrate in the short run and demonstrate in the long run. To illustrate: In a fiction by Steve Katz called "Oedipus," which is a revision and a boistrous vulgarization of the Oedipus myth, the protagonist puts out his eyes with a Py-Co-Pay toothbrush. The brand name in that context is indisputably comic—if not "experimental," at least nontraditional—and a use of detail incon-ceivable in an earlier writer.

I take *Madame Bovary* as being the quintessential nineteenth-century realistic novel, a legitimate base for considering how fiction now got to be what it is. Flaubert begins his second part with a chapter describing Yonville. It begins geographically, with town names, descriptions of roads, names of rivers. Much of the descrip-tion is rather remarkably cinematic, with the eye moving from pastures to plains to hills to horizon. It is a world both picturesque and suggestive of its backward agricultural economy. Flaubert moves us closer to the center of town and begins to register the outbuildings, the houses, the architectural details, ultimately a few decorative details. Inevitably, both for Flaubert and for Yonville, the church is described with particularity and scorn. There is the market. There is Homais' pharmacy. And the town is finished, ending with a paragraph describing the cemetery beyond its edge, in which the sexton makes use of the spare ground to plant potatoes.

Imagine a writer now in search of the images that would embody small-town vulgarity. I suggest a few. A Coca-Cola sign. A Dr. Pepper sign. The name of the local newspaper. A MacDonald's hamburger stand surrounded by time-killing teenagers. A movie theater, plaster-Moorish in style, now boarded up. A bus station. A tourist court with separate cabins. An automobile parts store that seems to specialize in chrome-plated tail pipes. Obviously I am selecting details from twentieth-century America, not nineteenth-century provincial France. But my point is that the imagination now turns easily and naturally to the commercial images which pervade small towns, the neon signs and the cheap diners, and that these are, for us, the iconography for the poverty of spirit that we find there. For Flaubert, no such commercial imagery comes to mind. Except for some quaint patent medicines listed in script on Homais' pharmacy, nothing in Yonville seems to be bought or sold. Despite the rural character of the town, the inhabitants' lives must have been filled with vulgar and trashy merchandise, most of it tasteless and some of it mass produced. Yet Flaubert does not see that particular kind of trash, useful though it might have been to his purpose, preferring instead to define the vulgarity of Yonville by describing the potato patch in the cemetery.

Consider a parallel situation in nineteenth-century England. Of that brilliant galaxy of prophets—Ruskin, Morris, Carlyle, Arnold, Pater (and, in America, Emerson and Thoreau), a painful awareness of the nature of mass-produced objects is central to the analysis of all of them. Yet one searches in vain in the fiction of the period for that pervasive consciousness of manufactured things. Dickens is as aware as anyone in his age of the debasement of work, the depredations of the factory system, the acquisitive motive, and the awesome power of acquired objects to transform the very soul of man. But people in Dickens do not buy brand-name merchandise; in fact, characters in Dickens do not go shopping at all. Although most of them live in a highly commercialized London, they do not read advertisements. They do not respond to newspapers except, for melodramatic purposes, to read a headline. Although Dickens shows the influence of mass entertainment, his characters do not; they do not chatter on about music hall celebrities in the way that people now talk about last night's television shows, although people in Victorian England surely did just that. Or take Hardy for a different imagination but a parallel case. No one in Victorian England was more aware of the transformation of England from an agricultural world with traditional folk values to a commercial world held together by the cash nexus. Yet he does not portray in his fiction, any more than Dickens does, the multitudinous objects of that new world. It is, of course, not my intention to fault the Victorian novelists, only to express surprise that it seems to have taken so long for novelists to learn how to make a fictional world that registers a kind of phenomenology of mass culture.

I suggest Joyce's *Ulysses* as a convenient base for considering the movement from the nineteenth century to the modernist period. Readers of Joyce will recall that people in his novel do, in fact, buy brand-name merchandise. People in *Ulysses* buy Plumtree's Potted Meat; Joyce himself was so fascinated with the name and the product that he used it as a motif, the name appearing dozens of times in the course of the book. People do, in fact, read newspapers: the multiplex stuff of a modern newspaper runs through the novel, world events, obituaries, gossip and scandal, editorial opinion, jingoistic posturing and stancetaking of all kinds, and advertisements. Furthermore, Leopold Bloom is an advertising canvasser. He is not only a consumer, registering on his consciousness the running thoughts of a mass man, but he is also a maker and seller of the imagery of mass culture.

In Joyce, the made coexists with the born, the well-made with the schlock, the classic with the disposable, and they are all rooted in a complicated tradition that extends from ancient origins to last week's events. Unlike Flaubert, who despises the banality of the bourgeois world he shows us, Joyce embraces his world, banality and all. Surely there are different pleasures, for Joyce and anyone else, in quoting Shakespeare and quoting music hall doggerel. And there is some legitimate sense in which the latter is banal, tasteless, and trashy, as Joyce would concede. But Joyce likes those music hall lyrics, remembers them with fondness, lays them before us with nothing of the patent contempt of Flaubert; and it would surprise no one to discover that Joyce was personally fond of Plumtree's Potted Meat. So it is that that older tradition of the realistic novel, with its base of frustrated desire, perverted will, and human corruption, all worked out in a largely junk-free world, is faded, replaced in the 1920's and 1930's by a novel imposed upon a background of cultural objects, most of which are vulgar and devoid of merit, but few of which are despised with the hearty loathing that Flaubert gave to the basic data of his fictional world.

Why the entry of what we have come to call mass culture into the texture of the art novel occurred when it did, and why it occurred at all, are questions to some extent beyond analysis. But I would suggest one relevant development in Western consciousness. The anthropologist Edmund Carpenter has pointed out how, for modern man, the reality of possessions comes often not from buying, owning, and using them, but from fulfilling their advertisements. People who own products for which they have seen no advertisements feel virtually as if they do not own those products. An object for which one knows the advertisement, however, becomes more than a function, more than a sensory object; it becomes a luminous polarity for the conscious mind, full of nuances and satisfactions.[1] Thus in the world of Joyce (or, for an American equivalent, the world of Dos Passos), the entry of mass culture into the most sophisticated fiction is often an entry of advertisements *for* mass culture. And thus the fiction of the 1920's and 1930's begins to respond not merely to the growth of mass culture, but to the manipulated consciousness *of* mass culture that results from the new power of mass advertising.

Of the fiction of the last twenty years, a rich sense of the possibilities of cultural junk plays across both the realists and the experimentalists. In realistic fiction, such as the early Roth and Updike, or in a large number of lesser-known recent novels like *Bijou* by David Madden, a large amount of the solidity of the realism is made up precisely of cultural junk: old movies, radio serials, brand names, advertising jingles. I turn idly through Updike's *Rabbit Redux* and find references to the black go-go dancer in *Laugh-In,* David Frost, *The Match Game,* TV dinners, Carol Burnett, Gomer Pyle, the Lone Ranger, Tonto, Wheaties, McDonald's, Mobil gas, Vitalis. It is a marvelously evocative base of details, fixing the action of the novel in its appropriate place and cultural milieu. For all of the differences between Joyce and contemporary realistic fiction, the use of such cultural junk is remarkably similar. In both, there is an obsessive accuracy and precision. In both, the details begin to become dated almost immediately. In both, there is an ambivalence

[1]Edmund Carpenter, *Oh, What a Blow That Phantom Gave Me!* (New York: Holt, Rinehart and Winston, 1973), p. 6.

of value that hovers over the details—fascination and repulsion, a full recognition of the mindless banality of that commercial trash and a nostalgic fondness for it, that ambiguity of value being a quality both of the author's imagination and of our response.

Moving from the realists to those kinds of recent fiction that seem non-traditional, supra-realistic, post-modernist, and experimental, a change occurs that is as dramatic as the change from the anger of Flaubert at the corruption of the world to the neutral assimilation of cultural junk into the fictional world of Joyce. The place to begin is with the fiction of Donald Barthelme, the writer who represents, in his own memorable phrase (a phrase perpetuated by William Gass), "the leading edge of the trash phenomenon." I quote a paragraph from a story by Barthelme called "City Life": "Everybody in the city was watching a movie about an Indian village menaced by a tiger. Only Wendell Corey stood between the village and the tiger. Furthermore Wendell Corey had dropped his rifle—or rather the tiger had knocked it out of his hands—and was left with only his knife. In addition, the tiger had Wendell Corey's left arm in his mouth up to the shoulder."[2] Judging from the summary, the movie described is a Grade B thriller, a fourth-rate jungle epic. (A friend tells me that the film referred to is "Man-Eater of Kumaon" [1948], starring Sabu, Wendell Corey, Joy Ann Page, Morris Carnovsky, and Argentina Brunetti, directed by Byron Haskin.) Joyce's cultural junk, one recalls, is done quickly—a few lines of a song, a passing book title, an advertising slogan—so that the cultural junk makes a background for the large movements of the central characters. The summary of the movie in Barthelme, however, is not background, not a part of a realistic texture against which the main action is presented. "Background" and "foreground" become meaningless terms in Barthelme. There is nothing before that ridiculous movie, nothing after it; nothing causes, nothing results from it; nobody in particular has made the movie, except for Wendell Corey, and Barthelme says "everybody" is watching it. The movie is not exactly foreground; but it is no longer background, as such a piece of cultural junk would be in Joyce, Updike, or a thousand novelists in the realistic tradition. Nothing is more important to keep in mind about junk in postmodern fiction than this fact: junk has moved

---

[2]Donald Barthelme, "City Life," in *City Life* (New York: Farrar, Straus and Giroux, 1970), p. 166.

forward in the perspective of the novel; it is no longer like designs in the wallpaper but is like a presence in the middle of the room.

The narration of Barthelme's story describes the movie in a way that can only be called naive, childlike, and undiscriminating. One effect of such narration is to eliminate any possibility of judgment: nothing in the description, not even the slightest connotation, suggests that it is a bad movie. That naive and value-free narration becomes an indirect way for Barthelme to suggest that a banal and tasteless movie need not be experienced as a banal and tasteless movie, need not be presented as such, need not be judged at all. Implicitly, Barthelme finds the movie oddly ingratiating, partly because it is so blatantly and audaciously tasteless. Analyses of "camp" tastes have diminished in the more than ten years since Susan Sontag gave the term its currency; although the word has all but disappeared, the phenomenon remains. Perhaps we talk about it less because we all participate in it more, and what seemed perverse and clever in Susan Sontag's analysis seems largely shared and commonplace now. Barthelme's implicit attitude, in any case, has relationships to what we used to call camp taste; yet in the story the passage becomes far more than a camp reference. Instead, it becomes an epistemological gesture, not simply a pointing at an object, but a way of apprehending the world.

Details in fiction have always had the function of making the world of the novel seem familiar and recognizable. When we say that a novel is realistic, we mean that the accumulated details of its narration convince us of the authenticity of the reported experience. "Had I been there," we say as we read, "that is the way the world would have looked to me." In Barthelme the effect is the opposite, to take a detail which we are prepared to accept as "realistic," even commonplace and banal, and give it a treatment and an emphasis that make it seem strange and ridiculous. Yet for all of its strangeness, the appropriate response, I think, is an amused recognition of kinship with the experience described. Joyce's *dreck* is *dreck* remembered, arranged, understood, and aesthetically deployed. Barthelme's narrator does not remember *dreck;* he is *in* the world of *dreck*. It is a placement the reader is encouraged to share. Joyce's best readers are those who were *not* alive in the Dublin of 1904. Barthelme's best readers are those, bored, idle, insomniac, or moved only by an unaccountable reflex action, who *do* habitually flip on a tasteless old movie.

For the sake of range, I will lay out some examples from elsewhere. Kurt Vonnegut, in *Breakfast of Champions,* describes a Colonel Sanders Kentucky Fried Chicken franchise. "A chicken," he writes, "was a flightless bird which looked like this:" here he inserts a drawing of a chicken, in the manner of a child's coloring book, done evidently by Vonnegut himself with a felt-tipped pen. "The idea," he continues, "was to kill it and pull out all its feathers, and cut off its head and feet and scoop out its internal organs—and then chop it into pieces and fry the pieces, and put the pieces in a waxed paper bucket with a lid on it, so it looked like this:" here Vonnegut draws a picture of a bucket of fried chicken.[3] Obviously somewhat different purposes are being served in Vonnegut's novel and Barthelme's story. But the junk is the same, naively narrated, without cause or consequence, an aspect no longer of the background, with a mixed sense of utter tastelessness and a bizarre kind of appeal, utterly familiar yet slightly "unreal" in the telling, commonplace and ignorable yet comic. Robert Coover begins a story entitled "Panel Game": "Situation: television panel game, live audience. Stage strobelit and cameras intersecting about. Moderator, bag-shape, corseted and black suited, behind desk-rostrum, blinking mockmodestly at lens and lamps, practiced pucker on his soft mouth and brows arched in mild goodguy astonishment. Opposite him, the panel."[4] Again, Coover's purposes are not identical with Barthelme's or Vonnegut's. But the junk is the same, front and center in the fiction, told in such a way as to make the episodes seem very like a rerun of *What's My Line,* yet fantastic, dream-like, and oddly comic.

The most dazzling display of the kinds of details I have been describing is in Thomas Pynchon's *Gravity's Rainbow.* I merely point, without comment, at some of the details that play across several representative pages: The Pause That Refreshes, Moxie (by which is meant, I assume from the context, a brand of soft drink still sold in parts of the United States), Baby Ruth, an early Kelvinator refrigerator still called by its owners an "ice box," the old radio commercial for United Fruit in which Chiquita Banana cautions us against putting bananas in the refrigerator, the look of Chiquita Banana in the magazine ads with a huge hat made of fruit, the Spike

---

[3]Kurt Vonnegut, Jr., *Breakfast of Champions* (New York: Delacorte, 1973), pp. 157–158.
[4]Robert Coover, "Panel Game," in *Pricksongs and Descants* (New York: E. P. Dutton, 1969), p. 79.

Jones record from early World War II days titled "Right in the Führer's Face," the facial configurations of Japanese fighter pilots in World War II movies, the movie actor William Bendix, a violin cadenza from a concerto by Rossini, a mass parachute jump by the 82nd Airborne Division, a popularized version of the Rossini violin cadenza played by a guitar-playing singer with a wiggling pelvis, the actress Fay Wray, the actress Norma Shearer, the actress Margaret O'Brien, Gimbel's basement, Frank Sinatra, Post Toasties, the shooting of John Dillinger outside the Biograph theater, Plasticman.

A certain code, pattern, or set of relationships lies behind the use of the fictional details whose history I have attempted to sketch. The code depends upon the intersection of three forces. The first is a linguistic force, by means of which names *qua* names, words *qua* words, syntactic structures *qua* syntactic structures exert their own comic energy, carrying a certain extravagance, a "foregrounded," attention-getting quality, a measure of grotesqueness or oddity. This, of course, is hardly an aspect peculiar to the recent comic effects I am describing. When Dickens names a character Mr. Fezziwig, we laugh before we find out what Mr. Fezziwig does. The second is a historical-cultural force, by means of which associations of age and obsolescence, chicness and novelty, the timeless and the dated, cultural centrality and marginality, popularity and elite exclusivity all bear on the comic intent and the comic effect. Although comedies have often dealt with the chic and the fashionable, the dated and the passé, the historical-cultural aspects of which I speak rarely inhere in a systematic way in the individual devices of the comic text. Classic theoreticians of the comic never, in fact, speak of such aspects, treating the characteristic events of comedy, instead, as if they were timeless and loosely attached to any cultural assumptions. The third is an evaluative force, by means of which a sense of eccentric value and patent worthlessness are at once brought into play. And this peculiar evaluative force, a consistent ambivalence toward the things of the world turned toward comic purposes, is, as I have tried to sketch in the previous section, new in postmodern fiction.

I suggest a range of possibilities as a way into that code. Let us imagine a character in a novel, in the middle station of life, proper, ambitious, conventional, suburban, slightly banal. At a certain point, as a nonessential, ancillary detail, by way of accompanying an episode in his characteristic but private life, he eats something, between meals, as a snack. A ham sandwich, which he makes himself, from some boiled ham in the refrigerator, is, whatever else it may be, not funny. A peanut butter and jelly sandwich is slightly eccentric, or childish perhaps, but not funny. A peanut butter and jelly sandwich made with Skippy peanut butter is nearer to being funny. Half a box of Cheese Tid-Bits is almost funny. A Clark Bar is almost funny. An Almond Joy is mildly funny. So is a box of Raisinettes, or a box of Jujubes. A Hostess Twinkie is funny.

There is, in some sense, an imagined, intended clientele for every advertised product in modern culture. That clientele may be more or less universal: surely the intent in naming many products is to stimulate the largest possible clientele, although the intent in the case of others is to create an artificially restricted group to which the consumer wishes to belong. The moment something is named, much less advertised, its universality is diminished, sometimes deliberately, sometimes in ways even the cleverest advertiser cannot control. There are those who would not wish to smoke Pall Malls or wear Hush Puppies, because the name of the product, in some magical and indescribable way, does not speak to them or seem to include them in its clientele. Our dailiness is filled with made objects, each with a rich and evocative name. And our half-conscious life is filled with trying out, accepting, or rejecting those names.

I suggest that it would be amusing for a proper, middle-class, middle-aged, conventional character to eat a Hostess Twinkie, first, because the name (never mind the product) does not seem to fit. Inserted into the life of such a character, the product's name has the effect of an object pasted in a collage. It startles the mind, calls attention to itself, intrigues us by its discontinuity with the rest of our field of attention. It would be amusing, second, because of the apparent value of the product, a bland, mass-produced sponge cake, individually wrapped, intended mainly, one supposes, for children's lunches, filled with a synthetic cream—again, in a word, *dreck*. In this case, the specificity of the brand name clearly has something to do with the comic effect. The abruptness of the presentation also has something to do with it: if we are prepared by the novelist to respond to a plausible character who has an explainable taste for mass-produced cakes, the use of the name is no longer comic, except in a broad and diffuse way. Furthermore, the continuity of reference with our own world has something to do with the comic effect: it is appropriate that we recall the thing named, not merely as an object in the world, but as an object from our own experience, acknowledged with silent amusement, repressed because of decorum. Most people have eaten a Hostess Twinkie, and some will again.

Naming the Hostess Twinkie is, in some respects, a classic maneuver. It exposes a slice of the character's private life, unmasking him, middle-brow though he may be, as, in unguarded moments, a lover of mass-produced sponge cakes. And it gives us a linguistic jolt, the idiotic trade name existing in a setting of well-made prose. That, too, is a classic strategy. In the twentieth century, S. J. Perelman has been making comedy out of such stylistic shifts since before most of the practitioners of experimental fiction were born. But when such a name is one element in what turns out to be an assemblage of such elements, the effect is, at the same time, comic and experimental, building upon our sense of conventional comic appeals—but also willing into existence a form which is not a vehicle in which those comic events can occur, but a texture which is *nothing but* those comic events, in which the very fabric of the form is *dreck*.

I have chosen to invent the easiest example of *dreck* to analyze, the named product in which the name itself cannot be spoken by a reasonable man without its being automatically foregrounded, the product being both mass-produced and unique, tasteless and unaccountably palatable. Other kinds of cultural scraps are not necessarily subject to the same analysis. Barthelme's "Indian Uprising," for example, contains, among a multitude of examples, Gabriel Fauré, a coffee table made from a hollow-core door, Korzybski, Jean-Luc Godard, and Bordentown, New Jersey. Still, I have promised a code by means of which such elements can be seen as parts of a pattern, notes toward a grammar, as it were, of *dreck*. The way to initiate such a code is by a series of categorical generalizations, none of which is wholly true but all of which are mostly true.

An object, alone, is potentially funny when it is named; that is, it can be made funny in an appropriate setting, if it evokes a small but real commitment of the past which the reader has long since transcended and which the writer knows the reader has transcended, the object being still remembered with a fondness which is at once nostalgic and embarrassed. The brightly colored stamps from such countries as Monaco and Mozambique from one's childhood stamp collection; Fleer's bubble gum; Winnie the Pooh; Eskimo Pies.

An object, alone, is potentially funny when it is named if the naming of it suggests an unusual degree of attention being given to a small, ignorable part of the flux of disposable objects, such as a third-rate actor in a forgotten film or an ignorable brand name. George Brent; Louise Allbritton; Vick's Vaporub; Shinola.

An object, alone, is potentially funny when it is named if the naming of it suggests a banal, tasteless, mass-produced quality which all of those bright enough to be reading the reference would recognize, along with a secret charm, or value, or durability, so that naming the object serves to suggest the possibility of a covert indulgence shared by writer and reader. Hydrox cookies; McDonald's hamburgers; Farah slacks; Bic ballpoint pens; Mary Tyler Moore.

An object, alone, is potentially funny when it is named if the naming of it compels the writer to reproduce the end result of an advertising campaign that necessarily has promised more power or gratification or ecstasy than the product can possibly deliver. The Plymouth Barracuda; Wheaties, Breakfast of Champions; Tabu perfume.

An object, alone, is potentially funny when it is named if the naming of it accomplishes a literalization, so that the metaphorical attributes of the product are imagined to be literally true. Tabu perfume is doubly amusing if one can imagine having to ask for it in a furtive whisper, receive it under the counter, pay for it surreptitiously, take it home in a plain brown bag. In a Barthelme story, a character wants to become an Untouchable, presumably in imitation of the police series that ran for several seasons on television, but somebody spoils his imagined ambition by touching him.

An object, alone, is potentially funny when it is named if the naming of it suggests a banal and tasteless quality which all of those bright enough to be reading the reference would recognize, but along with that banal and tasteless quality a certain flair and audacity that gives the object the special energy that used to be called "camp." A cocktail lounge located on U. S. Route 1 midway between Philadelphia and Trenton, made from a converted DC-3 airplane; an early James Cagney movie with a prison scene.

An object, alone, is potentially funny when it is named if the naming of it identifies a particular kind of cult object. The transaction between writer and reader, in this case, is almost impossibly complicated. The writer cannot know the relation of his reader to a given cult, and the reader will respond in different ways, according to his commitment to the cult. But, in general, the relationships operate in this way. A writer can cite a detail associated with a cult to which he expects few if any of his readers will have a commitment—an astrological chart, a framed picture of Father Divine, a copy of *Awake*—and the reader will respond with amused condescension, in ways not different from response to classic satire. A writer can cite a detail associated with a cult which he expects will be known by most of his readers, at a distance by some of them, with a degree of commitment by others, with fervent and total involvement by still others: Elaine's restaurant, the novels of Ronald Firbank, Godard's films, the literary criticism of Ronald Barthes, Coors beer. Most of those who are members of the cult will be aware of the fragility of the cult and be both amused and embarrassed to see the name of the cult object printed, "foregrounded," set into a fiction. Most of those who are not members of the cult will be aware of the cult's potency and its claim to our attention; they will also be aware of the specious fashionability of its membership, and will therefore be amused and startled to see the cult object named in a fiction.

An object, alone, is potentially funny when it is named if the naming of it revives the memory of something obsolescent, preferably with a certain mythic aura about it, toward which our moral and emotional response has changed almost beyond recall. A French tickler; spats; any song by Stephen Foster.

A series or collection of objects is potentially funny when it is named if the naming of it suggests an encyclopedic, enumerative, obsessively assimilative energy somewhat out of control. This is, of course, a source for comic effects which is at least as old as Rabelais. But the implications of the obsessive series change from time to time. In other periods, the effect has usually been directed toward the undermining of decorum in the interests of registering the richness and multiplicity of experience. In the fiction of the present time, such apparently obsessive serializing very often registers the ambivalent response to the junk of the world that I have tried to describe: an enumeration of the contents of somebody's medicine cabinet, for example, or the contents of a drugstore, as the speaker in Stanley Elkin's novel so manically and irrepressibly enumerates it in the passage I have used as an epigraph.

A word, phrase, or linguistic construct is potentially funny if it suggests a slight time lag in the adoption of a cant, chic vocabulary. To use the word "existential" more or less gratuitously now is hardly funny, because the word is out of fashion and a character in a fiction who uses it will seem either a crude parodist or a bore. But a character in a fiction who drops a reference to the *Tel Quel* school of French literary criticism will seem more appropriately comic, since his attempt at chic is not last decade's but last year's.

A word, phrase, or linguistic construct is potentially funny if it suggests an abortive attempt by a member of one speech community to communicate with a member of another speech community by mimicking a device of his dialect; a white who attempts black street talk, a middle-aged parent who attempts adolescent slang.

A word, phrase, or linguistic construct is potentially funny if it suggests the special stamp of another writer, so that its use creates a passing moment of parody. Hemingway and James can be mimicked in a phrase. And anybody with a good ear could integrate a passing, parodic quote, recognizable and funny, from a hundred living figures from R. D. Laing to Julia Child.

The permutations and categories of my subject are larger than I can exhaust, but the code emerges. Each of the categories I have proposed reinforces my initial assertion, that the humor of *dreck* depends upon the simultaneous interaction of a linguistic force, by means of which verbal elements carry a certain foregrounded, stylized, extravagant quality which inheres in the words *qua* words; a historical-cultural force, by means of which the vitality and obsolescence, centrality and eccentricity of an object are suggested; and an evaluative force, in which the worth of an object is ambivalently implied. Almost everything in the world is capable of becoming trash, or capable of being seen as trash. But not all of that real and potential trash is capable of being used as elements in a fiction of the kind now written by post-realistic writers, because most of that real and potential trash will merely lie there on the page, without the intricacy of intention and response that redeems that trash as art and transforms it into comedy.

A number of tendencies have converged in the 1970's to produce a fiction which is unconventional and strikingly anti-realistic in certain respects but, at the same time, evocative of the shared perceptions of the individual in mass society—a fiction, moreover, which is formally intricate and thoroughly serious about its status as art, but which is funny. One of the tendencies is simply the inevitable turn that art of any kind takes when its modes and sensibilities seem worked out and uncongenial; in this case, a shift in narrative art from the problematic intensity, the self-seriousness, the sheer "difficulty" of the dominant modernists to the non-problematic "fabulation" of the postmodernists. Or, to put the shift another way, from the ironic and distanced voice of the modernists to the naive, involved, vulnerable voice of the postmodernists. Or, to put it still differently, from the symbolic resonance and the multi-leveled depth of reference of the modernists to the fascination with surface in the postmodernists.

More than a shift from exhausted forms, the junk of current fiction represents a new way of giving fictional specificity to a meaningless quality of life. One recalls how hard earlier writers worked to evoke a spirit of hollowness and emptiness in modern life—the labored naturalism of Dos Passos, for example; or Marlow's journey to the heart of darkness, in the dense and devious prose of Conrad; or, more recently, Beckett's awesome voyage toward silence. How natural it is now, on the other hand, to suggest those qualities of disconnection and the absence of significance by making a fiction out of pop images, free floating, without context. Long after many of those naturalistic and existential fictions of an earlier day have ceased to be readable, striking us as heavy-handed, over-determined, overcome with the pathos of their condition, we can continue to take pleasure in the fictions of our own time which allow, in some marvelous equipoise, the coexistence of an appalling view of the meaninglessness of the world, along with a sense of wit and play that makes that meaningless quality bearable and often very funny.

The centrality of *dreck,* moreover, implies that writers of recent fiction recognize a new audience, an audience with none of the common bonds of earlier audiences for earlier fiction. Readers of the best new fiction do not necessarily share common social assumptions (as readers of Victorian three-volume novels tended to do) or metaphysical assumptions (as readers of naturalistic novels tended to do). We do not share a common education (as readers of French novels tended to do). We do not share a common susceptibility to certain stylistic effects (as readers of Scott or Thackeray tended to do), or a common interest in myth (as Joyce could assume of his readers). What most of us do share, along with an interest in wit, nuance, verbal play, the power and perversity of language, is a common mass culture, a misspent youth filled with trivial and nearly forgotten movies, comics, radio and television serials, and a whole range of public names, events, and faces known only as their contrived and stylized images have filtered down to us through the cultural media.

The use of junk, furthermore, means that fiction has re-energized itself by borrowing from the vulgar arts, as fiction has often done when its best writers see its possibilities turned toward ever narrower circles of self-imitation. Fiction from the Elizabethans to Defoe energized itself by superimposing upon romance the bad taste of true crime stories. Jane Austen energized her fiction by assimilating and ironizing melodrama. Melville and Conrad energized their works by borrowing from, and then transforming, a vacuous and simple-minded tradition of sea fiction. And when Twain is very good, it is because he has put to his own uses the frontier tall tale. It is a process that critics have sometimes called re-barbarization, the constant renewal of serious art by borrowing from the vulgar arts. That such a process happens with somewhat more rapidity and intensity than it used to need hardly surprise us.

Finally, it happens that the use of *dreck* is particularly suited to a structural principle central to the purposes of the post-modernists. An interviewer of Barthelme quotes an earlier sentence of Barthelme's, in which he said that "The principle of collage is the central principle of all art in the twentieth century in all media." Would he expand on that sentence, asks the interviewer? Replies Barthelme,

> "I was probably wrong, or too general. I point out however that New York City is or can be regarded as a collage, as opposed to, say, a tribal village in which all of the huts are the same hut, duplicated. The point of collage is that unlike things are stuck together to make, in the best case, a new reality. This new reality, in the best case, may be or imply a comment on the other reality from which it came, and may be also much else. It's an *itself*, if it's successful: Harold Rosenberg's

'anxious object,' which does not know whether it's a work of art or a pile of junk.''[5]

Barthelme was, no doubt, too general in his original statement. Collage is not the organizing principle of all art in the twentieth century. But it *is* the organizing principle of the art Barthelme practices, and of the narrative art of any of those writers to whom we would now easily give the epithets "experimental" or "anti-realistic" or "non-traditional." The implications of such a reorienting of narrative are considerable; and if verbal collage is the wave of the future, we will have to expand our ways of understanding narrative more radically than we have so far. But the implications of collage in relation to *dreck* are clear. A narrative structure that is analogous to visual collage opens itself to the assimilation of junk more easily than narrative has ever done. And a narrative structure that is analogous to Harold Rosenberg's "anxious object" opens itself to a range of comic effects which are powerfully rooted in our own uneasy time, but for which few of our classic descriptions of the comic have prepared us.

[5]Joe David Bellamy, *The New Fiction: Interviews with Innovative American Writers* (Urbana: University of Illinois Press, 1974), pp. 51–52.

RUBY COHN

Camp, Cruelty, Colloquialism

"Now, flagellation isn't my idea of good times," protests Nick in *Who's Afraid of Virginia Woolf?*, to which a skeptical George retorts: "but you can admire a good flagellator . . . a real pro." Such admiration has spread epidemically in the last decade or so. Modern audiences *do* find in verbal flagellation their "idea of good times," and Edward Albee is "a real pro."

Verbal flagellation is not a new sport. Greek Old Comedy may owe more to iambic poets of abuse than to fertility rites nostalgically resurrected in the twentieth century. Cursing matches are ingrained in cultures as diverse as Arabic, Celtic, Provençal. Conjugal quarrels beat their way through European medieval farce. But though American popular types—peddlers, frontiersmen, barkers, minstrels, medicine men—might stretch their language with imaginative insults, two centuries of American drama adhered to the polite genteel tradition.

Arthur Hobson Quinn, still the only historian of American drama, devotes chapters to American comic types: Harrigan, Hoyt, and the comedy of types; Clyde Fitch and the development of social comedy; Mitchell, Williams [Jesse Lynch], and the later social comedy; comedy types again. For Quinn, social comedy pivots on comic types, so that the two coalesce. And social comedy still thrives at the box office as sitcom laced with gags, although Neil Simon and Jules

Feiffer might not appreciate being placed in the same rubric. Less profitable than Simon-Feiffer, but far more telling, are contemporary dramas that explore rather than merely entertain. Rarely fulfilling academic definitions of comedy, these plays bleed humor through scenes of serious, sometimes deadly, import. What is contemporary about such humor is its blend of cruelty, colloquialism, and especially camp. Susan Sontag's 1964 "Notes on Camp" constitute the *locus classicus* for thoughtful understanding of camp. Though she offers no neat definition, she designates its essence as "love of the unnatural: of artifice and exaggeration."[1] In drama, camp is recognizable by its simultaneous nostalgia for and mockery of the artifacts of another era, its combination of satire and parody, its androgynous sexuality, its veneer of triviality, and especially its obstreperous self-consciousness of itself as play.

The cruelty and colloquialism of *Virginia Woolf* are instantly striking, but antennas have to be receptive to hear the camp vibes in Martha's imitation of Bette Davis in *Beyond the Forest,* George's Napoleonic pose, his burlesque of President Kennedy's phrase about Berlin, his quotation from Spengler's *Decline of the West.* The very names George and Martha look askance at a prototypical patriot couple. The assiduous drinking of the four characters is a form of "artifice and exaggeration," rather than a realistic depiction of alcoholism. Though the play attained some fame as academic satire, it reaches out to embrace and indict American middle-class culture, while it revels in cruelty, colloquialism, and touches of camp. However, it was not with *Virginia Woolf* that Albee's humor first erupted on the modern theater scene.

"Ich war im Zoo. Ich hab gesagt, ich war im Zoo. Sie, ich war im Zoo." Those were the first Albee words heard on any stage, when his *Zoo Geschichte* opened in Berlin, after the play was refused in America. Albee knows no German, and these words are only an approximation of what he wrote. Simple though the phrases seem, they betray Albee's colloquialisms: "I've been to the zoo. I said, I've been to the zoo. MISTER, I'VE BEEN TO THE ZOO!" "I've been" is not "Ich war," and "Mister" is not "Sie." Later in the play, the translator was evidently nonplussed by the camp resonance of "I mean, I was queer . . . queer, queer, queer . . . with bells ringing,

[1]Susan Sontag, *Against Interpretation* (New York: Dell, 1966), p. 275.

banners snapping in the wind. . . . But that was the jazz of a very special hotel, wasn't it?" So he omitted the passage.

Albee's *Zoo Story* dramatizes an old American theme—redskin bests paleface, to use Philip Rahv's metaphors.[2] But Albee's redskin speaks current city idiom: "*Time* magazine isn't for blockheads." "That particular vaudeville act is playing the cloud circuit now." Redskin Jerry's verbal flagellation of paleface Peter is climaxed by a shaggy-dog story without the bite of a punch line but with vivid evocation of detail—"But there he was; malevolence with an erection, waiting." In the man-animal contest, the dog wins; but Jerry wins the theater contest with Peter, forcing the respectable businessman to knife the permanent transient. Jerry's comic cruelty leads relentlessly to his noncomic, perhaps tragic, death.

Though Albee's Grandma calls *The American Dream* a comedy, that play's ending is *sourly* happy. Old garrulous Grandma is replaced in the family by a young handsome son-lover, the American Dream, after whom the play is named. Of the three comic C's, Mommy carries the cruelty, Grandma most of the colloquialisms. There is only a hint of camp in the exaggerated trivialization of the family as a hallowed institution; Daddy is rich and sterile, Mommy acquisitive and sadistic, and the handsome young American Dream will do anything but feel nothing. In contrast to these caricatures, Grandma straddles the fence between mythic frontierswoman and geriatric victim. It is she who remarks campily to the audience: "I mean, for better or worse, this is a comedy, and I don't think we'd better go any further." Nor need we go any further to realize that the American Dream (Albee's and ours) has curdled into nightmare beneath its comic surface—a nightmare propped on sex and success.

Sex and success lie at the base of the reciprocal cruelties of George and Martha in *Who's Afraid of Virginia Woolf?*, Albee's most skillful and celebrated play. Martha harps on George's failure in the History Department, and George jabs at Martha's physique and philandering. The hard-drinking, hard-playing, hard-fighting couple at once personify and satirize the inadequacies of modern America. Unlike the Mommy-Daddy couple of *The American Dream,* however, George and Martha inspire sympathy as well as laughter—a sympathy that has been growing with the years. When

[2]Philip Rahv, *Image and Idea* (New York: New Directions, 1949).

first performed, the drama shocked through its vitriolic idiom, but few critics today would echo Walter Sorell's opinion: "The two couples are revolting, the situations offensive. The play portrays the lower depths of a *dolce vita* at the point where it pukes over its own existence."[3]

Today it is clear that George and Martha are interdependent, nourishing their love on invective and invention. Their contemporary colloquialisms quicken with new life the old comic device of conjugal quarrels. This Mommy's Daddy boomerangs her every barb. However much Martha drinks, she can still aim accurately with verbal missiles, and George shoots more lethal ammunition than colored parasols. Some of his phrases are erudite, as befits a professor—"chromosomological partnership"—but he disdains his own erudition: "A.B. . . . M.A. . . . Ph.D. . . . Abmaphid." He can be deft with colloquialisms, as when he needles his guests: "this nice young couple comes out of the middle west . . . and they got to know each other when they was only *teensie little types,* and they used to get under the vanity table and *poke around*" (my italics). But it is his wife's vanity that George seeks to puncture with his forked tongue—her age, drinking, sexuality, and her own cruelties: "I thought you'd like it, sweetheart, it's sort of to your taste . . . blood, carnage and all. Why, I thought you'd get all excited . . . sort of heave and pant and come running at me, your melons bobbling." Which *is* Martha's intermittent reaction to George's flagellation. Her own assaults are more direct, and, except for momentary scorn at Nick's impotence, they aim relentlessly at George, whom she calls cluck, dumbbell, simp, pig, blank, cipher, zero, sour-puss, muckmouth, paunchy, a bog, a fen, a G. D. swamp, swampy, prick, coward, bastard, floozie, S.O.B., flop, cochon, canaille, son of a bitch, mother, mur . . . der . . . er, ending limply enough on the already used "Liar."

Who's Afraid of Virginia Woolf?—song and play—conceals fear beneath a party surface. Far from a mere *dolce vita* of offensive couples, however, the drama of four characters terminates in an act of exorcism. Though Martha claims that George no longer knows the difference between truth and illusion, he finally kills their child of illusion in the last darkly comic scene of the play. When first heard, the Latin service for the dead sounds like camp parody, but it

[3] Walter Sorell, *Facets of Comedy* (New York: Grosset and Dunlap, 1972), p. 216.

prepares for George's outrageous tale of the death telegram, corroborated by Honey. Unlike his namesake, Albee's George can tell a lie, but he implies that lies act in the service of truth. Possibly the dawn ending signals the birth of truth in marriage, and yet Martha's final words express fear rather than hope. Finally ambiguous, Albee's drama is comic not in its conclusion but in its verbal cruelties, lively colloquialisms, and such camp effects as Martha imitating Bette Davis, George imitating President Kennedy, a Latin burial service for an imaginary death, and a familiar tune with semi-nonsensical words—"Who's afraid of Virginia Woolf?"

After *Virginia Woolf,* Albee's humor drains away. Like *Zoo Story, Tiny Alice* ends in death, but Julian, the would-be apostate, lacks the self-irony of Jerry, a prophet with a nickname. The opening scene seems to continue the three comic C's of *Virginia Woolf*—as Cardinal and Lawyer fence verbally; as they lapse into such slang as diddle, pig, loot; as they seem to play at law and church, rather than belonging to these professions. With the entrance of humorless Julian, however, comedy sputters into martyrdom (Albee apparently takes the martyrdom as seriously as does Julian, since he threatened to sue ACT for shrinking Julian's dying monologue). In *Virginia Woolf,* Martha says: "I have a fine sense of the ridiculous, but no sense of humor." Unfortunately, both senses have deserted Albee in his plays of the 1970's.

Edward Albee has sometimes been called the last of the traditional playwrights, in that he gives the director a finished script, participates minimally during rehearsals, and has achieved success on Broadway. However, that combination almost holds true of two younger playwrights, Arthur Kopit and John Guare. In contrast, several of their contemporaries have worked in close collaboration with particular ensembles—Megan Terry and Jean-Claude van Itallie with the Open Theatre, Ed Bullins with the New Lafayette Theatre, Sam Shepard with Cafe LaMamma, and Kenneth Bernard, Ronald Tavel, and Charles Ludlam with the Ridiculous Theatre Company or its predecessor. The printed plays often evolved through exercises or workshops.[4]

A decade separates Edward Albee from Arthur Kopit and John Guare, but it might be a generation, so effortlessly do the younger

[4]For facility of reference, I discuss only plays that have been printed. For selection among modern dramatists, I, of course, am responsible.

dramatists wield disjunctive dialogue, minimal plots, and zany characters. Like Albee, the younger playwrights arrive at no unequivocally happy endings, and they pivot serious themes on obstreperous humor. Unlike Albee, however, Kopit and Guare imitate the loose structure of media programs, never attaining the dramatic drive of *Zoo Story* or *Virginia Woolf*.

Though younger than Albee, Kopit entered the theater scene earlier—in 1957, while he was a Harvard undergraduate. Inevitably, New York critics dubbed him an undergrad playwright, but Kopit graduated in 1960 with *Oh Dad, Poor Dad, Mama's Hung You in the Closet and I'm Feelin' So Sad: A Pseudoclassical Tragifarce in a Bastard French Tradition,* whose title sparked as much fun outside as in the theater. Gerald Weales describes it as "at once a successful sick joke and a good clean American absurdist comedy."[5] Since the play does not reflect on metaphysics, however, it is not absurdist but merely absurd in its several cruelties and early camp. In 1961 Albee would stage a Mommy who has systematically mutilated her son, but in 1960 Kopit staged a monstrous millionairess who imprisons her son among Venus fly-traps, a piranha fish, and a taxidermically stuffed husband (the titular Dad in the closet). Son Jonathan is buffeted like a tennis ball between Madame Rosepettle, his predatory chaste mother, and Rosalie, the promiscuous young *femme fatale*. His solution is to strangle the latter, enabling Madame Rosepettle to close the play in mockery of fashionable psychology: "As a mother to a son I ask you. *What is the meaning of this?*"

The meaning, of course, is that a neurotic society is sick at its center. Kopit dramatizes this meaning more comically (if less histrionically) in *The Day the Whores Came Out to Play Tennis,* produced in 1965. The whores' tennis game is viewed through the consternation of affluent Jewish country club members: "Instead of tennis whites they had on plaids and chartreuse and lavender. And when they bent over, it turns out they didn't have on any underpants, at *all*. Well! Of course! As soon as I saw all this vulgarity I knew they weren't members." The whores' effrontery does not stop at tennis; they fart in perfect unison, they use their tennis rackets to beat the chairman of the club sports, they invite the club butler to join their game, and they pelt the clubhouse with tennis balls. Instead of

[5]Gerald Weales, *The Jumping Off Place* (New York: Macmillan, 1969), p. 75.

confronting the whores, club members sting one another with cruel and funny barbs. Far from a united front against the whores' assault, two club members play cards, another drinks, and a fourth rides a child's hobby horse while "watch[ing] what we built collapse all about us."

Precocity notwithstanding, Kopit's humor was not taken seriously until *Indians* (1969), which so discerning a critic as John Lahr places on the high level of *Salesman, Streetcar,* and *Virginia Woolf.* Lahr believes that Kopit "demands complexity, not simplicity of vision."[6] Whatever Kopit may demand, however, *Indians* remains satirically simplistic. Today's fashion sides with Indians *against* cowboys, to little practical benefit for the native Americans. Kopit draws his Indians as nature's noblemen, eighteenth-century style, and he caricatures the palefaces as greedy buffoons, especially the Ol' Time President and his lady. Despite his title, Kopit centers his play not on Indians, but on Buffalo Bill, whose memories intrude upon his lavishly staged Wild West show. Believing in his own legendary heroism, Buffalo Bill is a camp character. Step by tricky step, he comes to accept the rape of the Indians, in order to publicize his mythic past. Mired in his own nostalgia, Buffalo Bill protests to Wild Bill Hickok: "I'm not being false to what I *was.* I'm simply *drawin'* on what I was . . . and liftin' it to a higher level." Finally, Buffalo Bill loses his Western colloquialisms as he rationalizes genocide.

Kopit's three major plays end unhappily—Jonathan trapped between his murdered seducer and his murderous mother in *Oh Dad Poor Dad,* the tennis-ball disintegration of the country club in *The Day the Whores,* and Buffalo Bill trembling over Indian trinkets before his glossy Wild West show usurps the stage. Each successive Kopit play dilutes his humor, but camp and cruelty enliven the three. Colloquialism is differently deployed: Madame Rosepettle's elegance and Jonathan's stuttering are deliberately anti-vernacular in *Oh Dad,* but in *The Day the Whores* the country club members speak crusty colloquialisms with Yiddish rhythms. In *Indians* Buffalo Bill retreats from his salty Western lingo to vapid political rhetoric. "Reminded o' somethin' tol' me once by General Custer. You remember him—one o' the great dumbass men in history"

---

[6]John Lahr, *Up Against the Fourth Wall* (New York: Grove Press, 1970), p. 150.

gives way to "I am sick and tired of these sentimental humanitarians who take no account of the difficulties under which this Government has labored in its efforts to deal fairly with the Indian."

Like Kopit, John Guare began with short sketches and graduated to full evenings in the theater. His three main plays focus on a hero who is at once ridiculous and sympathetic, and who is surrounded by more or less funny caricatures. Cumulatively, the plays satirize contemporary America as they sport, in varying proportions, camp, cruelty, colloquialism.

Muzeeka is named for the Muzak-type music with which Jack Argue betrays his ideal of a latter-day Etruscan civilization: "I'll wait with my tongue in my cheek here like a private smirking soul-kiss and when I'm piped into every elevator, every office, every escalator, every toilet, every home, airplane, bus, truck and car in this country, I'll strike." However, it is Jack Argue who is "struck" by his surrender to all-American jingoistic goals. Having enlisted in the army, he receives his wife's proud letter, hears his buddy's vision of a prosperous peacetime partnership. With a last thought of the Etruscans, Jack Argue stabs himself on the battlefield, while his campily catsup-splattered buddy calls out his name.

In *House of Blue Leaves* Guare attempts to blend Strindberg and Feydeau. Contemporary slang conveys not only marital cruelty (Artie Shaughnessy and his mad wife, Bananas) and erotic cruelty (Artie and his ambitious mistress, Bunny), but utter lack of charity (Artie and three nuns who come to see the Pope in New York City). Artie's son, AWOL from the army, intends to bomb the Pope, but he proves to be as ineffectual as his father, so that the bomb kills not the Pope but two nuns and a deaf movie star. After a scene of Feydeau-like farce, Artie is left alone with his mad wife, who behaves like a pet dog. Artie strokes her tenderly, then tightening his grip, "he squeezes the breath out of her throat." Unlike *Zoo Story*, where humor leads relentlessly to homicide, much of Guare's humor is gratuitous to the final homicide.

In *Rich and Famous*, playwright Bing Ringling faces the people he desires as stepping-stones toward becoming "rich and famous"—his actress girlfriend, a woman producer, a black homosexual who plays and betrays his protagonist, the aged but trendy composer who may set his play to music, the parents who are too ready to batten on his fame, and the childhood friend who *is*

rich and famous as a James Dean–type movie star. Each stereotype is delineated by his stereotyped jargon. Unlike *Muzeeka* and
House of Blue Leaves, Rich and Famous does not end in death or
insanity of the hero. After the suicide of the rich and famous
movie-star friend—"I'll be bigger in death than I ever was in life"
—Bing Ringling renounces riches and fame to write a play about
someone "who keeps seeing life through everyone else's eyes."
But Guare's three heroes seem to see life through *his* zany inventive temperament.

Before writing his full-length plays, Guare dipped into transformation technique. Originally conceived by the Second City Company in Chicago, the technique was developed in exercises of New
York's Open Theatre ensemble. In the words of director Peter
Feldman: "The transformation . . . is an improvisation in which the
established realities or 'given circumstances' (the Method phrase) of
the scene change several times during the course of the action. . . .
These changes occur swiftly and *almost without transition,* until
the audience's dependence upon any fixed reality is called into
question."[7] In Guare's *Cop-Out* an actor and actress assume several
roles with laughable abruptness. The roles parody those of media
characters, who in turn may parody contemporary social types: the
dedicated cop, whose first word is "Lease-Po," falls in love with the
dedicated radical. In a concurrent plot super-sleuth Brett Arrow
solves a murder mystery with the help of a *femme fatale.* The
murderer proves to be a little old lady who has killed her cat but is
hideously and hilariously avenged by cats united: "All that's left are
her crutches and the cats are using those for toothpicks." When the
masochistic *femme fatale* meets her own fate in Arrow's arms, he
resolves: "I'll get you all you Commie Jewo Niggo Dago Woppo
Mafio Faggo Russki." When the sterilized policeman shoots the
striker, she lies on the floor until the real theater audience departs.
Satire and parody dissolve into camp.

Guare experimented with transformation technique in a single
short play, but Megan Terry developed several plays in cooperation
with Open Theatre actors. Her first script, the twenty-six exercises
published as *Comings and Goings,* lacks a binding thematic thread,
but there are comic notes when two actors play five word-for-word
repetitions of a breakfast scene, tone transformations conveying five

[7]Quoted in Megan Terry, *Viet Rock* (New York: Simon and Schuster, 1967), pp. 200–201.

different relationships—matter-of-fact client and waitress, masterly waitress and submissive client, masterly customer and slavish waitress, automated robots, ecstatically symbolic customer and waitress. The humor is cumulative as the familiar colloquial phrases call attention to the artifice of roles.

More sustained are Terry's fifteen transformations in *Keep Tightly Closed in a Cool Dry Place*. The cool dry place is a prison, actual or metaphoric, in which three men are "closed" for the collaborative murder of the wife of one of them. Though the subject does not lend itself to humor, the swift transformations confer comic automatism on the scenes. According to director Peter Feldman: "The movie sequences, the vaudeville, the camped queen scene were all funny, often grotesque."[8] After the re-enactment of the murder, followed by a parody of contrition and frenzy, the self-created widower is probably meant to be taken seriously in his breakdown.

Terry uses transformation most ambitiously in *Viet Rock, a Folk War Movie*. Her production note specifies: "Every positive and comic value in the play must be played, and then the dark values will come through with twice the impact." An unspecified number of actors and actresses (Terry worked with thirteen to sixteen) become in turn mothers and newborn babies, doctors and new recruits, sweethearts and soldiers, protesters and policemen, an airplane and soldiers, the Lama and GIs, witnesses and senators, South Vietnamese and GIs, Viet Cong and GIs, mothers and their wounded sons, dancing couples, phantasmagoric echoes, celebrants of life. Through these transformations, Terry implies that the warring world is bereft of stability; people are mere roles in any given scene of an insane war. In Richard Schechner's description, as introduction to the published play, "Serious scene and parody, sentimental moment and satire, brutal death and vaudeville gag are all knitted into the complex crossweave of the sudden transformations." The crossweave is actually more complicated than complex, since satiric antiwar bias is never in doubt.

Like Megan Terry, Jean-Claude van Itallie participated in the Open Theatre workshops and gradually moved from comic transformation to graver and longer works. The swiftly changing roles in his short plays also accumulate into a satire on contemporary America—particularly on the media, in which he has worked. His

[8]*Ibid.*, p. 204.

dialogue, like Terry's, derives from everyday speech and cultural stereotypes. Of the three comic C's, he too indulges in camp—as satire, parody, and obstreperous insistence on its own artifice. Like Terry's *Comings and Goings* and especially *Viet Rock,* his *America Hurrah* trilogy depersonalizes character to indict America's depersonalized people. In performance, the Open Theatre actors avoided touching one another and talked past one another, to evoke horrified amusement in the audience.

"Interview," subtitled a fugue, plays variations on the relationship of brisk interviewer and timorous applicant. Actors and actresses transform in turn into priest-confessant, psychiatrist-patient, opponents in gymnastic exercise, subway, telephone switchboard, square dance. The whole mocks a mindless, mechanical system.

Juxtaposition replaces transformation in the next two parts of van Itallie's *America Hurrah* trio. "TV" juxtaposes a TV rating team against the TV programs they rate—the exploits of Wonderboy, Vietnamese deaths, cigarette commercials, Billy Graham sermons, soap opera. The programs are easily parodied, but the rating team members become depersonalized caricatures, as the stereotypical programs expose the stereotypicality of those who rate them.

"Motel," the last of the *America Hurrah* trilogy, turns on a simpler satiric juxtaposition—a grotesque Motel-Keeper doll incessantly chattering, and an equally grotesque but silent doll couple. The Motel-Keeper doll utters platitudes about rooms in general and this motel room in particular, with its hominess built of catalogue purchases. Emerging from behind headlights, a man and woman doll enter the praised motel room. The man doll proceeds to dismantle the room's furnishings, while from the offstage bathroom the woman throws toilet articles and fixtures. To TV rock music and the homey monologue of the Motel-Keeper doll—"Full with things, the world full up"—they write obscenities on the walls, then fornicate furiously. They "proceed methodically to greater and greater violence," smashing everything in the motel room, as a crescendo of miscellaneous noises overpowers the Motel-Keeper's monologue. Headlights, cacophony, and moving air simultaneously assault the audience, while onstage the man and woman dolls dismember the Motel-Keeper doll, before exiting down the theater aisle. Literally dehumanized, van Itallie's giant dolls are at once funny and horrifying; while the one doll intones homey colloquialisms, the other two destroy maniacally. The playwright uses the artifice of puppets very differently from traditional Punch and Judy or contemporary Bread and Puppets. Representatives of the triviality and artifice of a motel civilization, the dolls invite us, through uneasy laughter, to indict such triviality and artifice.

The genteel tradition of comedy obeyed set prescriptions for humor—situations, types, dialects, gags. Contemporary playwrights, in contrast, tend toward humor that is variously called sick, black, camp, and that many audiences do not find funny. Nothing is duller than arguing that humor *is* funny, so acceptance was slow for a theater ensemble dedicated to camp humor.

The very name, Playhouse of the Ridiculous, suggests its orientation—but only in part, for the name does not reveal the camp basis of performance. When founded in 1966, the Playhouse played the scripts of Ronald Tavel, who has written that "camp is a way of accepting ourselves in images, in stocks, in exaggerations that have in mind a pointing to a clear definition."[9] The clarity of definition is questionable, but the camp quality is not—neither in Tavel's scripts, nor in those of Kenneth Bernard, who also worked with the company. In 1969 actor-director-playwright Charles Ludlam founded his own group, the Ridiculous Theatrical Company, which continues to flourish. Very broadly, one can distinguish the three Ridiculous playwrights: Bernard originates his own stories in which cruelty is exhibited as part of a symbolic entertainment; Tavel parodies grade B movies—"Holly-would? Holly-did!"—and Ludlam parodies the classics: "We try imitating the great works and in our failure we find our own originality."[10] All three pun mercilessly, revel in transvestitism, exploit violence, and promulgate camp. Though the three playwrights use colloquialism and abuse cruelty, camp is their uneminent domain. Post-absurdist in dramatizing life's meaninglessness, the three playwrights diverge in that Bernard's characters suffer from such anarchy, whereas Tavel and Ludlam thrive on it. Examples from each writer suggest the respective flavors:

> GORILLA QUEEN (Tavel): That broad don't pull this boy's third leg—she ain't Karma Miranda—she's Queen Kong! And not

[9]Ronald Tavel, "The Theater of the Ridiculous," *Tri-Quarterly,* 6 (Spring, 1966), 93.
[10]Dan Isaac, "An Interview with Charles Ludlam, Norma Desmond and Laurette Bedlam," *The Drama Review,* 13 (Fall, 1968), 116.

married—what a break! If I can make her to the altar I'll be sable to shit the degrading job of chimney sweep and be King for a lay!

BLUEBEARD (Ludlam): Give up your passions, Bluebeard, and become the thing you claim to be. Is to end desire desire's chiefest end? Does sex afford no greater miracles? Have all my perversions and monstrosities, my fuckings and suckings led me to this? This little death at the climax followed by slumber? Yet chastity ravishes me. And yet the cunt gapes like the jaws of hell, an unfathomable abyss; or the boy-ass used to buggery spread wide to swallow me up its bung; or the mouth sucking out my life! Aaagh! If only there were some new and gentle genital that would combine with me and, mutually interpenetrated, steer me through this storm in paradise!

NIGHT CLUB (Bernard): You realize you don't deserve a girl like that. She has a perfect body. She was made to be loved.—And she loves to be made. Her mother was a maid of all work, and her father made millions. There's "made" in every bone and muscle of her.

With Rochelle Owens, much admired by Kenneth Bernard, we turn away from the determinedly ridiculous to a search for significance in humor and horror. Unlike van Itallie and Terry, however, who blend the two in satire, Owens writes dramas whose intentions are sometimes puzzling. Though she is light-years away from traditional situation comedy, her plays are anchored in exotic and painful situations, and her idiom explodes from these situations. Of the three comic C's she weights cruelty so heavily that her stage sadism borders on Grand Guignol, but is it *meant* to be laughable? Colloquialism is only one aspect of her verbal variety, when it suits such characters as Farmer Futz, the Greenland Eskimoes, the black singer Leadbelly. Though Owens hints at satire, parody, and sexual ambiguity, her plays lack the self-conscious sense of their own artifice—camp. In the introduction to her *Karl Marx Play* she has written: "Authentic theatre is always oscillating between joyousness and fiendishness." She achieves this pendulum movement only in her early plays. More recently, the balance leans toward fiendishness, which runs the risk of being unintentionally funny.

Her first play remains in delicate balance. Farmer Cyrus Futz is in love with his pig Amanda. But, far from *Tobacco Road*–type humor, his animality arouses audience sympathy by virtue of his neighbors' hostility. Majorie Satz, amendable to any perversions involving men, plots the death of Futz' pig-love. Oscar Loop, aroused by the man-pig orgy, kills Ann Fox and is hanged. In prison Futz is stabbed by Majorie's brother. Nevertheless, these passions and deaths are bathed in humor. Futz addresses his pig Amanda: "Lucky luck that I'm in love with you otherwise you'd be hanging in my pantry. Heeeehhhhehehehe when you're old you'll be sitting in my granny's rockin' chair readin' the Bible. Amanda you are of the world, known two kinds of male animals, pig and man! Sow I know you love me but I wonder whether you'd rather be with your own kind? Piglets I can't give you though I am a healthy man." The Narrator comments on Majorie Satz: "Hell hath no fury like a woman scorned by a man—for a pig." After Cyrus Futz is stabbed, the Narrator sums up tersely: "Amanda—there's someone here needs you. Yes." But animality is already dead.

In other short plays–*The String Game, Homo, Istanboul*–man's animality remains the central theme, but the violence is less wrenching, so that Owens's humor can govern the whole. In her first full-length play, bloodshed is as ubiquitous as in *Tamburlaine,* and as difficult to stage. The titular Beclch, a white woman who becomes an African queen, laughs uproariously at the tortures and murders she instigates as "sacrifices." Her glee is not contagious, in spite of her companion's opinion that she has a good sense of humor, in spite of the prediction that her own swan song "will be a horse laugh . . . loud enough to crack the dry earth."

After undertaking imaginary anthropology, Owens ventures into imaginary history, forcing into the same drama the black singer Leadbelly and Karl Marx with his entourage. A comic Karl Marx—with boils, prejudices, and feverish sex urges—succumbs to inaction. Leadbelly goads him, with cruel colloquialisms, to *be* Karl Marx: "Any time I look at your face, Karl Marx, I get mad! You're really nothing! You don't even have a lard ass! Not even no lard ass! Lemme see your gums! Blah! Yah! They red like the ass of a baboon! You white goo! Spewed out of a white bug! You—die —like a bug! Squish!" However, Marx does not die in Owens's play. Instead, literally inflamed when Leadbelly puts a torch to his intestines, Karl Marx "dashes off—to write *Das Kapital.*"

Though Owens does not accommodatingly use all three comic C's, she includes colloquialism in her several synthetic idioms. So specific is her stage cruelty that her tone can stumble uncertainly. At her best, she forces human animality into an aggrandized Guignol that demands the horse laugh merely predicted for Beclch.

In a different way, tone is a problem in the drama of Ed Bullins, a prolific playwright committed to the black theater movement. His so-called dynamite plays are simplistic, humorless agitprop, but his dramas of the black ghetto bear comparison with Chekhov's portrait of a dying aristocracy. Gorki describes Chekhov: "In front of that dreary, grey crowd of helpless people there passed a great, wise, and observant man [Chekhov]; he looked at all these dreary inhabitants of his country, and, with a sad smile, with a tone of gentle but deep reproach, with anguish in his face and in his heart, in a beautiful but sincere voice, he said to them: 'You live badly, my friends. It is shameful to live like that.' "[11] About such shameful lives Chekhov wrote what he sometimes called comedies. Bullins's blacks are never dreary, and he looks at their merrymaking with a similar loving reproach. Like Chekhov, Bullins dramatizes the foibles of his people, endearing them to us through their (and his) humor.

Bullins's blacks are criminal or bourgeois, speaking energetic slang and casual obscenity. The very title of an early play, *Clara's Ole Man,* is darkly humorous, since it refers to Big Girl, Clara's lover. Student Jack, attracted to Clara, is first mocked and then badly beaten on orders from his rival, "Clara's ole man." Explaining in educated English that he is a student on the GI bill, Jack is asked by a ghetto dweller: "Is that why you sound like you got a load of shit in your mouth?"

No one sounds that way in the underworld "tragifantasy," *Goin' a Buffalo,* where the outsider is victor rather than victim. Like Chekhov's three sisters who dream of going to Moscow, Bullins's pimps and whores dream of escaping from Los Angeles to Buffalo: "I heard that Buffalo is really boss." Through death and betrayal, the dream approaches reality by the end of the play. The outsider betrays his friend, annexes the pimps' black and white molls, Pandora and Mama Too Tight, and orders the women to pack. When asked where they are going, he replies: "To Buffalo, baby. Where else?" Rather than Owens's sustained exotic situations, Bullins sharply wrenches his dramas toward an ironic conclusion. And there is no dawn at the play's end.

[11]Quoted in *The Notebooks of Anton Tchekhov* (London: Hogarth Press, 1921) p. 108.

Most ambitious is Bullins's projected Twentieth-Century Cycle of twenty plays about Afro-Americans between 1900 and 1999. The five completed plays, set in the ghetto of Los Angeles, are mired in drinking, gambling, whoring, and violence, but the cool underworld idiom is imperturbable. The five completed plays involve Cliff Dawson and/or his half-brother, Steve Benson.

The first play chronologically (though not the first to be written) is the one-act *Corner*. Named for its setting, an urban streetcorner of a black Los Angeles ghetto of the 1950's, the play shows young blacks entering manhood by drinking and whoring. Twenty-two-year-old Cliff is their natural leader in this outpost of American culture, where Bummie declares: "I don't know nothin' bout no news. When that shit come on I'd have mah hand under some bitch's skirt or gettin' some popcorn." Drunk and desultorily flirting with Cliff's girl, Stella, the young blacks taunt each other with colloquial obscenities. Cliff, however, has learned that he has impregnated Lou, and he retreats from the corner, depositing Stella in the broken-down car where they usually fornicate: "Bitch so damn drunk she fell asleep on me. . . ." Giving the car keys to the whole gang to rape her at will, Cliff commands Bummie: "You can start callin' me Daddy Cliff," and admits that maybe he is changing. It is the most optimistic admission in the five cycle plays.

On the surface, Cliff does not change. *In the Wine Time* shows the ménage of Cliff and Lou, along with Lou's nephew Ray. Cliff drinks, whores, and lives on Lou's earnings. Drunk, he assaults God with his version of prayer: "You pour white heat on these niggers, these Derby Street Donkeys, in the daytime and roast and fry them while they shovel shit for nex' to nothin', and steam them at night like big black lobsters. . . ." Lou's fifteen-year-old nephew, Ray, imitates Cliff admiringly. By the end of the play Ray stabs another teenager, and Cliff takes the blame. He makes one serious and loving statement to Lou, in contrast to his usual macho taunts: "It won't be for long . . . I was protectin' my family . . . our family."

"Not for long" proves to be seven irretrievable years. *In New England Winter* finds Cliff after his prison sentence. His half-brother, Steve Benson, has masterminded a successful robbery, undertaken to enable him to head for an old love in New England winter. The play itself is a flashback that intercuts 1955 New England scenes with the 1960 rehearsal for the robbery—a four-man rehearsal demanding disguise and meticulous timing. Again Bullins's vivid idiom energizes the grim lives. In this play, tension, rather than wine, elicits the cryptically comic cross-taunts of the four black holdup men who have known each other since childhood on the Los Angeles corner. "When some guy bothers me I cut him. That's all," says Cliff, who still wields most authority. But it is Steve who cuts Bummie, splitting his throat to prevent the revelation of a Steve-Lou love affair while Cliff was in prison. "But it was for nothing, Steve . . . I knew . . ." Disposing of the corpse of Bummie, *three* men carry out the rehearsed robbery. In retrospect, the brothers' lines are mordantly ironic—Cliff's admiring: "You're a genius, Steve," and Steve's laconic: "Thanks, Cliff."

By the time of *The Duplex,* set in the 1960's, Cliff has disappeared, but his father is "an old man and Mamma's current man," of whom nameless Mamma says: "Clifton Slaughter Dawson . . . that's his name . . . his real name. But I just call him Pops now . . . like everybody else . . . not even 'Dawg.' Ha ha ha . . . 'Ole Dawg! . . . that's what I'd call him . . . was my special name for. . . . Poor Ole Dawg . . . cries and tells me how he's goin' to go find his son one day. . . . Before Ole Dawg dies . . . dies drunk . . . like an old drunken puppy." Unlike the play's main characters, Mamma and Pops do not live in the garishly ornamented Los Angeles duplex. The first-floor apartment is occupied by owner Velma and occasionally by her brutal husband O. D. The second floor apartment is shared by Marco Polo Henderson and Steve Benson, who has not gone to New England. Nominally students, the young men spend their time in the duplex, where they engage in pointless passing pleasures.

Bullins subtitles *The Duplex* "A Black Love Fable in Four Movements," which signals Steve's two approaches toward and retreats from Velma. (In the third movement Steve reads to Velma from *In The Wine Time,* but the remainder is lyrical rather than camp.) The love fable is enacted against a card-playing, wine-drinking, marijuana-smoking background in the second-floor apartment, with Montgomery Henderson meeting his adult son, Marco Polo, as Pops Dawson only dreams of meeting *his* son. The old couple occasionally visits. Marie Horton and niece Wanda drop in; Steve sleeps with Marie, and Marco seduces Wanda. Again the aimless lives are enlivened by the comic speech: "Don't want to hear of mah fat son fuggin' punks . . . Keep yo' dick outta dose fat round eyes, buddy boy." "Ya know I really do like skinny li'l honey girls, Montgomery . . . I don't see how ya can stand dose big fat elephant broads." After Velma's husband, O. D., almost strangles Steve, Marie remarks: "Damn . . . what caught hold of you, nigger? . . . You don't look good enough for an undertaker." After Steve is nearly murdered and Velma is marked for murder by O. D., old Montgomery Henderson arrives at the duplex to close the play: "'Hey, ev'vabody! Grab yo cards, whiskey 'n women! It's party time! . . . 'cause ole Montgomery . . . Saltspring . . . Henderson . . . just blew in!" He is utterly ignorant of the proximity of death.

In *The Fabulous Miss Marie* it is always party time; that is why Miss Marie is fabulous. Whatever the political or economic situation of her home or country, Miss Marie is hostess to drinking and fornication. Daughter of a college graduate, granddaughter of a schoolteacher, the pregnant Marie has married dancer Bill Horton. After World War II they have come to Los Angeles, where Bill parks cars for "two hundred stone cold dollars a week . . . We make almost as much as some colored doctors make . . . 'n we spend it too. 'Cause it's party time every day at Miss Marie's house." Husband and wife engage in free and easy drinking and fornication. Though all Miss Marie's Christmas party guests proclaim they are having a good time, boredom streaks through the tired language of schoolteacher, social worker, dress designer, and hangers on. Bullins's black bourgeoisie, living the consumer self-indulgence of the white bourgeoisie, lacks the loyalty and drive of the black criminals from the corner. Like Chekhov's dying aristocrats, Bullins's blacks have little left but their anachronistic style in a world that is passing them by.

The fulcrum of Ed Bullins's humor is black colloquialism and macho cruelty; but his plays are innocent of camp, since they faithfully reflect the fabric (rather than the facts) of twentieth-century black ghetto experience. In contrast, the plays of Sam Shepard revel in self-awareness of their artifice. Both playwrights stand high by the reach of their language. "I feel that language is a veil hiding demons and angels which the characters are always out of touch with," Shepard has written.[12] Shepard's dramatic dialogue shivers the veil. Through his plays runs the jargon of a youth culture

[12]Quoted in Kenneth Chubb, "Fruitful Difficulties of Directing Sam Shepard," *Theatre Quarterly*, 4 (August-October, 1974), 24.

addicted to drugs, rock music, detective stories, astrology, cowboy movies, and races of cars, horses, dogs.

The printing of Shepard's plays does not group them chronologically (or by any other rationale apparent to me), so it is difficult to trace his development. Widely divergent in quality, all his plays reveal his affinity for aspects of popular culture. Whereas the Ridiculous playwrights capitalize on sophisticated trivialization of pop art, Shepard smiles gently at its stereotypes. His first play, *Cowboys,* is lost, but its very title announces his affection. In his first surviving play, *Rock Garden,* the three comic C's blend; the dialogue is easy and colloquial, the self-conscious positions are redolent of camp, and the characters talk past each other cruelly. Unlike Chekhov's plays, where communication can occur in the interstices between speech, or Pinter's, where dialogue can deliberately veil communication, Shepard's competing monologues delineate the isolation of each character. This technique becomes deft in the *Five Plays,* each one pivoting on a single event: Joy gets a job in *Chicago;* a plane signals to picnickers and then crashes in *Icarus's Mother;* a bookcase for the titular *Fourteen Hundred Thousand* books is begun and then dismantled; crab lice attack husband and then wife in *Red Cross;* Floyd needs a new hit song in *Melodrama Play.* There is much rhythm but little reason to these exploratory sallies.

Within three years of these first efforts, in 1967, Shepard produced his first full-length play, *La Turista,* punning on the Spanish word for tourist and the diarrhea that attacks tourists in Mexico. Perhaps influenced by Beckett's *Godot, La Turista* is also composed of two acts in which the second almost repeats the first. However, shifting identities and mythic roles are at once more blatant and more realistic than in Beckett. Since Kent is sick, his wife Salem (both names for cigarette brands) sends for a doctor who, more or less aided by his son, essays a kind of cure. The first act takes place in a Mexican hotel room, the second in an American hotel room. In Act I Kent faints when he sees a Mexican boy in his bed; he never regains consciousness, despite the ministrations of the native witch-doctor and his son. Since there is talk in Act II of a trip to Mexico, it may precede Act I in time. Ill now from sleep-waking cycles, rather than from sunburn and diarrhea, Kent is able to rival the Doc in vocal patent-medicine salesman style. In Act I Salem and the boy form a new couple over Kent's body, whereas in Act II Kent escapes the others by leaping through the back wall of the set, "leaving a cut-out silhouette of his body in the wall." Leaning on satire of American marriage, American medicine, American tourism, *La Turista* plays with several colloquial idioms and displays Shepard's separate individuals, each locked within his own horrifyingly comic illness.

A series of shorter plays followed swiftly, published in two volumes in 1971. Each book is aptly named for its first and longest play. In the six plays of *Unseen Hand* the several main characters are threatened by unseen hands. In the title play a wheelless '51 Chevrolet is the setting for a reunion of a 120-year-old cowboy with his two dead brothers, to protect Willie of outer space. In *Forensic and the Navigators,* Forensic battles two exterminators whom he addresses as Forensic, while Oolan, in mental hospital garb, stuffs Emmet with endless Rice Krispies. In *Back Bog Beast Bait* man is first terrified, then terrifying when he realizes that he himself is the beast he fears. Cherry looks up from her pornographic book in *Shaved Splits* to watch her Chinese servant go berserk, her returned husband shot, and herself threatened by Geez, a revolutionary; but a narrator's voice indicates the camp quality of these contemporary roles. In these plays compounded of American life and legend, Shepard's dialogue pirouettes from cowboy to All-American kid, to sleuth, to cool youth, to modern rebel who dies in a fantasy of playing an orange guitar: "All the sounds of the fifties and sixties combined in one band and all making sense. All making music. . . . He was playing lead for the greatest band in the world. . . . The war was over and he was alive!"

Two plays in the *Mad Dog Blues* volume are madder and more musical. They are also more comically and self-consciously aware of themselves as theater pieces. In the title play, two friends, a rock star and a drug pusher, separate to seek their respective fortunes. Kosmo takes up with Mae West, and Yahoudi with Marlene Dietrich, those camp prima donnas. Each pair becomes a triangle when Yahoudi annexes Captain Kidd and Kosmo Waco Texas. Searching for Kidd's treasure, they tumble from one adventure to another: Yahoudi shoots Captain Kidd, Marlene Dietrich goes off with Paul Bunyan, Kosmo and Mae West find the treasure; but Jesse James robs Kosmo of treasure and Mae West, only to be detained by U.S. Customs. Mae West sparks a traditional comic ending, filling the stage with all the characters: "Wouldn't that be something, though?" Versatile is Shepard's idiomatic shift for each mythological character:

MAE WEST: Big surprises come in small packages.

PAUL BUNYAN: This is the North Woods. Ain't no highway for miles. Just lumber camps and diners and trucks and chain saws. Sell ya a good ax if ya need one. That's all I use. These new fellas they use the chain saws but not me. I can outchop the fastest chain saw around.

MARLENE DIETRICH: A mango in the morning is sometimes better than a man.

CAPTAIN KIDD: Aaah, laddie. 'Tis a treasure to make a man's eyes dance out of his head.

JESSE JAMES: Maybe we should just take what we can carry in our pockets and leave the rest hid. Then we can come back and pick it up some other time.

Shepard's extraordinarily inventive comic range needs the scope of longer plays. *The Unseen Hand* and *Mad Dog Blues,* with their different language blends and lonely agglomerations, outshine the briefer plays in their respective volumes. Preceding them was *La Turista,* a metaphysical farce before Shepard had heard of Ionesco. In later full-length plays Shepard again wields several kinds of colloquialism, cruelties born of isolation, and anachronistic legends that typify camp.

A longer play from 1969 is close to traditional comedy. The punning title of *Operation Sidewinder* refers to an American army computer in the shape of a sidewinder rattlesnake. By the play's end, it becomes an actual snake and Hopi Indian religious symbol through whose symbiotic power a disoriented young couple are integrated into an organic society—even as in Greek New Comedy. Before that comic ending, however, adventure runs rife: Honey, a young wife, is attacked by the sidewinder; a radical young man shoots her husband; an automobile mechanic, the halfbreed Mickey Free, beheads the sidewinder and rescues Honey; the young man is involved in a conspiracy based on drugs; black revolutionaries imprison and later free Honey and the young man; Mickey Free returns to his people with the head of the sidewinder, and soon the young man brings its long tail. The young man kneels to recite the Lord's Prayer while an Indian ritual is performed and army troops shoot into their midst. Reveling in several idioms—tall tales of an old cowboy, dog-breeding lingo of army officers, amoral jargon of an army scientist, revolutionary rhetoric of the blacks, semi-articulate sensuality of Honey, drug-induced paranoia of the young man, poetic imagery of Mickey Free—the play's words are cartoons in a comedy that converts a computer into a religious force. The several idioms dissolve into a wordless comic ending.

In spite of colloquial variety, the frankly comic ending is tainted by sentimentality. Only in *The Tooth of Crime* (written in London in 1971) does Shepard perfect the invention of a comic idiom that leads to tragedy. Susan Sontag has maintained that "camp and tragedy are antitheses," and this is almost always true, but Shepard molds these antitheses to a powerful intensity.

Hoss ("a killer's killer"), his henchman, and their opponent fuse the slangs of rock, crime, astrology, and car racing into a self-conscious camp language. Hoss has played by the code and moved by the charts, but he senses that he is doomed. In his opening song he sings: "All the heroes is dyin' like flies," like flies in the hands of wanton boys. Hoss's soliloquy has a comic edge because of its synthetic slang: "There's no sense of tradition in the game no more. There's no game. It's just back to how it was. Rollin' nightclubs, strip joints. Bustin' up poker games. Zip guns in the junk yard. Rock fights, dirt clods, bustin' windows. Vandals, juvies, *West Side Story*. Can't they see where they're goin'! Without a code it's just crime." And the tooth of crime turns out to be Crow, the young gypsy killer. Alerted through Eyes, warned by the charts of Galactic Jack, doped by his doctor, comforted by his moll, Hoss awaits his fate at Crow's hands: "Stuck in my image."

In Act II Hoss and Crow, has-been and would-be, confront each other with private names, Leathers and Crowbait. After preliminary skirmishing, the two combatants use microphones to duel with words and music—"Choose an argot"—as a referee keeps score. Round 1 is awarded to Crow on points, Round 2 is a draw, and in Round 3 the Ref calls a TKO after Crow's attack in rhyme. In rock-crime medley, a long way from academe, Crow's verbal flagellation is as skillful as that of Albee's George, and Hoss fights back as gamely as Martha. Until defeat.

Hoss then tries to bribe Crow into a partnership, but the young victor wants all glory to himself. Nevertheless, he gives Hoss veiled lessons in survival—how to walk, look, talk. Hoss is too old to learn new ways, and, like classical heroes, he chooses death. Unlike classical heroes, however, he casts an ironic shadow on death through his camp consciousness of his stance: "Now stand back and watch some true style. The mark of a lifetime. A true gesture that won't never cheat on itself 'cause it's the last of its kind. It can't be taught or copied or stolen or sold. It's mine. An original. It is my life and my death in one clean shot." Hoss then "raises one hand high in the air and pulls the trigger with the other." His death is self-inflicted, leading to a new era: "Now the power shifts and sits till a bigger wind blows." The stage lights fade to close *The Tooth of Crime*. There is no mention of dawn, as in *Virginia Woolf*. Separated by less than a decade, the two plays build tension through a humor that blends camp, cruelty, and crafty manipulation of colloquialism. *Virginia Woolf* hints at a traditional comic ending, but *The Tooth of Crime* cleaves to the noble tradition of tragedy.

In his recent *Culture Watch* Robert Brustein maintains that America is becoming a tragic nation: "A people who till very recently smiled at itself daily in the mirror, accentuated the positive, and demanded happy endings to its plays and movies is now being forced, against its will, to examine its soul and live with the knowledge that past sins are not easily redeemable, even with the best intentions. This is the knowledge that forms the basis for the tragic art."[13] This seems to me a curious confusion of life and art. Actual America continues to smile at itself, to accentuate the positive, and to demand happy endings. It is never "a people," but an artist, who creates tragic art. However, I have quoted Brustein not for the cheap pleasure of contradicting him, but for his insight in spite of himself. Against the smiling grain of the American people, its contemporary playwrights have carved a drama whose humor sometimes touches on the tragic.

[13]Robert Brustein, *The Culture Watch* (New York: Knopf, 1975), p. 68.

JOHN VERNON

Fresh Air: Humor in Contemporary American Poetry

I've never known anyone to fall out of his chair laughing while reading contemporary poetry; poetry today is dominated by the lyric, and the lyric is rooted in romantic melancholy. When contemporary poetry is funny, it is usually anti-lyrical, which means anti-poetic; hence, the title of Nicanor Parra's *Poemas y Antipoemas*. Moreover, the lyric for the most part lacks fiction's shadow connection with our "real" world, the connection that enables us to recognize ourselves long enough to sustain a belly laugh. This is another way of saying, of course, that poetry has things to do that fiction doesn't. Still, contemporary poets try to be humorous more often than most of their predecessors, the great and not-so-great modern poets. This is due in part to the dictum of one of those poets, Pound's "make it new," and in part to the influence of French surrealism. When thousands of poets want to be novel all at once, then we are inundated with mildly humorous images, in which the President smokes an orange or the moon is Hamlet on a motorcycle. In this way, the lyric mocks itself from within, while remaining at the same time essentially lyrical.

The most successful humorists in contemporary poetry are not always the funniest. In fact, their poems often have a quite serious intention. But this depends on the kind of humor involved. I can distinguish two kinds of humor in contemporary poetry. The first is that found in such poets as Kenneth Koch, John Ashbery, James Tate, poets of the so-called New York school,[1] and, to a lesser extent, in such Beat poets as Allen Ginsberg and Gregory Corso. The humor of these poets hovers between surrealism and a kind of epistemological skepticism, a refusal to mean or to respect meaning. Even though humor is often of the first importance in these poets, it appears to be a stopgap measure, a last resort. All of Kenneth Koch's poems, for example, seem to be telling us one thing: if poems can't mean, they can at least be ridiculous. There may or may not be a serious intention behind this poetry. The New York poets would be the last to admit it; they make an automatic series of associations: seriousness = high art = artificiality = pomposity. On the other hand, the title of one of James Tate's books, *Absences,* fits in nicely with the most serious of current philosophical jargons, that of the post-structuralists. For example, in Jacques Derrida's view, there is an unbridgeable gap between words and things; the word is the absence, not the presence, of what it designates. If we unpeel all the layers of language around us, tracing words back to their sources in other words, and still other words, what we find behind it all is not a "world" or "reality" or a presence of any kind, but simply an absence. Of the poets in this group, Ashbery is the most philosophical, and much of what he has to say agrees with this position. The others simply occupy a space in which this sense of things is part of the air they breathe. If there's a gap between words and things, then why not release words to play on their own, joke around, display themselves, invent, shuffle, entertain? The obligation to mean was an insufferable burden, these poets seem to say; it resulted usually in awkward, pompous, inflated poems dragging their rhetoric around like armor. Released from that burden, the words of these poets are lighter and more abundant than air. Surrealism has in fact become our light verse, in which the primary emphasis is upon novelty and inventiveness.

Of course, this kind of poetry isn't entirely new. It goes back through the Chilean poet Nicanor Parra, through some Americans of the 1920's and '30's, such as Kenneth Fearing, Harry Crosby, and

[1]The New York School: a loosely defined group, most of whom take the late Frank O'Hara as their patriarch. Most of them are also surrealists, and many are involved with the St. Mark's Poetry Project. Some names: James Schuyler, Kenneth Koch, John Ashbery, Michael Benedikt, Tom Clark, Peter Schjeldahl, Tony Towle, Ron Padget, Ted Berrigan.

Gertrude Stein, through the French surrealists and dadaists, through Alfred Jarry, and back, finally, to Arthur Rimbaud. Even anti-art has its history. I'll trace this history more carefully below.

The other kind of humor in contemporary poetry is more difficult to pin down or describe. It isn't as much a primary emphasis as it is part of a range of possibilities, and its style or employment isn't uniform from poet to poet. I see it in poets as different from each other as A. R. Ammons, John Berryman, Bill Knott, Russell Edson, David Ignatow, Jack Spicer, and Edward Dorn. Often it manifests itself simply as a tone, sudden and speculative—a bewilderment, a pause, a slip of the tongue—that throws the poem off balance. It usually seems accidental, or even tossed off, not the end of the poem but a means to the end. I think of it in contrast to the wit of poets of the 1940's and '50's. For John Crowe Ransom, Delmore Schwartz, Karl Shapiro, W. H. Auden, Richard Wilbur, and others who wrote (or still write) in that mode, humor was a means of achieving rather than losing balance and control. Humor took the forms of irony or satire, in which the writer was always strictly in control of the attitudes expressed, or of wit, in which a pleasurable word-play or turn of phrase served as ballast to keep the writer sane, upright, and firmly planted on his feet. Wit is always symmetrical and closes in on itself, like the circle of balls a juggler juggles. The humor I am trying to describe is assymmetrical and unstable. It is a form of bodily sabotage that throws you off balance the way laughter does, although it doesn't always necessarily result in laughter. Most of the poets in this group are engaged in a process of discovery, and humor is one of many tools that keeps the poem stumbling forward on a kind of sweeping, erratic, trial-and-error, zig-zag course. I am thinking now particularly of Ammons's long poems, or of Berryman's *Dream Songs* considered as one long poem. Their language is always engaged in a search, and humor is one of its several antennas. The theme of the search (rather than the fact of it) often occurs in poets of the first group, and its very presence as a theme illustrates the chief difference between the two groups. When Kenneth Koch describes a sheriff searching for a walnut, or when John Ashbery speaks of a group of assassins, maps in hand, spreading over a landscape at night, the search—like the language and the humor—exists for its own sake, not for the sake of what it might uncover or discover. Ashbery's maps are not keys to finding something, but signifiers cut off from their significance; in his "Rivers and Mountains," the landscape itself is a map. The search is purely linguistic and always ends where it begins, in language. In Berryman and Ammons, on the other hand, the search involves both words and things, each continually prying the other open. Humor in their poems is always a function of the possibility of meaning. Often the act of the poem is actually a birth of meaning, and humor is the catalyst which enables that birth to take place. In both groups, humor often involves sudden surprises, unusual juxtapositions, and puns, but the essential difference between them revolves around these contrasting attitudes toward meaning.

Of course, the distinction between the groups isn't absolute, and there are some poets, like Ginsberg and Spicer, who in a sense belong to both. Many of our best contemporary poets write an occasional humorous poem, often as a performance piece, but save most of their energy for their serious work; I am thinking primarily of Alan Dugan, or John Logan's poem to his liver, or some of Richard Hugo's letter poems. There are also poets who are humorless— W. S. Merwin, Galway Kinnell, Mark Strand, and Robert Lowell, for example—and others, such as Sylvia Plath and her followers, for whom humor is so transparently lacking in delight that they fail entirely to be humorous. This lack of humor isn't necessarily a failure in these poets, and in fact stems from a strong current in modern poetry that regards humor as superficial. The history of this attitude, and of reactions to it, is part of the ground out of which contemporary poetry emerges. To understand humor in contemporary poetry, we have to turn to that history.

The great modern poets—Hardy, Hopkins, Yeats, Eliot, Rilke, Valéry, Mallarmé—were rarely humorous. This isn't unusual or atypical; the great poets of history were rarely humorous. The chief form humor has taken in poetry is that of satire, which has always been regarded as important but secondary. So Horace is less than Virgil, Pope less than Milton, and so forth. Of course, the argument could be made that truly great poets exclude nothing from the scope of their voice, including humor; Shakespeare immediately comes to mind. Still, there is about poetry the aura of high art, which is probably why too few people read it. The poet is pictured as a priest, in touch with the gods but out of touch with human beings. Poets grow up in a culture in which this cliché is at least implicitly present, and so often come to fulfill it. The poet consecrates himself to his art, renounces the world, love, worldly possessions, and even suffers for the sake of his art (the latter requirement contributed by the Romantics). By the time we get to the end of the nineteenth century, and God's death, the substitution of poetry for religion is something the poets themselves talk a great deal about, particularly in France. The notion is strong enough that we have never completely abandoned it. Even today, going to a poetry reading has something of the flavor of going to church. It's not altogether a wrong-headed idea, either; poetry is, in its roots, oracular and prophetic, a magical use of words. Most primitive poems are expressions of religion. Still, the picture that we have of Mallarmé's hushed followers gathered around him like a congregation, or of Rilke walking the streets of Prague dressed in black, with a lily in his cupped hand, is enough to make it necessary to invent Rimbaud, if he hadn't done it himself.

Rimbaud is the only great modern poet for whom humor is important, and the first in a string of poets who take their primary energy not just from satirizing or parodying the dominant attitudes of poets, but from absolutely turning those attitudes inside out and scraping them clean. Once Rimbaud started writing, all other poets seemed pompous by comparison. Their poetry suddenly *became* serious; before that, it had simply been poetry. Here is one of his early poems, "Vénus Anadyomène," with a translation by Wallace Fowlie:

> Comme d'un cercueil vert en fer blanc, une tête
> De femme à cheveux bruns fortement pommadés
> D'une vieille baignoire émerge, lente et bête,
> Avec des déficits assez mal ravaudés;
>
> Puis le col gras et gris, les larges omoplates
> Qui saillent; le dos court qui rentre et qui ressort;
> Puis les rondeurs des reins semblent prendre l'essor;
> La graisse sous la peau paraît en feuilles plates;
>
> L'échine est un peu rouge; et le tout sent un goût
> Horrible étrangement; on remarque surtout
> Des singularités qu'il faut voir à la loupe . . .
>
> Les reins portent deux mots gravés: CLARA VENUS;
> —Et tout ce corps remue et tend sa large croupe
> Belle hideusement d'un ulcère à l'anus.
>
> (As from a green zinc coffin, a woman's

Head with brown hair heavily pomaded
Emerges slowly and stupidly from an old bathtub,
With bald patches rather badly hidden.

Then the fat gray neck, broad shoulder-blades
Sticking out; a short back which curves in and bulges;
Then the roundness of the buttocks seems to take off;
The fat under the skin appears in slabs;

The spine is a bit red; and the whole thing has a smell
Strangely horrible; you notice especially
Odd details you'd have to see with a magnifying glass . . .

The buttocks bear two engraved words: CLARA VENUS;
—And that whole body moves and extends its broad rump
Hideously beautiful with an ulcer on the anus.[2]

The center of this poem is the phrase "Belle hideusement." This is a love poem, but what the poet loves is not beauty but ugliness, and yet that ugliness is a kind of beauty. And he loves it with a merciless delight that makes most expressions of love in poetry seem fatuous by comparison. Rimbaud has taken the language, the tone, and the structure of the love lyric and turned them on their heads. The poem does have its antecedents: Baudelaire's "Une Charogne" and Shakespeare's sonnet, "My mistress's eyes . . ." The difference is that Rimbaud's microscopic eye absolutely refuses to allow the details of his subject any transcendence but a quantitative one: "on remarque surtout / Des singularités qu'il faut voir à la loupe . . ." This flat quality—which in the tone undermines the few references to conventional lyrical structures, such as the opening simile beginning with "comme"—gives Rimbaud's language a kind of anti-symbolist descriptive hollowness. The poet seems to be standing to one side, allowing the words of the poem simply to report; and the words, consequently, refuse to do anything more than that. All talk of mystery, subtle suggestiveness, multiple meanings, is of course made ridiculous by this kind of poem. Later, Rimbaud withdrew from his poems even the quality of referential meaning that gives the language in this poem its one focus. Without referential meaning, and without the notion of self or subjectivity that lends emotional depth, the lyric becomes a corpse devoured from the inside. In "Une Saison en Enfer" and particularly in "Les Illuminations," the shell

[2]Rimbaud, "Vénus Anadyomène," trans. Wallace Fowlie, in *Rimbaud: Complete Works, Selected Letters* (Chicago, 1966), pp. 40–41, © 1966 by the University of Chicago.

that is left disintegrates before our eyes. In three short years, Rimbaud acted out the entire exhaustion of a literary form. The first group of humorists in contemporary poetry—Koch, Ashbery, Tate—owe almost everything to him. In "Les Illuminations," the unity of self which is the foundation of all lyric poetry becomes increasingly fragmented by language. This is appropriate, since Rimbaud knew that that unity was probably a creation of language in the first place. As a result, poetry for him becomes not a spontaneous overflow of powerful feelings, but, to use Derrida's terms, a game, a play of language, a pure empty language with space all around it. This is not the most important tradition in modern poetry, but it certainly is an undercurrent, a kind of alternate tradition which has nurtured a whole group of poets today. It's enough of a *presence* in our literature that no poet can write without somehow coming to terms with it.

The dadaists and surrealists continue this tradition, as does Gertrude Stein. Any aesthetic which cultivates the dream and rejects reason, which loves sudden bizarre juxtapositions and values the free play of language over craftsmanship and form, is bound to continually border on humor, and often to spill over into it. Interestingly enough, however, the humor depends upon the very values the aesthetic rejects. To use Wallace Stevens's example, a clam playing an accordion is funny because there is a world, the one we usually live in, in which clams don't play accordions. Unfortunately, there is a world also where my love isn't like a red, red rose, let alone, say, like a fire hydrant, and that is also the world we usually live in. The tradition of Rimbaud can successfully call lyric poetry into question only because a world reduced to raw material—atoms and molecules, flat, without depth or resonance—also calls it into question. In this kind of world, imaginative richness easily becomes garish and sensational, just as a caress easily becomes a blow.

Although the kingdom of the dull isn't the only alternative to such richness, it is certainly one of them; in the 1930's, '40's, and '50's, it seemed to conquer American poetry, with the notable exceptions of Wallace Stevens, William Carlos Williams, and Theodore Roethke. Except for a few experimental poets of the twenties, and Kenneth Fearing, who wrote and published into the fifties, the Rimbaud tradition died with Gertrude Stein. As Kenneth Koch points out,

most poets in America were writing lines like "This Connecticut
landscape would have pleased Vermeer." Then, in the middle of the
"tranquilized fifties," in Robert Lowell's phrase, it was born again
with the Beat poets. Gregory Corso could have been Rimbaud's
double, and may even have thought of himself as such. Suppose,
in 1956, you are Gregory Corso and, say, Allen Ginsberg, hitchhiking across America; you are surrounded by raw material, but
you feel high, and the language feels good to you, and you remember that it was liberated three-quarters of a century ago from that
raw material anyway:

> Of course I tried to tell him
> but he cranked his head
>   without an excuse.
> I told him the sky chases
>   the sun
> And he smiled and said:
>   "What's the use."
> I was feeling like a demon
>   again
> So I said: "But the ocean chases
>   the fish."
> This time he laughed
>   and said: "Suppose the
>   strawberry were
>   pushed into a mountain."
> After that I knew the
>   war was on—
> So we fought:
> He said: "The apple-cart like a
>   broomstick-angel
>   snaps & splinters
>   old dutch shoes."
> I said: "Lightning will strike the old oak
>   and free the fumes!"
> He said: "Mad street with no name."
> I said: "Bald killer! Bald killer! Bald killer!"
> He said, getting real mad,
>   "Firestoves! Gas! Couch!"
> I said, only smiling,
>   "I know God would turn back his head

> if I sat quietly and thought."
> We ended by melting away,
> hating the air![3]

This wasn't humorous in the ways we expected poetry to be humorous. We had forgotten Rimbaud and never really knew surrealism, but we did know T. S. Eliot's *Old Possum's Book of Practical Cats;* now *that* was funny. This wasn't even poetry. Which was of course the point. It was anti-poetry, and that's why it was humorous. The emphasis upon balance, moderation, form, and wit had come to such a point by this time that the only alternative was a resurrection of insanity and a reaffirmed rejection of the lyric tradition.

Or suppose you are Kenneth Koch in 1955, thumbing through an issue of the *Hudson Review* at the New York Public Library, and you find yourself practically gagging for the lack of fresh air. The metaphor is so obvious and simple and true as to be, well, fresh —and funny as well:

> Blue air, fresh air, come in, I welcome you, you are an art
>   student,
> Take off your cap and gown and sit down on the chair.
> Together we shall paint the poets—but no, air! perhaps you
>   should go to them, quickly,
> Give them a little inspiration, they need it, perhaps they are out
>   of breath,
> Give them a little inhuman company before they freeze the
>   English language to death!
> (And rust their typewriters a little, be sea air! be noxious! kill
>   them, if you must, but stop their poetry!
> I remember I saw you dancing on the surf on the Côte d'Azur
> And I stopped, taking my hat off, but you did not remember me,
> Then afterwards, you came to my room bearing a handful of
>   orange flowers
> And we were together all through the summer night!)[4]

This poem, "Fresh Air," is still one of Koch's best and most lasting. The almost helpless and naively angry voice with its nervous, sudden outbursts, crazy rhapsodic asides, and, above all, its willingness to be silly—something Koch, I think, gradually lost as

---

[3]Gregory Corso, "Poets Hitchhiking on the Highway," *The Happy Birthday of Death* (New York, 1960), p. 28, © 1960 by New Directions Publishing Corp. Reprinted by permission of New Directions Publishing Corp.

[4]Kenneth Koch, "Fresh Air," *Thank You and Other Poems* (New York, 1962), pp. 54–60, © 1962 by Kenneth Koch. Reprinted by permission of Grove Press, Inc.

his humor became more confident, and his reputation more established—this voice was something American poetry had been without since Kenneth Fearing. The opening section of the poem, in fact, is a kind of homage to Fearing's "End of the Seer's Convention." Here is part of Fearing's poem:

> "I foresee a day," said the Idaho astrologer, "when human beings will live on top of flag-poles,
> And dance, at some profit, for weeks and months without any rest,
> And some will die very happily of eating watermelons, and nails, and cherry pies."
> "Why," said a bored numerologist, reaching for his hat, "can't these star-gazers keep their feet on the ground?"
> "Even if it's true," said a Bombay illusionist, "it is not, like the rope-trick, altogether practical."
> "And furthermore and finally," shouted the astrologer, with comets and halfmoons dropping from his pockets, and his agitated sleeves . . .[5]

And here is part of the opening section of "Fresh Air":

> At the Poem Society, a black-haired man stands up to say,
> "You make me sick with all your talk about restraint and mature talent!
> Haven't you ever looked out the window at a painting by Matisse,
> Or did you always stay in hotels where there were too many spiders crawling on your visages?
> Did you ever glance inside a bottle of sparkling pop,
> Or see a citizen split in two by lightning?
> I am afraid you have never smiled at the hibernation
> Of bear cubs except that you saw in it some deep relation
> To human suffering and wishes, oh what a bunch of crackpots!"
> The black-haired man sits down, and the others shoot arrows at him.
>
> . . . .
>
> The chairman stood up on the platform, oh he was physically ugly!
> He was small-limbed and -boned and thought he was quite seductive,
> But he was bald with certain hideous black hairs,

[5]Kenneth Fearing, "End of the Seer's Convention," *Afternoon of a Pawnbroker and Other Poems* (New York, 1943), pp. 35–37, © 1943 by Kenneth Fearing, © 1971 by Bruce Fearing.

> And his voice had the sound of water leaving a vaseline bathtub,
> And he said, "The subject for this evening's discussion is poetry
> On the subject of love between swans." And everyone threw
>   candy hearts
> At the disgusting man, and they stuck to his bib and tucker . . .

Not only is this funny; it is also, of course, the very fresh air Koch
was calling for. Whatever we think of poets like Corso and Koch
today, we have to admit that American poetry hasn't been the same
since. They—and others, like Ginsberg, Ferlinghetti, O'Hara,
Olsen, Duncan, Spicer, and Creeley—introduced a new freedom
into the very language of poetry, into the substance of that language.
Poets like Lowell, Berryman, Plath, Merwin, Bly, and many others
not associated with the Beats all underwent radical transformations
in their styles in the fifties and sixties, not necessarily in imitation of
the Beats, but simply because the atmosphere around them was so
electrically charged with change.

Koch's later work has moved more toward a kind of playful, pure
surrealism, prosaic like "Fresh Air," but usually eschewing both the
direct statement and the wonderful silliness of that poem. Like most
poets of the New York school, he often spices his poems with
references to pop culture, deliberate clichés, archaisms, or both
academic and romantic phrases and words, all for their campy,
ironic effect. These devices were first used by Frank O'Hara—to
whom Koch and Ashbery owe so much—and by now, ten years
after his death, have become somewhat stale through overuse. The
resulting campy surrealism sounds the same no matter who is
writing it. Here is a section from Koch's poem, "The Interpretation of Dreams":

> That autumn afternoon, when every affection came unsought
> As from an unstoppered lute and a glass of campari
> Was downed from a shimmering glass and quickly as if nothing
> Could harm the eternal beaver any more. But a policeman of
>   high reflection
> Suddenly stood up for the traffic crossings' protection
> And were we sad, lost in thought at our newfound abortionless-
>   ness
> In stages, because of a green kerchief stuck in your pocket
> As one asks What's the difference between that and a hand-
>   kerchief? and

Between each stop and its parenthesis? Let's assume we have
   too much
And pound on the marble table top. It has always gone best that
   way . . .[6]

The most curious and interesting aspect of this kind of poetry is that
the humor derives from attacking or undermining most of our fundamental notions about poetry and poetic language. If poetic language is concentrated, heightened, symbolic, and musical, then
poetry becomes humorous by being flat, prosaic, and deliberately
clumsy, the latter device learned from, of all people, Ogden Nash.
In fact, Koch's rhythms—especially the deliberate effect of having
too many words on a line—are strongly related to Nash's.

   In all of the poets of the first group, there is a fear of or distaste for
high language and poetic "effects," an aversion to language that is
in any way fashioned, carved, or charged with either meaning or
song. What's left is simply prose. We live in a culture in which one
of the chief ways poetry becomes funny is through the accident of
prose. This is ultimately a negative and cornered attitude if held
exclusively. Its most beneficial effect has been to expand the range
of possibilities available in the language for all poets. American
poetic language, in its freedom, covers more of a spectrum today
than it ever did before, from the extremely artificial and musical to
the extremely prosaic and conversational. I don't mean to imply by
this that our poetry is better than ever. The freedom often results,
paradoxically, in a great deal of conformity among poets. The
feeling that you can say anything in any way is actually quite
frightening, and usually drives poets to search for models out of
conscious or unconscious resentment. Still, the strong sense of
possibility is there in the language, particularly in the poets whom
I've labeled as belonging to the second group.

   It's difficult to trace a tradition for this second group. The poets
in it are not, in the first place, primarily humorists, and they don't
eschew the traditional devices of poetic language. So they are
perhaps more in the mainstream of modern poetry, but a mainstream
which has certainly undergone its own transformations precisely

---

[6]Kenneth Koch, "The Interpretation of Dreams," *The Pleasures of Peace and Other Poems* (New York, 1969), pp. 77–84, © 1969 by Kenneth Koch. Reprinted by permission of Grove Press, Inc.

because of the presence of the first group and the kind of anti-
tradition that they represent. John Berryman, for example, began as
a formalist, and moved gradually in the fifties and sixties to the
fractured, twisted, self-mocking free verse of the *Dream Songs*.
A. R. Ammons has moved more and more toward the rhythms of
prose in his work, particularly in his long poems. Rather than rejecting the lyric tradition, they have each tried to renew it, partly
by stretching the lyric impulse into an epic one, and partly by
opening up their language with devices and tonal modes not always associated with lyric poetry, humor being a chief one.

The humor in Berryman's *Dream Songs* is usually closely related
to the humor in minstrel shows: apologetic, foot-shuffling, self-
deprecating, self-conscious. The end men in minstrel shows are
strangely liberated by being treated as slaves; they have a space, and
the "massah" has a space, which they continually violate behind his
back. All their actions are self-consciously humorous because they
are human beings cut off from the possibility of response from other
human beings, confined in their space, observed, overheard,
overseen. Their humor oscillates between arrogance on the one hand
and false compliance and humility on the other, itself a kind of arrogance. Mr. Bones in the *Dream Songs* is of course such a figure
—but Berryman's very language, even when Mr. Bones isn't present, is a kind of end man, too. The language is unnaturally confined (by Berryman's arbitrary form: three stanzas of six lines),
syntactically turned in on itself, and cut off from reciprocity; it is
a kind of inner conversation we overhear, and often makes itself
most strongly felt (as end men do) by sudden interruptions, or at
least sudden shifts of pace and tone. In the act of creating a self—
for that is the chief job the language in the *Dream Songs* is given:
not to report on or confess a self, but to create one, out of the fragments of a broken life— in this act, the language is a kind of cripple
with rubbery limbs whose only self is bound to be cursed by both
alienation and self-consciousness. Humor is a natural by-product
of this self, inseparable from its pain and its sense of being im-
prisoned or confined, but probably at the same time the only thing
that keeps it alive. Here is "Dream Song # 5":

> Henry sats in de bar & was odd,
> off in the glass from the glass,
> at odds wif de world & its god,

> his wife is a complete nothing,
> St Stephen
> getting even.
>
> Henry sats in de plane & was gay.
> Careful Henry nothing said aloud
> but where a Virgin out of cloud
> to her Mountain dropt in light,
> his thought made pockets & the plane buckt.
> 'Parm me, lady,' 'Orright.'
>
> Henry lay in de netting, wild,
> while the brainfever bird did scales;
> Mr Heartbreak, the New Man,
> come to farm a crazy land;
> an image of the dead on the fingernail
> of a newborn child.[7]

This humor is often cruel, which is part of its pain. Almost always, it is a function of a self shattered into pieces, most likely by booze; thus, there are many shifts from humor to despair, as if they were only a thin line away from each other. This is in fact the classic emotional shift of the alcoholic, accompanied often by a transition of self-pity.[8] There is no one funnier and sadder than a drunk, and he won't let you forget it. The pain a reader feels in going through the *Dream Songs* is, in part, a function of this humor that always seems to be secretly asking for sympathy. This occurs in the very language itself, in the deliberate grammatical mistakes, the pronoun shifts, the reversals of word order, all usually funny, and all also a cry for help, because they are an extension of a self which is disintegrating as quickly as it is being created. "The poor man," as he says in "Dream Song 140," "is coming to pieces joint by joint."

Still, in the *Dream Songs* there is a sense of the language engaged in a struggle, continually pulling against the current, and of the language as an agent of change and creation, not just a transparent window through which we view things. This is another way of saying that, unlike the poets of the first group, Berryman uses a

[7]John Berryman, "Dream Song #5," *77 Dream Songs* (New York, 1964), p. 7, © 1959, 1962, 1963, 1964 by John Berryman. Reprinted with the permission of Farrar, Straus & Giroux, Inc.

[8]The best piece I have seen about Berryman traces some of the connections between alcoholism and the *Dream Songs,* particularly in terms of the alcoholic's self-pity: Lewis Hyde, "Alcohol and Poetry: John Berryman and the Booze Talking," *American Poetry Review,* 4 (January, 1975), pp. 7–12.

language which participates in the world, which is continually opening furrows in the world. His language *enacts* the terrible pain of
disintegration and the self-conscious humor that temporarily relieves
that pain. It also occasionally withdraws from the world, or gets
tangled in its own complexities and stumbles, like someone tangled
in his shoestrings. But it isn't a language which simply plays around
for its own sake, like someone making faces in front of a mirror.

Similarly, in A. R. Ammons, although there is a great deal of
playfulness, the play is inseparable from the natural wandering
movement of the mind engaging the world of things. Ammons's
main point—or one of them—seems to be that the mind and the
world, or language and the world, are finally inseparable. The world
is full of "syntax in thickets meshing" and "tangles of hypothesis
weaving / semantic currents." "Oh," he says in "The Marriage,"
"this caught thing! / It can't get loose from / meanings and the mind /
can't pull free of it." What's interesting, however, is that this isn't so
much a principle in Ammons's poems as it is an unavoidable inevita-
bility. He loves to play, speculate, wander, joke around, as much as
any surrealist, but words in his world always eventually drag things
along with them, so that the play usually opens up in discovery and
surprise. Stevens called surrealism invention without discovery.
Ammons has all the inventiveness of a surrealist, particularly when
he gives himself maximum room, in the longer poems, but that
inventiveness never finally exists only for its own sake, no matter
how self-delighting it is.

Both *Tape for the Turn of the Year* and *Sphere* are long strings of
language which move into and out of focus, suddenly shift direction,
widen or narrow or briefly flare up like patterns of light in a stream.
They contain much information and material, some of it undigested,
on various topics ranging from biology and zoology to comments on
the weather and lessons in government and society, all interspersed
with beautifully exact description of things, speculations of the mind
and imagination, dreams, and journal-like passages recording
everyday events, the food eaten at dinner, jokes told, and so forth.
Ammons loves weaving in and out of this heterogeneous material,
and he does it as easily and playfully as a fish in water. There is a
sense of mutual emergence in these poems: the world emerges from
and sheds its language, and language emerges from and sheds the
world. Their most essential medium is movement; the poems are

continually off balance, stumbling forward, falling behind, catching up, but always moving. Sometimes speculation or description carries the poems forward, and sometimes, when these peter out, there is a sudden bout of playful improvisation, often very funny, and always, like everything else, both a link to what comes after it and a chunk of language trying to find its own secure foothold, its own center of gravity. It's very difficult to quote from these poems, not because they are tightly woven (the opposite is true), but because their looseness is inseparable from the strange and beautiful movement of the whole, a movement which is both a kind of unravelling and a kind of accumulation. Even though the humorous passages are often interludes, their playfulness is usually inseparable from the continuous ongoing movement of the thought. Keep in mind that Ammons can only be quoted at length, if some flavor of the whole is to be preserved. Here are the opening sections of *Sphere*:

1

The sexual basis of all things rare is really apparent
and fools crop up where angels are mere disguises:
a penetrating eye (insight), a penetrating tongue (ah),

a penetrating penis and withal a penetrating mind,
integration's consummation: a com- or intermingling of parts,
heterocosm joyous, opposite motions away and toward

along a common line, the in-depth knowledge (a dilly),
the concentration and projection (firmly energized) and
the ecstasy, the pay off, the play out, the expended

nexus nodding, the flurry, cell spray, finish, the
haploid hungering after the diploid condition: the reconciler
of opposites, commencement, proliferation, ontogeny:

2

often those who are not good for much else turn to thought
and it's just great, part of the grand possibility, that
thought is there to turn to: camouflagy thought flushed

out of the bush, seen vaguely as potential form, and
pursued, pursued and perceived, declared: the savored
form, the known possession, knowledge carnal knowledge:

the seizure, the satiation: the heavy jaguar takes the
burro down for a foreleg or so: then, the lighter,
though still heavy, vultures pull and gulp: then, the
tight-bodied black crows peck and scratch: then ants

come out and run around the structure, picking bits:
finally, least bacteria boil the last grease mild:

3

so the lessening transformers arrive at the subtle condition
fine, the spiritual burro braying free, overwhelming
the hairy, and so must we all approach the fine, our

skinny house perpetual, where in total diminishment we will
last, elemental and irreducible, the matter of the universe:
slosh, slosh: vulnerability is merely intermediate: beyond

the autopsy and the worm, the blood cell, protein, amino acid,
the nervous atom spins and shines unsmirched: the total,
necessary arrival, the final victory, utterly the total loss:

we're haplessly one way the wrong way on the runway:
conglomerates, tongues or eyes or heel strings that
keep us, won't keep: we want to change without changing

4

out of change: actually, the imagination works pretty
diagrammatically into paradigm so one can ''see things'':
and then talk fairly tirelessly without going astray or

asunder: for me, for example, the one-many problem figures
out as an isoceles triangle (base: diversity and peak: unity)
or, even, equilateral, some rigor of rising: and this is

not to be distinguished from the center-periphery thing, in
that if you cut out a piece of pie from the center-periphery
circle, you have a triangle, a little rocky, but if you

cut off the arc, it sits up good, as (peak: center: unity)
and (base: periphery: diversity): actually, one could go even
so far so (peak: center: symbol: abstraction), etc., and the other:

5

this works in the bedrock, too, or undifferentiated gas:
one feels up the two legs of the possibility and, ever
tightening and steered, rises to the crux, to find

there the whole mystery, the lush squeeze, the centering
and prolongation: so much so that the final stone
never locks the peak but inlet:outlet opens unfolding

into nothingness's complete possibility, the strangling
through into the darkness of futurity: it is hard at this
point to avoid some feeling, however abstract the circumstance:

if one can get far enough this way where imagination

and flesh strive together in shocking splendors, one can
forget that sensibility is something dissociated and come:[9]

And so forth; it's practically impossible to interrupt this brilliant
and delightful poem. The humor is a kind of oil which keeps the
line moving and turning; it's also a prod, a sudden lurch off balance,
that forces the poem ahead. Just as walking is a process of losing and
regaining balance, so the poem moves forward, "balancing
imbalances," as Ammons says in section 90, playing off bawdy
humor against abstractions, the terror of death against the minute
details of the physical world, and playful improvisation against exact
description. No matter how abstract the poem becomes, materiality
clings to it, partly because of the humor which always is a carnal
thing even when it isn't bawdy, and partly because of the language
which always *enacts* as well as describes the twisting, meshing,
coalescing, separating, ensnaring activities of the world around it. In
fact, the humor is carnal for the same reason that the language enacts
the world: because both exist at that intersection of mind and body
where meaning disappears into activity and the joke becomes a smile
or the word a sound.

Ammons is a poet who has successfully *integrated* humor into his
poetry. Humor isn't the main business of his poems, but without it
they wouldn't be the same. I suspect this is a defining characteristic
of poets of the second group, and one of the things that makes
contemporary poetry refreshing even when it's very serious. I see it
in many younger poets. Russell Edson, for example, writes prose
poems which combine some of the theatrical silliness of Koch with a
world of things and people reminiscent of both Kafka and Grimm's
fairy tales. The result is a world in which cups refuse to hold coffee,
old men give themselves flowers, a jelly sandwich occupies the
center of the universe, and a woman plays the violin for mice. Here is
one of his poems, titled "When the Ceiling Cries":

> A mother tosses her infant so that it hits the ceiling.
> Father says, why are you doing that to the ceiling?
> Do you want my baby to fly away to heaven? the ceiling is
> there so the baby will come back to me, says mother.
> Father says, you are hurting the ceiling, can't you hear it
> crying?

[9]A. R. Ammons, *Sphere* (New York, 1974), pp. 11–13, © 1974 by A. R. Ammons.
Reprinted with the permission of W. W. Norton & Co., Inc.

So mother and father climb a ladder and kiss the ceiling.[10]

In Edson's world, the emotional responses of people are never appropriate to their objects, and screams occur as easily as sighs. His poems are humorous because they give us back our own world in reverse and slightly distorted, like curved mirrors do; so domestic objects are animate and people often passive and inanimate. But the poems are equally disturbing, not simply because we recognize our everyday world in them, but in fact because we recognize the distortions of our everyday world.

Similarly, many other contemporary poets include humor as one edge of their voice, usually where it spills over into the actual world of things. The humor in the poets of the first group is often an index of the split between language and the world. In the poets of the second group, it is often the chief means by which language and the world are re-connected. In Ammons, humor tugs against the tendency toward abstraction; in Edson, and in some of David Ignatow's poems, humor is an integral part of the allegory which reveals our own lives to us.

Of course, humor needn't always be this responsible; it doesn't always have to fit a scheme. Perhaps one of the reasons why it occurs more in contemporary poetry than in the past is precisely because it provides a vacation from responsibility. After an era in which the New Critics told us that every word in a poem had to be justified, and none wasted, humor often enters poetry today as that kind of relaxed playfulness by which in fact words *are* wasted, or call attention to themselves and fail to contribute to the whole. This vacation from responsibility can result in many boring, wordy, repetitious poems, but it can also result in a kind of supple, open, adaptable language, quick to respond to the unexpected because its range and its interests have been widened. This widening is in part a matter of form; poetic form has moved closer to that of prose. But it's also a matter of attitude; contemporary poets are willing to be funny because they are willing to allow the world to occur to them in a variety of shapes. This variety, in turn, results in an eclectic variety of styles, eclectic enough that my division of contemporary poets into two groups is a bit too simple. Still, I'll stay with it, keeping in mind that the best

[10]Russell Edson, "When the Ceiling Cries," *The Very Thing That Happens* (New York, 1964), p. 2, © 1964 by Russell Edson. Reprinted with the permission of New Directions Publishing Corp.

poets in each group often slip over the line between the two, as if the act of poetry today has become a kind of scanning back and forth, and language a radar to catch the world by surprise.

Contemporary
American Humor:
A Selected Checklist
of Criticism

Adams, Percy G. "Humor as Structure and Theme in Faulkner's Trilogy." *Wisconsin Studies in Contemporary Literature*, 5 (Autumn, 1964), 205–212.

Adler, Bill, and Jeffrey Feinman. *Woody Allen: Clown Prince of American Humor*. New York: Pinnacle Books, 1975.

Allsop, Kenneth. "Those American Sickniks." *The Twentieth Century*, 170 (July, 1961), 97–106.

Alter, Robert. "Jewish Humor and the Domestication of Myth." In *Veins of Humor*. Ed. Harry Levin. Cambridge: Harvard University Press, 1972. Pp. 255–268.

Altman, Sig. *The Comic Image of the Jew: Explorations of a Pop Culture Phenomenon*. Rutherford, N.J.: Fairleigh Dickinson University Press, 1971.

"American Humor: Hardly a Laughing Matter." *Time*, 87 (March 4, 1966), 46–47.

Anderson, Donald. "Comic Modes in Modern American Fiction." *Southern Review: An Australian Journal of Literary Studies* (University of Adelaide), 8 (1975), 549–560.

Appel, Alfred, Jr. "Lolita: The Springboard of Parody." *Wisconsin Studies in Contemporary Literature*, 8 (Spring, 1967), 204–241.

Arnez, Nancy Levi, and Clara B. Anthony. "Contemporary Negro Humor as Social Satire." *Phylon*, 29 (Winter, 1968), 33–46.

Barksdale, Richard K. "Black America and the Mask of Comedy." In *The Comic Imagination in American Literature*. Ed. Louis D. Rubin, Jr. New Brunswick, N.J.: Rutgers University Press, 1973. Pp. 349–360.

Bean, J. C. "John Barth and Festive Comedy: A Failure of Imagination in *The Sot-Weed Factor.*" *Xavier University Studies*, 10 (Spring, 1971), 3–15.

Beatts, Anne. "Can a Woman Get a Laugh and a Man Too?" *Mademoiselle*, 81 (November, 1975), 140, 182–186.

Beaver, Harold. "A Figure in the Carpet: Irony and the American Novel." *Essays and Studies*, 15 (1962), 101–114.

Bentley, Eric. "Comedy and the Comic Spirit in America." In *The American Theater Today.* Ed. Alan S. Downer. New York: Basic Books, 1967. Pp. 50–59.

Berger, Arthur Asa. *The Comic-Stripped American.* Baltimore: Penguin Books, 1973.

Bier, Jesse. *The Rise and Fall of American Humor.* New York: Holt, Rinehart, and Winston, 1968.

Bigsby, C. W. E. "The Impact of the 'Absurd' on American Literature." *Midcontinent American Studies Journal*, 8 (Fall, 1967), 72–79.

Blackwell, Louise. "Humor and Irony in the Works of Flannery O'Connor." *Reserches Anglaises et Americaines*, 4 (1971), 61–68.

Blair, Walter. "Aftermath: Twentieth Century Humorists." In *Native American Humor.* San Francisco: Chandler, 1960. Pp. 162–180.

———. "Laughter in Wartime America." *College English,* 6 (April, 1945), 361–367.

———. " 'A Man's Voice, Speaking': A Continuum in American Humor." In *Veins of Humor.* Ed. Harry Levin. Cambridge: Harvard University Press, 1972. Pp. 185–204.

———. "Some Values of American Humor." *American Humor,* 1, no. 2 (1974), 1–8.

———. "Urbanization of Humor." In *Thurber: A Collection of Critical Essays.* Ed. Charles Holmes. Englewood Cliffs, N.J.: Spectrum Books, 1975. Pp. 19–27.

Borgman, Paul. "Three Wise Men: The Comedy of O'Connor's *Wise Blood.*" *Christianity and Literature,* 24, no. 3 (1975), 36–48.

Boutrous, Laurence K. "Parody in Hawkes' *The Lime Twig.*" *Critique,* 15, no. 2 (1973), 49–56.

Bracher, Frederick. "John Cheever and Comedy." *Critique,* 6 (Spring, 1963), 66–77.

Brack, O. M., ed. *American Humor: Essays Presented to John C. Gerber.* Scottsdale, Ariz.: Arete Publications, 1977.

Brake, Robert. "The Lion Act Is Over: Passive/Aggressive Patterns of Communication in American Negro Humor." *Journal of Popular Culture,* 9 (1975), 549–560.

Brooks, A. Russell. "The Comic Spirit and the Negro's New Look." *CLA Journal,* 6 (September, 1962), 35–43.

Browning, Preston M., Jr. "Flannery O'Connor and the Grotesque of the Holy." In *Adversity and Grace*. Ed. Nathan A. Scott, Jr. Chicago: University of Chicago Press, 1968. Pp. 133–162.

Brustein, Robert. "The Healthiness of Sick Comedy." *New Republic,* December 15, 1962, pp. 28–30.

Buck, Lynn. "Vonnegut's World of Comic Futility." *Studies in American Fiction,* 3 (Autumn, 1975), 181–198.

Burke, Kenneth. "Caldwell: Maker of Grotesques." In *Psychoanalysis and American Fiction*. Ed. Irving Malin. New York: E. P. Dutton, 1965. Pp. 245–254.

Byrd, Scott. "A Separate War: Camp and Black Humor in Recent American Fiction." *Language Quarterly,* 7 (Fall-Winter, 1968), 7–10.

Cargas, H. J. "Are There Things a Novelist Shouldn't Joke About?" (Interview with Kurt Vonnegut, Jr.) *Christian Century,* 93 (November 24, 1976), 1048–50.

Cheney, Brainard. "Miss O'Connor Creates Unusual Humor out of Ordinary Sin." *Sewanee Review,* 71 (Autumn, 1963), 644–652.

Clark, Charlene Kerne. "Pathos with a Chuckle: The Tragi-comic Vision in the Novels of Carson McCullers." *Studies in American Humor,* 1 (January, 1975), 161–166.

Cohen, Sarah Blacher. *Saul Bellow's Enigmatic Laughter*. Urbana: University of Illinois Press, 1974.

––––––. "Sex: Saul Bellow's Hedonistic Joke." *Studies in American Fiction,* 2 (Autumn, 1974), 223–229.

Cox, J. M. "Toward Vernacular Humor." *Virginia Quarterly,* 46 (Spring, 1970), 311–330.

Cross, Richard K. "The Humor of *The Hamlet*." *Twentieth Century Literature,* 12 (January, 1967), 203–215.

Dance, Daryl C. "Contemporary Militant Black Humor." *Negro American Literature Forum,* 8 (1974), 217–222.

Davis, Douglas M., ed. *The World of Black Humor*. New York: E. P. Dutton, 1967.

DeMott, Benjamin. "The New Irony: Sickniks and Others." *The American Scholar,* 31 (Winter, 1961–62), 108–119.

DeVries, Peter. "Thurber: The Comic Prufrock." In *Thurber: A Collection of Critical Essays*. Ed. Charles Holmes. Englewood Cliffs, N.J.: Spectrum Books, 1975. Pp. 37–43.

Dickstein, Morris. "Black Humor and History: Fiction in the Sixties." *Partisan Review,* 43, no. 2 (1976), 185–211.

Edelstein, Mark G. "Flannery O'Connor and the Problem of Modern Satire." *Studies in Short Fiction,* 12 (1975), 139–144.

Falk, Robert P. *The Antic Muse*. New York: Grove Press, 1955.

Farwell, Harold. "John Barth's Tenuous Affirmation: The Absurd Unending Possibility of Love." *Georgia Review,* 28 (Summer, 1974), 290–306.

Foster, Frances S. "Charles Wright: Black Black Humorist." *CLA Journal,* 15 (September, 1971), 44–53.

Friedman, Bruce Jay, ed. *Black Humor.* New York: Bantam, 1965.

Frohock, W. M. "The Edge of Laughter: Some Modern Fiction and the Grotesque." In *Veins of Humor.* Ed. Harry Levin. Cambridge: Harvard University Press, 1972. Pp. 243–254.

Fuchs, Daniel. *The Comic Spirit of Wallace Stevens.* Durham, N.C.: Duke University Press, 1963.

Gallivan, Patricia. " 'The Comic Spirit' and *The Waste Land.* " *University of Toronto Quarterly,* 45 (Fall, 1975), 35–49.

Galloway, David D. "A Picaresque Apprenticeship: Nathanael West's *The Dream Life of Balso Snell* and *A Cool Million.*" *Wisconsin Studies in Contemporary Literature,* 5 (Summer, 1964), 110–126.

————. *The Absurd Hero in American Fiction: Updike, Styron, Bellow, Salinger.* Revised ed. Austin: University of Texas Press, 1970.

Gessel, Michael. "Katherine Anne Porter: The Low Comedy of Sex." In *American Humor: Essays Presented to John C. Gerber.* Ed. O. M. Brack. Scottsdale, Ariz.: Arete Publications, 1977. Pp. 139–152.

Gilliatt, Penelope. "Woody Allen." In *Unholy Fools, Wits, Comics, Disturbers of the Peace.* New York: Viking Press, 1973. Pp. 35–44.

Godshalk, W. W. "Cabell and Barth: Our Comic Athletes." In *The Comic Imagination in American Literature.* Ed. Louis D. Rubin, Jr. New Brunswick, N.J.: Rutgers University Press, 1973. Pp. 285–294.

Gold, Herbert. "Funny Is Money." *New York Times Magazine,* March 30, 1975, pp. 16–31.

Goldman, Albert. "Boy-man, *Schlemiel:* The Jewish Element in American Humour." In *Explorations.* Ed. Murray Mindlin and Chaim Bermant. London: Barrie and Rockliff, 1967. Pp. 3–17.

————. "The Comedy of Lenny Bruce." *Commentary,* 36 (October, 1963), 312–317.

————. "The Comic Prison." *Nation,* 200 (February 8, 1965), 142–144.

Goldman, Mark. "Bernard Malamud's Comic Vision and the Theme of Identity." *Critique,* 7 (Winter, 1964–65), 92–109.

Gossett, Louise Y. "Eudora Welty's New Novel: The Comedy of Loss." *Southern Literary Journal,* 3 (Fall, 1970), 122–137.

Gray, R. J. "Southwestern Humor, Erskine Caldwell, and the Comedy of Frustration." *Southern Literary Journal,* 8 (Fall, 1975), 3–26.

Greiner, Donald J. *Comic Terror: The Novels of John Hawkes.* Memphis: Memphis State University Press, 1974.

————. "Djuna Barnes' *Nightwood* and the American Origins of Black Humor." *Critique,* 17, no. 1 (1975), 41–54.

————. "Strange Laughter: The Comedy of John Hawkes." *Southwest Review,* 56 (Autumn, 1971), 318–328.

Gresham, James T. *"Giles Goat-Boy:* Satyr, Satire, and Tragedy Twined." *Genre,* 7 (June, 1974), 148–163.

Gross, Seymour L. "Eudora Welty's Comic Imagination." In *The Comic Imagination in American Literature.* Ed. Louis D. Rubin, Jr. New Brunswick, N.J.: Rutgers University Press, 1973. Pp. 319–328.

Guttmann, Allen. "The Black Humorists." In *The Jewish Writer in America.* New York: Oxford University Press, 1971. Pp. 76–84.

————. "Jewish Humor." In *The Comic Imagination in American Literature.* Ed. Louis D. Rubin, Jr. New Brunswick, N.J.: Rutgers University Press, 1973. Pp. 329–338.

Hall, James. "Play, the Fractured Self, and American Angry Comedy: From Faulkner to Salinger." In *The Lunatic Giant in the Drawing Room.* Bloomington: Indiana University Press, 1968. Pp. 56–80.

————. *The Tragic Comedians.* Bloomington: Indiana University Press, 1963. Pp. 151–163.

Hansen, A. J. "Entropy and Transformation: Two Types of American Humor." *American Scholar,* 43 (Summer, 1974), 405–421.

Harmon, William. " 'Anti-Fiction' in American Literature." In *The Comic Imagination in American Literature.* Ed. Louis D. Rubin, Jr. New Brunswick, N.J.: Rutgers University Press, 1973. Pp. 373–384.

Harris, Charles B. *Contemporary American Novelists of the Absurd.* New Haven: College and University Press, 1971.

Hasley, Louis. "Black Humor in Recent American Literature." In *Americana-Austriaca: Beitrage zur Amerikakunde.* Band 3. Wien: Braumuller, 1974. Pp. 33–42.

————. "James Thurber: Artist in Humor." *South Atlantic Quarterly,* 73 (Autumn, 1974), 504–515.

Hassan, Ihab. "Laughter in the Dark: The New Voice in American Fiction." *American Scholar,* 33 (Autumn, 1964), 636–640.

Hauck, Richard B. *A Cheerful Nihilism: Confidence and "The Absurd" in American Humorous Fiction.* Bloomington: Indiana University Press, 1971.

Haule, James M. *"Terra Cognita:* The Humor of Vladimir Nabokov." *Studies in American Humor,* 2 (October, 1975), 78–87.

Hausdorff, Don. "Thomas Pynchon's Multiple Absurdities." *Wisconsin Studies in Contemporary Literature,* 7 (Autumn, 1966), 258–269.

Hill, Hamlin. "Black Humor and the Mass Audience." In *American*

Humor: Essays Presented to John C. Gerber. Ed. O. M. Brack. Scottsdale, Ariz.: Arete Publications, 1977. Pp. 1–11.

———. "Black Humor: Its Cause and Cure." *Colorado Quarterly,* 17 (Summer, 1968), 57–64.

———. "Modern American Humor: The Janus Laugh." *College English,* 25 (December, 1963), 170–176.

Hoffman, Frederick J. "The Fool of Experience: Saul Bellow's Fiction." In *Contemporary American Novelists.* Ed. Harry T. Moore. Carbondale: Southern Illinois University Press, 1964. Pp. 80–94.

———. "The Questing Comedian: Thomas Pynchon's *V.* . . . ." *Critique,* 6 (Winter, 1963–64), 174–177.

Howell, Elmo. "Eudora Welty's Comedy of Manners." *South Atlantic Quarterly,* 69 (Autumn, 1970), 469–479.

Hunt, John W. "Comic Escape and Anti-Vision: The Novels of Joseph Heller and Thomas Pynchon." In *Adversity and Grace.* Ed. Nathan A. Scott, Jr. Chicago: University of Chicago Press, 1968. Pp. 87–112.

Hurley, Paul J. "France and America: Versions of the Absurd." *College English,* 26 (May, 1965), 634–640.

Irwin, W. R. "Robert Frost and the Comic Spirit." *American Literature,* 35 (November, 1963), 299–310.

Jacobs, Robert D. "Faulkner's Humor." In *The Comic Imagination in American Literature.* Ed. Louis D. Rubin, Jr. New Brunswick, N.J.: Rutgers University Press, 1973. Pp. 305–318.

———. "The Humor of *Tobacco Road.*" In *The Comic Imagination in American Literature.* Ed. Louis D. Rubin, Jr. New Brunswick, N.J.: Rutgers University Press, 1973. Pp. 285–294.

Janoff, Bruce. "Black Humor: Beyond Satire." *Ohio Review,* 14, no. 1 (1972), 5–20.

———. "Black Humor, Existentialism, and Absurdity: A Generic Confusion." *Arizona Quarterly,* 30 (1974), 293–304.

Josipovici, Gabriel. "*Lolita:* Parody and the Pursuit of Beauty." In *The World and the Book: A Study of Modern Fiction.* Palo Alto: Stanford University Press, 1971. Pp. 201–220.

Karl, Frederick R. "Joseph Heller's *Catch-22:* Only Fools Walk in Darkness." In *Contemporary American Novelists.* Ed. Harry T. Moore. Carbondale: Southern Illinois University Press, 1964. Pp. 134–142.

Katz, Naomi, and Eli Katz. "Tradition and Adaptation in American Jewish Humor." *Journal of American Folklore,* 84 (April, 1971), 215–220.

Kazin, Alfred. "Absurdity as a Contemporary Style: Ellison to Pynchon." In *Bright Book of Life.* New York: Dell, 1974. Pp. 243–282.

Klinkowitz, Jerome. "A Final Word for Black Humor." *Contemporary Literature,* 15 (Spring, 1974), 271–276.

Knickerbocker, Conrad. "Humor with a Mortal Sting." *New York Times Book Review,* September 27, 1964, pp. 3, 60–61.

Kostelanetz, Richard. "The Point Is That Life Doesn't Have Any Point." *New York Times Book Review,* June 6, 1965, pp. 3, 28–30.

Kristol, Irving. "Is Jewish Humor Dead?" In *Mid-Century.* Ed. Harold U. Ribalow. New York: Beechhurst Press, 1955. Pp. 428–432.

Kronenberger, Louis. "The American Sense of Humor." In *Company Manners.* New York: Bobbs-Merrill, 1954. Pp. 159–171.

Kunzle, David. "Self-Conscious Comics." *The New Republic,* 173 (July 19, 1975), 26–27.

Lahr, John. "Jules Feiffer: Satire as Subversion." In *Up Against the Fourth Wall: Essays on Modern Theater.* New York: Grove Press, 1968. Pp. 78–94.

———. "The Language of Laughter." In *Up Against the Fourth Wall: Essays on Modern Theater.* New York: Grove Press, 1968. Pp. 195–212.

Larner, Jeremy. "The New *Schlemiel.*" *Partisan Review,* 30 (Summer, 1963), 273–276.

LeClair, Thomas. "Death and Black Humor." *Critique,* 17, no. 1 (1975), 5–40.

Leech, Clifford. "When Writing Becomes Absurd." *Colorado Quarterly,* 13 (Summer, 1964), 6–24.

Leverence, W. John. "*Cat's Cradle* and Traditional American Humor." *Journal of Popular Culture,* 5 (Spring, 1972), 955–963.

Levin, Harry, ed. *Veins of Humor.* Cambridge: Harvard University Press, 1972.

Lewis, R. W. B. "Days of Wrath and Laughter." In *Trials of the Word.* New Haven: Yale University Press, 1965. Pp. 184–235.

Light, James F. "Varieties of Satire in the Art of Nathanael West." *Studies in American Humor,* 2 (April, 1975), 46–60.

Little, Matthew, "*As I Lay Dying* and 'Dementia Praecox' Humor." *Studies in American Humor,* 2 (April, 1975), 61–70.

Loukides, Paul. "New Directions in the Novel: Some Notes on the Novel of the Absurd." *CEA Critic,* 30 (January, 1968), 8, 13.

Macaree, D. "Study of Humorous Fiction and *The Education of H*Y*M*A*N K*A*P*L*A*N.*" *English Journal,* 57 (March, 1968), 334–338.

Maclachlan, John M. "Southern Humor as a Vehicle of Social Evaluation." *Mississippi Quarterly,* 13 (Fall, 1960), 157–162.

Martin, Carter. "Comedy and Humor in Flannery O'Connor's Fiction." *Flannery O'Connor Bulletin,* 4 (1975), 1–12.

Martin, Jay. "Nathanael West's Burlesque Comedy." *Studies in American Jewish Literature,* 2 (Spring, 1976), 4–13.

McCaffery, Larry. "Barthelme's *Snow White:* The Aesthetics of Trash." *Critique,* 16, no. 3 (1975), 19–32.

McDonald, Walter P. "Look Back in Horror: The Functional Comedy of *Catch-22." CEA Critic,* 35 (January, 1973), 18–21.

McFadden, George. *"Life Studies—*Robert Lowell's Comic Breakthrough." *PMLA,* 90 (January, 1975), 96–106.

McNamara, Eugene. "The Absurd Style in Contemporary American Literature." *The Humanities Association Bulletin,* 19 (Winter, 1968), 44–49.

Markfield, Wallace. "Yiddishization of American Humor." *Esquire,* 64 (October, 1965), 114, 115, 136.

May, John R. "Loss of World in Barth, Pynchon, and Vonnegut: The Varieties of Humorous Apocalypse." In *Toward a New Earth: Apocalypse in the American Novel.* South Bend: Notre Dame University Press, 1972, Pp. 172–200.

———. "Vonnegut's Humor and the Limits of Hope." *Twentieth Century Literature,* 18 (January, 1972), 25–36.

Meeker, Joseph W. "Comedy of Survival." *North American Review,* 9 (Summer, 1972), 11–17.

Mellard, J. M. "Faulkner's 'Golden Book': *The Reivers* as Romantic Comedy." *Bucknell Review,* 13 (December, 1965), 19–31.

———. "Soldier's Pay and the Growth of Faulkner's Comedy." In *American Humor: Essays Presented to John C. Gerber.* Ed. O. M. Brack. Scottsdale, Ariz.: Arete Publications, 1977, pp. 99–117.

Michaels, I. Lloyd. "A Particular Kind of Joking: Burlesque, Vaudeville, and Nathanael West." *Studies in American Humor,* 1 (January, 1975), 149–160.

Michelson, Peter. "Pop Goes America: Absurdity in Literature." *New Republic,* 157 (September 9, 1967), 23–26, 28.

Miller, Russell H. *"The Sot-Weed Factor:* A Contemporary Mock-Epic." *Critique,* 8, no. 2 (1966), 88–100.

Miller, Jonathan. "A Bit of a Giggle." *The Twentieth Century,* 170 (July, 1961), 39–45.

Miller, Russell H. *"The Sot-Weed Factor:* A Contemporary Mock-Epic." *Critique,* 8, no. 2 (1966), 88–100.

Miller, Vincent M. "The Serious Wit of Pound's *Homage to Sextus Propertius." Contemporary Literature,* 16 (Autumn, 1975), 452–462.

Mills, Nicolaus. "Ken Kesey and the Politics of Laughter." *The Centennial Review,* 16 (Winter, 1972), 82–90.

Morris, Christopher D. "Barth and Lacan: The World of the Moebius Strip." *Critique,* 17, no. 1 (1975), 69–77.

Muehl, Lois. "Faulkner's Humor in Three Novels and One 'Play.' " *Library Chronicle,* 34 (Spring, 1968), 78–93.

Muste, John M. "Better to Die Laughing: The War Novels of Joseph Heller and John Ashmead." *Critique,* 5 (Fall, 1962), 16–27.

Nagel, James. "*Catch-22* and Angry Humor: A Study of the Normative Values of Satire." *Studies in American Humor,* 1 (October, 1974), 99–106.

Noland, Richard W. "John Barth and the Novel of Comic Nihilism." *Wisconsin Studies in Contemporary Literature,* 7 (Autumn, 1966), 239–257.

Numasawa, Koji. "Black Humor: An American Aspect." *Studies in English Literature* (Tokyo Imperial University; English Seminar), 44 (1968), 177–193.

Oates, Joyce Carol. "Updike's American Comedies." *Modern Fiction Studies,* 21 (Autumn, 1975), 459–472.

Oberbeck, S. K. "John Hawkes: The Smile Slashed by a Razor." In *Contemporary American Novelists.* Ed. Harry T. Moore. Carbondale: Southern Illinois University Press, 1964. Pp. 193–204.

Payne, Ladell. "The Trilogy: Faulkner's Comic Epic in Prose." *Studies in the Novel,* 1 (Spring, 1969), 27–37.

Pearson, Carol. "The Cowboy Saint and the Indian Poet: The Comic Hero in Ken Kesey's *One Flew Over the Cuckoo's Nest.*" *Studies in American Humor,* 1 (October, 1974), 91–98.

Pinsker, Sanford. "Bernard Malamud's Ironic Heroes." In *Bernard Malamud: A Collection of Critical Essays.* Ed. Leslie A. Field and Joyce W. Field. Englewood Cliffs, N.J.: Prentice-Hall, 1975. Pp. 45–71.

———. *The Comedy That "Hoits": An Essay on the Fiction of Philip Roth.* Columbia: University of Missouri Press, 1975.

———. "The Greying of Black Humor." *Studies in the Twentieth Century,* 9 (Spring, 1972), 15–33.

———. *The Schlemiel as Metaphor: Studies in the Yiddish and American Jewish Novel.* Carbondale: Southern Illinois University Press, 1971.

Podhoretz, Norman. "Nathanael West: A Particular Kind of Joking." In *Nathanael West: A Collection of Critical Essays.* Ed. Jay Martin. Englewood Cliffs, N.J.: Prentice-Hall, 1971. Pp. 154–160.

Poirier, Richard. "The Politics of Self-Parody." *Partisan Review,* 35 (Summer, 1968), 339–353.

Popkin, Henry. "American Comedy." *Kenyon Review,* 16 (Spring, 1954), 329–334.

Rader, Dotson. "The Jewish Comedian." *Esquire,* 84 (December, 1975), 106–109, 192–199.

Ramsey, Vance. "From Here to Absurdity: Heller's *Catch-22.*" In *Seven Contemporary Authors*. Ed. Thomas Bacon Whitbread. Austin: University of Texas Press, 1966. Pp. 99–118.

Rexroth, Kenneth. "The Decline of American Humor." *Nation,* 184 (April 27, 1957), 374–376.

———. "Humor in a Tough Age." *Nation,* 188 (March 7, 1959), 211–213.

Rodgers, Bernard F., Jr. "*The Great American Novel* and 'the Great American Joke.' "*Critique,* 16, no. 2 (1974), 12–29.

Rosenblatt, Roger. "The 'Negro Everyman' and His Humor." In *Veins of Humor*. Ed. Harry Levin. Cambridge: Harvard University Press, 1972. Pp. 225–242.

Rother, James. "Modernism and the Nonsense Style." *Contemporary Literature,* 15 (Spring, 1974), 187–202.

Rourke, Constance. *American Humor: A Study of the National Character*. New York: Harcourt, Brace, 1931.

Rovit, Earl. "Jewish Humor and American Life." *The American Scholar,* 36 (Spring, 1967), 237–245.

———. "The Novel as Parody: John Barth." *Critique,* 6 (Fall, 1963), 77–85.

———. "Ralph Ellison and the American Comic Tradition." *Wisconsin Studies in Contemporary Literature,* 1 (Fall, 1960), 34–42.

Ruark, Robert. "Let's Nix the Sicknicks." *Saturday Evening Post,* 236 (June 29, 1963), 38–39.

Rubin, Louis D., Jr. "The Barber Kept on Shaving: The Two Perspectives of American Humor." In *The Comic Imagination in American Literature*. Ed. Louis D. Rubin, Jr. New Brunswick, N.J.: Rutgers University Press, 1973. Pp. 385–406.

———. "Introduction: 'The Great American Joke.' " In *The Comic Imagination in American Literature*. Ed. Louis D. Rubin, Jr. New Brunswick, N.J.: Rutgers University Press, 1973. Pp. 3–16.

Schmitz, Neil. "Donald Barthelme and the Emergence of Modern Satire." *Minnesota Review,* 1 (Fall, 1971), 109–118.

———. "What Irony Unravels." *Partisan Review,* 40 (Summer, 1973), 482–490.

Schoen, Elin. "Kiss, Kiss, *Kvetch, Kvetch:* What's Ailing the New Belles of Letters." *New York Magazine,* 10 (May 23, 1977), 59, 60, 62, 64–66, 68, 69.

Scholes, Robert. *The Fabulators*. New York: Oxford University Press, 1967.

———. " 'Mithridates, He Died Old': Black Humor and Kurt Vonnegut, Jr." *The Hollins Critic,* 3 (October, 1966), 1–12.

Schulz, Max F. *Black Humor Fiction of the Sixties: A Pluralistic Definition of Man and His World*. Athens: Ohio University Press, 1973.

———. "Pop, Op, and Black Humor: The Aesthetics of Anxiety." *College English,* 30 (December, 1968), 230–241.

———. "The Unconfirmed Thesis: Kurt Vonnegut, Black Humor, and Contemporary Art." *Critique,* 13, no. 3 (1971), 5–28.

Sheffey, Ruthe. "Wit and Irony in Militant Black Poetry." *Black World,* 22 (June 1973), 14–21.

Shelton, Frank W. "Humor and Balance in Coover's *The Universal Baseball Association, Inc.*" *Critique,* 17, no. 1 (1975), 78–90.

———. "Nathanael West and Theatre of the Absurd: A Comparative Study." *Southern Humanities Review,* 10 (Summer, 1976), 225–234.

Sherwood, Terry G. "*One Flew over the Cuckoo's Nest* and the Comic Strip." *Critique,* 13, no. 1 (1971), 96–109.

Shulman, Max. "American Humor: Its Cause and Cure." *Yale Review,* 51 (October, 1961), 119–124.

Shulman, Robert. "Myth, Mr. Eliot and the Comic Novel." *Modern Fiction Studies,* 12 (Winter, 1966–67), 315–403.

———. "The Style of Bellow's Comedy." *PMLA*, 83 (March, 1968), 109–117.

Siegel, Ben. "Saul Bellow and Mr. Sammler: Absurd Seekers of High Qualities." In *Saul Bellow: A Collection of Critical Essays.* Ed. Earl Rovit. Englewood Cliffs, N.J.: Prentice-Hall, 1975. Pp. 122–134.

———. "Victims in Motion: Bernard Malamud's Sad and Bitter Clowns." In *Recent American Fiction: Some Critical Views.* Ed. Joseph J. Waldmeir. Boston: Houghton Mifflin, 1963. Pp. 203–214.

Smith, Gerald J. "Medicine Made Palatable: An Aspect of Humor in *The Reivers.*" *Notes on Mississippi Writers,* 8 (1975), 58–62.

Southern, Terry. "Dark Laughter in the Towers." *Nation,* 190 (April 23, 1960), 348–350.

Sterling, Philip. *Laughing on the Outside: The Intelligent White Reader's Guide to Negro Tales and Humor.* New York: Grossett and Dunlap, 1965.

Stern, J. P. "War and the Comic Muse: *The Good Soldier Schweik* and *Catch-22.*" *Comparative Literature,* 20 (Summer, 1968), 193–216.

Sullivan, Walter. "Southerners in the City: Flannery O'Connor and Walker Percy." In *The Comic Imagination in American Literature.* Ed. Louis D. Rubin, Jr. New Brunswick, N.J.: Rutgers University Press, 1973. Pp. 339–348.

Tanner, Stephen L. "Salvation through Laughter: Ken Kesey and the Cuckoo's Nest." *Southwest Review,* 58 (Spring, 1973), 125–137.

Tanner, Tony. "The Hoax That Joke Bilked." *Partisan Review,* 34 (Winter, 1967), 102–109.

———. "On Lexical Playfields." In *City of Words: American Fiction 1950–1970*. London: Jonathan Cape, 1971. Pp. 33–49.

Tharpe, Jac. *John Barth: The Comic Sublimity of Paradox*. Carbondale: Southern Illinois University Press, 1974.

Thorp, Willard. *American Humorists*. University of Minnesota pamphlets on American Writers, #42. Minneapolis: University of Minnesota Press, 1964.

———. "Suggs and Sut in Modern Dress: The Latest Chapter in Southern Humor." *Mississippi Quarterly*, 13 (Winter, 1959–60), 169–175.

Thurber, James. "The Case for Comedy." *Atlantic Monthly*, 206 (November, 1960), 97–99.

———. "The Future, If Any, of Comedy (Or Where Do We Non-Go from Here?)" *Harper's*, 223 (December, 1961), 40–45.

Trachtenberg, Stanley. "Counterhumor: Comedy in Contemporary American Fiction." *The Georgia Review*, 27 (Spring, 1973), 33–48.

———. "Vonnegut's Cradle: The Erosion of Comedy." *Michigan Quarterly Review*, 12 (Winter, 1973), 66–71.

Turner, Arlin. "The Many Sides of Southern Humor." *Mississippi Quarterly*, 13 (Fall, 1960), 155–156.

Wakefield, Dan. "Heavy Hand of College Humor: Superman, Sex, and Salinger." *Mademoiselle*, 55 (August, 1962), 288–289.

Waldmeir, Joseph J. "Two Novelists of the Absurd: Heller and Kesey." *Wisconsin Studies in Contemporary Literature*, 5 (Autumn, 1964), 192–204.

Weber, Brom. "The Mode of 'Black Humor.' " In *The Comic Imagination in American Literature*. Ed. Louis D. Rubin, Jr. New Brunswick, N.J.: Rutgers University Press, 1973. Pp. 361–372.

Weber, Ronald. "Tom Wolfe's Happiness Explosion." *Journal of Popular Culture*, 8 (Summer, 1974), 71–79.

Weinstein, Sharon R. "Comedy and the Absurd in Ralph Ellison's *Invisible Man*." *Studies in Black Literature*, 3 (Autumn, 1972), 12–16.

———. "Don't Women Have a Sense of Comedy They Can Call Their Own?" *American Humor*, 1 no. 2 (1974), 9–12.

Weixlmann, Joseph. " '. . . such a devotee of Venus is our Capt . . .': The Use and Abuse of Smith's *Generall Historie* in John Barth's *The Sot-Weed Factor*." *Studies in American Humor*, 2 (October, 1975), 105–115.

West, Paul. *The Wine of Absurdity*. University Park: Pennsylvania State University Press, 1966.

Wheeler, Otis B. "Some Uses of Folk Humor by Faulkner." *Mississippi Quarterly*, 17 (Winter, 1963–64), 107–122.

Widmer, Kingsley. "The Academic Comedy." *Partisan Review,* 28 (Summer, 1960), 526–535.

Wilde, Larry. *How the Great Comedy Writers Create Laughter.* Chicago: Nelson-Hall, 1976.

Williams, M. "Comedy of Lenny Bruce." *Saturday Review,* 45 (November 24, 1962), 60–61.

Winston, Mathew. *"Humour noir* and Black Humor." In *Veins of Humor.* Ed. Harry Levin. Cambridge: Harvard University Press, 1972. Pp. 269–284.

Wisse, Ruth R. *The Schlemiel as Modern Hero.* Chicago: University of Chicago Press, 1971.

Wynne, Judith F. "The Sacramental Irony of Flannery O'Connor." *Southern Literary Journal,* 7 (Spring, 1975), 33–49.

Yates, Norris. *The American Humorist: Conscience of the Twentieth Century.* Ames: Iowa State University Press, 1964.

Notes on Contributors

SARAH BLACHER COHEN, associate professor of English at the State University of New York at Albany, is the author of *Saul Bellow's Enigmatic Laughter* and essays on the humor of Henry James and Philip Roth. She is currently writing a book on the city in contemporary American literature and editing a collection of essays on Jewish-American drama.

MAX F. SCHULZ, chairman of the English department at the University of Southern California, has written extensively on contemporary American humor and literature. His books include *Black Humor Fiction of the Sixties* and *Radical Sophistication: Studies in Contemporary Jewish-American Novelists*.

RICHARD PEARCE, professor of English at Wheaton College, Norton, Massachusetts, is the author of *Stages of the Clown: Perspectives on Modern Fiction from Dostoevsky to Beckett* and *William Styron*. Among his works in progress is *Enter the Frame: A Study of Modernism*.

STANLEY TRACHTENBERG is director of graduate studies and professor of English at Northeastern University, Boston. He has written on Freud's *Jokes and Their Relation to the Unconscious,* and is the author of articles on humor in the fiction of Herman Melville, Nathanael West, John Barth, Kurt Vonnegut, and Saul Bellow.

DAVID KETTERER is an Englishman whose areas of expertise are American literature and science fiction. An associate professor of English at Concordia University, Montreal, he is the author of *New Worlds for Old: The Apocalyptic Imagination* and *Science Fiction and American Literature*. His new book, *The Rationale of Deception in Poe,* is forthcoming.

C. HUGH HOLMAN is Kenan Professor of English at the University of North Carolina at Chapel Hill. His many books include studies of southern literature, literary criticism, Thomas Wolfe, John P. Marquand, and others. One of his most recent books is *The Roots of Southern Writing*.

CHARLES H. NICHOLS, professor of English at Brown University, is the author of *Many Thousand Gone: The Ex-Slaves' Account of Their Bondage and Freedom*. He is the editor of *African Nights: Black Erotic Folk Tales* and *Black Men in Chains: An Anthology of Slave Narratives*. He is presently editing the correspondence of Langston Hughes and Arna Bontemps and working on a biography of Theodore Parker.

ALLEN GUTTMANN, chairman of the American Studies department at Amherst College, is the author of *The Wound in the Heart: America and the Spanish Civil War; The Conservative Tradition in America;* and *The Jewish Writer in America*. His new book is *From Ritual to Record: The Nature of Modern Sports*.

SHELDON GREBSTEIN, dean of arts and science and professor of English at the State University of New York at Binghamton, has written books on Sinclair Lewis, John O'Hara, and Ernest Hemingway and has edited several critical anthologies. He is now writing a book on Jewish-American literature for the University of Illinois Press.

WENDY MARTIN teaches American literature at Queens College of the City University of New York. In addition to her essays on early American fiction, she has published articles on the American woman writer from Susanna Rowson to Adrienne Rich. She has edited *The American Sisterhood* and is the editor of *Women's Studies: An Interdisciplinary Journal*.

GEORGE GARRETT, professor of English and Fellow of the Creative Writing Program at Princeton University, is a master of many genres of WASP literature. He has written four novels, five collections of short stories, four volumes of poetry, and one children's play, and has edited fourteen critical and literary anthologies. His most recent novel is *Death of the Fox,* and his latest collection of short stories is *The Magic Striptease*.

EARL ROVIT, professor of English at the City College of New York, is both critic and novelist. In addition to his three novels, he has written widely on humor in American literature. He has also published books on Elizabeth Madox Roberts, Ernest Hemingway, and Saul Bellow.

SANFORD PINSKER, associate professor of English at Franklin & Marshall College, is the author of *The Schlemiel as Metaphor: Studies in the Yiddish and American-Jewish Novel* and *The Comedy That "Hoits": An Essay on the Fiction of Philip Roth*. His book on *The Languages of Joseph Conrad* will soon appear.

PHILIP STEVICK, whose specialties are experimental fiction and literary theory, is professor of English at Temple University. He has written *The Chapter in Fiction: Theories of Narrative Division* and has edited *The Theory of the Novel* and *Anti-Story: An Anthology of Experimental Fiction*.

RUBY COHN, professor of comparative drama at the University of California, Davis, is a most prolific drama critic. She has written *Samuel Beckett, the Comic Gamut; Currents in Contemporary Drama; Dialogue in American Drama; Back to Beckett;* and, most recently, *Modern Shakespeare Offshoots*.

JOHN VERNON, associate professor of English, is a poet who teaches creative writing and modern poetry at the State University of New York at Binghamton. He is the author of *The Garden and the Map: Schizophrenia in Twentieth-Century Literature and Culture* and *Poetry and the Body*.